Tabular Modeling in Microsoft SQL Server Analysis Services, Second Edition

Marco Russo
and Alberto Ferrari

PUBLISHED BY

Microsoft Press

A division of Microsoft Corporation

One Microsoft Way

Redmond, Washington 98052-6399

Library of Congress Control Number: 2016931110

ISBN: 978-1-5093-0277-2

Printed and bound in the United States of America.

1   17

Microsoft Press books are available through booksellers and distributors worldwide. If you need support related to this book, email Microsoft Press Support at mspinput@microsoft.com. Please tell us what you think of this book at *https://aka.ms/tellpress*.

This book is provided "as-is" and expresses the author's views and opinions. The views, opinions and information expressed in this book, including URL and other Internet website references, may change without notice.

Some examples depicted herein are provided for illustration only and are fictitious. No real association or connection is intended or should be inferred.

Microsoft and the trademarks listed at *https://www.microsoft.com* on the "Trademarks" webpage are trademarks of the Microsoft group of companies. All other marks are property of their respective owners.

Acquisitions Editor: Devon Musgrave

Editorial Production: Polymath Publishing

Technical Reviewer: Ed Price

Copy Editor: Kate Shoup

Layout Services: Shawn Morningstar

Proofreader: Corina Lebegioara

Indexing Services: Kelly Talbot Editing Services

Illustrator: Daniele Perilli

Cover: Twist Creative • Seattle

Contents at a Glance

Contents

Chapter 3   Loading data inside Tabular   83

Chapter 10   Security   269

Chapter 13   Interfacing with Tabular   373

Chapter 14   Monitoring and tuning a Tabular service   395

Foreword

For most people who have already worked with Analysis Services, the names Marco Russo and Alberto Ferrari probably need little introduction. They have worked on some of the most challenging Analysis Services projects, written multiple books about the product, and put together fascinating blog posts on best practices and other technical topics. Besides all of the above, they are frequent presenters at conferences and hold popular training courses on a wide range of topics related to business intelligence and Analysis Services. I've met with Alberto and Marco many times over the years and they have a wonderful passion for the BI space and a pure love of learning and teaching.

As a long-term member of the Analysis Services engineering team, I've worked on a large spectrum of the SSAS engine as well as parts of Power BI. I've truly loved building Analysis Services. The strong and enthusiastic engineering team combined with our amazing partners and customers make it so worthwhile!

Having designed and built features in Analysis Services over so many releases, I sometimes think I know exactly what customers need and want from the product. But my conversations with Marco and Alberto usually remind me how much more they know about BI in the real world. Our discussions are always fascinating and thought-provoking because both of them have a tendency to provide unexpected viewpoints that shatter my preconceived notions. The questions are wild and wide-ranging, the debates often rage on in emails, and the consequences are always positive for the product and our customers.

Every product team is occasionally accused of "living in ivory towers" and ignoring what is important to customers. Having our MVPs and experts act as our sounding board, throw cold water on our bad ideas, and show support for our good ideas is more valuable than even they realize. But I believe that the biggest value they bring to our Analysis Services world is acting as our proxies and translating our documentation and other communications (which can sometimes be too technical or abstract for non-developers), and creating examples and solutions that show people how things should really be done. This book is an excellent example of our expert community leading the way.

As always, Marco and Alberto have put in a massive amount of effort to research the new Analysis Services 2016 release. You can benefit from their expertise and hard work and take advantage of all the lessons that they have learned since they started using the new product.

I'm personally very proud of the Analysis Services 2016 release, which includes the release of so many new features and performance improvements that I can name only a few of my favorites: Tabular metadata, the TOM object model, SuperDAX, Parallel Partition Processing, BiDirectional CrossFiltering, etc. After reviewing many of the chapters of this new book, I'm confident that it will be a truly useful and educational companion to the product, and readers will quickly be able to start taking advantage of the potential of this new version of Analysis Services.

I look forward to more collaboration with Marco and Alberto and wish them all success with this new book!

Akshai Mirchandani
Principal Software Engineer
Microsoft Corporation

Introduction

The first edition of this book was published in 2012, when Microsoft released the first version of SQL Server Analysis Services (SSAS) working in Tabular mode. Previously, SSAS ran a different engine, now called Multidimensional mode; since 2012, users are given the option to choose which one to install. In 2016, Microsoft issued the second major release of Analysis Services Tabular, introducing many new features and important improvements. For this reason, we decided to write the second edition of our SSAS Tabular book, which is what you are reading now.

Notice that we omitted the Analysis Services version number from the book title. This is because things are moving faster and faster. At the time of this writing, we are using the 2016 version of SSAS, but a technical preview of the next version is already available. Does that mean this book is already out-of-date? No. We took on this challenge, and we included notes related to features that could change soon. These are exceptions, however. You will probably see new features added to the product, but not many changes to the existing ones.

If you already read the previous edition of this book, is it worth reading this new one? Yes. There is a lot of new content and updates. Indeed, you should read almost all the chapters again, because we updated the entire book using the new version of Analysis Services. Moreover, with this second edition, we decided to focus on SSAS only. We removed all the advanced chapters about the DAX language, adding several new chapters and extending the existing ones to cover new features and to provide more insights into the SSAS engine. We also leveraged the experience we gained in the intervening years helping many customers around the world to deploy solutions based on Analysis Services Tabular. In case you are missing the DAX part, we wrote a comprehensive book about DAX only, *The Definitive Guide to DAX*, where you can find everything you need to master this beautiful language—much more than what was available in the previous edition of this book.

Finally, if you are a new developer, why should you invest on learning Analysis Services Tabular? These days, Power BI looks like a good alternative for smaller models, it is easier to use, and it is free. But it may be that one day, your Power BI–based solution will need to scale up, serve multiple users, handle more information, and grow in size and complexity. When that happens, the natural move will be to migrate to a full Tabular solution. The engine in Power BI and Power Pivot is the very same as in SSAS Tabular, so the more you know about it, the better.

We hope this book will be useful to you, and that you will enjoy reading it.

Who should read this book

This book is aimed at professional business intelligence (BI) developers: consultants or members of in-house BI development teams who are about to embark on a project using the tabular model.

We are going to start with the basics of Tabular, so in a sense, this is an introductory book. However, we assume that you already know certain core BI concepts such as dimensional modeling and data warehouse design. Some previous knowledge of relational databases, especially SQL Server, will be important when it comes to understanding how Tabular is structured and how to load data into it, and for topics such as DirectQuery. Previous experience with Analysis Services Multidimensional is not necessary, but because we know most readers of this book have some, we occasionally refer to its features and compare them with equivalent features in Tabular.

Who should not read this book

No book is suitable for every possible audience, and this book is no exception. Those with no BI experience will find themselves out of their depth very quickly, as will managers who do not have a technical background.

Organization of this book

This book is organized as follows:

- Chapter 1, "Introducing the tabular model," introduces the tabular model—what it is and when it should (and should not) be used.

- Chapter 2, "Getting started with the tabular model," and Chapter 3, "Loading data inside Tabular," cover the basics of building a tabular model.

- Chapter 4, "Introducing calculations in DAX," introduces the DAX language to enable you to create simple calculations.

- Chapter 5, "Building hierarchies," Chapter 6, "Data modeling in Tabular," Chapter 8, "The tabular presentation layer," Chapter 10, "Security," and Chapter 15, "Optimizing tabular models" deal with numerous Tabular design topics, such as hierarchies, relationships, many-to-many, and security.

- Chapter 7, "Tabular Model Scripting Language (TMSL)" discusses TMSL, while Chapter 13, "Interfacing with Tabular," provides insight into yet more methods for accessing tabular models programmatically.

- Chapter 9, "Using DirectQuery," and Chapter 12, "Inside VertiPaq," provide several insights into the DirectQuery and VertiPaq engines.

- Chapter 11, "Processing and partitioning tabular models," Chapter 14, "Monitoring and tuning a Tabular service," and Chapter 16, "Choosing hardware and virtualization," deal with operational issues such as hardware sizing and configuration, processing, partitioning, and monitoring.

Conventions and features in this book

This book presents information using conventions designed to make information readable and easy to follow:

- Boxed elements with labels such as "Note" provide additional information or alternative methods for completing a step successfully.

- Text that you type (apart from code blocks) appears in bold.

- A plus sign (+) between two key names means you must press those keys at the same time. For example, "Press Alt+Tab" means that you hold down the Alt key while you press the Tab key.

- The definition of measures, calculated columns, and calculated tables uses the following standard, which does not correspond to the syntax used in Visual Studio, but it is a simpler convention for the book (more details about that in Chapter 4, "Introducing calculations in DAX"):

```
Table[MeasureName] := <expression>
Table[CalculatedColumnName] = <expression>
CalculatedTable = <expression>
```

System requirements

You will need the following hardware and software to install the code samples and sample database used in this book:

- Windows 7, Windows Server 2008 SP2, or greater. Either 32-bit or 64-bit editions will be suitable.

- At least 6 GB of free space on disk.

- At least 4 GB of RAM.

- A 2.0GHz x86 or x64 processor or better.

- An instance of SQL Server Analysis Services 2016 Tabular plus client components.

Full instructions on how to install this are given in Chapter 2, "Getting started with the tabular model."

Code samples

The databases used for examples in this book are based on Microsoft's Adventure Works 2012 DW and on ContosoDW sample databases. All sample projects and the sample databases can be downloaded from the following page:

https://aka.ms/tabular/downloads

Follow these steps to install the code samples on your computer so that you can follow the examples in this book:

1. Unzip the samples file onto your hard drive.

2. Restore the two SQL Server databases from the .bak files that can be found in the Databases directory. Full instructions on how to do this can be found here: *http://msdn.microsoft.com/en-us/library/ms177429.aspx*.

3. Each chapter has its own subdirectory containing code samples within the Models directory. In many cases this takes the form of a project, which must be opened in SQL Server Data Tools. Full instructions on how to install SQL Server Data Tools are given in Chapter 2, "Getting started with the tabular model."

4. Scripts in PowerShell and TMSL are included in the directories Script PowerShell and Script TMSL, respectively.

Acknowledgments

We would like to thank the following people for their help and advice: Bret Grinslade, Christian Wade, Cristian Petculescu, Darren Gosbell, Jeffrey Wang, Kasper de Jonge, Marius Dumitru, Kay Unkroth, and TK Anand.

A special mention to Akshai Mirchandani for the incredible job he did answering all our questions, completing accurate technical reviews, and providing us the foreword for the book.

Finally, we want to thank Ed Price and Kate Shoup, who worked as technical reviewer and editor. You will find fewer mistakes thanks to their work. The remaining ones (hopefully very few) are on us.

Errata and book support

We have made every effort to ensure the accuracy of this book and its companion content. Any errors that have been reported since this book was published are listed on our Microsoft Press site at:

https://aka.ms/tabular/errata

If you find an error that is not already listed, you can report it to us through the same page.

If you need additional support, email Microsoft Press Book Support at *mspinput@microsoft.com*.

Please note that product support for Microsoft software is not offered through the addresses above.

We want to hear from you

At Microsoft Press, your satisfaction is our top priority and your feedback our most valuable asset. Please tell us what you think of this book at:

https://aka.ms/tellpress

The survey is short, and we read every one of your comments and ideas. Thanks in advance for your input!

Stay in touch

Let's keep the conversation going! We're on Twitter: @MicrosoftPress.

Introducing the tabular model

This chapter introduces SQL Server Analysis Services (SSAS) 2016, provides a brief overview of what the tabular model is, and explores its relationship to the multidimensional model, to SSAS 2016 as a whole, and to the wider Microsoft business intelligence (BI) stack. This chapter will help you make what is probably the most important decision in your project's life cycle: whether you should use a tabular model or a multidimensional model. Finally, it includes a short description of the main differences in tabular models between SSAS 2016 and previous versions.

> **What's new in SSAS 2016**   New compatibility levels and a new implementation of DirectQuery have improved performance and removed limitations present in previous versions.

Semantic models in Analysis Services

In the Microsoft ecosystem, BI is not a single product, but a set of features distributed across several products. The following sections explain the role of SSAS in this ecosystem. The tabular model is one of the two types of semantic models you can create in SSAS. (The other is the multidimensional model.)

What is Analysis Services and why should I use it?

SSAS is an online analytical data engine—a type of service that is highly optimized for the kinds of queries and calculations that are common in a business intelligence environment. It does many of the same things that a relational database can do, but it differs in many respects. In most cases, it will be easier to develop your BI solution by using SSAS in combination with a relational database, such as Microsoft SQL Server, than by using SQL Server alone. SSAS does not replace the need for a relational database or a properly designed data warehouse, however.

One way of thinking about SSAS is as an extra layer of metadata, or a semantic model, that sits on top of a data warehouse in a relational database. This extra layer contains information about how fact tables and dimension tables should be joined, how measures should aggregate up, how users should be able to explore the data through hierarchies, the definitions of common calculations, and so on. This layer also includes one or more models containing the business logic of your data warehouse. End users query these models rather than the underlying relational database. With all this information stored in a central place and shared by all users, the queries that users need to write become much simpler.

In most cases, all a query needs to do is describe which columns and rows are required, and the model applies the appropriate business logic to ensure that the numbers that are returned make sense. Most important, it becomes impossible to write a query that returns "incorrect" results due to a mistake by end users. This, in turn, means that end-user reporting and analysis tools must do much less work and can provide a clearer visual interface for end users to build queries. It also means that different tools can connect to the same model and return consistent results.

Another way of thinking about SSAS is as a kind of cache that you can use to speed up reporting. In most scenarios in which SSAS is used, it is loaded with a copy of the data in the data warehouse. Subsequently, all reporting and analytic queries are run against SSAS instead of the relational database. Even though modern relational databases are highly optimized and contain many features specifically aimed at BI reporting, SSAS specifically designed for this type of workload and can, in most cases, achieve much better query performance. For end users, optimized query performance is extremely important because it allows them to browse through data without waiting a long time for reports to run and without any breaks in their chain of thought.

For the IT department, the biggest benefit of all this is that it becomes possible to transfer the burden of authoring reports to end users. A common problem with BI projects that do not use Online Analytical Processing (OLAP) is that the IT department must build not only a data warehouse but also a set of reports to go with it. This increases the amount of time and effort involved, and can be a cause of frustration for the business when it finds that IT is unable to understand its reporting requirements or to respond to them as quickly as is desirable. When an OLAP database such as SSAS is used, the IT department can expose the models it contains to end users and enable them to build reports themselves, using whatever tool with which they feel comfortable. By far the most popular client tool is Microsoft Excel. Ever since Office 2000, Excel PivotTables have been able to connect directly to SSAS multidimensional models (also known as *cubes*), and Excel 2016 has some extremely powerful capabilities as a client for SSAS.

All in all, Analysis Services not only reduces the IT department's workload but also increases end-user satisfaction. Users now find they can build the reports they want and explore the data at their own pace, without having to go through an intermediary.

A short history of Analysis Services

SQL Server Analysis Services—or OLAP Services, as it was originally called when it was released in 1998 with SQL Server 7.0—was the first foray by Microsoft into the BI market. When it was released, many people saw it as an indicator that BI software was ready to break out of its niche and reach a mass market. Over the past 16 years, the success of Analysis Services and the rest of the Microsoft BI stack has proved them correct.

SQL Server Analysis Services 2000 was the first version of Analysis Services to gain significant traction in the marketplace. Analysis Services 2005 became the biggest-selling OLAP tool not long after its release. As Analysis Services 2008 and 2008 R2 improved scalability and performance still further, more and more companies started to adopt it as a cornerstone of their BI strategy. By 2010, terabyte-sized cubes were not uncommon. The famous example of the 24-terabyte (TB) cube Yahoo! built shows just what can be achieved.

Microsoft Analysis Services 2012 leveraged an existing infrastructure to introduce a new engine and a new type of data model, essentially becoming two products in one. It still contains Analysis Services from the SQL Server 2008 R2 release and before, but that has become known as the *multidimensional model*. Although Analysis Services has seen a few improvements since the 2008 R2 release, related to performance, scalability, and manageability, no new major functionality has been introduced since then. Meanwhile, Analysis Services 2012 has a new data-modeling experience and a new engine that closely resembles the Power Pivot and Power BI data modeling experience. This is called the *tabular model*.

The following version of SQL Server did not introduce new BI features, so there are no differences between Analysis Services 2012 and 2014, provided you run the latest service packs and cumulative updates. However, Analysis Services 2016 introduces many new features and improvements to the tabular model, to the point that we considered it necessary to write a new book about it.

The tabular model in Analysis Services 2016 is the subject of this book. We will cover migration issues from tabular models created in former versions of Analysis Services, but if you are not planning to upgrade to 2016, then we recommend you read our previous book, *Microsoft SQL Server 2012 Analysis Services: The BISM Tabular Model*.

Understanding Tabular and Multidimensional

This section explains a little about the architecture of Analysis Services, which since SQL Server 2012 has been split into two modes: Tabular and Multidimensional.

When installing Analysis Services, you must choose between installing an instance that runs in Tabular mode and one that runs in Multidimensional mode. (For more details on the installation process, see Chapter 2, "Getting started with the tabular model.") A Tabular mode instance can support only databases containing tabular models, and a Multidimensional mode instance can support only databases containing multidimensional models. Although these two parts of Analysis Services share much of the same code underneath, in most respects they can be treated as separate products. The concepts involved in designing the two types of models are very different. You cannot convert a tabular database into a multidimensional database, or vice versa, without rebuilding everything from scratch. That said, it is important to emphasize the fact that, from an end user's point of view, the two models do almost exactly the same things and appear almost identical when used through client tools such as Excel and Power BI.

The following sections compare the functionalities available in the tabular and multidimensional models and define some important terms that are used throughout the rest of this book.

The tabular model

A *database* is the highest-level object in the tabular model. It is very similar to the concept of a database in the SQL Server relational database. An instance of Analysis Services can contain many databases, and each database can be thought of as a self-contained collection of objects and data relating to a single business solution. If you are writing reports or analyzing data and find that you need to run queries on multiple databases, you have probably made a design mistake somewhere because everything you need should be contained in a single database. If you face a situation where data is scattered across different tabular databases, you should consider refactoring the analytical models into one. Discussing the correct design of analytical databases and of underlying data warehouse and/ or data marts is beyond the scope of this book. You can find more information about this in the "SQLBI Methodology" whitepaper (*http://www.sqlbi.com/articles/sqlbi-methodology/*).

You design tabular models using SQL Server Data Tools (SSDT) for Visual Studio (VS). A project in SSDT maps onto a database in Analysis Services. After you have finished designing a project in SSDT, it must be deployed to an instance of Analysis Services. This means SSDT executes numerous commands to create a new database in Analysis Services or alters the structure of an existing database. You can also use SQL Server Management Studio (SSMS), a tool that can be used to manage databases that have already been deployed, to write queries against databases.

Databases are made up of one or more tables of data. Again, a *table* in the tabular model is very similar to a table in the relational database world. A table in the tabular model is usually loaded from a single table in a relational database or from the results of a SQL SELECT statement. A table has a fixed number of *columns* that are defined at design time and can have a variable number of rows, depending on the amount of data that is loaded. Each column has a fixed type. For example, a single column could contain only integers, only text, or only decimal values. Loading data into a table is referred to as *processing* that table.

It is also possible to define relationships between tables at design time. Unlike in SQL, it is not possible to define relationships at query time; all queries must use these preexisting relationships. However, relationships between tables can be marked as active or inactive, and at query time it is possible to choose which relationships between tables are actually used. It is also possible to simulate the effect of relationships that do not exist inside queries and calculations. All the relationships are one-to-one or one-to-many, and must involve just one column from each of two tables. A relationship can propagate a filter in one or both directions. It is not possible to design relationships based on more than one column from a table or recursive relationships that join a table to itself.

The tabular model uses a purely memory-based engine and stores only a copy of its data on disk. That way, no data is lost if the service is restarted. Whereas the multidimensional model, like most relational database engines, stores its data in a row-based format, the tabular model uses a column-oriented database called the *in-memory analytics engine*. In most cases, this offers significant improvements in query performance. (For more details on the column-based type of database, see *http://en.wikipedia.org/wiki/Column-oriented_DBMS*.)

> **Note** The in-memory analytics engine was known as the *VertiPaq* engine before the public release of Analysis Services 2012. Many references to the VertiPaq name remain in documentation, blog posts, and other material online. It even persists inside the product itself in property names and Profiler events. For these reasons and for brevity, we will use the term *VertiPaq* in this book when referring to the in-memory analytics engine.

Queries and calculations in the tabular model are defined in Data Analysis eXpressions (DAX), the native language of a model created in the tabular model, Power Pivot, or Power BI. The multidimensional model has internal calculations defined in Multi Dimensional eXpressions (MDX) language. Client tools can generate DAX or MDX queries to retrieve data from a semantic model, regardless of whether it is a tabular or a multidimensional one. This means the tabular model is backward-compatible with the large number of existing Analysis Services client tools designed for the multidimensional model that are available from Microsoft, such as Excel and SQL Server Reporting Services, as well as tools from third-party software vendors that use MDX to query a semantic model. At the same time, the multidimensional model is compatible with new client tools such as Power BI, which generates queries in DAX.

You can add derived columns, called *calculated columns*, to a table in a tabular model. They use DAX expressions to return values based on the data already loaded in other columns or other tables in the same Analysis Services database. You can add derived tables, called *calculated tables*, to a tabular model as if they were new tables. They use DAX table expressions to return values based on data already loaded in other tables in the same Analysis Services database. Calculated columns and calculated tables are populated at processing time. After processing has taken place, they behave in exactly the same way as regular columns and tables.

You can also define *measures* on tables by using DAX expressions. You can think of a measure as a DAX expression that returns some form of aggregated value based on data from one or more columns. A simple example of a measure is one that returns the sum of all values from a column of data that contains sales volumes. *Key performance indicators* (*KPIs*) are very similar to measures, but are collections of calculations that enable you to determine how well a measure is doing relative to a target value and whether it is getting closer to reaching that target over time.

Most front-end tools such as Excel use a pivot table–like experience for querying tabular models. For example, you can drag columns from different tables onto the rows axis and columns axis of a pivot table so that the distinct values from these columns become the individual rows and columns of the pivot table, and measures display aggregated numeric values inside the table. The overall effect is something like a Group By query in SQL, which aggregates rows by selected fields. However, the definition of how the data aggregates up is predefined inside the measures and is not necessarily specified inside the query itself.

To improve the user experience, it is also possible to define *hierarchies* on tables inside the tabular model. These create multilevel, predefined drill paths. *Perspectives* can hide certain parts of a complex model, which can aid usability, and *security roles* can be used to deny access to specific rows of data from tables to specific users. Perspectives should not be confused with security, however. Even if an object is hidden in a perspective, it can still be queried, and perspectives themselves cannot be secured.

The multidimensional model

At the highest level, the multidimensional model is very similar to the tabular model: Data is organized in databases, and databases are designed in SSDT (formerly BI Development Studio, or BIDS) and managed using SQL Server Management Studio.

The differences become apparent below the database level, where multidimensional rather than relational concepts are prevalent. In the multidimensional model, data is modeled as a series of *cubes* and *dimensions*, not tables. Each cube is made up of one or more *measure groups*, and each measure group in a cube is usually mapped onto a single fact table in the data warehouse. A measure group contains one or more *measures*, which are very similar to measures in the tabular model. A cube also has two or more dimensions. One special dimension, the *measures dimension*, contains all the measures from each of the measure groups. Various other dimensions such as time, product, geography, customer, and so on, map onto the logical dimensions present in a dimensional model. Each of these non-measures dimensions consists of one or more *attributes* (for example, on a date dimension, there might be attributes such as date, month, and year), and these attributes can themselves be used as single-level hierarchies or to construct multilevel *user hierarchies*. Hierarchies can then be used to build queries. Users start by analyzing data at a highly aggregated level, such as a year level on a time dimension, and can then navigate to lower levels such as quarter, month, and date to look for trends and interesting anomalies.

As you would expect, because the multidimensional model is the direct successor to versions of Analysis Services before 2016, it has a very rich and mature set of features representing the fruit of more than a decade of development (even if some of them are not used very often). Most of the features available in the tabular model are present in the multidimensional model, but the multidimensional model also has many features that have not yet been implemented in the tabular one. A detailed feature comparison between the two models appears later in this chapter.

In terms of data storage, the multidimensional model can store its data in three ways:

- **Multidimensional OLAP (MOLAP)** In this model, all data is stored inside Analysis Services' own disk-based storage format.

- **Relational OLAP (ROLAP)** In this model, Analysis Services acts purely as a metadata layer. No data is stored in Analysis Services itself. Instead, SQL queries are run against the relational source database when a cube is queried.

- **Hybrid OLAP (HOLAP)** This is the same as ROLAP but some pre-aggregated values are stored in MOLAP.

MOLAP storage is used in the vast majority of implementations, although ROLAP is sometimes used when there is a requirement for so-called real-time BI. HOLAP is almost never used.

One area in which the multidimensional and tabular models differ is in the calculation languages they support. The native language of the multidimensional model is MDX. Only MDX can be used for defining calculations, whereas queries can be in either MDX or DAX. The MDX language has been successful and is supported by numerous third-party client tools for Analysis Services. It was also promoted as a semi-open standard by a cross-vendor industry body called the XMLA Council (now effectively defunct). As a result, it has also been adopted by many other OLAP tools that are direct competitors to Analysis Services. The problem with MDX, however, is the same problem many people have with the multidimensional model in general: Although it is extremely powerful, many BI professionals have struggled to learn it because the concepts it uses, such as dimensions and hierarchies, are very different from the ones they are accustomed to using in SQL.

Why have two models?

Why has this split happened? There are several reasons:

- The Analysis Services multidimensional model was designed in an age of 32-bit servers with one or two processors and less than a gigabyte of RAM, when disk-based storage was the only option for databases. Times have changed, however, and modern hardware is radically different. Now, a new generation of memory-based, columnar databases has set the standard for query performance with analytic workloads, and Analysis Services must adopt this new technology to keep up. Retrofitting the new in-memory analytics engine into the existing multidimensional model was not, however, a straightforward job, so it was necessary to introduce the new tabular model to take full advantage of VertiPaq.

- Despite the success of the Analysis Services multidimensional model, there has always been a perception that it is difficult to learn. Some database professionals, accustomed to relational data modeling, struggle to grasp multidimensional concepts—and those who manage it find the learning curve is steep. Therefore, if Microsoft wants to bring BI to an ever-wider audience, it must simplify the development process—hence the move from the complex world of the multidimensional model to the relatively simple and familiar concepts of the tabular model.

- Microsoft sees self-service BI as a huge potential source of growth, where Power Pivot and Power BI are its entry into this market. (Self-service BI enables less-technical business users to build BI solutions.) It is also important to have consistency between the Microsoft self-service and corporate BI tools. Therefore, if Analysis Services must be overhauled, it makes sense to make it compatible with Power Pivot and Power BI, with a similar design experience, so self-service models can easily be upgraded to full-fledged corporate solutions.

- Some types of data are more appropriate or more easily modeled using the tabular approach, and some types of data are more appropriate or more easily modeled for a multidimensional approach. Having different models gives developers the choice to use whichever approach suits their circumstances.

What is the BI Semantic Model (BISM)?

One term that was mentioned a lot in discussions about Analysis Services 2012 before its release was *BI Semantic Model* (*BISM*). This term does not refer to either the multidimensional or tabular model specifically. Instead, it describes the function of Analysis Services in the Microsoft BI stack—the fact that it acts as a semantic layer on top of a relational data warehouse, adding a rich layer of metadata that includes hierarchies, measures, and calculations. In that respect, it is very similar to the term *Unified Dimensional Model* (*UDM*) that was used around the time of the SQL Server 2005 launch. In some cases, BISM has been used to refer only to the tabular model, but this is not correct. Because this book is specifically concerned with the tabular model, we will not use this term very often. Nevertheless, we believe it is important to understand exactly what it means and how it should be used.

The future of Analysis Services

Having two models inside Analysis Services, plus two query and calculation languages, means you must choose which model to use at the start of your project. The only problem is, at that early stage, you might not know enough about your requirements to know which one is appropriate. We will address this dilemma in the next section. Having two models also means that anyone who decides to specialize in Analysis Services must learn two technologies or else specialize in just one of the modeling types.

Microsoft has been very clear in saying that the multidimensional model is not deprecated and that the tabular model is not its replacement. It is likely that new features for the multidimensional model will be released in future versions of Analysis Services. The fact that the tabular and multidimensional models share some of the same code suggests that some new features could easily be developed for both models simultaneously. In the very long term, the two models might converge and offer much the same functionality, so the decision about which model to use will be based on whether the developer prefers to use a multidimensional or relational way of modeling data. For example, support for DAX queries in the multidimensional model was introduced with an update of Analysis Services 2012 (Cumulative Update 3 for Service Pack 1), and it represented one important step in this direction. In fact, thanks to this feature, the Power BI client can establish a live connection to a multidimensional model.

Azure Analysis Services

Analysis Services is also available as a service on Azure, named Azure Analysis Services (Azure AS). You can create an instance of Azure AS that is deployed in a very short amount of time, and you pay only when said instance is active. When you pause the service, there is no charge, even if data is still loaded in the instance and ready to be queried as soon as you restart the service. As of February 2017, only the tabular model is available on Azure. For the purposes of this book, you can consider an instance of Azure AS to be an instance of an on-premises version of Analysis Services. You can just skip all the details about the installation of the services, because the provisioning is automatically managed by the Azure infrastructure.

Choosing the right model for your project

It might seem strange to address the question of whether the tabular model is appropriate for your project at this point in the book, before you have even learned anything about it. But you must answer this question at an equally early stage of your BI project. At a rough guess, either model will work equally well for about 60 to 70 percent of projects, but for the remaining 30 to 40 percent, the correct choice of model will be vital.

As stated, after you have started developing with one model in Analysis Services, there is no way to switch over to use the other. You would have to start all over again from the beginning, possibly wasting much precious development time. Therefore, it is very important to make the correct decision as soon as possible. When making this decision, you must take many factors into account. This section discusses all of them in a reasonable amount of detail. You can then bear these factors in mind as you read the rest of this book. When you finish it, you will be in a position to determine whether to use a tabular or multidimensional model.

Licensing

Analysis Services 2016 is available in SQL Server Standard and SQL Server Enterprise editions. In the SQL Server Standard edition, both multidimensional and tabular models are available, even with certain limitations for cores, memory, and features available. This means several important features needed for scaling up a model, such as partitioning, are *not* available in the SQL Server Standard edition. This is a short recap of the limitations of the Standard edition. (Please refer to official Microsoft licensing documentation for a more detailed and updated description, and remember that the Enterprise edition does not have such limitations.)

- **Memory** An instance in the multidimensional model can allocate up to 128 gigabytes (GB), whereas an instance in the tabular model can allocate up to 16 GB. This limitation mainly affects tabular models. Because all the data must be allocated in memory, the compressed database must consume no more than 16 GB. Considering the compression ratio and the need for memory during query, this limit corresponds to an uncompressed relational database of 100 to 150 GB. (The exact compression ratio depends on many factors. You can increase compression using best practices described in Chapter 12, "Inside VertiPaq," and Chapter 15, "Optimizing tabular models.")

- **Cores** You cannot use more than 24 cores. Considering the limit in database size, this limitation should not affect more than the memory constraint.

- **Partitions** You cannot split a table in multiple partitions regardless of whether you use a multidimensional or tabular model. This affects both processing and query performance in the multidimensional model, whereas it only affects processing performance in the tabular model. Usually, you use partitions to process only part of a large table—for example, the current and the last month of a transactions table.

- **DirectQuery** You cannot use DirectQuery—a feature that transforms a query sent to the semantic model in one or more queries to the underlying relational database—in the tabular model. The correspondent feature in the multidimensional model is ROLAP, which is supported in the Standard edition. This affects semantic models that must expose data changing in real-time.

- **Perspectives** You cannot use perspectives, regardless of whether you use a multidimensional or tabular model.

Note In Analysis Services 2012 and 2014, the features that enabled the sending of DAX queries to a multidimensional model were available only in the Enterprise and Business Intelligence editions of the product. In Analysis Services 2016, this feature is also available in the Standard edition. Azure Analysis Services supports all the features of the Enterprise edition.

Upgrading from previous versions of Analysis Services

As mentioned, there is no easy way to turn a multidimensional model into a tabular model. If any tool existed that claimed to make this transition with a few mouse clicks, it could only ever work for very simple multidimensional models and would not save much development time. Therefore, if you already have a mature Multidimensional mode implementation and the skills in-house to develop and maintain it, it probably makes no sense to abandon it and move over to the tabular model unless you have specific problems with the multidimensional model that the tabular model is likely to solve, such as several measures based on distinct count.

Ease of use

If you are starting an Analysis Services 2012 project with no previous multidimensional or OLAP experience, it is very likely that you will find the tabular model much easier to learn than the multidimensional model. Not only are the concepts much easier to understand, especially if you are used to working with relational databases, but the development process is also much more straightforward and there are far fewer features to learn. Building your first tabular model is much quicker and easier than building your first multidimensional model. It can also be argued that DAX is easier to learn than MDX, at least when it comes to writing basic calculations, but the truth is that both MDX and DAX can be equally confusing for anyone used to SQL.

Compatibility with Power Pivot

The tabular model and Power Pivot are almost identical in the way their models are designed. The user interfaces for doing so are practically the same, and both use DAX. Power Pivot models can also be imported into SQL Server Data Tools to generate a tabular model, although the process does not work the other way around. That is, a tabular model cannot be converted to a Power Pivot model. Therefore, if you have a strong commitment to self-service BI by using Power Pivot, it makes sense to use Tabular for your corporate BI projects because development skills and code are transferable between the two. However, in Tabular you can only import Power Pivot models loading data straight from a data source without using Power Query. This feature might be added in a future update of Analysis Services 2016.

Compatibility with Power BI

Despite models in Tabular and Power BI being identical and using the same core engine, Power BI uses a feature equivalent to Power Query to import data into the data model, and this feature is not supported by Analysis Services 2016 in its first release. As soon as this feature is added in a future update of Analysis Services 2016, it will be possible to import a Power BI model in Tabular, too.

Query performance characteristics

Although it would be dangerous to make sweeping generalizations about query performance, it's fair to say that the tabular model will perform at least as well as the multidimensional model in most cases and will outperform it in some specific scenarios. For example, distinct count measures—a particular weakness of the multidimensional model—perform extremely well in the tabular model. Anecdotal evidence also suggests that queries for detail-level reports (for example, queries that return numerous rows and return data at a granularity close to that of the fact table) will perform much better in the tabular model as long as they are written in DAX and not MDX. Unfortunately, when more complex calculations are involved, it is much more difficult to say whether the multidimensional or tabular model will perform better. A proper proof of concept will be the only way to tell whether the performance of either model will meet the requirements.

Processing performance characteristics

Comparing the processing performance of the multidimensional and tabular models is difficult. The number of rows of raw data that can be processed per second, for a single partition, is likely to be similar between the two models—*if* you disregard the different, incomparable operations that each model performs when processing data, such as building aggregations and indexes in a multidimensional model.

However, the tabular model has the following significant advantages over the multidimensional model when it comes to processing:

- There are no aggregations in the tabular model. This means there is one less time-consuming task to be performed at processing time.

- Processing one table in a tabular model has no direct impact on any of the other tables in the model, whereas in the multidimensional model, processing a dimension has consequential effects. Doing a full process on a dimension in the multidimensional model means you must do a full process on any cubes in which that dimension is used. Even doing a process update on a dimension requires a process index on a cube to rebuild aggregations.

Both of these factors can cause major headaches on large Multidimensional mode deployments, especially when the window available for processing is small. One similar bottleneck in the tabular model is calculated columns, which are always computed for the entire table, even when you refresh a single partition. Thus, you should not use calculated columns in large fact tables of a data model.

Hardware considerations

The multidimensional and tabular models have very different hardware-specification requirements. The multidimensional model's disk-based storage means it's important to have high-performance disks with plenty of space on those disks. It also caches data, so having sufficient RAM is very useful, although not essential. For the tabular model, the performance of disk storage is much less of a priority because it is an in-memory database. For this very reason, though, it is much more important to have enough RAM to hold the database and to accommodate any spikes in memory usage that occur when queries are running or when processing is taking place.

The multidimensional model's disk requirements will probably be easier to accommodate than the tabular model's memory requirements. Buying a large amount of disk storage for a server is relatively cheap and straightforward for an IT department. Many organizations have storage area networks

(SANs) that, although they might not perform as well as they should, make providing enough storage space (or increasing that provision) very simple. However, buying large amounts of RAM for a server can be more difficult. You might find that asking for half a terabyte of RAM on a server raises some eyebrows. If you find you need more RAM than you originally thought, increasing the amount that is available can also be awkward. Based on experience, it is easy to start with what seems like a reasonable amount of RAM. But as fact tables grow, new data is added to the model, and queries become more complex, you might start to encounter out-of-memory errors. Furthermore, for some extremely large Analysis Services implementations with several terabytes of data, it might not be possible to buy a server with sufficient RAM to store the model. In that case, the multidimensional model might be the only feasible option.

Real-time BI

Although not quite the industry buzzword that it was a few years ago, the requirement for real-time or near–real-time data in BI projects is becoming more common. Real-time BI usually refers to the need for end users to be able to query and analyze data as soon as it has been loaded into the data warehouse, with no lengthy waits for the data to be loaded into Analysis Services.

The multidimensional model can handle this in one of the following two ways:

- Using MOLAP storage and partitioning your data so that all the new data in your data warehouse goes to one relatively small partition that can be processed quickly

- Using ROLAP storage and turning off all caching so that the model issues SQL queries every time it is queried

The first of these options is usually preferred, although it can be difficult to implement, especially if dimension tables and fact tables change. Updating the data in a dimension can be slow and can also require aggregations to be rebuilt. ROLAP storage in the multidimensional model can often result in very poor query performance if data volumes are large, so the time taken to run a query in ROLAP mode might be greater than the time taken to reprocess the MOLAP partition in the first option.

The tabular model offers what are essentially the same two options but with fewer shortcomings than their multidimensional equivalents. If data is being stored in the in-memory engine, updating data in one table has no impact on the data in any other table, so processing times are likely to be faster and implementation much easier. If data is to remain in the relational engine, then the major difference is the equivalent of ROLAP mode, called *DirectQuery*. A full description of how to configure DirectQuery mode is given in Chapter 9, "Using DirectQuery."

Client tools

In many cases, the success or failure of a BI project depends on the quality of the tools that end users employ to analyze the data being provided. Therefore, it is important to understand which client tools are supported by which model.

Both the tabular model and the multidimensional model support both MDX and DAX queries. In theory, then, most Analysis Services client tools should support both models. Unfortunately, this is not true in practice. Although some client tools such as Excel and Power BI do work equally well on both, some third-party client tools might need to be updated to their latest versions to work, and some older tools that are still in use but are no longer supported might not work properly or at all. In general, tools designed to generate MDX queries (such as Excel) work better with the multidimensional model, and tools designed to generate DAX queries (such as Power BI) work better with the tabular model, even if the support of both query languages guarantees all combinations to work.

Feature comparison

One more thing to consider when choosing a model is the functionality present in the multidimensional model that either has no equivalent or is only partially implemented in the tabular model. Not all this functionality is important for all projects, however, and it must be said that in many scenarios it is possible to approximate some of this multidimensional functionality in the tabular model by using some clever DAX in calculated columns and measures. In any case, if you do not have any previous experience using the multidimensional model, you will not miss functionality you have never had.

The following list notes the most important functionality missing in the tabular model:

- **Writeback** This is the ability of an end user to write values back to a multidimensional database. This can be very important for financial applications in which users enter budget figures, for example.

- **Dimension security on measures** This enables access to a single measure to be granted or denied.

- **Cell security** This enables access to individual cells to be granted or denied. Again, there is no way of implementing this in the tabular model, but it is only very rarely used in the multidimensional model.

- **Ragged hierarchies** This is a commonly used technique for avoiding the use of a parent/child hierarchy. In a multidimensional model, a user hierarchy can be made to look something like a parent/child hierarchy by hiding members if certain conditions are met—for example, if a member has the same name as its parent. This is known as creating a *ragged hierarchy*. Nothing equivalent is available in the tabular model.

- **Role-playing dimensions** These are designed and processed once, then appear many times in the same model with different names and different relationships to measure groups. In the multidimensional model, this is known as using *role-playing dimensions*. Something similar is possible in the tabular model, by which multiple relationships can be created between two tables. (See Chapter 3, "Loading data inside Tabular," for more details on this.) Although this is extremely useful functionality, it does not do exactly the same thing as a role-playing dimension. In the tabular model, if you want to see the same table in two places in the model simultaneously, you must load it twice. This can increase processing times and make maintenance more difficult.

However, it is also true that using role-playing dimensions is not a best practice in terms of usability. This is because attribute and hierarchy names cannot be renamed for different roles. This creates confusion in the way data is displayed, using multiple roles of the same dimension in a report.

- **Scoped assignments and unary operators**   Advanced calculation functionality is present in MDX in the multidimensional model but it is not possible—or at least not easy—to re-create it in DAX in the tabular model. These types of calculations are often used in financial applications, so this and the lack of writeback and true parent/child hierarchy support mean that the tabular model is not suited for this class of application. Workarounds are possible in the tabular model, but at the cost of an increased development effort for each data model requiring these features.

The following functionality is only partially supported in the tabular model:

- **Parent/child hierarchy support**   In the multidimensional model, this is a special type of hierarchy built from a dimension table with a self-join on it by which each row in the table represents one member in the hierarchy and has a link to another row that represents the member's parent in the hierarchy. Parent/child hierarchies have many limitations in the multidimensional model and can cause query performance problems. Nevertheless, they are very useful for modeling hierarchies, such as company organization structures, because the developer does not need to know the maximum depth of the hierarchy at design time. The tabular model implements similar functionality by using DAX functions, such as PATH (see Chapter 5, "Building hierarchies," for details). Crucially, the developer must decide what the maximum depth of the hierarchy will be at design time.

- **Drillthrough**   This enables the user to click a cell to see all the detail-level data that is aggregated to return that value. Drillthrough is supported in both models, but in the multidimensional model, it is possible to specify which columns from dimensions and measure groups are returned from a drillthrough. In the tabular model, no interface exists in SQL Server data tools for doing this. By default, a drillthrough returns every column from the underlying table.

Understanding DAX and MDX

A tabular model defines its calculations using the DAX language. However, you can query a tabular model by using both DAX and MDX. In general, it is more efficient to use DAX as a query language, but the support for MDX is important to enable compatibility with many existing clients designed for the Analysis Services multidimensional model. (Keep in mind that any version of Analysis Services prior to 2012 only supported multidimensional models.) This section quickly describes the basic concepts of these two languages, guiding you in the choice of the query language (and client tools) to consume data from a tabular model.

The DAX language

DAX is a functional language that manipulates table and scalar expressions. A query in DAX always returns a table made by a variable number of rows (depending on the data) and a fixed number of typed columns (depending on the query statement). From this point of view, the result of a DAX query is very similar to that of a SQL query, and we can say that DAX is more similar to SQL than to MDX in its principles. The bigger difference is that SQL queries always express any relationship between tables in an explicit way, whereas DAX implicitly uses relationships existing in the data model, making it necessary to read the data model definition to understand the meaning of a query.

Similar to SQL, DAX does not have any semantic to operate with hierarchies. DAX manipulates only tables, rows, columns, and relationships. Even if a tabular model can include metadata defining hierarchies, the DAX language cannot use such information (which can be used by client tools to display data and has a semantic meaning only in MDX expressions).

As a pure functional language, DAX does not have imperative statements, but it leverages special functions called *iterators* that execute a certain expression for each row of a given table expression. These arguments are close to the lambda expressions in functional languages. However, there are limitations in the way you can combine them, so we cannot say they correspond to a generic lambda expression definition. Despite its functional nature, DAX does not allow you to define new functions and does not provide recursion.

The MDX language

The MDX language evaluates expressions in a multidimensional space. A query in MDX can return another multidimensional array, where the number of members of each axis of the result might depend on the data and could be not constrained to a limited number of members. Even if in most cases the result of an MDX expression is produced using two axes (rows and columns), you can easily build a query returning a variable number of columns, depending on context and filters used. The result of an MDX query is designed for client tools, such as a PivotTable. It could require extra effort to make sure the result of an MDX query will fit in a predefined structure with a fixed number (and type) of columns.

Every column in a table of a tabular model corresponds to an attribute of a dimension of a single cube, and the cube corresponds to the tabular model itself. Every hierarchy in a tabular model corresponds to a user hierarchy for MDX, and each measure in a tabular model corresponds to a measure for MDX that belongs to a measure group, having the same name as the table that includes the measure's definition. Relationships in the tabular model are implicitly considered relationships between measure groups and dimensions. If you are used to star schemas, which are the best relational model for both multidimensional and tabular databases, you will see a very similar result obtained by importing the same data in Multidimensional and Tabular mode. However, the presence of user hierarchies within a table enables the use of MDX functions to navigate hierarchies that do not have any correspondent feature in DAX.

An MDX query can use scope and local measures defined in MDX, as well as local measures defined in DAX. The opposite is not true. You cannot evaluate an MDX expression from a DAX query. MDX enables recursive calculations, even if such a technique might be limited when applied to a tabular model, because defining MDX measures embedded in the data model is not supported.

Choosing the query language for Tabular

In general, the default choice for querying a tabular model should be DAX. It provides the best performance, regardless of the granularity of the calculation (aggregated or leaf-level). However, most existing client tools for Analysis Services generate queries in MDX, so it is important to evaluate what the limitations are in using MDX for a tabular model.

Any leaf-level calculation applied to the data model, such as a multiplication made row-by-row in a table, has a better definition (and query plan) in DAX. The navigation of a user hierarchy has a shorter syntax in MDX, whereas it requires numerous constructs in DAX. From a performance point of view, usually MDX does not provide a real advantage, even if it offers a second-level cache (in the formula engine) that is not available in DAX.

If you must choose a language to query data for a table-based report (such as reporting services), you should use DAX. MDX could be the language of choice if you generate results in a dynamic matrix with a variable number of rows and columns, and nested levels of aggregation and subtotals (such as in a pivot table). If you choose a client that generates MDX queries, be aware of the possible performance issues when you place a high number of attributes in rows and columns of the result set. This is a typical problem using an Excel PivotTable querying a tabular or multidimensional model and trying to get a table with detailed information with many descriptive and grouping attributes. DAX is far more efficient for such kinds of queries.

Introduction to Tabular calculation engines

Every query sent to the tabular model in Analysis Services 2016 is executed by two layers of calculation engines. Analysis Services parses both DAX and MDX queries, transforming them in query plans executed by the formula engine, which can execute any function or operation of the two languages. To retrieve the raw data and perform calculations, the formula engine makes one or more calls to the storage engine, which could be either the in-memory analytics engine (VertiPaq) or the external relational database (DirectQuery). Each data model (corresponding to a database in Analysis Services) defines which storage engine to use. As shown in Figure 1-1, the VertiPaq engine contains a copy of the data read from the data source when you refresh the data model, whereas DirectQuery forwards requests to the external data source when necessary, reducing the latency between data updates in the data source and availability of updated data in Analysis Services. The VertiPaq engine receives requests in an internal binary structure (externally described using a human-readable format called *xmSQL*), whereas requests sent through DirectQuery are in the SQL language supported by the data source.

In this section, you will find an introduction to the two storage engines so you can make an initial choice for your data model. Later in this book, you will find dedicated chapters for each of the two storage engines, with a practical guide to their use and optimization: Chapter 9 and Chapter 12.

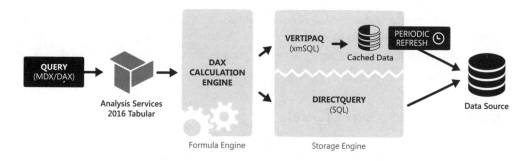

FIGURE 1-1 Formula and storage engines in the Analysis Services tabular model.

Introduction to VertiPaq

The in-memory analytics engine used by the tabular model, also known as the VertiPaq engine, is an in-memory columnar database. Being *in-memory* means that all the data handled by a model reside in RAM. Being *columnar* means that data is organized in a separate-columns structure, optimizing vertical scanning and requiring a greater effort if an entire row must be materialized with all its columns. VertiPaq does not have additional structures to optimize queries, such as indexes in a relational database. Since a complete logical scan of a column is required for any query, data is also compressed in memory (using algorithms that allow a quick scan operation) to reduce the scan time and the memory required.

The VertiPaq engine is only one part of the execution engine that provides results to DAX and MDX queries and expressions. In fact, VertiPaq is only the storage engine that has physical access to the compressed data and performs basic aggregations, filters, and joins between tables. The more complex calculations expressed in DAX or MDX are in charge of the formula engine, which receives intermediate results from the storage engine (VertiPaq or DirectQuery) and executes the remaining steps to complete the calculation. The formula engine is often the bottleneck of a slow query using the VertiPaq storage engine (with DirectQuery this might be different). This is because the formula engine usually executes a query in a single thread (but it handles requests from different users in parallel, if necessary). In contrast, VertiPaq can use multiple cores if the database is large enough to justify the usage of multiple threads (usually requiring a minimum of 16 million rows in a table, but this number depends on the segment size used at processing time).

VertiPaq storage processing is based on a few algorithms: hash encoding, value encoding, and run-length encoding (RLE). Each value in a column is always mapped into a 32-bit integer value. The mapping can be done in one of two ways: value encoding or hash encoding. Value encoding uses a dynamic arithmetic calculation to convert from the real value into an integer and vice versa. Hash encoding inserts new values into a hash table. The 32-bit integer value is then compressed before it is stored in the columns. Using RLE, the engine sorts data so that contiguous rows having the same values in a column will get a better compression, storing the number of rows with duplicated values instead of repeating the same value multiple times.

Note Whether you select value encoding or hash encoding depends on various factors, which are explained in more depth in Chapter 12. In that chapter, you will also learn how to improve the compression, reduce the memory usage, and improve the speed of data refresh.

Introduction to DirectQuery

The in-memory analytics engine (VertiPaq) is the default choice for any tabular model you create. However, you also have the option to avoid storing a copy of the data in memory. To do so, you use an alternative approach that converts a query to a tabular model into one or more SQL queries to the data source, without using the VertiPaq engine. This option is called *DirectQuery*. In this section, you learn its purpose. You will learn how to use it in your tabular model in Chapter 9.

The main benefit of using DirectQuery is to guarantee that data returned by a query is always up to date. Moreover, because Analysis Services does not store a copy of the database in memory, the size of the database can be larger than the memory capacity of the server. The performance provided by DirectQuery strongly depends on the performance and optimization applied to the relational database used as a data source. For example, if you use Microsoft SQL Server, you can take advantage of the columnstore index to obtain faster response times. However, it would be wrong to assume that a generic existing relational database could provide better performance than a properly tuned Analysis Services server for a tabular model. Usually you should consider using DirectQuery for small databases updated frequently, or for very large databases that cannot be stored in memory. However, in the latter case, you should set expectations of query refresh in the order of magnitude of seconds (or more). This reduces the user-friendliness of an interactive navigation of data.

DirectQuery is supported for a limited number of relational databases: Microsoft SQL Server (version 2008 or later), Microsoft Azure SQL Database, Microsoft Azure SQL Data Warehouse, Microsoft Analytics Platform System (APS), Oracle (version 9i and later), and Teradata (V2R6 and later). Other relational databases and/or versions are also supported, and more might be supported in the future. To verify the latest news about databases and versions supported, refer to the Microsoft documentation (*https://msdn.microsoft.com/en-us/library/gg492165.aspx*).

DirectQuery does not support all the features of a tabular data model or of MDX or DAX. From a data-model point of view, the main limitation of DirectQuery is that it does not support calculated tables. You can, however, use calculated columns, although with some limitations (which we will describe later).

From a DAX point of view, there are numerous functions that have a different semantic because they are converted in correspondent SQL expressions, so you might observe an inconsistent behavior across platforms by using time intelligence and statistical functions. From an MDX point of view, there are numerous limitations that affect only the MDX coding style. For example, you cannot use relative names, session-scope MDX statements, or tuples with members from different levels in MDX subselect clauses. However, there is one limitation that affects the design of a data model: You cannot reference user-defined hierarchies in an MDX query sent to a model using DirectQuery. This affects the usability of DirectQuery from Excel because such a feature works without any issue when you use VertiPaq as a storage engine.

Note DirectQuery had many more limitations in Analysis Services 2012/2014. For example, it worked only for Microsoft SQL Server, MDX was not supported, and every DAX query was converted in a complete SQL query, without using the formula engine of the Analysis Services tabular model. And features like calculated columns and time-intelligence functions were not supported at all. For this reason, the list of restrictions for using DirectQuery was much longer. However, DirectQuery received a complete overhaul in Analysis Services 2016. In this book, you will find only information about DirectQuery used in Analysis Services with the new compatibility level, which is described in the next section.

Tabular model compatibility level (1200 vs. 110*x*)

Analysis Services 2016 introduced a new compatibility level, which refers to a set of release-specific behaviors in the Analysis Services engine. Databases created with previous versions of Analysis Services have a different compatibility level, and Analysis Services 2016 also supports all these. This means you can easily migrate existing databases created in previous versions to Analysis Services 2016, but you must migrate to the new data model if you want to use specific features available only in this new release. You can also create new databases in Analysis Services using an older compatibility level in case you need to use certain features that were available in a previous compatibility level (even if they were not officially supported), as you will see later in this section.

The following compatibility levels are available for tabular models:

- **1100** This is available in SQL Server 2012, SQL Server 2014, and SQL Server 2016.

- **1103** This is available in SQL Server 2012 SP1, SQL Server 2014, and SQL Server 2016.

- **1200** This is available in SQL Server 2016 and Azure Analysis Services.

You can create and deploy any compatibility level using SQL Server Data Tools (SSDT) for VS 2015. You can use only compatibility levels 1100 and 1103 if you use SQL Server Data Tools for Business Intelligence (SSDT-BI) for VS 2012 or 2013.

The new compatibility level 1200 stores the data model using a JSON format, whereas the previous compatibility levels 110*x* use an XML-based format that was inherited from the Multidimensional version of Analysis Services. Such a model was adapted for the tabular model in its first version (Analysis Services 2012), but it required a useless overhead and redundancy in code. It also had numerous effects in performance (longer time to deploy data models) and manageability (small changes in a data model produced numerous differences in files, complicating the comparison of different versions and the use of source-control systems).

Many new features in Analysis Services 2016 are available only using the new compatibility level. Therefore, it is generally a good idea to use the compatibility level 1200 when you start a new project or migrate an existing one. Such a compatibility level is also required to deploy a database on Azure

Analysis Services. However, certain tools and extensions that were available in SSDT-BI for VS 2012 and VS 2013 are no longer available in SSDT for VS 2015. If you used any of these, you should consider carefully when to upgrade an existing model to the new compatibility level and to the new version of VS. The following two open-source tools are the most affected by this change:

- **BIDS Helper** You can no longer use BIDS Helper (*http://bidshelper.codeplex.com/*) to edit Actions or the HideMemberIf property because these features are no longer supported in the compatibility level 1200. If you use BIDS Helper to edit display folders or translations, you should rely on the new equivalent features for the tabular model now supported in Analysis Services 2016.

- **DAX Editor** If you use DAX Editor (*http://www.sqlbi.com/tools/dax-editor/*) to edit the list of measures of a tabular model in a single text file, make sure you download the latest version (2.0 or newer), which is compatible with both XML and JSON formats.

You can still use BIDS Helper when deploying a model to Analysis Services 2016, taking advantage of the new engine and DAX functions available in this version. However, you must use SSDT-BI for VS 2012 or VS 2013, without accessing the features available in the new data model. If you make this choice, consider it a temporary situation and define a plan for a future migration to the new model compatibility level.

> **Note** This book is based on the features available in the new compatibility level 1200. If you want to create a model using a 110*x* compatibility level, you might find differences in features, performance, and the user interface of the development tools. In that case, we suggest you rely on the documentation available for Analysis Services 2012/2014 and refer to our previous book, *Microsoft SQL Server 2012 Analysis Services: The BISM Tabular Model*, as a reference.

Analysis Services and Power BI

Power BI is an excellent client tool for Analysis Services. As of now, Power BI is the only widely available client tool that generates queries in DAX, so it can take full advantage of a tabular model. In fact, the engine used internally by Power BI is the same engine as Analysis Services 2016 for tabular models. Power BI is available online, consuming reports through a web browser or a mobile device. It is also available as a free desktop application called *Power BI Desktop*.

You can connect Power BI Desktop to Analysis Services using the Connect Live mode in Get Data. If you want to use the same database online, you must install the on-premises data gateway, which creates a bridge between the online client tool and your Analysis Services database installed on-premises, as shown in Figure 1-2.

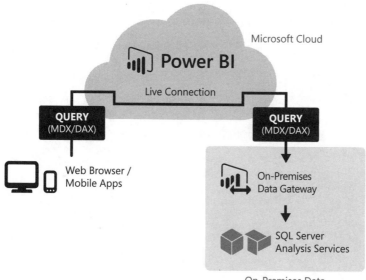

FIGURE 1-2 SQL Server Analysis Services connected to Power BI through the On-Premises Data Gateway.

Although you can connect any version of the Analysis Services tabular model to Power BI, you should be aware that Power BI creates optimized DAX queries for Analysis Services 2016, using many new DAX features designed expressly to improve the performance of Power BI. When Power BI connects to Analysis Services 2012/2014, it must use an older version of the DAX language, producing less-efficient queries and slower user interaction in complex reports. This performance difference is not related to the compatibility version level. Also, databases deployed with an older compatibility level can get the full benefits of the new DAX syntax available in Analysis Services 2016. Thus, consider upgrading the server to Analysis Services 2016 as an existing data model if you want to consume it with Power BI—even if you don't want to or cannot upgrade the model compatibility level.

Summary

This chapter discussed the tabular and multidimensional models in Analysis Services, their strengths and weaknesses, and when they should be used. The key point to remember is that the two models are very different—they're practically separate products. You should not make the decision to use the tabular model on a project without considering whether it is a good fit for your requirements, or whether you should use a multidimensional model instead. In the next chapter, you will take a first look at how to build tabular models.

CHAPTER 2

Getting started with the tabular model

Now that you have been introduced to the Analysis Services tabular model, this chapter shows you how to get started developing tabular models yourself. You will discover how to install Analysis Services, how to work with projects in SQL Server Data Tools, what the basic building blocks of a tabular model are, and how to build, deploy, and query a very simple tabular model.

What's new in SSAS 2016   There are new model and development features, such as integrated workspace in SQL Server Data Tools, and calculated tables. In addition, this chapter has been updated to describe how to use Power BI to test the model and the importance of DAX Studio and other free development tools.

Setting up a development environment

Before you can start working with the tabular model, you must set up a development environment.

Components of a development environment

A development environment has the following three logical components:

- A development workstation

- A development server

- A workspace database, which might be hosted on a separate workspace server

You may install each of these components on separate machines or on a single machine. Each component has a distinct role to play, and it is important for you to understand these roles.

Development workstation

You will design your tabular models on your development workstation. Tabular models are designed using SQL Server Data Tools (SSDT). This is essentially Visual Studio 2015 plus numerous SQL Server–related project templates. You can download and install SSDT from the Microsoft web site (*https:// msdn.microsoft.com/en-us/library/mt204009.aspx*). No separate license for Visual Studio is required.

To create and modify a tabular model, SSDT needs a workspace database. This is a temporary database that can be created on the same development workstation using Integrated Workspace Mode or on a specific instance of Analysis Services. (For more on this, see the section "Workspace database server installation" later in this chapter.)

After you finish designing your tabular model in SSDT, you must build and deploy your project. Building a project is like compiling code. The build process translates all the information stored in the files in your project into a data definition language called *Tabular Model Scripting Language* (*TMSL*). Deployment involves executing this TMSL on the Analysis Services tabular instance running on your development server. The result will either create a new database or alter an existing database.

> **Note** Previous versions of Analysis Services used XML for Analysis (XMLA), which is XML-based, as a data definition language. Analysis Services 2016 introduced a new language, TMSL, which is JSON-based instead of XML-based. However, the JSON-based script is still sent to Analysis Services using the XMLA protocol. (The XMLA.Execute method accepts both TMSL and XMLA definitions.)

Development server

A *development server* is a server with an installed instance of Analysis Services running in Tabular mode that you can use to host your models while they are being developed. You can also use an instance of Azure Analysis Services (Azure AS) as a development server. You deploy your project to the development server from your development workstation.

A development server should be in the same domain as your development workstation. After you deploy your project to your development server, you and anyone else to whom you give permission will be able to see your tabular model and query it. This will be especially important for any other members of your team who are building reports or other parts of your BI solution.

Your development workstation and your development server can be two machines, or you can use the same machine for both roles. It is best, however, to use a separate, dedicated machine as your development server for the following reasons:

- A dedicated server will likely have a much better hardware specification than a workstation. In particular, as you will soon see, the amount of available memory can be very important when developing with tabular. Memory requirements also mean that using a 64-bit operating system is important. Nowadays, you can almost take this for granted on new servers and workstations, but you might still find legacy computers with 32-bit versions of Windows.

- A dedicated server will make it easy for you to grant access to your tabular models to other developers, testers, or users while you work. This enables them to run their own queries and build reports without disturbing you. Some queries can be resource-intensive, and you will not want your workstation grinding to a halt unexpectedly when someone else runs a huge query. And, of course, no one would be able to run queries on your workstation if you have turned it off and gone home for the day.

- A dedicated server will enable you to reprocess your models while you perform other work. As noted, reprocessing a large model is very resource-intensive and could last for several hours. If you try to do this on your own workstation, it is likely to stop you from doing anything else.

- A dedicated development server will (probably) be backed up regularly. This reduces the likelihood that hardware failure will result in a loss of work or data.

There are a few occasions when you might consider *not* using a separate development server. Such instances might be if you do not have sufficient hardware available, if you are not working on an official project, or if you are only evaluating the tabular model or installing it so you can learn more about it.

Workspace database

One way the tabular model aims to make development easier is by providing a what-you-see-is-what-you-get (WYSIWYG) experience for working with models. That way, whenever you change a model, that change is reflected immediately in the data you see in SSDT without you having to save or deploy anything. This is possible because SSDT has its own private tabular database, called a *workspace database*, to which it can deploy automatically every time you make a change. You can think of this database as a kind of work-in-progress database.

Do not confuse a workspace database with a development database. A development database can be shared with the entire development team and might be updated only once or twice a day. In contrast, a workspace database should never be queried or altered by anyone or anything but the instance of SSDT (and Excel/Power BI clients) that you are using. Although the development database might not contain the full set of data you are expecting to use in production, it is likely to contain a representative sample that might still be quite large. In contrast, because it must be changed so frequently, the workspace database might contain only a very small amount of data. Finally, as you have seen, there are many good reasons for putting the development database on a separate server. In contrast, there are several good reasons for putting the workspace database server on the same machine as your development database.

A workspace database for a tabular project can have either one of these following two configurations:

- **Integrated workspace** In this configuration, SSDT runs a private instance of Analysis Services (installed by SSDT setup) hosting the workspace database.

- **Workspace server** In this configuration, the workspace database is hosted on an explicit instance of Analysis Services, which is a Windows service that must be installed using the SQL Server setup procedure.

Note Previous versions of Analysis Services required an explicit instance of Analysis Services for the workspace database. SSDT introduced the integrated workspace option in October 2016. When you use the integrated workspace, SSDT executes a separate 64-bit process running Analysis Services using the same user credentials used to run Visual Studio.

Licensing

All the installations in the developer environment should use the SQL Server Developer Edition. This edition has all the functionalities of Enterprise Edition, but is free! The only limitation is that the license cannot be used on a production server. For a detailed comparison between all the editions, see *https://www.microsoft.com/en-us/cloud-platform/sql-server-editions*.

Installation process

This section discusses how to install the various components of a development environment. If you use only Azure AS, you can skip the next section, "Development server installation," and go straight to the "Development workstation installation" section. If you are interested in provisioning an instance of Azure AS, you can find detailed instructions at *https://azure.microsoft.com/en-us/documentation/services/analysis-services/*.

Development server installation

To install an instance of Analysis Services in Tabular mode on your development server, follow these steps:

1. Ensure that you are logged on to Windows as a user with administrative rights.

2. Double-click SETUP.EXE to start the SQL Server Installation Center.

3. On the left side of the SQL Server Installation Center window, click **Installation**, as shown in Figure 2-1.

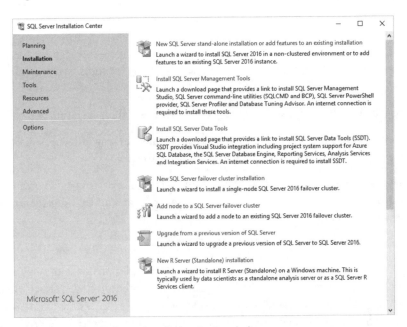

FIGURE 2-1 The SQL Server Installation Center window.

4. Click the first option on the right side of the window, **New SQL Server Stand-Alone Installation or Add Features to an Existing Installation**.

5. The wizard opens the SQL Server 2016 Setup window. On the Product Key page, select **Enter a Product Key** and type the key for your SQL Server Developer license. Alternatively, if you want to install an evaluation-only version, select the **Evaluation** option in the Specify a Free Edition section. Then click **Next**.

6. On the License Terms page, select the **I Accept the License Terms** check box and click **Next.**

7. The wizard runs Setup Global Rules to see whether any conditions might prevent the setup from succeeding. If there are, it will display the Global Rules page, shown in Figure 2-2. (You will not see this page if there are no warnings or errors.) If there are any issues, you must address them before the installation can proceed. After you do so, click **Next**.

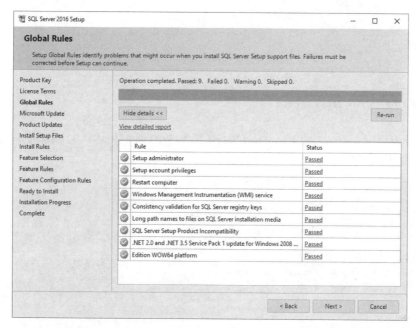

FIGURE 2-2 The Global Rules page.

8. On the Microsoft Update page, select the **Use Microsoft Update to Check for Updates** check box (assuming you are connected to the Internet) and then click **Next**. The wizard checks for any SQL Server updates, such as service packs that you might also want to install.

9. The Product Updates and Install Setup Files pages update you on the setup preparation progress. After that, the wizard runs Install Rules to see whether any conditions might prevent the setup from succeeding. If there are, it will display the Install Rules page, shown in Figure 2-3. (You will not see this page if there are no warnings or errors.) If there are any failures, you must address them before the installation can proceed. Warnings (marked by a yellow triangle icon) can be ignored if you feel they are not relevant. When you are finished, click **Next**.

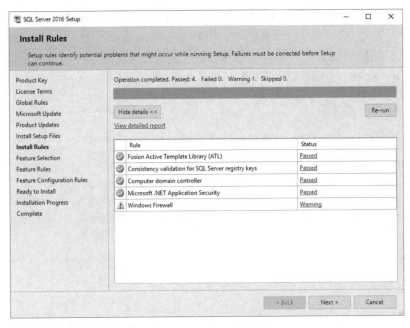

FIGURE 2-3　The Install Rules page.

10. On the Feature Selection page, select the **Analysis Services** check box in the Features list, as shown in Figure 2-4.

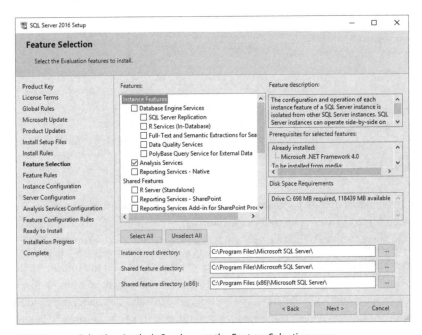

FIGURE 2-4　Selecting Analysis Services on the Feature Selection page.

Note With the given selections, SQL Server 2016 Setup skips the Feature Rules page and continues to the Instance Configuration.

11. On the Instance Configuration page, shown in Figure 2-5, choose either the **Default Instance** or **Named Instance** option button to create either a default instance or a named instance. A named instance with a meaningful name (for example, *TABULAR*, as shown in Figure 2-5) is preferable because if you later decide to install another instance of Analysis Services (but run it in multidimensional mode on the same server), it will be much easier to determine the instance to which you are connecting. When you are finished, click **Next**.

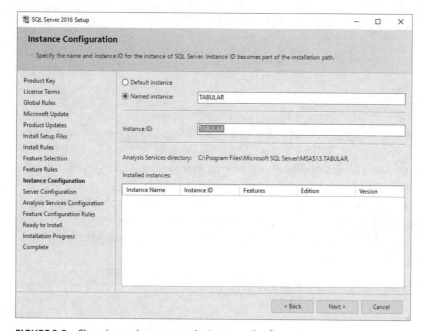

FIGURE 2-5 Choosing an instance on the Instance Configuration page.

12. On the Server Configuration page, in the **Service Accounts** tab, enter the user name and password under which the Analysis Services Windows service will run. This should be a domain account created especially for this purpose.

13. Click the **Collation** tab and choose which collation you want to use. We suggest *not* using a case-sensitive collation. Otherwise, you will have to remember to use the correct case when writing queries and calculations. Click **Next**.

14. On the Analysis Services Configuration page, in the Server Mode section of the Server Configuration tab, select the **Tabular Mode** option button, as shown in Figure 2-6. Then click either the **Add Current User** button or the **Add** button (both are circled in Figure 2-6) to add a user as an Analysis Services administrator. At least one user must be nominated here.

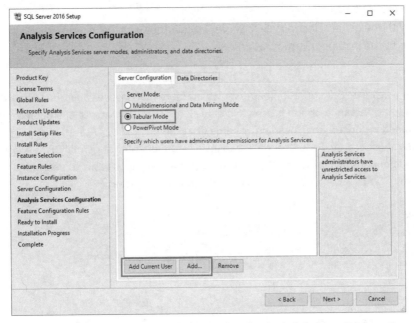

FIGURE 2-6 Selecting the Tabular Mode option on the Analysis Services Configuration page.

15. Click the **Data Directories** tab to specify the directories Analysis Services will use for its Data, Log, Temp, and Backup directories. We recommend that you create new directories specifically for this purpose, and that you put them on a dedicated drive with lots of space (*not* the C: drive). Using a dedicated drive makes it easier to find these directories if you want to check their contents and size. When you are finished, click **Next**. (SQL Server 2016 Setup skips the Feature Configuration Rules page.)

16. On the Ready to Install page, click **Install** to start the installation. After it finishes, close the wizard.

Note It is very likely you will also need to have access to an instance of the SQL Server relational database engine for your development work. You might want to consider installing one on your development server.

Development workstation installation

On your development workstation, you need to install the following:

- SQL Server Data Tools and SQL Server Management Studio

- A source control system

- Other useful development tools such as DAX Studio, DAX Editor, OLAP PivotTable Extensions, BISM Normalizer, and BIDS Helper

SQL Server Data Tools and SQL Server Management Studio installation

You can install the components required for your development workstation from the SQL Server installer as follows:

1. Repeat steps 1–3 in the "Development server installation" section.

2. In the SQL Server Installation Center window (refer to Figure 2-1), select **Install SQL Server Management Tools**. Then follow the instructions to download and install the latest version of SQL Server Management Studio, SQL Server Profiler, and other tools.

3. Again, in the SQL Server Installation Center window, select **Install SQL Server Data Tools**. Then follow the instructions to download and install the latest version of SQL Server Data Tools (SSDT) for Visual Studio 2015. If you do not have Visual Studio 2015, SSDT will install the Visual Studio 2015 integrated shell.

Source control system installation

At this point, you must ensure that you have some form of source control set up that integrates well with Visual Studio, such as Team Foundation Server. That way, you can check any projects you create by using SSDT. Developing a BI solution for Analysis Services is no different from any other form of development. It is vitally important that your source code, which is essentially what an SSDT project contains, is stored safely and securely. Also, make sure you can roll back to previous versions after any changes have been made.

Installing other tools

After you have deployed your tabular model, you cannot browse it inside SSDT. To browse your deployed tabular model, you should install Microsoft Excel on your development workstation. As you will see later in this chapter, SSDT will attempt to launch Excel when you are ready to do this. The browser inside SQL Server Management Studio is very limited, as it is based on the MDX query generator control in SQL Server Reporting Services.

In addition, you should install the following free tools on your development workstation. These provide useful extra functionality and are referenced in upcoming chapters:

- **DAX Studio** This is a tool for writing, running, and profiling DAX queries against data models in Excel Power Pivot, the Analysis Services tabular model, and Power BI Desktop. You can download it from *http://daxstudio.codeplex.com/*.

- **DAX Editor** This is a tool for modifying the DAX measures of a tabular model in a text file. You can download it from *http://www.sqlbi.com/tools/dax-editor/*.

- **OLAP PivotTable Extensions** This Excel add-in adds extra functionality to PivotTables connected to Analysis Services data sources. Among other things, it enables you to see the MDX generated by the PivotTable. It can be downloaded from *http://olappivottableextend.codeplex.com/*.

- **BISM Normalizer**   This is a tool for comparing and merging two tabular models. It is particularly useful when trying to merge models created in Power Pivot with an existing tabular model. You can download it from *http://bism-normalizer.com/*.

- **BIDS Helper**   This is an award-winning, free Visual Studio add-in developed by members of the Microsoft BI community to extend SSDT. It includes functionalities for both tabular and multidimensional models. The updated version of BIDS Helper for Visual Studio 2015 is available in the Visual Studio Gallery. You can find more information at *http://bidshelper.codeplex.com/*.

Workspace database server installation

You need not install a workspace database server if you plan to use the integrated workspace. If you do want to install it, it involves following similar steps as installing a development database server. First, however, you must answer the following two important questions:

- **On what type of physical machine do you want to install your workspace database server?**   Installing it on its own dedicated server would be a waste of hardware, but you can install it on either your development workstation or the development server. There are pros and cons to each option, but in general, we recommend installing your workspace database server on your development workstation if possible. By doing so, you gain the following features, which are not available if you use a remote machine as the workspace server:

  - SSDT has the option to back up a workspace database when you save a project (although this does not happen by default).

  - It is possible to import data and metadata when creating a new tabular project from an existing Power Pivot workbook.

  - It is easier to import data from Excel, Microsoft Access, or text files.

- **Which account will you use to run the Analysis Services service?**   In the previous section, we recommended that you create a separate domain account for the development database installation. For the workspace database, it can be much more convenient to use the account with which you normally log on to Windows. This will give the workspace database instance access to all the same file system locations you can access, and will make it much easier to back up workspace databases and import data from Power Pivot.

If you choose the integrated-workspace route, you have a situation that is similar to a workspace server installed on the same computer that is running SSDT, using your user name as a service account for Analysis Services. Consider that with the integrated workspace, the workspace database is saved in the bin\Data directory of the tabular project folder. When you open the project, this database is read in memory, so storing the project files in a remote folder could slow down the process of opening an existing project. In general, you should consider using the integrated workspace, because it is easier to manage and provides optimal performance. You might still consider an explicit workspace when you know the workspace database will be large or you need to host it on a separate machine from the developer workstation.

Note If you do not use an integrated workspace, you can find more details on using an explicit workspace server on Cathy Dumas's blog, at *https://blogs.msdn.microsoft.com/ cathyk/2011/10/03/configuring-a-workspace-database-server/*.

Working with SQL Server Data Tools

After you set up the development environment, you can start using SQL Server Data Tools to complete several tasks. First, though, there are some basic procedures you will need to know how to perform, such as creating a new project, configuring a new project, importing from Power Pivot or Power BI, and importing a deployed project from Analysis Services. You will learn how to do all these things in this section.

Creating a new project

To start building a new tabular model, you must create a new project in SSDT. Follow these steps:

1. Start SSDT.

2. If this is the first time you have started SSDT, you will see the dialog box shown in Figure 2-7, asking you to choose the default development settings. Select **Business Intelligence Settings** and then click **Start Visual Studio**.

FIGURE 2-7 Choosing Business Intelligence Settings on the initial dialog box.

3. After the start page appears, open the **File** menu, choose **New**, and select **Project**.

4. The New Project dialog box shown in Figure 2-8 opens. In the left pane, click **Installed**, choose **Templates**, select **Business Intelligence**, and click **Analysis Services** to show the options for creating a new Analysis Services project.

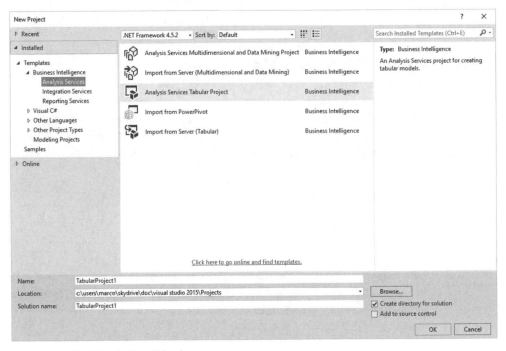

FIGURE 2-8   The New Project dialog box.

5. Explore the options in the center pane. The first two options are for creating projects for the multidimensional model, so they can be ignored. That leaves the following three options:

- **Analysis Services Tabular Project**   This creates a new, empty project for designing a tabular model.

- **Import from PowerPivot**   This enables you to import a model created by using Power Pivot into a new SSDT project.

- **Import from Server (Tabular)**   This enables you to point to a model that has already been deployed to Analysis Services and import its metadata into a new project.

6. Click the **Analysis Services Tabular Project** option to create a new project. (You will explore the other two options in more detail later in this chapter.)

Editing projects online

Readers with experience with the Analysis Services multidimensional model know that there is another option for working with multidimensional models in SSDT: online mode. This enables you to connect to a multidimensional database that has already been deployed and edit it live on the server. That way, every time you save, the changes are immediately made on the server. Using this option has always been strongly discouraged because it is dangerous to update a running model. For this reason, it is no longer supported for tabular models.

Configuring a new project

Now that your new project has been created, the next thing to do is to configure various project properties.

Tabular Model Designer dialog box

The first time you create a new tabular project in SSDT, a dialog box will help you set a few important properties for your projects. These include where you want to host the workspace database and the compatibility level of the tabular model, as shown in Figure 2-9. You can change these settings later in the model's properties settings.

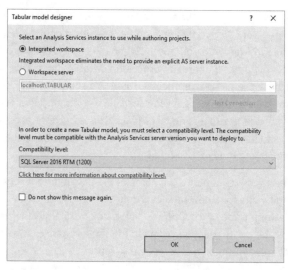

FIGURE 2-9   Setting the workspace database and the compatibility level of the tabular model.

> **Note**   You can choose a compatibility level lower than 1200 to support older versions of Analysis Services. This book discusses the models created in the compatibility level greater than or equal to 1200 (for SQL Server 2016 RTM or newer versions).

Project Properties

You set project properties using the Project Properties dialog box, shown in Figure 2-10. To open this dialog box, right-click the name of the project in the Solution Explorer window and choose **Properties** from the menu that appears.

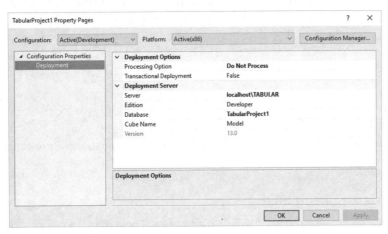

FIGURE 2-10   The project's Properties Pages dialog box.

Now you should set the following properties. (We will deal with some of the others later in this book.)

- **Deployment Options > Processing Option**   This property controls which type of processing takes place after a project has been deployed to the development server. It controls if and how Analysis Services automatically loads data into your model when it has been changed. The default setting, Default, reprocesses any tables that are not processed or tables where the alterations you are deploying would leave them in an unprocessed state. You can also choose Full, which means the entire model is completely reprocessed. However, we recommend that you choose **Do Not Process** so that no automatic processing takes place. This is because processing a large model can take a long time, and it is often the case that you will want to deploy changes either without reprocessing or reprocessing only certain tables.

- **Deployment Server > Server**   This property contains the name of the development server to which you wish to deploy. The default value for a new project is defined in the Analysis Services Tabular Designers > New Project Settings page of the Options dialog box of SSDT. Even if you are using a local development server, be aware that you will need the same instance name of Analysis Services in case the project is ever used on a different workstation.

- **Deployment Server > Edition**   This property enables you to specify the edition of SQL Server you are using on your production server and prevents you from developing by using any features that are not available in that edition. You should set this property to Standard if you want to be able to deploy the model on any version of Analysis Services. If you set this property to Developer, you have no restrictions in features you have available, which corresponds to the full set of features available in the Enterprise edition.

- **Deployment Server > Database**   This is the name of the database to which the project will be deployed. By default, it is set to the name of the project, but because the database name will be visible to end users, you should check with them about what database name they would like to see.

- **Deployment Server > Cube Name**   This is the name of the cube that is displayed to all client tools that query your model in MDX, such as Excel. The default name is *Model*, but you might consider changing it, again consulting your end users to see what name they would like to use.

Model properties

There are also properties that should be set on the model itself. You can find them by right-clicking the Model.bim file in the Solution Explorer window and selecting **Properties** to display the Properties pane inside SSDT, as shown in Figure 2-11. Several properties are grayed out because they cannot be modified in the model's Properties pane. To change them, you must use the **View Code** command to open the Model.bim JSON file and manually edit the properties in that file.

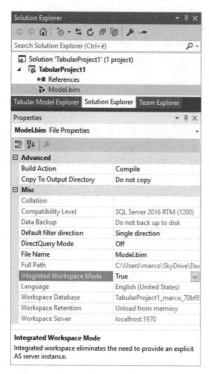

FIGURE 2-11   The model's Properties pane in Solution Explorer.

The properties that should be set here are as follows:

- **Data Backup** This controls what happens to the workspace database when you close your project. You can change it only if you use an explicit workspace server. This property is disabled if you use the integrated workspace because the workspace database is already saved in the project's bin\Data folder, so no additional backup is required. The default setting is Do Not Back Up to Disk, which means that nothing is backed up when the project is closed. However, you might consider changing this property to Back Up to Disk if all of the following are true:

  - You are working with a local workspace database server.

  - The instance on the workspace database server is running as an account with sufficient permissions to write to your project directory (such as your own domain account, as recommended earlier in this chapter).

  - The data volumes in the workspace database are small.

 Note When you close your project, the workspace database is backed up to the same directory as your SSDT project. This could be useful for the reasons listed in the blog post at *https://blogs.msdn.microsoft.com/cathyk/2011/09/20/working-with-backups-in-the-tabular-designer/*, but the reasons are not particularly compelling, and backing up the data increases the amount of time it takes to save a project.

- **Default Filter Direction** This controls the default direction of the filters when you create a new relationship. The default choice is Single Direction, which corresponds to the behavior of filters in Analysis Services 2012/2014. In the new compatibility level 1200, you can choose **Both Directions**, but we suggest you leave the default direction as is and modify only the specific relationships where enabling the bidirectional filter makes sense. You will find more details about the filter direction of relationships in Chapter 6, "Data modeling in Tabular."

- **DirectQuery Mode** This enables or disables DirectQuery mode at the project level. A full description of how to configure DirectQuery mode is given in Chapter 9, "Using DirectQuery."

- **File Name** This sets the file name of the .bim file in your project. (The "Contents of a Tabular Project" section later in this chapter explains exactly what this file is.) This could be useful if you are working with multiple projects inside a single SSDT solution.

- **Integrated Workspace Mode** This enables or disables the integrated workspace. Changing this property might require a process of the tables (choose **Model** > **Process** > **Process All**) if the new workspace server never processed the workspace database.

- **Workspace Retention** This setting can be edited only if you use an explicit workspace server. When you close your project in SSDT, this property controls what happens to the workspace database (its name is given in the read-only Workspace Database property) on the workspace database server. The default setting is Unload from Memory. The database itself is detached, so it is still present on disk but not consuming any memory. It is, however, reattached quickly when the project is reopened. The Keep in Memory setting indicates that the database is not detached and nothing happens to it when the project closes. The Delete Workspace setting indicates that the database is completely deleted and must be re-created when the project is reopened. For temporary projects created for testing and experimental purposes, we recommend using the Delete Workspace setting. Otherwise, you will accumulate numerous unused workspace databases that will clutter your server and consume disk space. If you are working with only one project or are using very large data volumes, the Keep in Memory setting can be useful because it decreases the time it takes to open your project. If you use the integrated workspace, the behavior you have is similar to Unload from Memory, and the database itself is stored in the bin\Data folder of the tabular project.

- **Workspace Server**   This is the name of the Analysis Services tabular instance you want to use as your workspace database server. This setting is read-only when you enable the Integrated Workspace Mode setting. Here you can see the connection string to use if you want to connect to the workspace database from a client, such as Power BI or Excel.

Options dialog box

Many of the default settings for the properties mentioned in the previous three sections can also be changed inside SSDT. That means you need not reconfigure them for every new project you create. To do this, follow these steps:

1. Open the **Tools** menu and choose **Options** to open the Options dialog box, shown in Figure 2-12.

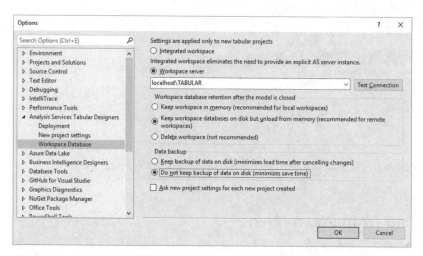

FIGURE 2-12   The Options dialog box, with the Workspace Database page displayed.

2. On the left side of the Options dialog box, click **Analysis Services Tabular Designers** in the left pane and choose **Workspace Database**.

3. In the right pane, choose either **Integrated Workspace** or **Workspace Server**. If you choose Workspace Server, also set the default values for the **Workspace Server**, **Workspace Database Retention**, and **Data Backup** model properties.

4. Optionally, select the **Ask New Project Settings for Each New Project Created** check box.

> **Note** The Analysis Services Tabular Designers > Deployment page enables you to set the name of the deployment server you wish to use by default. The Business Intelligence Designers > Analysis Services Designers > General page enables you to set the default value for the Deployment Server Edition property.

5. Click **Analysis Services Tabular Designers** and choose **New Project Settings** to see the page shown in Figure 2-13. Here, you can set the default values for the Default Compatibility Level and Default Filter Direction settings, which will apply to new projects. The check boxes in the Compatibility Level Options section enable a request to check the compatibility level for every new project as well as a check of the compliance of the compatibility level with the server chosen for project deployment.

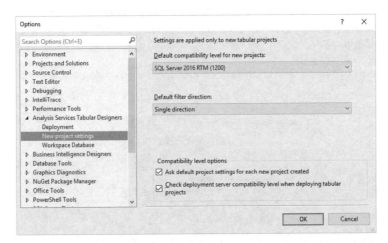

FIGURE 2-13 The Options dialog box with the New Project Settings page displayed.

Importing from Power Pivot

Instead of creating an empty project in SSDT, it is possible to import the metadata and, in some cases, the data of a model created in Power Pivot into a new project. A Power Pivot workbook contains a semantic model that can be converted in a corresponding Analysis Services tabular model, and this could be very useful to create first prototypes.

To import a model from Power Pivot, follow these steps:

1. Create a new project.

2. Choose **Import from PowerPivot** in the New Project dialog box (refer to Figure 2-8).

3. Choose the Excel workbook that contains the Power Pivot model you want to import. A new project containing a tabular model identical to the Power Pivot model will be created.

If you use an integrated workspace, this operation should run smoothly. However, if you use an explicit workspace server, and the service account you are using to run it does not have read permissions on the directory where you are storing the new project, the dialog box shown in Figure 2-14 will appear, indicating that the model will not be imported. This is common when you save the project in the local user folder (usually C:\users\username\... in Windows 10), which is commonly used for the standard Documents folder of your computer. Usually, only your user name has access to this folder, but a local service account used by default for the Analysis Services service does *not* have such access. Moreover, you typically cannot use a remote workspace server because the remote service usually does not have access to the directory where you store the project files. These are yet more good reasons you should consider using the integrated workspace or installing a local workspace server on your computer, providing your user name to run the service instance.

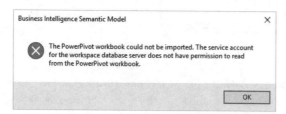

FIGURE 2-14   This error message appears when the Power Pivot workbook cannot be imported.

Importing from Power BI

As of this writing, the ability to import a Power BI model in Analysis Services is not supported. However, this feature is expected to be released in a future update of Analysis Services. When this happens, you will probably see an Import from Power BI choice in the New Project dialog box (refer to Figure 2-8).

Importing a Deployed Project from Analysis Services

It is also possible to create a new project from an existing Analysis Services tabular database that has already been deployed on a server. This can be useful if you need to quickly create a copy of a project or if the project has been lost, altered, or corrupted, and you were not using source control. To do this, choose **Import from Server (Tabular)** in the New Project dialog box (refer to Figure 2-8). You will be asked to connect to the server and the database from which you wish to import, and a new project will be created.

Contents of a tabular project

It is important to be familiar with all the different files associated with a tabular project in SSDT. Figure 2-15 shows all the files associated with a new, blank project in the Solution Explorer pane.

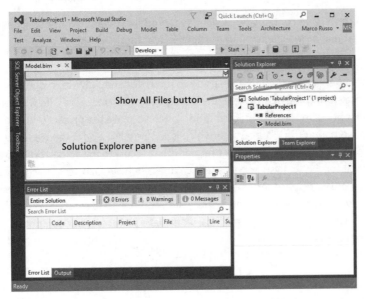

FIGURE 2-15   The Solution Explorer pane.

At first glance, it seems like the project contains only one file: Model.bim. However, if you click the **Show All Files** button at the top of the Solution Explorer pane (refer to Figure 2-15), you see there are several other files and folders there, as shown in Figure 2-16. (Some of these are only created the first time the project is built.) It is useful to know what these are.

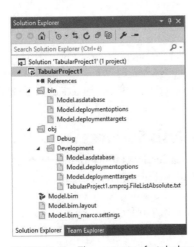

FIGURE 2-16   The contents of a tabular project in the Solution Explorer pane.

The following files are the contents of a tabular project:

- **Model.bim**   This file contains the metadata for the project, plus any data that has been copied or pasted into the project. (For more details on this, see Chapter 3 "Loading data inside Tabular.") This metadata takes the form of a TMSL script, which is JSON-based if the project is in a compatibility version that is greater than or equal to 1200. For previous compatibility versions, it takes the form of an XMLA `alter` command. (XMLA is XML-based.) Note that this metadata was used to create the workspace database. This is not necessarily the same as the metadata used when the project is deployed to the development server. If for any reason your Model.bim file becomes corrupted and will not open, you can re-create it by following the steps in the blog post at *https://blogs.msdn.microsoft.com/cathyk/2011/10/06/recovering-your-model-when-you-cant-save-the-bim-file/*.

- **The .asdatabase, .deploymentoptions, and .deploymenttargets**   These files contain the properties that might be different if the project were to be deployed to locations such as the development database server rather than the workspace database server. They include properties that can be set in the Project Properties dialog box (refer to Figure 2-10), such as the name of the server and database to which it will be deployed. For more details on what these files contain, see *https://msdn.microsoft.com/en-us/library/ms174530(v=sql.130).aspx*.

- **.abf**   This file contains the backup of the workspace database, which is created if the Data Backup property on the Model.bim file is set to Back Up to Disk.

- **.settings**   This file contains a few properties that are written to disk every time a project is opened. For more information on how this file is used, see *https://blogs.msdn.microsoft.com/cathyk/2011/09/23/where-does-data-come-from-when-you-open-a-bim-file/*. If you wish to make a copy of an entire SSDT project by copying and pasting its folder to a new location on disk, you must delete this file manually, as detailed in the blog post at *http://sqlblog.com/blogs/alberto_ferrari/archive/2011/09/27/creating-a-copy-of-a-bism-tabular-project.aspx*.

- **.layout**   This file contains information on the size, position, and state of the various windows and panes inside SSDT when a project is saved. For more information about this file, see *https://blogs.msdn.microsoft.com/cathyk/2011/12/02/new-for-rc0-the-layout-file/*.

Building a simple tabular model

To help you get your bearings in the SSDT user interface, and to help illustrate the concepts introduced in the preceding sections, this section walks you through the process of creating and deploying a simple model. This is only a very basic introduction to the process; of course, all these steps are dealt with in much more detail throughout the rest of this book.

Before you start, make sure that you—and the accounts you have used to run instances of Analysis Services on your workspace and development servers—have access to an instance of SQL Server and the Contoso DW sample database on your development server. (You can find the Contoso DW sample database for SQL Server in the companion content.)

Loading data into tables

To load data into tables, follow these steps:

1. Create a new tabular project in SSDT. Your screen should resemble the one shown in Figure 2-15, with the Model.bim file open.

2. You now have an empty project and are ready to load data into tables. Open the **Model** menu along the top of the screen (this is visible only if the Model.bim file is open) and select **Import from Data Source** to launch the Table Import wizard, shown in Figure 2-17.

FIGURE 2-17   The first page of the Table Import wizard.

3. In the first page of the Table Import wizard, the Connect to a Data Source page, select **Microsoft SQL Server** in the Relational Databases section and click **Next**.

4. On the Connect to a Microsoft SQL Server Database page, connect to the ContosoDW database in SQL Server after you select the proper server name, as shown in Figure 2-18. (Replace the server name "Demo" with the server and instance name of your own SQL Server.) Then click **Next**.

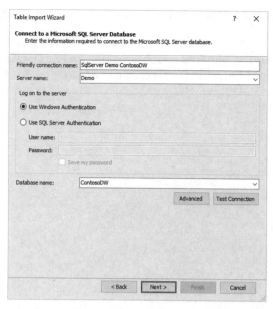

FIGURE 2-18   Connecting to SQL Server in the Table Import wizard.

5.   On the Impersonation Information page, configure how Analysis Services will connect to SQL
     Server to load data. At this point, the easiest thing to do is to choose the **Specific Windows
     User Name and Password** option and enter the user name and password you used to log in to
     your current session, as shown in Figure 2-19. (Chapter 3 gives a full explanation of this process.)
     Then click **Next**.

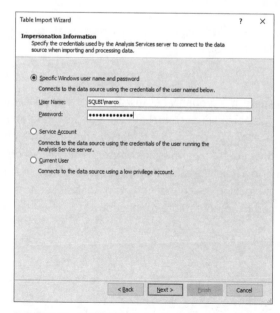

FIGURE 2-19   Setting impersonation information in the Table Import wizard.

6. Make sure the **Select from a List of Tables and Views** option is selected and click **Next**.

7. On the Select Tables and Views page, select the following tables, as shown in Figure 2-20: **DimProduct**, **DimProductCategory**, **DimProductSubcategory**, and **FactSalesSmall**. (You can update the Friendly Name and Filter Details columns as needed.) Then click **Finish**.

FIGURE 2-20   Selecting tables and views in the Table Import wizard.

8. You will see data from these tables being loaded into your workspace database. This should take only a few seconds. Click **Close** to finish the wizard.

Note   If you encounter any errors here, it is probably because the Analysis Services instance you are using for your workspace database cannot connect to the SQL Server database. To fix this, repeat all the previous steps. When you get to the Impersonation Information page, try a different user name that has the necessary permissions or use the service account. If you are using a workspace server on a machine other than your development machine, check to make sure firewalls are not blocking the connection from Analysis Services to SQL Server and that SQL Server is enabled to accept remote connections.

You will be able to see data in a table in grid view. Your screen should look something like the one shown in Figure 2-21.

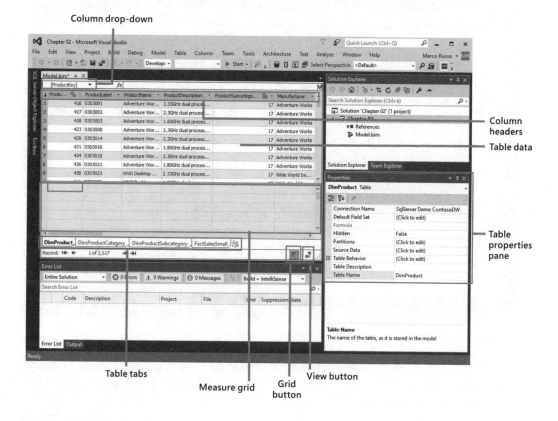

FIGURE 2-21 The grid view.

You can view data in a different table by clicking the tab with that table's name on it. Selecting a table makes its properties appear in the Properties pane. You can set some of the properties, plus the ability to delete a table and move it around in the list of tabs, by right-clicking the tab for the table.

Within a table, you can find an individual column by using the horizontal scrollbar immediately above the table tabs or by using the column drop-down list above the table. To explore the data within a table, you can click the drop-down arrow next to a column header, as shown in Figure 2-22. You can then sort the data in the table by the values in a column, or filter it by selecting or clearing individual values or by using one of the built-in filtering rules. Note that this filters only the data displayed on the screen, not the data that is actually in the table itself.

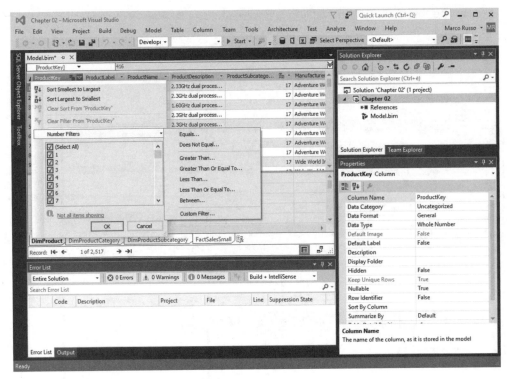

FIGURE 2-22 Filtering a column in the grid view.

Right-clicking a column enables you to delete, rename, freeze, and copy data from it. (When you freeze a column, it means that wherever you scroll, the column will always be visible, similar to freezing columns in Excel.) When you click a column, you can modify its properties in the Properties pane. After importing a table, you might want to check the Data Type property. This is automatically inferred by SSDT depending on the data type of the source database, but you might want to change it according to the calculation you want to perform when using that column. You will find many other properties described in Chapter 8, "The tabular presentation layer." Chapter 4, "Introducing calculations in DAX," includes descriptions of the available data types.

Creating measures

One of the most important tasks for which you will use the grid view is to create a measure. *Measures*, you might remember, are predefined ways of aggregating the data in tables. The simplest way to create a measure is to click the **Sum (Σ)** button in the toolbar and create a new measure that sums up the values in a column (look ahead at Figure 2-23). Alternatively, you can click the drop-down arrow next to that button and choose another type of aggregation.

To create a measure, follow these steps:

1. In the model you have just created, select the **SalesAmount** column in the FactSalesSmall table.

2. Click the **Sum** button. Alternatively, click the drop-down arrow next to the **Sum** button and choose **Sum** from the menu that appears, as shown in Figure 2-23.

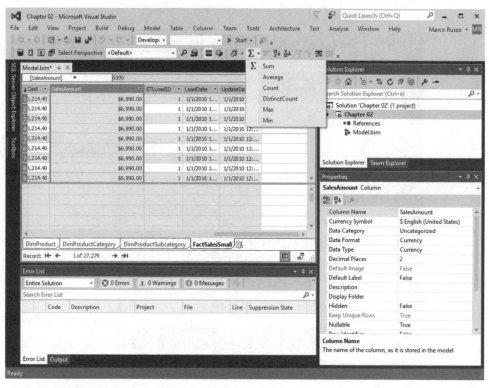

FIGURE 2-23   Creating a measure in the grid view.

3. The new measure appears in the measure grid underneath the highlighted column, as shown in Figure 2-24. When a measure is selected in the measure grid, its properties are displayed in the Properties pane. The measure name and a sample output (which is the aggregated total of the rows that are currently being displayed) are shown in the measure grid. Click the cell that contains the measure name and sample output to display the DAX definition of the measure in the formula bar. There, it can be edited.

> **Note**   Measure definitions in the formula bar take the following form:
>
> ```
> <Measure name> := <DAX definition>
> ```
>
> You can resize the formula bar to display more than a single line. This is a good idea if you are dealing with more complex measure definitions; you can insert a line break in your formulas by pressing **Shift+Enter**.

Measure in the
measure grid

Measure definition
in the formula bar

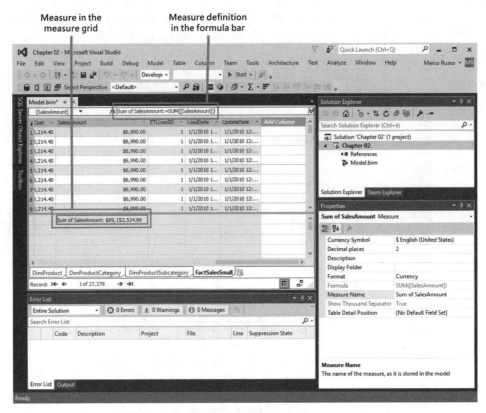

FIGURE 2-24 A measure in the measure grid.

4. Repeat steps 1–3 for the TotalCost column. You now have two measures in the data model.

5. By default, a measure appears in the measure grid underneath the column that was selected when it was created. Its position in the measure grid is irrelevant, however. You can move it somewhere else if you want to. To move a measure in the measure grid, right-click it, choose **Cut**, select the cell to which you want to move it, and choose **Paste**.

Note It is very easy to lose track of all the measures that have been created in a model. For this reason, it is a good idea to establish a standard location in which to keep your measures—for example, in the first column in the measure grid.

6. To help you write your own DAX expressions in the formula bar, Visual Studio offers extensive IntelliSense for tables, columns, and functions. As you type, SSDT displays a list of all the objects and functions available in the current context in a drop-down list underneath the formula bar, as shown in Figure 2-25. Select an item in the list and then press Tab to insert that object or function into your expression in the formula bar.

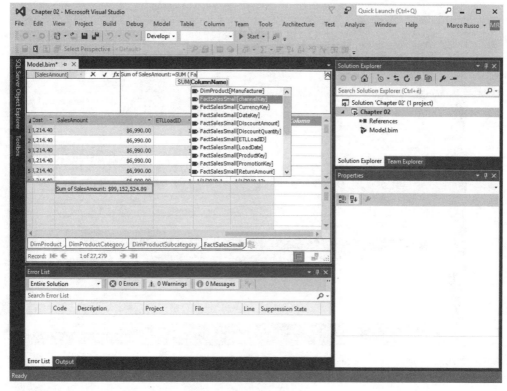

FIGURE 2-25 Using IntelliSense when defining a measure.

Creating calculated columns

You can create calculated columns in the grid view in one of two ways. The first method is as follows:

1. Scroll to the far right of the table and click **Add Column**, as shown in Figure 2-26.

2. Enter a new DAX expression for that column in the formula bar in the following format and press **Enter**. (Note that IntelliSense works the same way for calculated columns as it does for measures.)

```
= <scalar DAX expression>
```

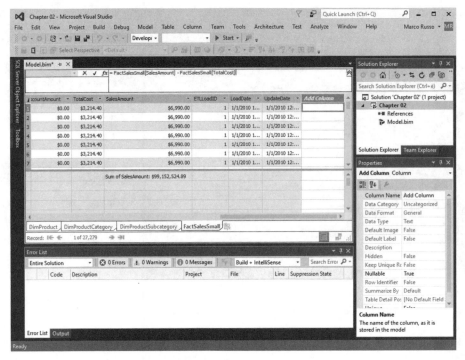

FIGURE 2-26 Creating a calculated column.

3. A new calculated column is created with a name such as *CalculatedColumn1*. To rename the calculated column to something more meaningful, double-click the column header and type the new name. Alternatively, edit the value for the **Column Name** property in the Properties pane on the right.

Note Editing the DAX expression for a calculated column in the formula bar is done in the same way as editing the expression for a measure, but the name of a calculated column cannot be edited from within its own expression.

The second method is as follows:

1. Right-click an existing column and select **Insert Column** from the menu that appears. This creates a new calculated column next to the column you have just selected.

Before moving on to the next section, follow these steps:

1. In your model, create a new calculated column called *Margin*, with the following definition:

   ```
   = FactSalesSmall[SalesAmount] - FactSalesSmall[TotalCost]
   ```

2. Create a new measure from it by using the **Sum** button in the same way you did in the previous section.

Creating Calculated Tables

Calculated tables are a new feature in compatibility level 1200. You can create a new calculated table by opening the **Table** menu and choosing **New Calculated Table** or by clicking on the small plus symbol on the right of the last table in the table tabs. In both cases, you enter a new DAX expression for that table in the formula bar in the following format:

```
= <table DAX expression>
```

You specify a DAX expression returning a table, which is evaluated and stored when you refresh the data model. This is similar to what you do for a calculated column. The only difference is that you must specify an expression that generates columns and rows of the table you want to store in the model. A new calculated table is created, with a name such as CalculatedTable1. You can give it a more meaningful name by either double-clicking the name in the table tabs and entering the new name or editing the Table Name property in the Properties pane. For example, you can create a table named Dates containing all the dates required for the fact table by using the following definition, obtaining the result shown in Figure 2-27:

```
= ADDCOLUMNS (
    CALENDARAUTO(),
    "Year", YEAR ( [Date] ),
    "Month", FORMAT ( [Date], "MMM yyyy" ),
    "MonthNumber", YEAR ( [Date] ) * 100 + MONTH ( [Date] )
)
```

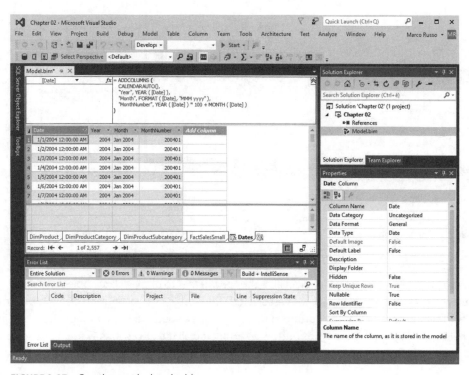

FIGURE 2-27   Creating a calculated table.

Working in the diagram view

To see an alternative way of looking at a tabular model, you can click the **Diagram View** button at the bottom-right corner of the measure grid (marked on the right side of Figure 2-28). This displays the tables in your model laid out in a diagram with the relationships between them displayed. Clicking the **Diagram View** button for the model you have created in this section should show you something like what is displayed in Figure 2-28. It is also possible to switch to diagram view by opening the **Model** menu, choosing **Model View**, and selecting **Diagram View**.

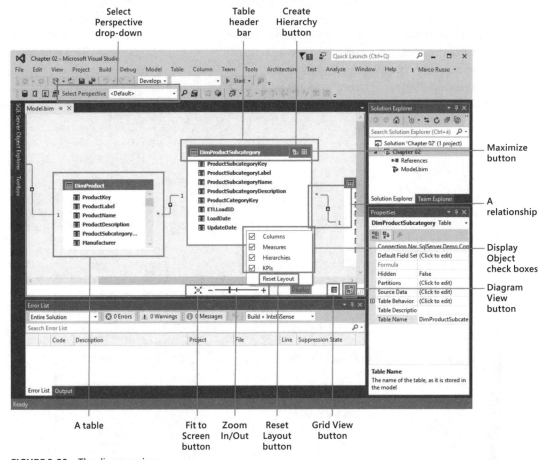

FIGURE 2-28 The diagram view.

In the diagram view, you can opt to display all the tables in your model or only the tables that are present in a particular perspective. You can also choose whether to display all the object types or just the columns, measures, hierarchies, or KPIs associated with a table by selecting and clearing the boxes in the **Display** pop-up menu at the bottom of the pane. You can automatically arrange the tables in the model by clicking the **Reset Layout** button, by arranging all the tables so they fit on one screen (by clicking the **Fit to Screen** button), and by zooming in and out (by dragging the slider at bottom edge of the pane). In the diagram view, you can rearrange tables manually by dragging and dropping them if you click and drag their blue table header bars. You can resize a table by clicking its bottom-left corner, and you can maximize a table so that all the columns in the table are displayed by clicking the **Maximize** button in the right corner of the table header bar. Each of these interface elements is shown in Figure 2-28.

Creating relationships

You can create relationships between tables in grid view, but it is easier to create them in diagram view because they are actually visible there after you have created them. To create a relationship, click the column on the "many" side of the relationship (usually the Dimension Key column on the Fact table) and drag it onto the column on another table that will be on the "one" side of the relationship (for example, the column that will be the lookup column, which is usually the primary key column on a dimension table). As an alternative, select the table in the diagram view and, from the **Table** menu at the top of the screen, select **Create Relationship**.

After a relationship has been created, you can delete it by clicking it to select it and pressing the **Delete** key. You can also edit it by double-clicking it or by selecting **Manage Relationships** from the **Table** menu. This displays the Manage Relationships dialog box, shown in Figure 2-29. There, you can select a relationship for editing. This displays the Edit Relationship dialog box (also shown in Figure 2-29).

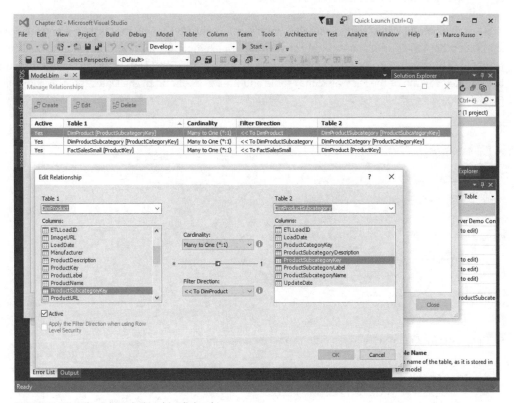

FIGURE 2-29 The Edit Relationship dialog box.

The model you have been building should already have the following relationships:

- Between FactSalesSmall and DimProduct, based on the ProductKey column.

- Between DimProduct and DimProductSubcategory, based on the ProductSubcategoryKey column.

- Between DimProductSubcategory and DimProductCategory, based on the ProductCategoryKey column.

These relationships were created automatically because they were present as foreign key constraints in the SQL Server database. If they do not exist in your model, create them now.

The Edit Relationship dialog box shows the following additional information about the relationship that you will see in more detail in Chapter 6:

- **Cardinality**   This can be Many to One (*:1), One to Many (1:*), or One to One (1:1).

- **Filter Direction**   This can have a single direction (from the table on the One side to the table on the Many side of a relationship) or can be bidirectional (the filter propagates to both tables).

- **Active**   You can enable this on only one relationship connecting two tables in case more than one relationship's path connects two tables.

The table named Dates that you created before (as a calculated table) does not have any relationship with other tables until you explicitly create one. For example, by clicking **Create Relationship** from the **Table** menu, you can create a relationship between the FactSalesSmall and Dates tables using the DateKey column of the FactSalesSmall table and the Date column of the Dates table, as shown in Figure 2-30.

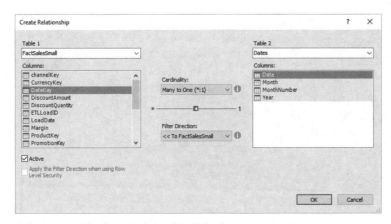

FIGURE 2-30   The Create Relationship dialog box.

Creating hierarchies

Staying in the diagram view, the last task to complete before the model is ready for use is to create a hierarchy. Follow these steps:

1. Select the DimProduct table and click the **Maximize** button so that as many columns as possible are visible.

2. Click the **Create Hierarchy** button on the table.

3. A new hierarchy will be created at the bottom of the list of columns. Name it **Product by Color**.

4. Drag the **ColorName** column down onto it to create the top level. (If you drag it to a point after the hierarchy, nothing will happen, so be accurate.)

5. Drag the **ProductName** column below the new ColorName level to create the bottom level, as shown in Figure 2-31.

> **Note** As an alternative, you can multiselect all these columns and then, on the right-click menu, select **Create Hierarchy**.

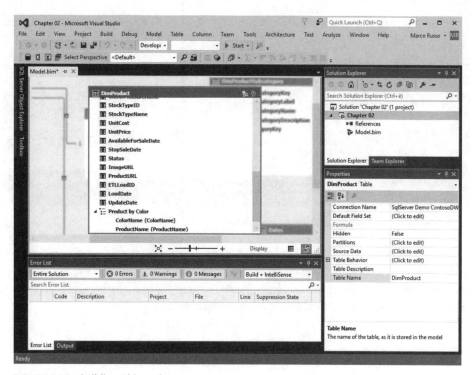

FIGURE 2-31 Building a hierarchy.

6. Click the **Restore** button (which is in the same place the Maximize button was) to restore the table to its original size.

Navigating in Tabular Model Explorer

You can browse the entities of a data model by using the Tabular Model Explorer pane, which is available next to the Solution Explorer pane. In this pane, you can see a hierarchical representation of the objects defined in the tabular model, such as data sources, KPIs, measures, tables, and so on. Within a table, you can see columns, hierarchies, measures, and partitions. The same entity could be represented in multiple places. For example, measures are included in a top-level Measures folder, and in a Measures folder for each table. By double-clicking an entity, you also set a correspondent selection in the data view or grid view (whichever is active). You can see in Figure 2-32 that when you select the ProductCategoryName column in the Tabular Model Explorer pane, SSDT selects the correspondent column in the DimProductCategory table.

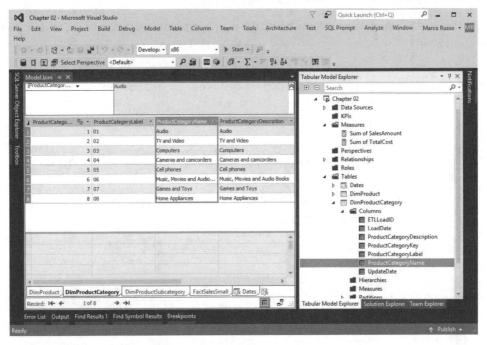

FIGURE 2-32 Navigation using Tabular Model Explorer.

You can enter text in the Search box in the Tabular Model Explorer pane to quickly locate any entity in the data model that includes the text you typed. For example, Figure 2-33 shows only the entities containing the word *Sales* in any part of the name. You can see the measures, relationships, tables, columns, and partitions that include the word *Sales* in their name.

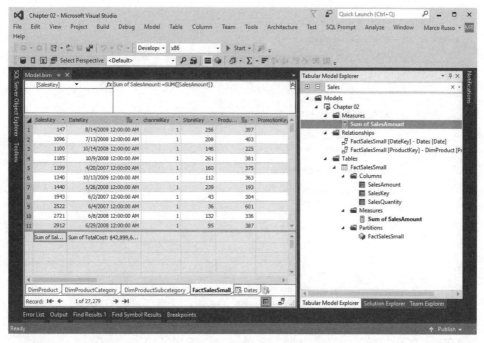

FIGURE 2-33 The filtered entities selected using the Search box in Tabular Model Explorer.

Deploying a tabular model

The simple model you have been building is now complete and must be deployed. To do this, follow these steps:

1. Open the **Build** menu and click **Deploy**. The metadata for the database is deployed to your development server. Then it is processed automatically if you have left the project's Processing Option property set to Default.

> **Note** If you have changed this property to Do Not Process, you must process your model by connecting in SQL Server Management Studio (SSMS) to the server where you deployed the database and selecting **Process Database** in the context menu of the deployed database. You will find an introduction to SSMS later in this chapter, in the "Working with SQL Server Management Studio" section.

2. If you chose to use a Windows user name on the Impersonation Information screen of the Table Import wizard for creating your data source, you might need to reenter the password for your user name at this point. After processing has completed successfully, you should see a large green check mark with the word *Success*, as shown in Figure 2-34.

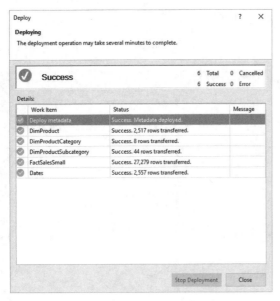

FIGURE 2-34 The end of a successful deployment.

The model is now present on your development server and ready to be queried.

Querying tabular models with Excel

Excel is the client tool your users are most likely to want to use to query your tabular models. It is also an important tool for an Analysis Services developer. During development, you must browse the model you are building to make sure it works in the way you expect. That means it is important to understand how to use the Excel built-in functionality for querying Analysis Services. This section provides an introductory guide on how to do this, even though it is beyond the scope of this book to explore all the Excel BI capabilities.

This section focuses on Excel 2016 as a client tool. End users can use an earlier version of Excel, but it will not have the same functionality. Excel versions from 2007 to 2013 are very similar to Excel 2016, but Excel 2003 and earlier versions provide only basic support for querying Analysis Services and have not been fully tested with Analysis Services tabular models.

Connecting to a tabular model

Before you can query a tabular model in Excel, you must first open a connection to the model. There are several ways to do this.

Browsing a workspace database

While you are working on a tabular model, you can check your work very easily while browsing your workspace database in Excel. To do so, follow these steps:

1. Open the **Model** menu and click **Analyze in Excel**. (There is also a button on the toolbar with an Excel icon on it that does the same thing.) This opens the Analyze in Excel dialog box, shown in Figure 2-35.

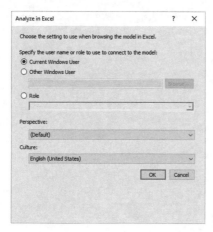

FIGURE 2-35   The Analyze in Excel dialog box.

2. Choose one of the following options:

   - **Current Windows User**   This is the default setting. It enables you to connect to your workspace database as yourself and see all the data in there.

   - **Other Windows User or Role**   These settings enable you to connect to the database as if you were another user to test security. They are discussed in more detail in Chapter 10, "Security."

   - **Perspective**   This option enables you to connect to a perspective instead of the complete model.

   - **Culture**   This option allows you to connect using a different locale setting, displaying data in a different language if the model includes translations. Translations are discussed in Chapter 8.

3. Click **OK**. Excel opens and a blank PivotTable connected to your database is created on the first worksheet in the workbook, as shown in Figure 2-36.

Note Remember that this is possible only if you have Excel installed on your development workstation and there is no way of querying a tabular model from within SSDT.

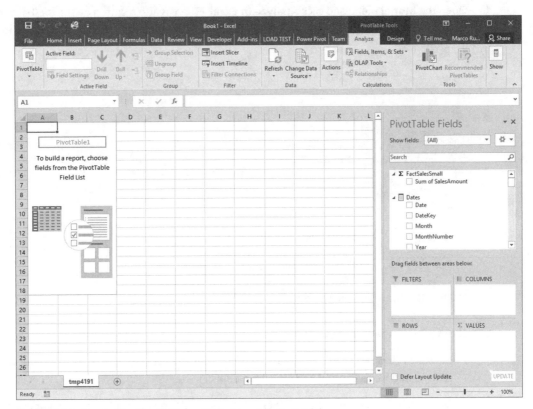

FIGURE 2-36 Excel with a PivotTable connected to a tabular model.

Connecting to a deployed database

You can also connect to a tabular model without using SSDT. This is how your end users will connect to your model. To do this, follow these steps:

1. Start Excel.

2. Click the **Data** tab on the ribbon and click the **From Other Sources** button in the Get External Data group.

3. Select **From Analysis Services**, as shown in Figure 2-37.

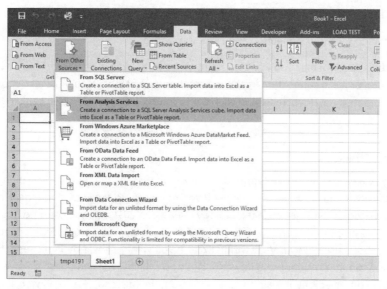

FIGURE 2-37 Connecting to Analysis Services from Excel.

4. This starts the Data Connection wizard. On the first page, enter the name of the instance of Analysis Services to which you wish to connect and click **Next**. (Do not change the default selection of Use Windows Authentication for logon credentials.)

5. Choose the database to which you want to connect and the cube you want to query. (If you are connecting to a workspace database, you will probably see one or more workspace databases with long names incorporating globally unique identifiers, or GUIDS.) There are no cubes in a tabular database, but because Excel predates the tabular model and generates only MDX queries, it will see your model as a cube. Therefore, choose the item on the list that represents your model, which, by default, will be called Model, as shown in Figure 2-38. If you defined perspectives in your model, every perspective will be listed as a cube name in the same list.

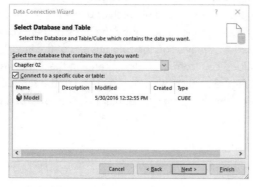

FIGURE 2-38 The Data Connection wizard.

6. Click **Next**.

7. Click **Finish** to save the connection and close the wizard.

8. You will be asked whether you want to create a new PivotTable, a new PivotChart, a new Power View report, or just a connection. If you are creating a PivotTable, you must also choose where to put it. Create a new PivotTable and click **OK** to return to the point shown back in Figure 2-36.

Power View in Excel

Excel 2016 and Excel 2013 have an integrated visualization tool called Power View, which is designed explicitly to query tabular and Power Pivot models using the DAX language. However, Power View is based on Silverlight 5, a technology released in 2011 that Microsoft no longer develops and will support only until October 2021. For this reason, you must consider carefully creating new reports using Power View within Excel. If you want a similar dynamic reporting experience, you should consider using Power BI Desktop, which is the evolution of Power View and is not based on Silverlight. It is a free download from the Microsoft Power BI web site. You will find more details about it later in this chapter in the section "Querying tabular models with Power BI Desktop."

Using PivotTables

Building a basic PivotTable is very straightforward. In the PivotTable Fields pane on the right side of the screen is a list of measures grouped by table (there is a Σ before each table name, which shows these are lists of measures), followed by a list of columns and hierarchies, which are again grouped by table.

You can select measures either by choosing them in the PivotTable Fields pane or dragging them down into the Values area in the bottom-right corner of the PivotTable Fields pane. In a similar way, you can select columns either by clicking them or by dragging them to the Columns, Rows, or Filters areas in the bottom half of the PivotTable Fields pane. Columns and hierarchies become rows and columns in the PivotTable, whereas measures display the numeric values inside the body of the PivotTable. By default, the list of measures you have selected is displayed on the columns axis of the PivotTable, but it can be moved to rows by dragging the Values icon from the Columns area to the Rows area. You cannot move it to the Filters area, however. Figure 2-39 shows a PivotTable using the sample model you have built with two measures on columns, the Product by Color hierarchy on rows, and the ProductCategoryName field on the filter.

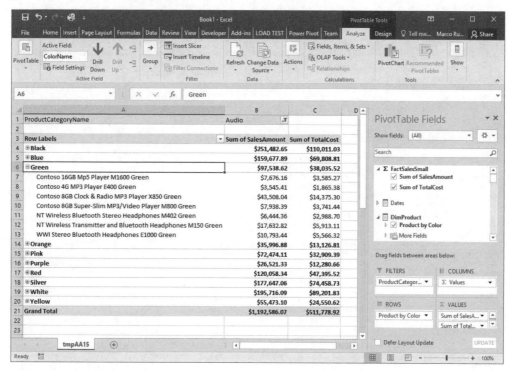

FIGURE 2-39 A sample PivotTable.

Using slicers

Slices are an alternative to the Report Filter box you have just seen. Slicers are much easier to use and a more visually appealing way to filter the data that appears in a report. To create a slicer, follow these steps:

1.   From the **Insert** tab on the ribbon, click the **Slicer** button in the **Filters** group.

2.   In the Insert Slicers dialog box, select the field you want to use, as shown in Figure 2-40, and click **OK**. The slicer is added to your worksheet.

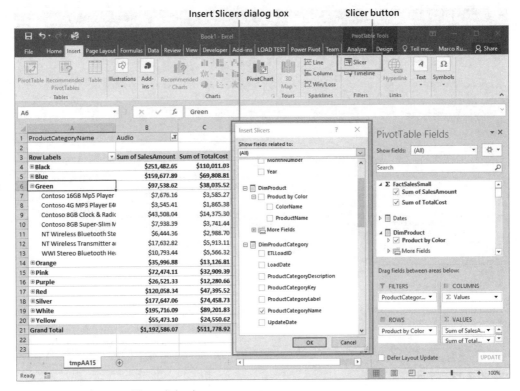
Insert Slicers dialog box   Slicer button

FIGURE 2-40 The Insert Slicers dialog box.

After the slicer is created, you can drag it wherever you want in the worksheet. You then only need to click one or more names in the slicer to filter your PivotTable. You can remove all filters by clicking the **Clear Filter** button in the top-right corner of the slicer. Figure 2-41 shows the same PivotTable as Figure 2-40 but with the filter ProductCategoryName replaced by a slicer and with an extra slicer added, based on ProductSubcategoryName.

When there are multiple slicers, you might notice that some of the items in a slicer are shaded. This is because, based on the selections made in other slicers, no data would be returned in the PivotTable if you selected the shaded items. For example, in Figure 2-41, on the left side, the TV And Video item on the ProductCategoryName slicer is grayed out. This is because no data exists for that category in the current filter active in the PivotTable above the slicers, which includes only Pink, Red, and Transparent as possible product colors. (Such a selection is applied straight to the product colors visible on the rows of the PivotTable.) In the ProductSubcategoryName slicer, all the items except Cell Phones Accessories and Smart Phones & PDAs are shaded because these are the only two subcategories in the Cell Phones category (which is selected in the ProductCategoryName slicer on the left) for the product colors selected in the PivotTable.

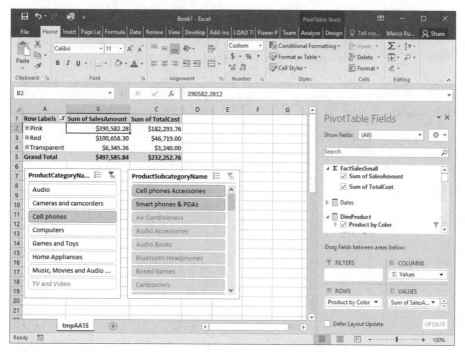

FIGURE 2-41 Using slicers.

Putting an attribute on a slicer enables you to use it on rows, on columns, or in the Filter area of the PivotTable. This is not the case of an attribute placed in the Filter area, which cannot be used on rows and columns of the same PivotTable. You can also connect a single slicer to many PivotTables so that the selections you make in it are applied to all those PivotTables simultaneously.

Sorting and filtering rows and columns

When you first drag a field into either the Rows area or Columns area in the PivotTable Fields pane, you see all the values in that field displayed in the PivotTable. However, you might want to display only some of these values and not others. There are numerous options for doing this.

When you click any field in the PivotTable Fields list or in the drop-down arrow next to the Row Labels or Column Labels box in the PivotTable, you can choose individual items to display and apply sorting and filtering, as shown in Figure 2-42.

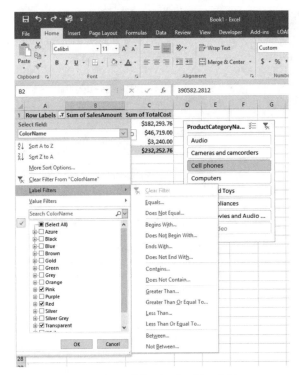

FIGURE 2-42 Sorting and filtering in a PivotTable.

Selecting and clearing members in the list at the bottom of the dialog box selects and clears members from the PivotTable. It is also possible to filter by the names of the items and by the value of a measure by using the **Label Filters** and **Value Filters** options.

If you need more control over which members are displayed and in which order they are shown, you must use a named set. To create a named set, follow these steps:

1. Click the **Analyze** tab in the PivotTable Tools section on the ribbon.

2. In the Calculations group, click **Fields, Items, & Sets** and select either **Create Set Based on Row Items** or **Create Set Based on Column Items**, as shown in Figure 2-43.

Named set options

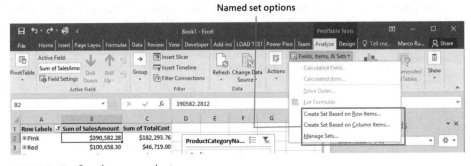

FIGURE 2-43 Creating a named set.

3. The New Set dialog box then appears, as shown in Figure 2-44. Here, you can add, delete, and move individual rows in the PivotTable. If you have some knowledge of MDX, click the **Edit MDX** button (in the lower-right portion of the dialog box) and write your own MDX set expression to use.

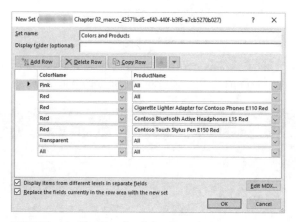

FIGURE 2-44 The New Set dialog box.

4. Click **OK** to create a new named set.

You can think of a named set as being a predefined selection that is saved with the PivotTable, but does not necessarily need to be used. After you create the named set, it appears under a folder called Sets in the PivotTable Fields list, as shown in Figure 2-45. As long as you leave the **Replace the Fields Currently in The Row/Column Area with the New Set** option selected in the bottom of the New Set dialog box (refer to Figure 2-44), your set will control what appears on the rows in the PivotTable.

FIGURE 2-45 Sets in the PivotTable Fields list.

Using Excel cube formulas

The last important bit of Analysis Services–related functionality to mention in Excel is the Excel cube formulas. These enable Excel to retrieve a single cell of data from a cube—for example, a reference to an individual item name or a measure value. The easiest way to understand how they work is to convert an existing PivotTable to cells containing formulas. To do so, follow these steps:

1. Click the **Analyze** tab on the PivotTables Tools section of the ribbon.

2. Click the **OLAP Tools** button in the Calculations group and select **Convert to Formulas** from the drop-down menu, as shown in Figure 2-46. The result is also shown in Figure 2-46.

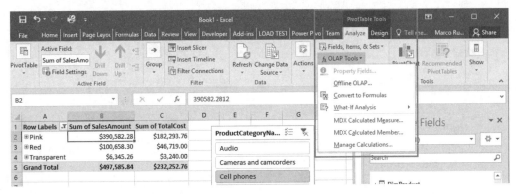

FIGURE 2-46 Converting a PivotTable to formulas.

Notice how in Figure 2-46 the B2 cell returns the value of the measure Sum of SalesAmount for pink products, but this value is returned now by the following formula:

```
=CUBEVALUE("localhost_Tabular Chapter 02_marco_42571bd5-ef40-440f-b3f6-a7cb5270b027",$A2,B$1,
Slicer_ProductCategoryName)
```

The four parameters used in the CubeValue() function here are as follows:

- The name of the Excel connection to Analysis Services

- A cell reference to cell A2, which contains another function that returns the item name Pink

- Another cell reference to cell B1, which returns the measure Sum of SalesAmount

- A reference to the slicer containing the product category names

As a result, this cell returns the value from the cube for the Sum of SalesAmount, Pink products, and the product category Cell Phones.

Cube formulas are a very powerful way of displaying free-form reports in Excel and allow much greater flexibility in layout and formatting than PivotTables. Their one drawback is that they do not allow as much interactivity as PivotTables. Users can no longer change what appears on rows and columns by dragging and dropping, nor can they navigate down through hierarchies (although slicers and report filters still work as expected).

It is beyond the scope of this book to provide a full description of what Excel cube formulas can do. If you would to learn more about them, Excel help, found at *https://support.office.com/en-us/article/ Cube-functions-reference-2378132b-d3f2-4af1-896d-48a9ee840eb2*, is a good place to start.

> **Note** Excel cube formulas are designed for multidimensional models in Analysis Services, and their performance is less than optimal with tabular models. If you have hundreds of cells or more computed by cube functions, you should consider loading in a PivotTable all the data you need at a proper granularity level, and then reference it using GetPivotData() instead of the CubeValue() function.

Querying tabular models with Power BI Desktop

In addition to Excel, another tool you might want to use to query your tabular model locally is Power BI Desktop. This free tool inherits and empowers the data discovery and navigation experience provided by Power View. As with Excel, it is beyond the scope of this book to provide more than a basic introduction to Power BI in general and Power BI Desktop in particular. However, this section should give you an idea of the capabilities of this powerful tool. You can freely download Power BI Desktop from *https:// powerbi.microsoft.com/desktop/*. Describing the setup for this tool is beyond the scope of this book.

> **Note** Power BI Desktop has a monthly release cycle, adding new features every time. For this reason, certain screenshots included in this section might be different from what you see on your screen.

Creating a connection to a tabular model

Before you can create a new report in Power BI Desktop, you must create a new connection to your tabular model. To do this, follow these steps:

1. Open Power BI Desktop.

2. In the Home tab's External Data group on the ribbon, click the **Get Data** drop-down arrow and select **Analysis Services**, as shown in Figure 2-47.

FIGURE 2-47 Creating a connection to Analysis Services in Power BI Desktop.

3. The SQL Server Analysis Services Database opens. Enter the server name corresponding to the tabular instance of Analysis Services (see Figure 2-48).

4. Select the **Connect Live** option button, as shown in Figure 2-48, to create a report that interactively queries Analysis Services. Then click **OK**.

Note If you were to choose **Import Data** instead of Connect Live, you would create a new Power BI data model, copying data from the tabular database. You might choose this option if you want to create a report that can also be interactive when you are offline and if the tabular server is not accessible, but this is beyond the scope of this section.

FIGURE 2-48 The SQL Server Analysis Services Database dialog box.

5. The Navigator dialog box opens, displaying a list of the databases available in the Analysis Services. For each one, you can see the models and perspectives available. As shown in Figure 2-49, choose the model (named **Model**) in the Chapter 02 database. Then click **OK**.

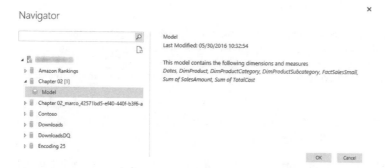

Navigator

Model
Last Modified: 05/30/2016 10:32:54

This model contains the following dimensions and measures
*Dates, DimProduct, DimProductCategory, DimProductSubcategory, FactSalesSmall,
Sum of SalesAmount, Sum of TotalCost*

- Amazon Rankings
- Chapter 02 [1]
  - Model
- Chapter 02_marco_42571bd5-ef40-440f-b3f6-a
- Contoso
- Downloads
- DownloadsDQ
- Encoding 25

OK   Cancel

FIGURE 2-49   Selecting the model (named Model) in the Navigator dialog box.

> **Note**   Similar to Excel, the procedure to connect to Analysis Services is identical for tabular and multidimensional connections. However, Excel generates queries using the MDX language, whereas Power BI generates queries in DAX, regardless of the model type they are connected to.

Building a basic Power BI report

With the connection created, you have an empty report based on the tabular model, as shown in Figure 2-50. A report consists of one or more pages, which are similar to slides in a Microsoft PowerPoint deck. What you see on the screen is a new blank page in your report. On the right side of the screen in Figure 2-50, you can see a list of the tables in the model you created earlier (in the Fields pane). Clicking the arrows next to the names shows the columns and measures in each table (such as Dates, DimProduct, and so on).

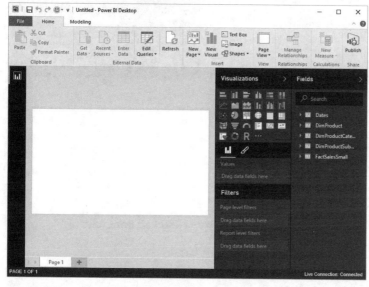

FIGURE 2-50   A blank page in a Power BI report.

To add a table to the report, follow these steps:

1. Drag the **ProductCategoryName** column from the DimProductCategory table into the Values area in the Visualizations pane.

2. Repeat step 1 with the **ProductSubcategoryName** column from the DimProductSubcategory table.

3. Repeat step 1 with the **Sum of SalesAmount** measure defined in the FactSalesSmall table. This creates a new table in the report page.

4. Resize the table by clicking the bottom-left edge and expanding it, so all the data is visible. The result should look like the report shown in Figure 2-51.

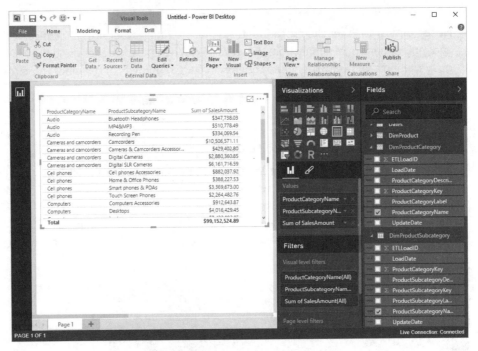

FIGURE 2-51 A report with a table.

Adding charts and slicers

To turn a table into a chart, follow these steps:

1. Click somewhere inside the table.

2. In the Visualizations pane, select a chart type, such as a **Stacked Bar Chart**.

You can add a slicer inside the page to provide another way of filtering the chart you have just created. Follow these steps:

1. Drag the **Color** column from the DimProduct table into the empty space to the right of the chart to create a new table.

2. Click inside the table.

3. In the Visualizations pane, click the **Slicer** button (the bottom-left corner icon in the Visualizations pane) to turn the table into a slicer.

In addition to resizing the controls, you can also move them around to improve the layout of the view by hovering over the top-right side of a control until the mouse turns into a figure icon and then dragging it. Selecting a color name inside the slicer filters the values that are used in the chart.

One of the coolest visualizations available in Power BI is the animated scatter chart. To create one on your report, follow these steps:

1. Click the empty space at the bottom of the report.

2. Click the **Scatter Chart** button in the Visualizations pane (the third row down on the far left).

3. Assign to each visualization property the following columns or measures (you can use drag and drop to do this):

   - **Details** Drag the **ProductSubcategoryName** column from the DimProductSubcategory table.

   - **Legend** Drag the **ProductCategoryName** column from the DimProductCategory table.

   - **X Axis** Drag the **UnitPrice** column from the FactSalesSmall table. Then click the drop-down arrow next to it and select **Average**. This creates a new measure just for this report that returns the average price of sales transactions.

   - **Y Axis** Drag the **SalesQuantity** column from the FactSalesSmall table. This creates a new measure just for this report that returns the sum of the quantity in sales.

   - **Size** Drag the sum of the **SalesAmount** measure from the FactSalesSmall table.

   - **Play Axis** Drag the **MonthNumber** column from the Dates table.

4. The report should now look like the one shown in Figure 2-52. To save the report, open the **File** menu and choose **Save**.

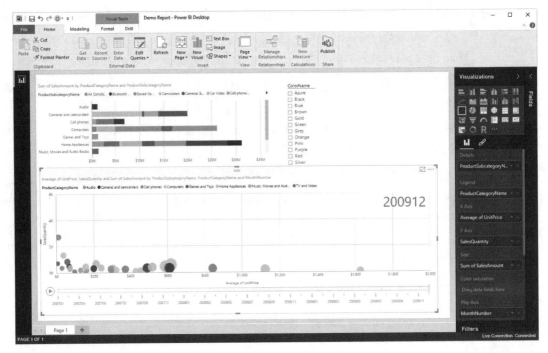

FIGURE 2-52 A report with a scatter chart.

Interacting with a report

To give you as much screen surface as possible to view a report, follow these steps:

1. Click the up-arrow button in the top-right corner of the ribbon, next to the Help button, to minimize the ribbon.

2. The scatter chart still does not have much space. To make more room for it, click the **Focus Mode** button in the top-right corner of the chart to expand it to the full screen, as shown in Figure 2-53.

FIGURE 2-53 An example of a full-screen scatter chart.

3. Click the **Play** button in the bottom-left corner to show an animation of how the sales of the product categories, their order volumes, and their average product costs change over time.

4. To return the scatter chart to its original size, again click the **Focus Mode** button in the top-right corner of the report.

In the Filters area of the Visualizations pane, you can apply filters to individual charts, individual pages or the whole report. In Figure 2-53 you can see a filter of three product categories applied to the scatter chart visualization only.

More Info For more information about how to use Power BI, see the documentation at *https://powerbi.microsoft.com/documentation/*.

Working with SQL Server Management Studio

Another tool with which you need to familiarize yourself is SQL Server Management Studio (SSMS), which you use to manage Analysis Services instances and databases that have already been deployed. To connect to an instance of Analysis Services, follow these steps:

1. Open SSMS.

2. In the Connect to Server dialog box that appears, choose **Analysis Services** in the **Server Type** drop-down box.

3. Enter your instance name in the **Server Name** box, as shown in Figure 2-54.

4. Click **Connect**.

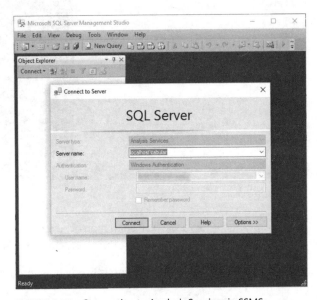

FIGURE 2-54 Connecting to Analysis Services in SSMS.

5. A new connection to Analysis Services opens in the Object Explorer pane. Expand all the available nodes on a tabular instance to see something similar to what is displayed in Figure 2-55, which shows the database you created and deployed earlier in this chapter.

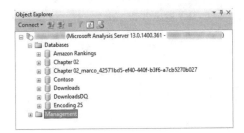

FIGURE 2-55 The Object Explorer pane in SSMS.

At the top of the pane is the Instance node, showing the name of the instance, the version number, and your user name. Underneath that is a folder containing a list of databases. Inside each database, you can see the connections, tables, and security roles inside that database. Right-clicking any of these objects enables you to view and edit their properties. In the case of the instance, this is the only place in which Analysis Services server properties can be edited in a user interface. In addition, you can process databases and individual tables, and you can script out objects to XMLA or JSON. All this functionality is covered in more detail in Chapter 11, "Processing and partitioning tabular models," and in Chapter 13, "Interfacing with Tabular."

It is also possible to execute both DAX and MDX queries against a tabular model in SSMS. Although confusing, both must be executed through an MDX query pane. To open one, you can do one of the following:

- **Click the New MDX Query button on the toolbar**   The same Connect to Server dialog box appears as when you opened a connection in Object Explorer.

- **Right-click a database in the Object Explorer pane, select New Query, and choose MDX**   You will be connected directly to the database you have clicked, but you can change the database to which you are connected by using the Database drop-down box in the toolbar.

After you have connected, your new MDX query pane appears, where you can enter your MDX or DAX query (see Figure 2-56).

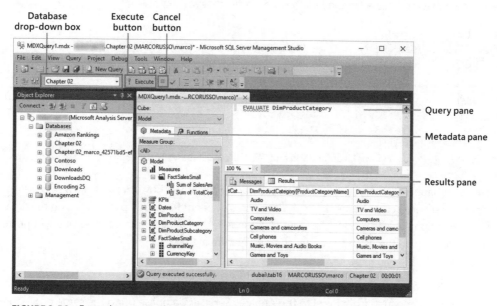

FIGURE 2-56   Executing a query in SQL Server Management Studio.

To run the query, click the **Execute** button on the toolbar or press **F5**. To cancel a query during execution, click the red **Cancel** button next to the Execute button. You can try this yourself by running the following DAX query against the model you have built, which returns the DimProductCategory table:

EVALUATE DimProductCategory

The subject of writing DAX queries is part of the larger topic of the DAX language, which is introduced in Chapter 4. Detailed coverage of DAX is available in *The Definitive Guide to DAX*, written by the authors of this book and published by Microsoft Press.

> **Note** The Metadata pane in SSMS currently provides metadata for MDX queries only. If you drag and drop any entity from the Metadata pane to the query pane, the MDX syntax will appear there. Thus, even if the query pane accepts queries written in DAX, the version of SSMS available as of this writing does not provide any help to write correct DAX queries. Such support might appear in future versions of SSMS. In the meantime, we suggest you to consider using DAX Studio for this purpose. For more information, see the section, "Using DAX Studio as an alternative to SSMS" later in this chapter.

Importing from Power Pivot

Previously in this chapter, you saw that you can create a new Analysis Services tabular project by importing an existing Power Pivot model using SSDT. You can also import an existing Power Pivot model in an Analysis Services tabular database by using SSMS. You do this through the Restore from Power-Pivot feature available in the right-click menu on the Databases folder in the Object Explorer pane, as shown in Figure 2-57. In this case, you will keep the tabular model compatibility level 110x of the Power Pivot model that is contained in the Excel workbook file that you import.

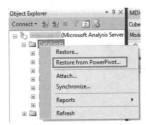

FIGURE 2-57 Restoring a Power Pivot model in an SSAS tabular database.

Like what happens when you create a new tabular project in SSDT by starting from a Power Pivot model, if the service account running Analysis Services does not have read permissions on the data sources, you might have to modify the security settings in the connection properties of the imported database. You can do this using the corresponding feature in SSMS.

> **Note** Once a Power Pivot data model has been imported into a tabular database, you can access it by connecting from Excel to the Analysis Services database using the same procedure described previously in this chapter, in the section "Querying tabular models with Excel." However, there are a few differences in the user interface. In particular, a PivotTable connected to Analysis Services no longer allows the user to create new implicit measures. Before restoring a database from a Power Pivot model, make sure that all the measures required for analysis have been already created.

Importing from Power BI Desktop

As of this writing, the feature for importing a Power BI model in Analysis Services is not available. However, this feature is expected to be released in an upcoming update of Analysis Services 2016. When this is possible, you will probably see a Restore from Power BI choice in the context menu of the Databases folder shown in Figure 2-57.

Using DAX Studio as an alternative to SSMS

DAX Studio is a free open-source tool to write, execute, and analyze DAX queries in Power BI Desktop, Power Pivot for Excel, and the Analysis Services tabular model. It includes an object browser, query editing and execution, formula and measure editing, syntax highlighting and formatting, integrated tracing, and query execution breakdowns. You can download the latest version of this tool from *https://daxstudio.codeplex.com*.

As you see in Figure 2-58, its layout is similar to SSMS. It also allows the execution of MDX and DAX queries, but it provides features that help the DAX syntax only. The Metadata pane shows tables, columns, and measures of the database and perspective selected in the drop-down lists above. Clicking the **Run** button on the toolbar or pressing F5 executes the query, and you can cancel a running execution by clicking the **Cancel** button in the ribbon. DAX Studio also offers an integrated environment to analyze the query plan and the timings of the internal operations that are executed within a query, without having to open SQL Profiler to capture such events.

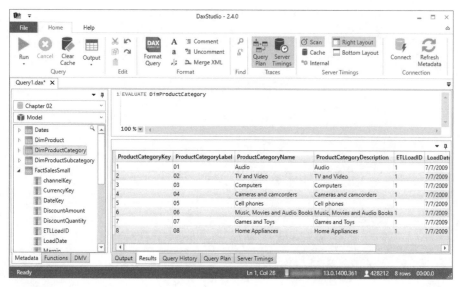

FIGURE 2-58 Executing a query in DAX Studio.

> **Note** DAX Studio is not intended to be a replacement for SSMS. The only goal of DAX Studio is to support writing, executing, and profiling DAX queries and expressions. SSMS is a tool for database administrators that offers features such as managing security roles, partitions, process data, backups, and more. You must use SSMS if you want a graphical user interface (GUI) for administrative tasks on Analysis Services.

Summary

In this chapter, you saw how to set up a development environment for the Analysis Services tabular model and had a whirlwind tour of the development process and the tools you use, such as SQL Server Data Tools, Excel, Power BI, SQL Server Management Studio, and DAX Studio. You should now have a basic understanding of how a tabular model works and how you build one. In the rest of the book you will learn in detail about loading data (Chapter 3), DAX, data modeling, deployment, scalability, security, and optimizations.

Loading data inside Tabular

As you learned in Chapter 2, "Getting started with the tabular model," the key to producing a tabular model is to load data from one or many sources that are integrated in the analysis data model. This enables users to create their reports by browsing the tabular database on the server. This chapter describes the data-loading options available in Tabular mode. You have already used some of the loading features to prepare the examples of the previous chapters. Now you will move a step further and examine all the options for loading data so you can determine which methods are the best for your application.

> **What's New in SSAS 2016** SSAS 2016 offers new impersonation options and a different way to store data copied from the clipboard in the data model.

Understanding data sources

In this section, you learn the basics of data sources, starting with the interfaces between SQL Server Analysis Services (SSAS) and databases. These interfaces provide the abstraction layer that Analysis Services needs to communicate with different sources of data. Analysis Services provides several kinds of data sources, which can be divided into the following categories:

- **Relational databases** Analysis Services can load data hosted in relational databases, such as Microsoft Access, Microsoft SQL Server, Microsoft Azure SQL Database, Oracle, Teradata, Sybase, IBM Informix, IBM DB2, and many others. You can load tables, views, and queries from the server that hosts the data sources in this category.

- **Multidimensional sources** You can load data into your tabular model from an Analysis Services multidimensional model by using these data sources. Currently, SQL Server Analysis Services is the only multidimensional database for which there is an available data source. The same data source can also load data from queries issued to Power Pivot data contained in a Microsoft Excel workbook that is published on Microsoft SharePoint or from a tabular data model hosted on a server.

- **Data feeds**   This category of data sources enables you to load data from dynamic feeds, such as Open Data Protocol (OData) feeds from the Internet, or data feeds tied to reports stored in Reporting Services.

- **Text files**   Data sources in this category can load data that is stored in comma-separated text files, Excel files, fixed-length files, or any other file format that can be interpreted by Analysis Services.

- **Other sources**   Data can be loaded from the clipboard and stored statically inside the .bim file.

In a tabular data model, you can freely mix different data sources to load data from various media. It is important to remember that after data is loaded, it must be refreshed by the server on a scheduled basis, depending on your needs, during the database processing.

If you want to see the complete list of all the data sources available in Tabular mode, you can open the Table Import wizard (see Figure 3-1). To do so, open the **Model** menu and choose **Import from Data Source**.

FIGURE 3-1   Using the Table Import wizard to connect to a workspace database.

The first page of the Table Import wizard lists all the data sources available in Tabular mode. Each data source has specific parameters and dialog boxes. The details for connecting to the specialized data sources can be provided by your local administrator, and are outside the scope of this book. It is interesting to look at the differences between loading from a text file and from a SQL Server query, but it is of little use to investigate the subtle differences between Microsoft SQL Server and Oracle, which are both relational database servers and behave in much the same way.

Understanding impersonation

Some data sources only support what is known as *basic authentication*, where the user must provide a user name and password in the connection string. For those types of data sources, the impersonation settings are not critical, and you can usually use the service account. Whenever Analysis Services uses Windows authentication to load information from a data source, it must use the credentials of a Windows account so that security can be applied and data access can be granted. Stated more simply, SSAS impersonates a user when opening a data source. The credentials used for impersonation might be different from both the credentials of the user currently logged on—that is, from the user's credentials—and the ones running the SSAS service.

For this reason, it is very important to decide which user will be impersonated by SSAS when accessing a database. If you fail to provide the correct set of credentials, SSAS cannot correctly access the data, and the server will raise errors during processing. Moreover, the Windows account used to fetch data might be a higher-privileged user, such as a database administrator (DBA), and therefore expose end users to more data from the model than you may have intended. Thus, it is necessary to properly evaluate which credentials should be used.

Moreover, it is important to understand that impersonation is different from SSAS security. Impersonation is related to the credentials the service uses to refresh data tables in the database. In contrast, SSAS security secures the cube after it has been processed, to present different subsets of data to different users. Impersonation comes into play during processing; security is leveraged during querying.

Impersonation is defined on the Impersonation Information page of the Table Import wizard, which is described later (and shown in Figure 3-3). From this page, you can choose the following options:

- **Specific Windows User Name and Password**

- **Service Account**

- **Current User**

If you use a specific Windows user, you must provide the credentials of a user who will be impersonated by SSAS. If, however, you choose **Service Account**, SSAS presents itself to the data source by using the same account that runs SSAS (which you can change by using SQL Configuration Manager to update the service parameters in the server). Current User is used only in DirectQuery mode and connects to the data source using the current user logged to Analysis Services, when it is querying the data model. For the purposes of this book, we will focus on the first two options.

Impersonation is applied to each data source. Whether you must load data from SQL Server or from a text file, impersonation is something you must understand and always use to smooth the process of data loading. Each data source can have different impersonation parameters.

It is important, at this point, to digress a bit about the workspace server. As you might recall from Chapter 2, the *workspace server* hosts the workspace database, which is the temporary database that SQL Server Data Tools (SSDT) uses when developing a tabular solution. If you choose to use Service

Account as the user running SSAS, you must pay attention to whether this user is different in the workspace server from the production server, which leads to processing errors. You might find that the workspace server processes the database smoothly, whereas the production server fails.

The workspace database

It is worth noting that when you develop the solution, data is loaded inside the workspace database. However, when the project is deployed on the development server, data will be loaded inside the development server database. Thus, even if you can work with data when you develop a solution, you must remember that the data (that you see when you are inside SSDT) comes from the workspace database and not from the deployed database on the development server.

Understanding server-side and client-side credentials

As you have learned, SSAS impersonates a user when it accesses data. Nevertheless, when you are authoring a solution in SSDT, some operations are executed by the server and others are executed by SSDT on your local machine. Operations executed by the server are called *server-side operations*, whereas the ones executed by SSDT are called *client-side operations*. Even if they appear to be executed in the same environment, client and server operations are in fact executed by different software and therefore might use different credentials. The following example should clarify the scenario.

When you import data from SQL Server, you follow the Table Import wizard, by which you can choose the tables to import and preview and filter data. Then, when the selection is concluded, you have loaded data from the database into the tabular model.

The Table Import wizard runs inside SSDT and is executed as a client-side operation. That means it uses the credentials specified for client-side operations—that is, the credentials of the current user. The final data-loading process, however, is executed by the workspace server by using the workspace server impersonation settings, and it is a server-side operation. Thus, in the same logical flow of an operation, you end up mixing client-side and server-side operations, which might lead to different users being impersonated by different layers of the software.

Note In a scenario that commonly leads to misunderstandings, you specify Service Account for impersonation and try to load some data. If you follow the default installation of SQL Server, the account used to execute SSAS does not have access to the SQL engine, whereas your personal account should normally be able to access the databases. Thus, if you use the Service Account impersonation mode, you can follow the wizard up to when data must be loaded (for example, you can select and preview the tables). At that point, the data loading starts and, because this is a server-side operation, Service Account cannot access the database. This final phase raises an error.

Although the differences between client-side and server-side credentials are difficult to understand, it is important to understand how connections are established. To help you understand the topic, here is a list of the components involved when establishing a connection:

- The connection can be initiated by an instance of SSAS or SSDT. You refer to server and client operations, respectively, depending on who initiated the operation.

- The connection is established by using a connection string, defined in the first page of the wizard.

- The connection is started by using the impersonation options, defined on the second page of the wizard.

When the server is trying to connect to the database, it checks whether it should use imperson-ation. Thus, it looks at what you have specified on the second page and, if requested, impersonates the desired Windows user. The client does not perform this step; it operates under the security context of the current user who is running SSDT. After this first step, the data source connects to the server by using the connection string specified in the first page of the wizard, and impersonation is no longer used at this stage. Therefore, the main difference between client and server operations is that the impersonation options are not relevant to the client operations; they only open a connection through the current user.

This is important for some data sources, such as Access. If the Access file is in a shared folder, this folder must be accessible by both the user running SSDT (to execute the client-side operations) and the user impersonated by SSAS (when processing the table on both the workspace and the deployment servers). If opening the Access file requires a password, both the client and the server use the password stored in the connection string to obtain access to the contents of the file.

Working with big tables

In a tabular project, SSDT shows data from the workspace database in the model window. As you have learned, the workspace database is a physical database that can reside on your workstation or on a server on the network. Wherever this database is, it occupies memory and resources and needs CPU time whenever it is processed.

Processing the production database is a task that can take minutes, if not hours. The workspace database, however, should be kept as small as possible. This is to avoid wasting time whenever you must update it, which happens quite often during development.

To reduce the time it takes, avoid processing the full tables when working with the workspace data-base. You can use some of the following hints:

- You can build a development database that contains a small subset of the production data. That way, you can work on the development database and then, when the project is deployed, change the connection strings to make them point to the production database.

- When loading data from a SQL Server database, you can create views that restrict the number of returned rows, and later change them to retrieve the full set of data when in production.

- If you have SQL Server Enterprise Edition, you can rely on partitioning to load a small subset of data in the workspace database and then rely on the creation of new partitions in the production database to hold all the data. You can find further information about this technique at *https://blogs.msdn.microsoft.com/cathyk/2011/09/01/importing-a-subset-of-data-using-partitions-step-by-step/*.

Your environment and experience might lead you to different mechanisms to handle the size of the workspace database. In general, it is a good practice to think about this aspect of development before you start building the project. This will help you avoid problems later due to the increased size of the workspace model.

Loading from SQL Server

The first data source option is SQL Server. To start loading data from SQL Server, follow these steps:

1. Open the **Model** menu and choose **Import from Data Source** to open the Table Import wizard.

2. Select **Microsoft SQL Server** and click **Next**.

3. The Connect to a Microsoft SQL Server Database page of the Table Import wizard asks you the parameters by which to connect to SQL Server, as shown in Figure 3-2. Enter the following information and then click **Next**:

   - **Friendly Connection Name**   This is a name that you can assign to the connection to recall it later. We suggest overriding the default name provided by SSDT because a meaningful name will be easier to remember later.

   - **Server Name**   This is the name of the SQL Server instance to which you want to connect.

   - **Log On to the Server**   This option enables you to choose the method of authentication to use when connecting to SQL Server. You can choose between **Use Windows Authentication**, which uses the account of the user who is running SSDT to provide the credentials for SQL Server, and **Use SQL Server Authentication**. In the latter case, you must provide your user name and password in this dialog box. You can also select the **Save My Password** check box so that you do not have to enter it again during future authentication.

   - **Database Name**   In this box, you specify the name of the database to which you want to connect. You can click **Test Connection** to verify you are properly connected.

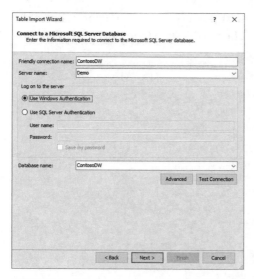

FIGURE 3-2 Entering the parameters by which to connect to SQL Server in the Table Import wizard.

4. The Impersonation Information page of the Table Import wizard requires you to specify the impersonation options, as shown in Figure 3-3. Choose from the following options and then click **Next**:

- **Specific Windows User Name and Password**   SSAS will connect to the data source by impersonating the Windows user specified in these text boxes.

- **Service Account**   SSAS will connect to the data source by using the Windows user running the Analysis Services service.

- **Current User**   This option is used only when you enable the DirectQuery mode in the model.

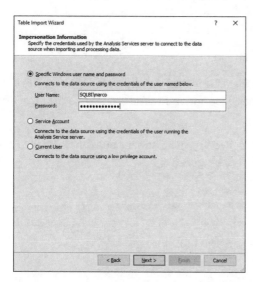

FIGURE 3-3 Choosing the impersonation method on the Impersonation Information page.

5. In the Choose How to Import the Data page of the wizard (see Figure 3-4), choose **Select from a List of Tables and Views to Choose the Data to Import** or **Write a Query That Will Specify the Data to Import**. Then click **Next**.

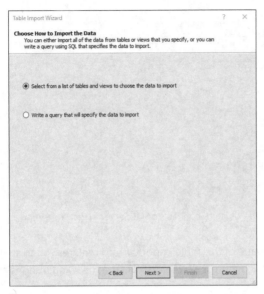

FIGURE 3-4 Choosing the preferred loading method.

What happens next depends on which option you choose. This is explored in the following sections.

Loading from a list of tables

If you choose to select the tables from a list, the Table Import wizard displays the Select Tables and Views page. This page shows the list of tables and views available in the database, as shown in Figure 3-5. Follow these steps:

1. Click a table in the list to select it for import.

2. Optionally, type a friendly name for the table in the **Friendly Name** column. This is the name that SSAS uses for the table after it has been imported. (You can change the table name later, if you forget to set it here.)

3. Click the **Preview & Filter** button to preview the data, to set a filter on which data is imported, and to select which columns to import (see Figure 3-6).

FIGURE 3-5 Choosing from the list of tables to import.

Selecting related tables

One feature in the Table Import wizard is the **Select Related Tables** button (refer to Figure 3-5). When you click this button, the wizard automatically includes all the tables that are directly related to the ones already selected. Although it might save some time during the model definition, it is always better to decide up front which tables to load. That way, you avoid loading useless tables that will later be deleted, which is a common scenario that might arise when you use this feature.

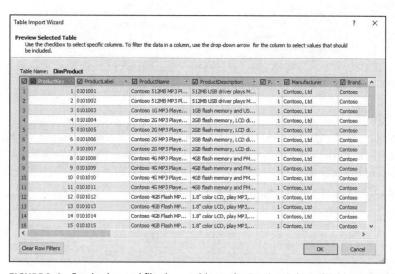

FIGURE 3-6 Previewing and filtering a table on the Preview Selected Table page of the wizard.

4. To limit the data in a table, apply either of the following two kinds of filters. Both column and data filters are saved in the table definition, so that when you process the table on the server, they are applied again.

- **Column filtering**   You can add or remove table columns by selecting or clearing the check box before each column title at the top of the grid. Some technical columns from the source table are not useful in your data model. Removing them helps save memory space and achieve quicker processing.

- **Data filtering**   You can choose to load only a subset of the rows of the table, specifying a condition that filters out the unwanted rows. In Figure 3-7, you can see the data-filtering dialog box for the Manufacturer column. Data filtering is powerful and easy to use. You can use the list of values that are automatically provided by SSDT. If there are too many values, you can use text filters and provide a set of rules in the forms, such as greater than, less than, equal to, and so on. There are various filter options for several data types, such as date filters, which enable you to select the previous month, last year, and other specific, date-related filters.

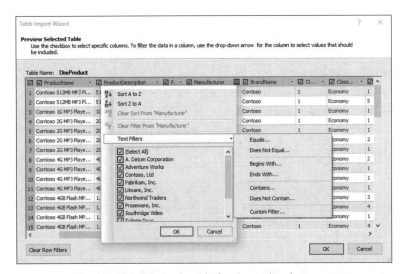

FIGURE 3-7   The filter values in a column before importing data.

Note   Pay attention to the date filters. The query they generate is always relative to the creation date, and not to the execution date. Thus, if you select Last Month, December 31, you will always load the month of December, even if you run the query on March. To create queries relative to the current date, rely on views or author-specific SQL code.

5. When you finish selecting and filtering the tables, click **Finish** for SSDT to begin processing the tables in the workspace model, which in turn fires the data-loading process. During the table processing, the system detects whether any relationships are defined in the database, among the tables currently being loaded, and, if so, the relationships are loaded inside the data model. The relationship detection occurs only when you load more than one table.

6. The Work Item list, in the Importing page of the Table Import wizard, is shown in Figure 3-8. On the bottom row, you can see an additional step, called Data Preparation, which indicates that relationship detection has occurred. If you want to see more details about the found relationships, you can click the **Details** hyperlink to open a small window that summarizes the relationships created. Otherwise, click **Close**.

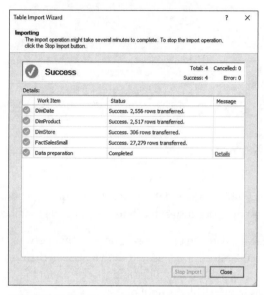

FIGURE 3-8 The Data Preparation step of the Table Import wizard, showing that relationships have been loaded.

Loading from a SQL query

If you chose the **Write a Query That Will Specify the Data to Import** option in the Choose How to Import the Data page of the Table Import wizard (refer to Figure 3-4), you have two choices:

- **Write the query in a simple text box**   You normally would paste it from a SQL Server Management Studio (SSMS) window, in which you have already developed it.

- **Use the Table Import wizard's query editor to build the query**   This is helpful if you are not familiar with SQL Server.

To use the query editor, click the **Design** button in the Table Import wizard. The Table Import wizard's query editor is shown in Figure 3-9.

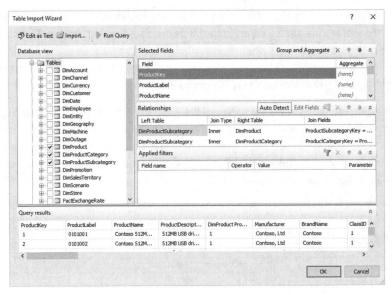

FIGURE 3-9 The Table Import wizard's query editor, which enables you to design a SQL query visually as the data source.

Loading from views

Because you have more than one option by which to load data (a table or SQL query), it is useful to have guidance on which method is the best one. The answer is often neither of these methods.

Linking the data model directly to a table creates an unnecessary dependency between the tabular data model and the database structure. In the future, it will be harder to make any change to the physical structure of the database. However, writing a SQL query hides information about the data source within the model. Neither of these options seems to be the right one.

It turns out, as in the case of multidimensional solutions, that the best choice is to load data from views instead of from tables. You gain many advantages by using views. Going into the details of these advantages is outside the scope of this book, but we will provide a high-level overview (you can find a broader discussion about best practices in data import that is valid also for Analysis Services at *https://www.sqlbi.com/articles/data-import-best-practices-in-power-bi/*). The advantages can be summarized in the following way:

- Decoupling the physical database structure from the tabular data model

- Declarative description in the database of the tables involved in the creation of a tabular entity

- The ability to add hints, such as NOLOCK, to improve processing performance

Thus, we strongly suggest you spend some time defining views in your database, each of which will describe one entity in the tabular data model. Then you can load data directly from those views. By using this technique, you will get the best of both worlds: the full power of SQL to define the data to be loaded without hiding the SQL code in the model definition.

More Info Importing data from views is also a best practice in Power Pivot and Power BI. To improve usability, in these views you should include spaces between words in a name and exclude prefixes and suffixes. That way, you will not spend time renaming names in Visual Studio. An additional advantage in a tabular model is that the view simplifies troubleshooting because if the view has exactly the same names of tables and columns used in the data model, then any DBA can run the view in SQL Server to verify whether the lack of some data is caused by the Analysis Services model or by missing rows in the data source.

Opening existing connections

In the preceding section, you saw all the steps and options of data loading, by creating a connection from the beginning. After you create a connection with a data source, it is saved in the data model so that you can open it without providing the connection information again. This option is available from the **Model** menu under **Existing Connections**.

Choosing this option opens the Existing Connections dialog box shown in Figure 3-10, in which you can select the connections saved in the model. From this window, you can choose a connection and then decide to use the connection to load data from other tables, to edit the connection parameters, to delete the connection, or to process all the tables linked to that connection.

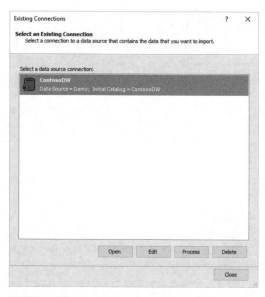

FIGURE 3-10 The Existing Connections dialog box, which lists all the connections saved in the project.

Note It is very important to become accustomed to reopening existing connections whenever you must import more tables from the same database. That way, if you create a new connection each time you intend to load data, you create many connections in the same model. If you have many connections, and you need to modify some of the connection parameters, you will have extra work to update all the connections.

Loading from Access

Now that you have seen all the ways that data can be loaded from relational databases, you can examine other data sources, the first of which is the Access data source.

When you open the Table Import wizard by using the Access data source, the connection parameters are different because the Access databases are stored in files on disk instead of being hosted in server databases. In Figure 3-11, you can see the Table Import wizard requesting that you identify an Access file.

FIGURE 3-11 The Table Import wizard with Access-specific parameters.

There is no practical difference between Access and any other relational database in loading tables, but be aware that the server uses the 64-bit Access Database Engine (ACE) driver, whereas in SSDT, you are using the 32-bit version. It is worth noting that the SQL Server designer of Access is limited because it does not offer a visual designer for the SQL query. When you query Access, you must write the query in a plain text editor.

Because the Table Import wizard for Access does not have a query designer, if you must load data from Access and need help with SQL, it might be better to write the query by using the query designer from inside Access. Then, after the query has been built in Access, you can load the data from that query. By doing so, you add an abstraction layer between the Access database and the tabular data model, which is always a best practice to follow.

When using an Access data source, pay attention to the following points:

- The file path should point to a network location that the server can access when it processes the data model.

- When processing the table, the user that is impersonated by the SSAS engine should have enough privileges to be able to access that folder.

- The workspace database uses the ACE driver installed on that server, so be aware of the bit structure of SSAS versus the bit structure of Office.

If the file is password protected, you should enter the password on the first page of the wizard and save it in the connection string so that the SSAS engine can complete the processing without errors.

Loading from Analysis Services

In the preceding sections, you learned how to load data from relational databases. Different relational data sources might have some slight differences among them, but the overall logic of importing from a relational database remains the same. This section explains the SQL Server Analysis Services data source, which has some unique features.

In the Table Import wizard for SSAS (see Figure 3-12), you must provide the server name and the database to which you want to connect.

FIGURE 3-12 Connecting to an Analysis Services database.

Click **Next** on the first page to open the Multidimensional Expressions (MDX) query editor. The MDX editor is similar to the SQL editor. It contains a simple text box, but the language you must use to query the database is MDX instead of SQL. You can write MDX code in the text box or paste it from an SSMS window in which you have already developed and tested it. As with the SQL editor, you do not need to know the MDX language to build a simple query. SSDT contains an advanced MDX query designer, which you can open by clicking the **Design** button.

> **Note**   As you might have already noticed, you cannot import tables from an Analysis Services database. The only way to load data from an Analysis Services database is to write a query. The reason is very simple: Online analytical processing (OLAP) cubes do not contain tables, so there is no option for table selection. OLAP cubes are composed of measure groups and dimensions, and the only way to retrieve data from these is to create an MDX query that creates a dataset to import.

Using the MDX editor

Using the MDX editor (see Figure 3-13) is as simple as dragging measures and dimensions into the result panel, and it is very similar to querying a multidimensional cube by using Excel. After you have designed the query, click **OK**; the user interface returns to the query editor, showing the complex MDX code that executes the query against the server.

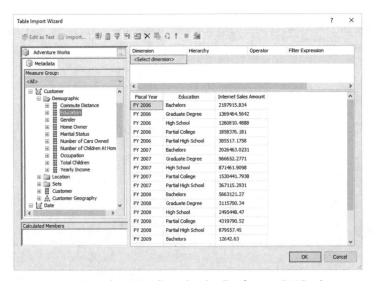

FIGURE 3-13   Using the MDX editor when loading from an OLAP cube.

Because this book is not about MDX, it does not include a description of the MDX syntax or MDX capabilities. The interested reader can find several good books about the topic from which to start learning MDX, such as *Microsoft SQL Server 2008 MDX Step by Step* by Brian C. Smith and C. Ryan Clay (Microsoft Press), *MDX Solutions with Microsoft SQL Server Analysis Services* by George Spofford (Wiley), and *MDX with SSAS 2012 Cookbook* by Sherry Li (Packt Publishing). A good reason to learn MDX is to use the MDX editor to define new calculated members, which help you load data from the SSAS cube. A calculated member is similar to a SQL calculated column, but it uses MDX and is used in an MDX query.

If you have access to an edition of Analysis Services that supports DAX queries over a multidimensional model, you can also write a DAX query, as explained in the next section, "Loading from a tabular database."

More Info   Analysis Services 2016 supports the ability to perform a DAX query over a multidimensional model in all available editions (Standard and Enterprise). However, Analysis Services 2012 and 2014 require the Business Intelligence edition or the Enterprise edition. Analysis Services 2012 also requires Microsoft SQL Server 2012 Service Pack 1 and Cumulative Update 2 or a subsequent update.

Loading from a tabular database

As you have learned, you can use the SSAS data source to load data from a multidimensional database. An interesting and, perhaps, not-so-obvious feature is that you can use the same data source to load data from a tabular data model. The tabular model can be either a tabular database in SSAS or a Power Pivot workbook hosted in Power Pivot for SharePoint.

To load data from Tabular mode, you connect to a tabular database in the same way you connect to a multidimensional one. The MDX editor shows the tabular database as if it were multidimensional, exposing the data in measure groups and dimensions, even if no such concept exists in a tabular model. In Figure 3-14, you can see the MDX editor open over the tabular version of the Adventure Works SSAS database.

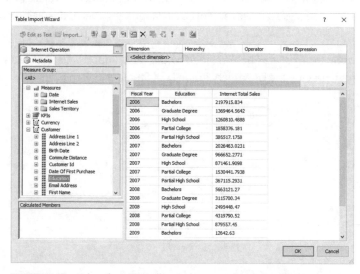

FIGURE 3-14   Using the MDX editor to browse tabular models.

At this point, you might be wondering whether you can query a tabular database using DAX. After all, DAX is the native language of Tabular mode, and it seems odd to be able to load data from Tabular mode by using MDX only. It turns out that this feature, although well hidden, is indeed available. The MDX editor is not capable of authoring or understanding DAX queries. Nevertheless, because the SSAS server in Tabular mode understands both languages, you can write a DAX query directly in the Table Import wizard in the place of an MDX statement, as shown in Figure 3-15.

FIGURE 3-15   Using DAX instead of MDX when querying a tabular data model.

The DAX query shown in Figure 3-15 is a very simple one. It loads the sales aggregated by year and model name. When you click the **Validate** button, the message, "The MDX statement is valid" appears, even if the query is in DAX. In reality, Analysis Services accepts both languages, even if the dialog box does not acknowledge that.

Authoring the DAX query inside the small text box provided by the Table Import wizard is not very convenient. Nevertheless, you can prepare the DAX query inside DAX Studio and then paste it inside the text box.

Column names in DAX queries

When using DAX to query the tabular data model, the column names assigned by the data source contain the table name as a prefix (if they come from a table). They represent the full name if they are introduced by the query. For example, the query in Figure 3-15 produces the results shown in Figure 3-16.

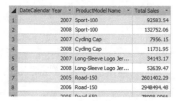

FIGURE 3-16   The column names from the result of DAX queries, as adjusted after data loading.

The DateCalendar Year and ProductModel Name columns must be adjusted later, removing the table name and renaming them to Calendar Year and Model Name, but the Total Sales column is already correct. A possible workaround is using the SELECTCOLUMNS function to rename the column names in DAX, but such a function is available only when querying an Analysis Services 2016 server. It is not available in previous versions of Analysis Services.

Loading from an Excel file

Data such as budgets or predicted sales is often hosted inside Excel files. In such cases, you can load the data directly from the Excel workbook into the tabular data model.

It might be worthwhile to write an Integration Services package to load that Excel workbook into a database and keep historical copies of it. Tabular models are intended for corporate business intelligence (BI), so you likely will not need to load data from Excel as often as self-service users do. There are a few issues to look out for when loading data from Excel. If you are loading from a range in which the first few rows are numeric, but further rows are strings, the driver might interpret those rows as numeric and return the string values as null. However, the rest of this section explains possible workarounds if you insist on loading from Excel.

Suppose that you have an Excel workbook that contains predicted sales in an Excel table named PredictedSales, as shown in Figure 3-17. To load this workbook into the tabular data model, follow these steps:

Year	Model	Amount
2005	Mountain-500	196,558.94
2005	Mountain-400-W	323,185.80
2005	Road-750	566,314.51
2005	Road-350-W	1,299,131.11
2005	Touring-3000	296,940.00
2005	Touring-1000	2,416,850.96
2005	Touring-2000	320,416.69
2005	Touring Tire	21,090.23
2005	HL Road Tire	18,867.25
2005	ML Road Tire	15,640.50

FIGURE 3-17   Loading a sample Excel table, which contains predicted sales, in Tabular mode.

1. Open the Table Import wizard.

2. Select the Excel data source and click **Next**. This opens the page shown in Figure 3-18.

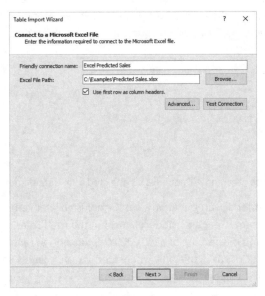

FIGURE 3-18   Loading an Excel file in the Table Import wizard.

3. In the **Excel File Path** box, type the file path of the file containing the data.

4. If your table contains column names in the first row (as is the case in this example), select the **Use First Row as Column Headers** check box to ensure that SSDT automatically detects the column names of the table. Then click **Next**.

5. In the Impersonation page, leave the settings as is, and click **Next**.

6. In the Select Tables and Views page (see Figure 3-19), define the worksheets and/or ranges from the workbook to load inside the data model.

Important   Only worksheets and named ranges are imported from an external Excel workbook. If multiple Excel tables are defined on a single sheet, they are not considered. For this reason, it is better to have only one table for each worksheet and no other data in the same worksheet. SSDT cannot detect Excel tables in a workbook. The wizard automatically removes blank space around your data.

7. The wizard loads data into the workspace data model. You can click the **Preview & Filter** button to look at the data before the data loads and then apply filtering, as you learned to do with relational tables. When you are finished, click **Finish**.

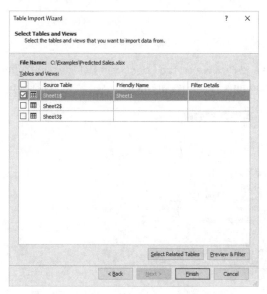

FIGURE 3-19 Choosing the worksheet to import from an Excel workbook.

Note Similar to Access files, you must specify a file path that will be available to the server when processing the table, so you should not use local resources of the development workstation (such as the C: drive), and you must check that the account impersonated by SSAS has enough privileges to reach the network resource in which the Excel file is located.

Loading from a text file

A common data format from which to load is text files. Data in text files often comes in the form of comma separated values (CSV), a common format by which each column is separated from the previous one by a comma, and a newline character is used as the row separator.

If you have a CSV file that contains some data, you can import it into the data model by using the text file data source. If your CSV file contains the special offers planned for the year 2005, it might look like the following data sample:

```
Special Offer,Start,End,Category,Discount
Christmas Gifts,12/1/2005,12/31/2005,Accessory,25%
Christmas Gifts,12/1/2005,12/31/2005,Bikes,12%
Christmas Gifts,12/1/2005,12/31/2005,Clothing,24%
Summer Specials,8/1/2005,8/15/2005,Clothing,10%
Summer Specials,8/1/2005,8/15/2005,Accessory,10%
```

Usually, CSV files contain the column header in the first row of the file, so that the file includes the data and the column names. This is the same standard you normally use with Excel tables.

To load this file, follow these steps:

1. Start the Table Import wizard.

2. Choose the **Text File** data source and click **Next**. The Connect to Flat File page of the Table Import wizard (see Figure 3-20) contains the basic parameters used to load from text files.

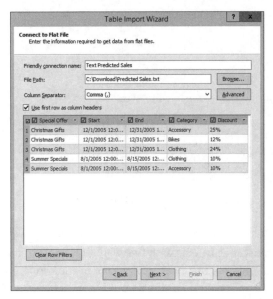

FIGURE 3-20 The basic parameters for loading a CSV file in the Table Import wizard.

3. Choose the column separator, which by default is a comma, from the **Column Separator** list. This list includes Comma, Colon, Semicolon, Tab, and several other separators. The correct choice depends on the column separator that is used in the text file.

Handling more complex CSV files

You might encounter a CSV file that contains fancy separators and find that the Table Import wizard cannot load it correctly because you cannot choose the necessary characters for the separators. It might be helpful, in such a case, to use the schema.ini file, in which you can define advanced properties of the comma separated file. Read *https://msdn.microsoft.com/en-us/library/ms709353.aspx* to learn this advanced technique for loading complex data files. At the same link, you will find information about how to load text files that do not follow the CSV schema, but use a fixed width instead.

1. If your CSV file contains column names in the first row, select the **Use First Row as Column Headers** check box to ensure that SSDT automatically detects the column names of the table. (By default, this check box is cleared, even if most CSV files follow this convention and contain the column header.) Then click **Next**.

2. As soon as you fill the parameters, the grid shows a preview of the data. You can use the grid to select or clear any column and to set row filters, as you can do with any other data source you have seen. When you finish the setup, click **Finish** to start the loading process.

> **Note** After the loading is finished, check the data to see whether the column types have been detected correctly. CSV files do not contain, for instance, the data type of each column, so SSDT tries to determine the types by evaluating the file content. Because SSDT is making a guess, it might fail to detect the correct data type. In the example, SSDT detected the correct type of all the columns except the *Discount* column. This is because the flat file contains the percentage symbol after the number, causing SSDT to treat it as a character string and not as a number. If you must change the column type, you can do that later by using SSDT or, in a case like this example, by using a calculated column to get rid of the percentage sign.

Loading from the clipboard

This section explains the clipboard data-loading feature. This method of loading data inside a tabular database has some unique behaviors—most notably, the fact that it does not rely on a data source.

To load data from the clipboard, follow these steps:

1. Open a sample workbook (such as the workbook shown in Figure 3-17).

2. Copy the Excel table content into the clipboard.

3. In SSDT, from inside a tabular model, open the **Edit** menu and choose **Paste**. SSDT analyzes the contents of the clipboard.

4. If the contents contain valid tabular data, SSDT opens the Paste Preview dialog box (see Figure 3-21). It displays the clipboard as it will be loaded inside a tabular table. You can give the table a meaningful name and preview the data before you import it into the model. Click **OK** to end the loading process and to place the table in the data model.

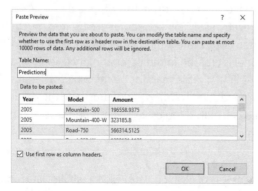

FIGURE 3-21 Loading from the clipboard to open the Paste Preview dialog box.

> **Note** You can initiate the same process by copying a selection from a Word document or from any other software that can copy data in the tabular format to the clipboard.

How will the server be able to process such a table if no data source is available? Even if data can be pushed inside the workspace data model from SSDT, when the project is deployed to the server, Analysis Services will reprocess all the tables, reloading the data inside the model. It is clear that the clipboard content will not be available to SSAS. Thus, it is interesting to understand how the full mechanism works in the background.

If the tabular project contains data loaded from the clipboard, this data is saved in the DAX expression that is assigned to a calculated table. The expression uses the DATATABLE function, which creates a table with the specified columns, data types, and static data for the rows that populate the table. As shown in Figure 3-22, the Predictions table is imported in the data model, with the corresponding DAX expression that defined the structure and the content of the table itself.

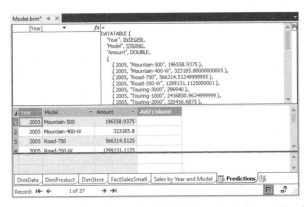

FIGURE 3-22 The calculated table that is created after pasting data in SSDT.

> **Note** In compatibility levels lower than 1200, a different technique is used to store static data that is pasted in the data model. It creates a special connection that reads the data saved in a particular section of the .bim file, in XML format. In fact, calculated tables are a new feature in the 1200 compatibility level. In SSDT, linked tables are treated much the same way as the clipboard is treated, but when you create a tabular model in SSDT by starting from a Power Pivot workbook, the model is created in the compatibility level 110x, so the former technique is applied. This means linked tables cannot be refreshed when the Excel workbook is promoted to a fully featured tabular solution. If you upgrade the data model to 1200, these tables are converted into calculated tables, exposing the content in the DAX expression that is assigned to the table.

Although this feature looks like a convenient way of pushing data inside a tabular data model, there is no way, apart from manually editing the DAX expression of the calculated table, to update this data later.

In a future update of SSDT (this book currently covers the November 2016 version), a feature called Paste Replace will allow you to paste the content of the clipboard into a table created with a Paste command, overwriting the existing data and replacing the DATATABLE function call.

Moreover, there is absolutely no way to understand the source of this set of data later on. Using this feature is not a good practice in a tabular solution that must be deployed on a production server because all the information about this data source is very well hidden inside the project. A much better solution is to perform the conversion from the clipboard to a table (when outside of SSDT), create a table inside SQL Server (or Access if you want users to be able to update it easily), and then load the data inside tabular from that table.

We strongly discourage any serious BI professional from using this feature, apart from prototyping. (For prototyping, it might be convenient to use this method to load the data quickly inside the model to test the data.) Nevertheless, tabular prototyping is usually carried out by using Power Pivot for Excel. There you might copy the content of the clipboard inside an Excel table and then link it inside the model. Never confuse prototypes with production projects. In production, you must avoid any hidden information to save time later when you will probably need to update some information.

There is only one case when using this feature is valuable for a production system: if you need a very small table with a finite number of rows, with a static content set that provides parameters for the calculations that are used in specific DAX measures of the data model. You should consider that the content of the table is part of the structure of the data model, in this case. So to change it, you must deploy a new version of the entire data model.

Loading from a Reporting Services report

When you work for a company, you are likely to have many reports available to you. You might want to import part or all of the data of an existing report into your model.

You might be tempted to import the data by copying it manually or by using copy-and-paste techniques. However, these methods mean that you always load the final output of the report and not the original data that has been used to make the calculations. Moreover, if you use the copy-and-paste technique, you often have to delete the formatting values from the real data, such as separators, labels, and so on. In this way, it is difficult—if not impossible—to build a model that can automatically refresh the data extracted from another report; most of the time, you end up repeating the import process of copying data from your sources.

If you are using reports published by SQL Server Reporting Services 2008 R2 and later, SSAS can connect directly to the data the report uses. In this way, you have access to a more detailed data model, which can also be refreshed. Furthermore, you are not worried by the presence of separators or other decorative items that exist in the presentation of the report. You get only the data. In fact, you can use a report as a special type of data feed, which is a more general type of data source described in the next section. You can import data from Reporting Services in two ways: using a dedicated user interface in SSDT or through the data feed output in the report itself.

Loading reports by using the report data source

Look at the report shown in Figure 3-23. The URL in the Web browser, at the top of the image, points to a sample Reporting Services report. (The URL can be different, depending on the installation of Reporting Services sample reports, which you can download from *http://msftrsprodsamples.codeplex.com/*.)

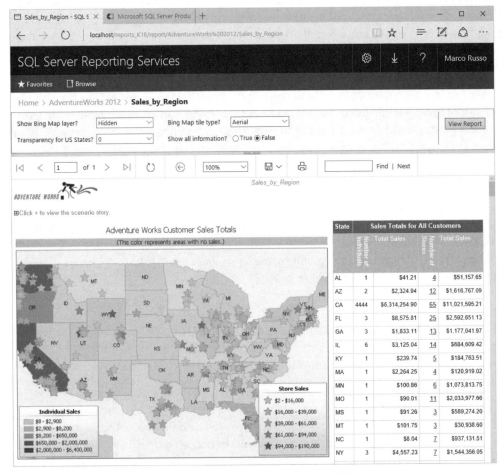

FIGURE 3-23 The report for Sales by Region from Reporting Services 2016.

This report shows the sales divided by region and by individual stores using a chart and a table. If you click the Number of Stores column's number of a state, the report scrolls down to the list of shops in the corresponding state. So you see another table, not visible in Figure 3-23, which appears when you scroll down the report.

You can import data from a report inside SSDT by using the report data source. Follow these steps:

1. Start the Table Import wizard.

2. On the Connect to a Data Source page, select **Report** and click **Next**. This opens the Connect to a Microsoft SQL Server Reporting Services Report page of the Table Import wizard (see Figure 3-24).

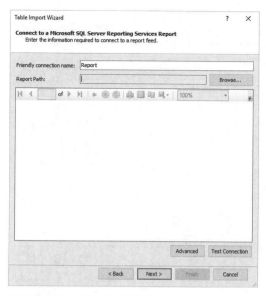

FIGURE 3-24 Using the Table Import wizard to import data from a report.

3. Click the **Browse** button next to the **Report Path** box and select the report to use, as shown in Figure 3-25.

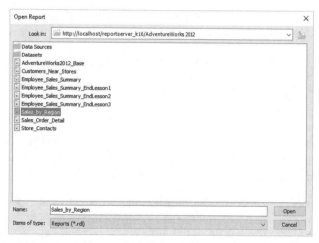

FIGURE 3-25 Using the Table Import wizard to select from the available reports on the server.

4. Click **Open**. The selected report appears in the Table Import wizard, as shown in Figure 3-26.

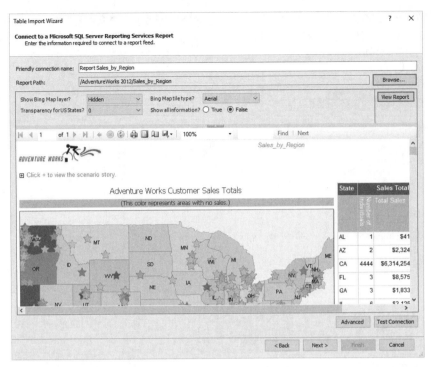

FIGURE 3-26 Previewing a report in the Table Import wizard.

Report pathnames

Figure 3-26 shows the report previously shown in Figure 3-23. However, the URL is a little bit different. The URL for the report shown in the browser was as follows:

http://localhost/reports_K16/report/AdventureWorks%202012/Sales_by_Region

However, the URL to load data from a report in Tabular mode was different:

http://localhost/reportserver_K16/AdventureWorks 2012

This is because the URL that SSAS used (the second URL) is a direct pointer to the report, which bypasses the user interface of Report Manager that you used earlier. You should ask for the assistance of your IT department to get the right URL for your reports.

As a rule, if you can navigate in the reports available through a browser by starting at *http://SERVERNAME/Reports_INSTANCENAME*, you can do the same by using the name *ReportServer* in place of *Reports* when you want to navigate to the available reports by using the Open Report dialog box at *http://SERVERNAME/ReportServer_INSTANCENAME*.

The *SERVERNAME* and *INSTANCENAME* parts of the path must be replaced by the real names used on your server. In our examples, *LOCALHOST* replaces *SERVERNAME*, and *K16* replaces *INSTANCENAME*. If you worked with the default instance of Reporting Services, the instance name would be empty. If the instance name is omitted, the underscore character also must be eliminated. You can deduce the server name and instance name by looking at the URL for the reports in your company.

However, if the URL used for your reports has a different nomenclature and is actually a SharePoint path, you should be able to use the same URL in both the browser and the Open Report dialog box.

5. Optionally, you can change the friendly connection name for this connection. Then click **Next**.

6. Set up the impersonation options to instruct which user SSAS has to use to access the report when refreshing data and click **Next**.

7. The Select Tables and Views page opens. Choose which data table to import from the report, as shown in Figure 3-27. The report shown here contains four data tables. The first two contain information about the graphical visualization of the map, on the left side of the report in Figure 3-26. The other two are interesting: Tablix1 is the source of the table on the right side, which contains the sales divided by state, and tblMatrix_StoresbyState contains the sales of each store for each state.

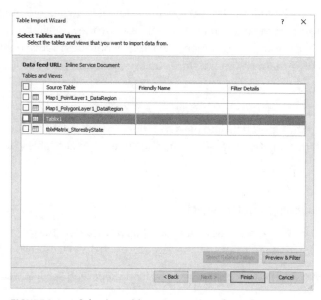

FIGURE 3-27 Selecting tables to import from a data feed.

8. The first time you import data from a report, you might not know the content of each of the available data tables. In this case, you can click the **Preview & Filter** button to preview the table. (Figure 3-28 shows the preview.) Or, you can click **Finish** to import everything, and then remove all the tables and columns that do not contain useful data.

Table Import Wizard

Preview Selected Table
Use the checkboxes to select specific columns.

Table Name: **Tablix1**

	Distance	ShowBingMaps	BingMapTileType	US...	ShowAll	StateProvinceCode	CustomerID	TotalDue	Textbox8	Textbox10
1	50	Hidden	Aerial	0	FALSE	AL	1	41.2055	4	51157.6464
2	50	Hidden	Aerial	0	FALSE	AZ	2	2324.9417	12	1616767.0850
3	50	Hidden	Aerial	0	FALSE	CA	4444	6314254.9...	65	11021595.2...
4	50	Hidden	Aerial	0	FALSE	FL	3	8575.8053	25	2592651.1315
5	50	Hidden	Aerial	0	FALSE	GA	3	1833.1067	13	1177041.9682
6	50	Hidden	Aerial	0	FALSE	IL	6	3125.0391	14	684609.4209
7	50	Hidden	Aerial	0	FALSE	KY	1	239.7408	5	184763.5116
8	50	Hidden	Aerial	0	FALSE	MA	1	2264.2536	4	120919.0238
9	50	Hidden	Aerial	0	FALSE	MN	1	100.8645	6	1073813.7472
10	50	Hidden	Aerial	0	FALSE	MO	1	90.0133	11	2033977.6593
11	50	Hidden	Aerial	0	FALSE	MS	1	91.2620	3	589274.2025
12	50	Hidden	Aerial	0	FALSE	MT	1	101.7484	3	30938.6006
13	50	Hidden	Aerial	0	FALSE	NC	1	8.0444	7	937131.5111
14	50	Hidden	Aerial	0	FALSE	NY	3	4557.2300	7	1544356.0461
15	50	Hidden	Aerial	0	FALSE	OH	4	396.8941	12	1074209.0811
16	50	Hidden	Aerial	0	FALSE	OR	1073	1293945.6...	17	1708955.3610

OK   Cancel

FIGURE 3-28 Some sample rows imported from the report.

Note You can see in Figure 3-28 that the last two columns do not have meaningful names. These names depend on the discipline of the report author. Because they usually are internal names that are not visible in a report, it is common to have such non-descriptive names. In such cases, you should rename these columns before you use these numbers in your data model.

Now that you have imported the report data into the data model, the report will be queried again each time you reprocess it, and the updated data will be imported to the selected tables, overriding previously imported data.

Loading reports by using data feeds

You have seen how to load data from a report by using the Table Import wizard for the report data source. There is another way to load data from a report, however: by using data feeds. Follow these steps:

1. Open the report that contains the data you want to load in the Reporting Services web interface.

2. Click the **Save** button and choose **Data Feed** from the export menu that appears, as shown in Figure 3-29. Your browser will save the report as a file with the .atomsvc extension.

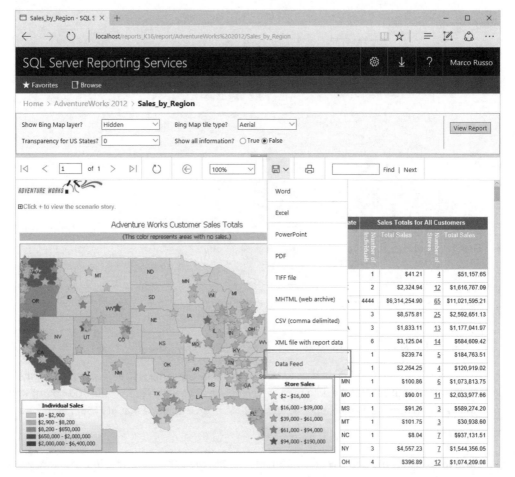

FIGURE 3-29 The Reporting Services web interface, showing the Data Feed item in the export drop-down menu (Save).

Note The .atomsvc file contains technical information about the source data feeds. This file is a data service document in an XML format that specifies a connection to one or more data feeds.

3. Start the Table Import wizard.

4. On the Connect to a Data Source page, choose **Other Feeds** and then click **Next**.

5. In the Connect to a Data Feed page of the Table Import wizard, click the **Browse** button next to the Data Feed URL box. Then select the .atomsvc file you saved in step 2. Figure 3-30 shows the result.

FIGURE 3-30 Providing the path to the .atomsvc file in the Table Import wizard's Connect to a Data Feed page.

6. Click **Next**. Then repeat steps 5–8 in the preceding section.

Loading report data from a data feed works exactly the same way as loading it directly from the report. You might prefer the data feed when you are already in a report and you do not want to enter the report parameters again, but it is up to you to choose the one that fits your needs best.

Note After the .atomsvc file has been used to grab the metadata information, you can safely remove it from your computer because SSDT does not use it anymore.

Loading from a data feed

In the previous section, you saw how to load a data feed exported by Reporting Services in Tabular mode. However, this technique is not exclusive to Reporting Services. It can be used to get data from many other services. This includes Internet sources that support the Open Data Protocol (OData; see *http://odata.org* for more information) and data exported as a data feed by SharePoint 2010 and later (described in the next section).

Note Analysis Services supports OData until version 3. It does not yet support version 4.

To load from one of these other data feeds, follow these steps:

1. Start the Table Import wizard.

2. On the Connect to a Data Source page, click **Other Feeds** and then click **Next**.

3. The Connect to a Data Feed page of the Table Import wizard (shown in Figure 3-31) requires you to enter the data feed URL. You saw this dialog box in Figure 3-30, when you were getting data from a report. This time, however, the Data Feed URL box does not have a fixed value provided by the report itself. Instead, you enter the URL of whatever source contains the feed you want to load. In this example, you can use the following URL to test this data source:

   http://services.odata.org/V3/OData/OData.svc/

FIGURE 3-31 Entering a data feed URL in the Table Import wizard.

4. Optionally, you can change the friendly connection name for this connection. Then click **Next**.

5. Set up the impersonation options to indicate which user SSAS must use to access the data feed when refreshing data and then click **Next**.

6. Select the tables to import (see Figure 3-32), and then follow a standard table-loading procedure.

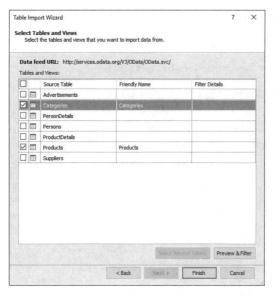

FIGURE 3-32 Selecting tables to load from a data feed URL.

7. Click **Finish**. The selected tables are imported into the data model. This operation can take a long time if you have a high volume of data to import and if the remote service that is providing the data has a slow bandwidth.

Loading from SharePoint

Microsoft SharePoint might contain several instances of data you would like to import into your data model. There is no specific data source dedicated to importing data from SharePoint. Depending on the type of data or the document you want to use, you must choose one of the methods already shown.

A list of the most common data sources you can import from SharePoint includes the following:

- **Report** A report generated by Reporting Services can be stored and displayed in SharePoint. In this case, you follow the same procedure described in the "Loading from a Reporting Services report" section earlier in this chapter, by providing the report pathname or by using OData.

- **Excel workbook** You can import data from an Excel workbook that is saved in SharePoint, the same way you would if it were saved on disk. Refer to the "Loading from an Excel file" section earlier in this chapter, and use the path to the library that contains the Excel file that you want.

- **Power Pivot model embedded in an Excel workbook** If an Excel workbook contains a Power Pivot model and is published in a Power Pivot folder, you can extract data from the model by querying it. To do that, you can follow the same steps described in the "Loading from Analysis Services" section earlier in this chapter, with the only difference being that you use the complete path to the published Excel file instead of the name of an Analysis Services server. (You do not have a Browse help tool; you probably need to copy and paste the complete URL from a browser.)

- **SharePoint list**   Any data included in a SharePoint list can be exported as a data feed. So you can use the same instructions described in the "Loading from a Reporting Services report" and "Loading from a data feed" sections earlier in this chapter. When you click the **Export as Data Feed** button in SharePoint, an .atomsvc file is downloaded, and you see the same user interface previously shown for reports.

Choosing the right data-loading method

SSDT makes many data sources available, each with specific capabilities and scenarios of usage. Nevertheless, as seasoned BI professionals, we (the authors) think it is important to warn our readers about some issues they might encounter during the development of a tabular solution.

The problems with the clipboard method of loading data were discussed earlier. The fact that it is not reproducible should discourage you from adopting it in a production environment. The only exception is loading very small tables with fixed lists of parameters to be used in particular measures.

Other data sources should be used only with great care. Whenever you develop a BI solution that must be processed by SSAS, you must use data sources that are the following:

- **Well typed**   Each column should have a data type clearly indicated by the source system. Relational databases normally provide this information. Other sources, such as CSV files, Excel workbooks, and the clipboard, do not. SSDT infers this information by analyzing the first few rows of data and assumes the rest of the data matches that type. However, it might be the case that later rows contain different data types, which will cause the loading process to fail.

- **Consistent**   The data types and columns should not change over time. For example, if you use an Excel workbook as the data source, and you let users freely update the workbook, then you might encounter a situation in which the workbook contains the wrong data or the user has changed the column order. SSAS will not handle these changes automatically, and the data will not be loaded successfully.

- **Time predictable**   Some data sources, such as certain OData feeds, might take a very long time to execute. Just how long this takes will vary depending on the network bandwidth available and any problems with the Internet connection. This might make the processing time quite unpredictable, or it might create problems due to timeouts.

- **Verified**   If the user can freely update data, as is the case in Excel workbooks, the wrong data might be added to your tabular data model, which would produce unpredictable results. Data entering Analysis Services should always be double-checked by some kind of software that ensures its correctness.

For these reasons, we discourage our readers from using the following data sources:

- **Excel** The data is often not verified, not consistent, and not well typed.

- **Text file** The data is often not well typed.

- **OData** The data is often not time predictable when the data comes from the web.

For all these kinds of data sources, a much better solution is to create some kind of extract, transform, load (ETL) process that loads the data from these sources, cleans the data, and verifies that the data is valid and available. Then it puts all the information inside tables in a relational database (such as SQL Server), from which you can feed the tabular data model.

Using DirectQuery requires a relational database as a data source

Another excellent reason to use a relational database to hold all the data that feeds your data model is that if data is stored in a supported server type, you always have the freedom to activate Direct-Query mode, which is prevented if you decide to load data directly from the various data sources.

Of course, it is important to remember that having the option to do something does not mean that you must do it. SSAS Tabular offers many options to load data. All these options are relevant and important for Power BI, Power Pivot for Excel, and Power Pivot for SharePoint. However, we think that corporate BI, addressed by SSAS tabular running in Server mode, has different needs, and you can avoid using these self-service data sources. We are not saying you should avoid using these features; we are saying you must use them with care, understanding the pros and cons of your choice.

Summary

In this chapter, you were introduced to all the various data-loading capabilities of Tabular mode. You can load data from many data sources, which enables you to integrate data from the different sources into a single, coherent view of the information you must analyze.

The main topics you must remember are the following:

- **Impersonation** SSAS can impersonate a user when opening a data source, whereas SSDT always uses the credentials of the current user. This can lead to server-side and client-side operations that can use different accounts for impersonation.

- **Working with big tables** When you are working with big tables, the data needs to be loaded in the workspace database. Therefore, you must limit the number of rows that SSDT reads and processes in the workspace database so that you can work safely with your solution.

- **Data sources** There are many data sources to connect to different databases. Choosing the right one depends on your source of data. That said, if you must use one of the discouraged sources, remember that if you store data in a relational database before moving it into Tabular mode, you permit data quality control, data cleansing, and more predictable performances.

Introducing calculations in DAX

Now that you have seen the basics of the SQL Server Analysis Services (SSAS) tabular model, it is time to learn the fundamentals of Data Analysis Expressions (DAX). DAX has its own syntax for defining calculation expressions. It is somewhat similar to a Microsoft Excel expression, but it has specific functions that enable you to create more advanced calculations on data that is stored in multiple tables.

The goal of this chapter is to provide an overview of the main concepts of DAX without pretending to explain in detail all the implications of every feature and function in this language. If you want to learn DAX, we suggest reading our book, *The Definitive Guide to DAX*, published by Microsoft Press.

> **What's new in SSAS 2016**   DAX has a new syntax for variables, and table expressions can be used in calculated tables. You will also find an updated reference of tools to edit and format DAX expressions.

Introduction to the DAX language

DAX is a functional language, specifically designed to compute business formulas over a data model. The tabular model contains tables, columns, and relationships. A DAX expression can leverage an existing relationship without having to define it explicitly, as you have to do in a SQL query. Moreover, a DAX expression is evaluated in a particular context, where there are filters automatically applied to the tables in the data model. For this reason, an aggregation does not necessarily include all the rows of a table, but only those that appear active in the current evaluation context.

You can write a DAX expression to define the following entities:

- **Measure**   The DAX expression is evaluated in a filter context, where rows of one or more tables in the data model are aggregated and filtered according to implicit filters defined in a filter context. For example, a cell in a PivotTable in Excel displays the value of a measure, computed in an implicit filter context that is defined by the selection of slices, filters, rows, and columns of the PivotTable itself. The following expression is valid in a measure:

```
SUM ( Sales[Line Amount] )
```

- **Calculated column** The DAX expression is evaluated for each row in a table and the DAX syntax can implicitly reference the value of each column of the table. The result of a calculated column is persisted in the data model and is automatically refreshed every time there is a refresh operation on any table of the data model. The following expression is valid in a calculated column:

```
Sales[Quantity] * Sales[Net Price]
```

- **Calculated table** The DAX expression returns a table that is persisted in the data model and it is automatically refreshed every time there is a refresh operation on any table in the data model. The following example is an expression for a calculated table:

```
ADDCOLUMNS (
    ALL ( Product[Manufacturer] ),
    "Quantity", CALCULATE ( SUM ( Sales[Line Amount] ) )
)
```

- **Query** The DAX expression returns a table that is materialized in the result of the query itself. The following example is a DAX query:

```
EVALUATE
SUMMARIZECOLUMNS (
    Product[Manufacturer],
    'Order Date' [Order Year Number],
    "Sales", SUM ( Sales[Line Amount] )
)
```

A DAX expression for a measure or calculated column must return a scalar value such as a number or a string. In contrast, a DAX expression for a calculated table or query must return a table (an entity with one or more columns and zero or more rows). You will see more examples of these entities later in this chapter.

To write DAX expressions, you need to learn the following basic concepts of DAX:

- The syntax

- The different data types that DAX can handle

- The basic operators

- How to refer to columns and tables

These and other core DAX concepts are discussed in the next few sections.

DAX syntax

You use DAX to compute values using columns of tables. You can aggregate, calculate, and search for numbers, but in the end, all the calculations involve tables and columns. Thus, the first syntax to learn is how to reference a column in a table.

The general format of a column reference is to write the table name enclosed in single quotes, followed by the column name enclosed in square brackets, such as the following example:

```
'Sales'[Quantity]
```

You can omit the single quotes if the table name does not start with a number, does not contain spaces, and is not a reserved word (like Date or Sum).

> **Note**   It is common practice to not use spaces in table names. This way, you avoid the quotes in the formulas, which tend to make the code harder to read. Keep in mind, however, that the name of the table is the same name that you will see when browsing the model with PivotTables or any other client tool, such as Power View. Thus, if you like to have spaces in the table names in your report, you need to use single quotes in your code.

You can also avoid writing the table name at all, in case you are referencing a column or a measure in the same table where you are defining the formula. Thus, [SalesQuantity] is a valid column reference if written in a calculated column or in a measure of the FactSalesSmall table. Even if this technique is syntactically correct (and the user interface might suggest its use when you select a column instead of writing it), we strongly discourage you from using it. Such a syntax makes the code rather difficult to read, so it is better to always use the table name when you reference a column in a DAX expression.

DAX data types

DAX can perform computations with different numeric types, of which there are seven. In the list that follows, we show both the DAX name that is visible in the user interface of Visual Studio and the name of the same data type that is used internally in the *Tabular Model Scripting Language (TMSL)*. The latter is indicated between parentheses. Certain data types are named differently than the standard terminology used in database jargon. Boolean values, for example, are called TRUE/FALSE in DAX terminology. We prefer to adhere to the internal definition that is close to the de-facto naming standard, and we refer to them as Boolean values. Wherever possible, we will also provide the corresponding data type used by SQL Server (Transact-SQL, or T-SQL), which could be helpful to understand the similarities and the differences between the two worlds.

The following list explains the different DAX data types:

- **Whole Number (int64)**   An integer number.

- **Decimal Number (double)**   A floating point number.

- **Currency (decimal)**   A fixed decimal number, with four decimal digits of fixed precision. It is internally stored as an integer. This is also known as a *Fixed Decimal Number* in the user interface of Power BI.

- **Date (dateTime)**   A date and time value.

- **TRUE/FALSE (boolean)**   A logical value.

- **Text (string)**   A string.

- **Binary (binary)**   A *binary large object*, also known as *BLOB*; it is usually used to store pictures and documents.

DAX has a powerful type-handling system so that you do not have to worry about data types. When you write a DAX expression, the resulting type is based on the type of terms used in the expression. You need to be aware of this in case the type returned from a DAX expression is not the expected one. Then you must investigate the data type of the terms used in the expression itself.

For example, if one of the terms of a sum is a date, then the result is a date too. In contrast, if the same operator is used with integers, the result is an integer. This is known as *operator overloading*. You can see an example of this in the following expression, which returns a date, adding seven days to the original value in the Order Date column. The result is, as we mentioned, a date.

```
'Dates'[Date] + 7
```

In addition to operator overloading, DAX automatically converts strings into numbers and numbers into strings whenever required by the operator. For example, if you use the & operator, which concatenates strings, DAX converts its arguments into strings. Look at the following formula:

```
5 & 4
```

It returns "54" as a string. On the other hand, observe the following formula:

```
"5" + "4"
```

It returns an integer result with the value of 9.

The resulting value depends on the operator and not on the source columns, which are converted following the requirements of the operator. Even if this behavior looks convenient, errors might happen during these automatic conversions. We suggest avoiding automatic conversions. If some kind of conversion needs to happen, then it is much better if you take control over it and make the conversion explicit. To be more explicit, the previous example should instead be written as follows:

```
VALUE ( "5" ) + VALUE ( "4" )
```

DAX data types might be familiar to people who are used to working with Excel or other languages. You can find specifications of DAX data types at *https://msdn.microsoft.com/en-us/library/gg492146. aspx*. However, it is useful to share a few considerations about each of these data types.

Whole Number (int64)

DAX has only one integer data type that can store a 64-bit value. All the internal calculations between the integer values in DAX also use a 64-bit value. This data type stores the corresponding T-SQL data types `bigint`, `int`, `smallint`, and `tinyint`.

Decimal Number (double)

A decimal number is always stored as a double-precision, floating point value. Do not confuse this DAX data type with the `decimal` and `numeric` data type of T-SQL. The corresponding data types of a DAX decimal number in T-SQL are `float` and `real`. However, consider that any `decimal` and `numeric` data type in SQL Server is converted to a decimal number data type in DAX when you import a table from SQL Server. You might want to consider the conversion to a currency data type in DAX of these columns whenever the precision required by T-SQL is available in such a data type in DAX.

Currency (decimal)

The currency data type in DAX stores a fixed decimal number. It can represent four decimal points, and it is internally stored as a 64-bit integer value, divided by 10,000. All calculations performed between currency data types always ignore decimals beyond the fourth decimal point. If you need more accuracy, you must do a conversion to the decimal data type in DAX.

The default format of the currency data type includes the currency symbol. You can also apply the currency formatting to whole and decimal numbers, and you can use a format without the currency symbol for a currency data type.

The currency data type in DAX stores the corresponding T-SQL data types: `money` and `smallmoney`.

Date (dateTime)

DAX stores dates in a date data type. This format uses a floating-point number internally, where the integer corresponds to the number of days since December 30, 1899, and the decimal part identifies the fraction of the day. Hours, minutes, and seconds are converted to the decimal fractions of a day. Thus, the following expression returns the current date plus one day (exactly 24 hours):

```
NOW () + 1
```

Its result is the date of tomorrow, at the same time of the evaluation. If you need only the date and not the time, use `TRUNC` to get rid of the decimal part. In the user interface of Power BI, you can see three different data types: Date/Time, Date, and Time. All these data types correspond to the date data type in DAX. To avoid confusion, we prefer to reference to this data type as dateTime, which is the name of the data type in TMSL. However, date and dateTime are the same concept when referring to the data type in a tabular model.

The date data type in DAX stores the corresponding T-SQL data types: `date`, `datetime`, `datetime2`, `smalldatetime`, and `time`. However, the range of values stored by the DAX data type does not correspond to the range of dates supported in T-SQL because DAX supports only dates between 1900 and 9999, and precision of time is of 3.33 ms.

TRUE/FALSE (boolean)

The boolean data type is used to express logical conditions. For example, a calculated column, defined by the following expression, is of the boolean type:

```
Sales[Unit Price] > Sales[Unit Cost]
```

You can also see boolean data types as numbers, where TRUE equals 1 and FALSE equals 0. This might be useful for sorting purposes, because TRUE > FALSE. The boolean data type in DAX stores the corresponding `bit` data type in T-SQL.

Text (string)

Every string in DAX is stored as a *Unicode* string, where each character is stored in 16 bits. The comparison between strings follows the collation setting of the database, which by default is case-insensitive. (For example, the two strings "Power Pivot" and "POWER PIVOT" are considered equal.) You can modify the collation in a database property `Collation`, which must be set before deploying the database to the server.

The text data type in DAX stores the corresponding T-SQL data types: char, varchar, text, nchar, nvarchar, and ntext.

Binary (binary)

The binary data type is used in the data model to store images, and it is not accessible in DAX. It is mainly used by Power BI or other client tools to show pictures stored directly in the data model.

The binary data type in DAX stores the corresponding T-SQL data types: binary, varbinary, and image.

DAX operators

Having seen the importance of operators in determining the type of an expression, you can now see a list of the operators that are available in DAX, as shown in Table 4-1.

Table 4-1 Operators

Operator Type	Symbol	Use	Example
Parenthesis	( )	Precedence order and grouping of arguments	`(5 + 2) * 3`

Arithmetic	+
	−
	*
	/
		Addition
		Subtraction/negation
		Multiplication
		Division
			`4 + 2`
			`5 − 3`
			`4 * 2`
			`4 / 2`

Comparison	=
	<>
	>
	>=
	<
	<=
		Equal to
		Not equal to
		Greater than
		Greater than or equal to
		Less than
		Less than or equal to
			`[CountryRegion] = "USA"`
			`[CountryRegion] <> "USA"`
			`[Quantity] > 0`
			`[Quantity] >= 100`
			`[Quantity] < 0`
			`[Quantity] <= 100`

Text concatenation	&	Concatenation of strings	`"Value is " & [Amount]`
Logical	&&	AND condition between two Boolean expressions	`[CountryRegion] = "USA" &&` `[Quantity] > 0`
	||	OR condition between two Boolean expressions	`[CountryRegion] = "USA" ||` `[Quantity] > 0`

Moreover, the logical operators are also available as DAX functions, with syntax that is very similar to Excel. For example, you can write the following lines:

```
AND ( [CountryRegion] = "USA", [Quantity] > 0 )
OR ( [CountryRegion] = "USA", [Quantity] > 0 )
```

Those expressions are equivalent, respectively, to the following lines:

```
[CountryRegion] = "USA" && [Quantity] > 0
[CountryRegion] = "USA" || [Quantity] > 0
```

The use of functions instead of operators for Boolean logic becomes very beneficial when you have to write complex conditions. In fact, when it comes to formatting large sections of code, functions are much easier to format and read than operators. However, a major drawback of functions is that you can only pass in two parameters at a time. This requires you to nest functions if you have more than two conditions to evaluate.

Column reference and measures reference

A table in the data model includes columns and measures, which are all accessible with the following syntax:

```
'TableName'[ColumnOrMeasureName]
```

The table name can be omitted if the expression is written in the same context as the table that includes the referenced column or measure. However, it is very important to follow these simple guidelines:

- **Always include the table name for a column reference** For example:

  ```
  'TableName'[ColumnName]
  ```

- **Always omit the table name for a measure reference** For example:

  ```
  [MeasureName]
  ```

There are many reasons for these guidelines, mainly related to readability and maintainability. A column name is always unique in a table, but you can have the same column name in different tables. A measure name is unique for the entire data model, and it cannot be the same as any other column or measure that is defined in any table of the data model. For this reason, the guideline produces an unambiguous definition in any context. Last, but not least, a measure reference implies a context transition (explained later in this chapter in the "Context transition" section), which has an important impact in the execution of the calculation. It is important to not confuse column references and measure references because they have a different calculation semantic.

Aggregate functions

Almost every data model needs to operate on aggregated data. DAX offers a set of functions that aggregate the values of a column or an expression in a table and then return a single value (also known as a *scalar value*). We call this group of functions *aggregate functions*. For example, the following measure calculates the sum of all the numbers in the SalesAmount column of the Sales table:

```
SUM ( Sales[SalesAmount] )
```

However, SUM is just a shortcut for the more generic expression called SUMX, which has two arguments: the table to scan and a DAX expression to evaluate for every row of the table, summing up the results obtained for all the rows considered in the evaluation context. Write the following corresponding syntax when using SUMX:

```
SUMX ( Sales, Sales[SalesAmount] )
```

Usually, the version with the X suffix is useful when you compute longer expressions row by row. For example, the following expression multiplies quantity and unit price row by row, summing up the results obtained:

```
SUMX ( Sales, Sales[Quantity] * Sales[Unit Price] )
```

Aggregation functions are SUMX, AVERAGEX, MINX, MAXX, PRODUCTX, GEOMEANX, COUNTX, COUNTAX, STDEVX, VARX, MEDIANX, PERCENTILEX.EXC, and PERCENTILEX.INC. You can also use the corresponding shorter version without the X suffix whenever the expression in the second argument is made by only one column reference.

The first argument of SUMX (and other aggregate functions) is a table expression. The simplest table expression is the name of a table, but you can replace it with a table function, as described in the next section.

Table functions

Many DAX functions require a table expression as an argument. You can also use table expressions in calculated tables and in DAX queries, as you will see later in this chapter. The simplest table expression is a table reference, as shown in the following example:

```
Sales
```

A table expression may include a table function. For example, FILTER reads rows from a table expression and returns a table that has only the rows that satisfy the logical condition described in the second argument. The following DAX expression returns the rows in Sales that have a value in the Unit Cost column that is greater than or equal to 10:

```
FILTER ( Sales, Sales[Unit Cost] >= 10 )
```

You can combine table expressions in the scalar expression, which is a common practice when writing measures and calculated columns. For example, the following expression sums up the product of quantity and unit price for all the columns in the Sales table with a unit cost greater than or equal to 10:

```
SUMX (
    FILTER ( Sales, Sales[Unit Cost] >= 10 ),
    Sales[Quantity] * Sales[Unit Price]
)
```

There are complex table functions in DAX that you can use to manipulate the rows and columns of the table you want as a result. For example, you can use ADDCOLUMNS and SELECTCOLUMNS to manipulate the projection, whereas SUMMARIZE and GROUPBY can join the tables and group rows by using the relationships in the data model and column specified in the function.

DAX also includes functions to manipulate sets (UNION, INTERSECT, and EXCEPT), to manipulate tables (CROSSJOIN and GENERATE), and to perform other specialized actions (such as TOPN).

An important consideration is that the most efficient way to apply filters in a calculation is usually by leveraging the CALCULATE and CALCULATETABLE functions. These transform the filter context before evaluating a measure. This reduces the volume of materialization (the intermediate temporary tables) that are required for completing the calculation.

Evaluation context

Any DAX expression is evaluated inside a context. The *context* is the environment under which the formula is evaluated. The evaluation context of a DAX expression has the following two distinct components:

- **Filter context**   This is a set of filters that identifies the rows that are active in the table of the data model.

- **Row context**   This is a single row that is active in a table for evaluating column references.

These concepts are discussed in the next two sections.

Filter context

Consider the following simple formula for a measure called Total Sales:

```
SUMX ( Sales, Sales[Quantity] * Sales[UnitPrice] )
```

This formula computes the sum of a quantity multiplied by the price for every row of the Sales table. If you display this measure in a PivotTable in Excel, you will see a different number for every cell, as shown in Figure 4-1.

Total Sales	Column Labels			
Row Labels	Deluxe	Economy	Regular	Grand Total
Azure	$19,495.00	$19,156.00	$69,722.20	$108,373.20
Black	$1,338,207.22	$1,003,414.79	$4,155,034.50	$6,496,656.51
Blue	$943,441.67	$392,559.86	$1,366,676.97	$2,702,678.50
Brown	$177,454.69	$201,688.00	$761,821.23	$1,140,963.92
Gold	$54,234.00	$60,506.70	$283,136.92	$397,877.62
Green	$305,129.98	$199,253.74	$1,050,431.16	$1,554,814.88
Grey	$1,129,843.26	$398,856.70	$2,310,613.09	$3,839,313.05
Orange	$148,178.77	$97,464.67	$693,563.82	$939,207.26
Pink	$104,783.00	$133,521.21	$678,488.52	$916,792.73
Purple	$4,405.38	$980.00	$1,179.95	$6,565.33
Red	$248,461.68	$273,355.94	$684,353.65	$1,206,171.27
Silver	$2,040,744.43	$1,091,694.59	$4,369,627.63	$7,502,066.65
Silver Grey	$67,605.00	$61,824.00	$281,417.00	$410,846.00
Transparent		$3,677.94		$3,677.94
White	$1,967,475.88	$1,040,408.68	$3,355,627.97	$6,363,512.53
Yellow	$35,335.22	$24,807.40	$40,488.50	$100,631.12
Grand Total	$8,584,795.18	$5,003,170.22	$20,102,183.11	$33,690,148.51

FIGURE 4-1   Displaying the Total Sales measure in a PivotTable.

Because the product color is on the rows, each row in the PivotTable can see, out of the whole database, only the subset of products of that specific color. The same thing happens for the columns of the PivotTable, slicing the data by product class. This is the surrounding area of the formula—that is, a set of filters applied to the database prior to the formula evaluation. Each cell of the PivotTable evaluates the DAX expression independently from the other cells. When the formula iterates the Sales table, it does not compute it over the entire database because it does not have the option to look at all the rows. When DAX computes the formula in a cell that intersects the White color and Economy class, only the products that are White and Economy are visible. Because of that, the formula only considers sales pertinent to the white products in the economy class.

Any DAX formula specifies a calculation, but DAX evaluates this calculation in a context that defines the final computed value. The formula is always the same, but the value is different because DAX evaluates it against different subsets of data. The only case where the formula behaves in the way it has been defined is in the grand total. At that level, because no filtering happens, the entire database is visible.

Any filter applied to a table automatically propagates to other tables in the data model by following the filter propagation directions, which were specified in the relationships existing between tables.

We call this context the *filter context*. As its name suggests, it is a context that filters tables. Any formula you ever write will have a different value depending on the filter context that DAX uses to perform its evaluation. However, the filter context is only one part of the evaluation context, which is made by the interaction of the filter context and row context.

Row context

In a DAX expression, the syntax of a column reference is valid only when there is a notion of "current row" in the table from which you get the value of a column. Observe the following expression:

```
Sales[Quantity] * Sales[UnitPrice]
```

In practice, this expression is valid only when it is possible to identify something similar to the generic concept of "current row" in the Sales table. This concept is formally defined as *row context*. A column reference in a DAX expression is valid only when there is an active row context for the table that is referenced. You have a row context active for the DAX expressions written in the following:

- A calculated column

- The argument executed in an iterator function in DAX (all the functions with an X suffix and any other function that iterates a table, such as FILTER, ADDCOLUMNS, SELECTCOLUMNS, and many others)

- The filter expression for a security role

If you try to evaluate a column reference when there is no row context active for the referenced table, you get a syntax error.

A row context does not propagate to other tables automatically. You can use a relationship to propagate a row context to another table, but this requires the use of a specific DAX function called RELATED.

CALCULATE and CALCULATETABLE

DAX has two functions that can modify a filter context before executing an expression: CALCULATE and CALCULATETABLE. The only difference between the two functions is that the former returns a single value (string or numeric), whereas the latter executes a table expression and returns a table.

The filter context is a set of filters that are applied to columns and/or tables of the data model. Each filter corresponds to a list of the values allowed for one or more columns, or for the entire table. By invoking CALCULATE or CALCULATETABLE, you modify the existing filter context, overriding any existing filters and/or adding new filters. To simplify the explanation, we consider the syntax of CALCULATE, but all the considerations apply to CALCULATETABLE, too.

The syntax for CALCULATE is as follows:

```
CALCULATE ( expression, filter1, filter2, …, filterN )
```

CALCULATE accepts any number of parameters. The only mandatory one is the first parameter in the expression. We call the conditions following the first parameter the *filter arguments*.

CALCULATE does the following:

- It places a copy of the current filter context into a new filter context.

- It evaluates each filter argument and produces for each condition the list of valid values for that specific column.

- If two or more filter arguments affect the same column filters, they are merged together using an AND operator (or, in mathematical terms, using the set intersection).

- It uses the new condition to replace the existing filters on the columns in the model. If a column already has a filter, then the new filter replaces the existing one. If, on the other hand, the column does not have a filter, then DAX simply applies the new column filter.

- After the new filter context is evaluated, CALCULATE computes the first argument (the expression) in the new filter context. At the end, it will restore the original filter context, returning the computed result.

The filters accepted by CALCULATE can be of the following two types:

- **List of values** This appears in the form of a table expression. In this case, you provide the exact list of values that you want to see in the new filter context. The filter can be a table with a single column or with many columns, as is the case of a filter on a whole table.

- **Boolean conditions** An example of this might be Product[Color] = "White". These filters need to work on a single column because the result must be a list of values from a single column.

If you use the syntax with a Boolean condition, DAX will transform it into a list of values. For example, you might write the following expression:

```
CALCULATE (
    SUM ( Sales[SalesAmount] ),
    Product[Color] = "Red"
)
```

Internally, DAX transforms the expression into the following one:

```
CALCULATE (
    SUM ( Sales[SalesAmount] ),
    FILTER (
        ALL ( Product[Color] ),
        Product[Color] = "Red"
    )
)
```

> **Note** The ALL function ignores any existing filter context, returning a table with all the unique values of the column specified.

For this reason, you can reference only one column in a filter argument with a Boolean condition. DAX must detect the column to iterate in the FILTER expression, which is generated in the background automatically. If the Boolean expression references more columns, then you must write the FILTER iteration in an explicit way.

Context transition

CALCULATE performs another very important task: It transforms any existing row context into an equivalent filter context. This is important when you have an aggregation within an iterator or when, in general, you have a row context. For example, the following expression (defined in the No CT measure shown later in Figure 4-2) computes the quantity of all the sales (of any product previously selected in the filter context) and multiplies it by the number of products:

```
SUMX (
    Product,
    SUM ( Sales[Quantity] )
)
```

The SUM aggregation function ignores the row context on the Product table produced by the iteration made by SUMX. However, by embedding the SUM in a CALCULATE function, you transform the row context on Product into an equivalent filter context. This automatically propagates to the Sales table thanks to the existing relationship in the data model between Product and Sales. The following expression is defined in the Explicit CT measure:

```
SUMX (
    Product,
    CALCULATE ( SUM ( Sales[Quantity] ) )
)
```

When you use a measure reference in a row context, there is always an implicit CALCULATE function surrounding the expression executed in the measure, so the previous expression corresponds to the following one, defined in the Implicit CT measure:

```
SUMX (
    Product,
    [Total Quantity]
)
```

The measure from Total Quantity in the previous expression corresponds to the following expression:

```
SUM ( Sales[Quantity] )
```

As you see in the results shown in Figure 4-2, replacing a measure with the underlying DAX expression is not correct. You must wrap such an expression within a CALCULATE function, which performs the same context transition made by invoking a measure reference.

Row Labels	Total Sales	Total Quantity	No CT	Explicit CT	Implicit CT
Azure	$108,373.20	546	7,644	546	546
Black	$6,496,656.51	33,618	20,238,036	33,618	33,618
Blue	$2,702,678.50	8,859	1,771,800	8,859	8,859
Brown	$1,140,963.92	2,570	197,890	2,570	2,570
Gold	$397,877.62	1,393	69,650	1,393	1,393
Green	$1,554,814.88	3,020	223,480	3,020	3,020
Grey	$3,839,313.05	11,900	3,367,700	11,900	11,900
Orange	$939,207.26	2,203	121,165	2,203	2,203
Pink	$916,792.73	4,921	413,364	4,921	4,921
Purple	$6,565.33	102	612	102	102
Red	$1,206,171.27	8,079	799,821	8,079	8,079
Silver	$7,502,066.65	27,551	11,488,767	27,551	27,551
Silver Grey	$410,846.00	959	13,426	959	959
Transparent	$3,677.94	1,251	1,251	1,251	1,251
White	$6,363,512.53	30,543	15,424,215	30,543	30,543
Yellow	$100,631.12	2,665	95,940	2,665	2,665
Grand Total	$33,690,148.51	140,180	352,833,060	140,180	140,180

FIGURE 4-2 The different results of a similar expression, with and without context transition.

Variables

When writing a DAX expression, you can avoid repeating the same expression by using variables. For example, look at the following expression:

```
VAR
    TotalSales = SUM ( Sales[SalesAmount] )
RETURN
    ( TotalSales - SUM ( Sales[TotalProductCost] ) ) / TotalSales
```

You can define many variables, and they are local to the expression in which you define them. Variables are very useful both to simplify the code and because they enable you to avoid repeating the same subexpression. Variables are computed using lazy evaluation. This means that if you define a variable that, for any reason, is not used in your code, then the variable will never be evaluated. If it needs to be computed, then this happens only once. Later usages of the variable will read the previously computed value. Thus, they are also useful as an optimization technique when you use a complex expression multiple times.

Measures

You define a *measure* whenever you want to aggregate values from many rows in a table. The following convention is used in this book to define a measure:

```
Table[MeasureName] := <expression>
```

This syntax does not correspond to what you write in the formula editor in Visual Studio because you do not specify the table name there. We use this writing convention in the book to optimize the space required for a measure definition. For example, the definition of the Total Sales measure in the Sales table (which you can see in Figure 4-3) is written in this book as the following expression:

```
Sales[Total Sales] := SUMX ( Sales, Sales[Quantity] * Sales[Unit Price] )
```

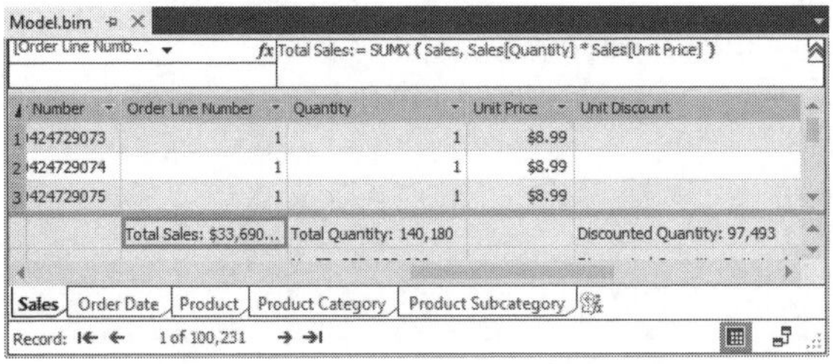

FIGURE 4-3   Defining a measure in Visual Studio that includes only the measure name; the table is implicit.

A measure needs to be defined in a table. This is one of the requirements of the DAX language. However, the measure does not really belong to the table. In fact, you can move a measure from one table to another one without losing its functionality.

The expression is executed in a filter context and does not have a row context. For this reason, you must use aggregation functions, and you cannot use a direct column reference in the expression of a measure. However, a measure can reference other measures. You can write the formula to calculate the margin of sales as a percentage by using an explicit DAX syntax, or by referencing measures that perform part of the calculation. The following example defines four measures, where the Margin and Margin % measures reference other measures:

```
Sales[Total Sales] := SUMX ( Sales, Sales[Quantity] * Sales[Unit Price] )
Sales[Total Cost]  := SUMX ( Sales, Sales[Quantity] * Sales[Unit Cost] )
Sales[Margin]      := [Total Sales] - [Total Cost]
Sales[Margin %]    := DIVIDE ( [Margin], [Total Sales] )
```

The following Margin % Expanded measure corresponds to Margin %. All the referenced measures are expanded in a single DAX expression without the measure references. The column references are always executed in a row context generated by a DAX function (always SUMX in the following example):

```
Sales[Margin % Expanded] :=
DIVIDE (
    SUMX ( Sales, Sales[Quantity] * Sales[Unit Price] )
        - SUMX ( Sales, Sales[Quantity] * Sales[Unit Cost] ),
    SUMX ( Sales, Sales[Quantity] * Sales[Unit Price] )
)
```

You can also write the same expanded measure using variables, making the code more readable and avoiding the duplication of the same DAX subexpression (as it is the case for TotalSales, in this case):

```
Sales[Margin % Variables]:=
VAR TotalSales =
    SUMX ( Sales, Sales[Quantity] * Sales[Unit Price] )
VAR TotalCost =
    SUMX ( Sales, Sales[Quantity] * Sales[Unit Cost] )
VAR Margin = TotalSales - TotalCost
RETURN
    DIVIDE ( Margin, TotalSales )
```

Calculated columns

A calculated column is just like any other column in a table. You can use it in the rows, columns, filters, or values of a PivotTable or in any other report. You can also use a calculated column to define a relationship. The DAX expression defined for a calculated column operates in the context of the current row of the table to which it belongs (a *row context*). Any column reference returns the value of that column for the current row. You cannot directly access the values of the other rows. If you write an aggregation, the initial filter context is always empty (there are no filters active in a row context).

The following convention is used in this book to define a calculated column:

```
Table[ColumnName] = <expression>
```

This syntax does not correspond to what you write in the formula editor in Visual Studio because you do not specify the table and column names there. We use this writing convention in the book to optimize the space required for a calculated column definition. For example, the definition of the Price Class calculated column in the Sales table (see Figure 4-4) is written in this book as follows:

```
Sales[Price Class] =
SWITCH (
    TRUE,
    Sales[Unit Price] > 1000, "A",
    Sales[Unit Price] > 100, "B",
    "C"
)
```

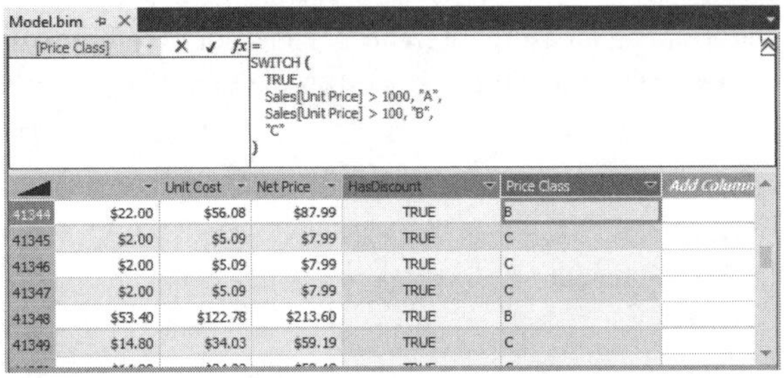

FIGURE 4-4   How the definition of a calculated column in Visual Studio does not include the table and column names.

Calculated columns are computed during the database processing and then stored in the model. This might seem strange if you are accustomed to SQL-computed columns (not persisted), which are computed at query time and do not use memory. In Tabular, however, all the calculated columns occupy space in memory and are computed during table processing.

This behavior is helpful whenever you create very complex calculated columns. The time required to compute them is always at process time and not query time, resulting in a better user experience. Nevertheless, you must remember that a calculated column uses precious RAM. If, for example, you have a complex formula for a calculated column, you might be tempted to separate the steps of computation in different intermediate columns. Although this technique is useful during project development, it is a bad habit in production because each intermediate calculation is stored in RAM and wastes precious space.

For example, if you have a calculated column called LineAmount, it is defined as follows:

```
Sales[LineAmount] = Sales[Quantity] * Sales[UnitPrice]
```

You might create the following Total Amount measure:

```
Sales[Total Amount] := SUM ( Sales[LineAmount] )
```

However, you should be aware that in reality, the last expression corresponds to the following:

```
Sales[Total Amount] := SUMX ( Sales, Sales[LineAmount] )
```

You can create the same Total Amount measure by writing a single formula in the following way:

```
Sales[Total Amount] :=
SUMX (
    Sales,
    Sales[Quantity] * Sales[UnitPrice]
)
```

Replacing a column reference pointing to a calculated column is usually a good idea if the column has a relatively large cardinality, as is the case in LineAmount. However, you might prefer to implement a calculated column instead of writing a single dynamic measure whenever you use a column reference to the calculated column in a filter argument of CALCULATE.

For example, consider the following expression of the Discounted Quantity measure, returning the sum of Quantity for all the sales having some discount:

```
Sales[Discounted Quantity] :=
CALCULATE (
    SUM ( Sales[Quantity] ),
    Sales[Unit Discount] <> 0
)
```

You can create a calculated column HasDiscount in the Sales table using the following expression:

```
Sales[HasDiscount] = Sales[Unit Discount] <> 0
```

Then, you can use the calculated column in the filter of CALCULATE, reducing the number of values pushed in the filter context (one value instead of all the unique values of Unit Discount except zero):

```
Sales[Discounted Quantity Optimized] :=
CALCULATE (
    SUM ( Sales[Quantity] ),
    Sales[HasDiscount] = TRUE
)
```

Using a calculated column that produces a string or a Boolean to filter data is considered a good practice. It improves query performances with a minimal cost in terms of memory, thanks to the high compression of a column with a low number of unique values.

Calculated tables

A calculated table is the result of a DAX table expression that is materialized in the data model when you refresh any part of it. A calculated table can be useful to create a lookup table from existing data to create meaningful relationships between entities.

The following convention is used in this book to define a calculated table:

```
Table = <expression>
```

This syntax does not correspond to what you write in the formula editor in Visual Studio because you do not specify the table name there. We use this writing convention in the book to optimize the space required for a calculated table definition. For example, the definition of the calculated table Colors, as shown in Figure 4-5, is written in this book as follows:

```
Colors =
UNION (
    ALL ( 'Product'[Color] ),
    DATATABLE (
        "Color", STRING,
        {
            { "*custom*" },
            { "Cyan" },
            { "Magenta" },
            { "Lime" },
            { "Maroon" }
        }
    )
)
```

FIGURE 4-5 The definition of a calculated column in Visual Studio, which does not include the table and column names.

Calculated tables are computed at the end of the database processing and then stored in the model. In this way, the engine guarantees that the table is always synchronized with the data that exists in the data model.

Writing queries in DAX

You can use DAX as both a programming language and a query language.

A DAX query is a DAX expression that returns a table, used with the EVALUATE statement. The complete DAX query syntax is as follows:

```
[DEFINE { MEASURE <tableName>[<name>] = <expression> }]
EVALUATE <table>
[ORDER BY {<expression> [{ASC | DESC}]} [, …]
    [START AT {<value>|<parameter>} [, …]]
]
```

The initial DEFINE MEASURE part can be useful to define measures that are local to the query (that is, they exist for the lifetime of the query). It becomes very useful when you are debugging formulas, because you can define a local measure, test it, and then put it in the model once it behaves as expected. This is very useful when using DAX Studio to test your measures, as shown in Figure 4-6.

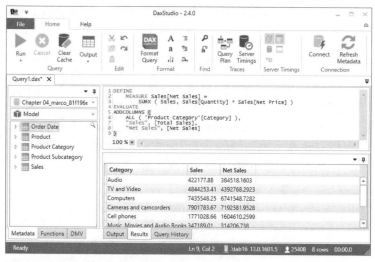

FIGURE 4-6 The execution of a DAX query using DAX Studio.

For example, the following query evaluates the Total Sales and Net Sales measures for each product category. The Total Sales measure is defined in the data model, whereas Net Sales is defined within the query and would override any measure with the same name defined in the data model.

```
DEFINE
    MEASURE Sales[Net Sales] =
        SUMX ( Sales, Sales[Quantity] * Sales[Net Price] )
EVALUATE
ADDCOLUMNS (
    ALL ( 'Product Category'[Category] ),
    "Sales", [Total Sales],
    "Net Sales", [Net Sales]
)
```

Writing DAX queries is useful to test and debug your measures. It is also required to create efficient reports in Microsoft SQL Server Reporting Services. This is because DAX is more efficient than MDX for producing the type of tabular results required in datasets for Reporting Services.

Formatting DAX code

A very important aspect of DAX is formatting the code. DAX is a functional language, meaning that no matter how complex it is, a DAX expression is always a single function call with some parameters. The complexity of the code translates into the complexity of the expressions that you use as parameters to the outermost function.

For this reason, it is normal to see expressions that span 10 lines or more. Seeing a 20-line DAX expression is not unusual, as you will see. As formulas start to grow in length and complexity, it is extremely important that you learn how to format them so they are easier to read and identify.

To understand why formatting is very important, we show a formula that computes the sum of account balances for the last available date of each account. It is a somewhat complex formula, but definitely not the most complex one you can author. The following example shows you what it can look like if you do not format the expression:

```
IF (COUNTX (BalanceDate, CALCULATE (COUNT( Balances[Balance] ), ALLEXCEPT ( Balances,
BalanceDate[Date] ))) > 0, SUMX (ALL ( Balances[Account] ), CALCULATE (SUM(
Balances[Balance] ), LASTNONBLANK (DATESBETWEEN (BalanceDate[Date], BLANK(),LASTDATE(
BalanceDate[Date] )), CALCULATE ( COUNT( Balances[Balance] ))))), BLANK ())
```

It is nearly impossible to understand what this formula computes. It is not clear what the outermost function is, nor how DAX evaluates the different parameters to create the complete flow of execution. It is very hard to read the formula and try to correct it (in case there is some error) or to modify it for whatever reason.

The following example is the same expression, properly formatted:

```
IF (
    COUNTX (
        'Date',
        CALCULATE (
            COUNT ( Balances[Balance] ),
            ALLEXCEPT ( Balances, 'Date'[Date] )
        )
    ) > 0,
    SUMX (
        VALUES ( Balances[Account] ),
        CALCULATE (
            SUM ( Balances[Balance] ),
            LASTNONBLANK (
                DATESBETWEEN ( 'Date'[Date], BLANK (), LASTDATE ( 'Date'[Date] ) ),
                CALCULATE ( COUNT ( Balances[Balance] ) )
            )
        )
    ),
    BLANK ()
)
```

The code is the same. This time, however, it is much easier to look at the three parameters of IF. More importantly, it is easier to follow the blocks that arise naturally by indenting lines, and you can more easily see how they compose the complete flow of execution. Yes, the code is still hard to read, and it is longer. But now the problem lies in using DAX, not the formatting.

We use a consistent set of rules to format DAX code, which we employed in this book. The complete list is available at *http://sql.bi/daxrules*.

Help with formatting DAX

SSDT and SSMS still do not provide a good text editor for DAX. Nevertheless, the following hints might help in writing your DAX code:

- If you want to increase the font size, you can hold down **Ctrl** while rotating the wheel button on the mouse, making it easier to look at the code.

- If you want to add a new line to the formula, you can press **Shift+Enter**.

- If you are having difficulty editing in the text box, you can always copy the code in another editor, like Notepad, and then paste the formula back into the text box.

DAX Formatter, DAX Studio, and DAX Editor

We created a website that is dedicated to formatting DAX code. We did it for ourselves, because formatting the code is a time-consuming operation, and we do not want to spend our time formatting every formula we write. Once the tool was working, we decided to donate it to the public domain so that users can format their own DAX code. (By the way, we have been able to promote our formatting rules this way.) You can find it at *http://www.daxformatter.com*. The user interface is simple: Just copy your DAX code into the formatter at the top and click **Format**. The page refreshes, showing a nicely formatted version of your code, which you can then copy and paste back into the original window.

The formatting provided by DAX Formatter is also available as a service that can be used by other tools. For example, DAX Studio uses the DAX Formatter service. You can use DAX Studio (*http://daxstudio.codeplex.com/*) as an editor for your DAX expressions, and use the Format Query button in the ribbon to format the code as required. You can also use DAX Editor (*http://www.sqlbi.com/tools/dax-editor*) to edit multiple measures of a tabular project in a single text file within Visual Studio. Also, DAX Editor uses the DAX Formatter service to properly format DAX expressions.

Summary

In this chapter, you explored the syntax of DAX, its data types, and the available operators and functions. The most important concepts you have learned are the difference between a calculated column and a measure, and the components of an evaluation context, which are the filter context and the row context. You also learned the following:

- CALCULATE and CALCULATETABLE are efficient functions that compute an expression in a modified filter context.

- There is a syntax to define variables in DAX.

- You should always include the table name in a column reference, and always omit the table name in a measure reference.

- Table expressions can be used in calculated tables and DAX queries.

CHAPTER 5

Building hierarchies

Hierarchies are a much more important part of a tabular model than you might think. Even though a tabular model can be built without any hierarchies, hierarchies add a lot to the usability of a model—and usability issues often determine the success or failure of a business intelligence (BI) project. The basic process of building a hierarchy was covered in Chapter 2, "Getting started with the tabular model." This chapter looks at the process in more detail and discusses some of the more advanced aspects of creating hierarchies: when you should build them, what the benefits and disadvantages of using them are, how you can build ragged hierarchies, and how you can model parent-child relationships.

 What's New in SSAS 2016   This chapter describes features that were already present in previous versions. SSAS 2016 does not provide new features in this area.

Basic hierarchies

First, we will look at what a hierarchy is and how to build basic hierarchies.

What are hierarchies?

By now, you are very familiar with the way a tabular model appears to a user in a front-end tool, such as Microsoft Excel, and the way the distinct values in each column in your model can be displayed on the rows or columns of a Microsoft Excel PivotTable. This provides a very flexible way of building queries, but it has the disadvantage that every new level of nesting that you add to the row or column axis requires a certain amount of effort for the user. First, the user must find what he or she wants to add and then click and drag it to where it should appear. More importantly, it requires the user to have a basic level of understanding of the data he or she is using. To build meaningful reports, the user must know information—such as the fact that a fiscal semester contains many fiscal quarters, but a fiscal quarter can be in only one fiscal semester—so that he or she can order these items appropriately on an axis.

Hierarchies provide a solution to these problems. You can think of them as predefined pathways through your data that help your users explore down from one level of granularity to another in a meaningful way. A typical example of a hierarchy would be on a Date table, in which users often start to view data at the Year level and then navigate down to Quarter, Month, and Date level. A hierarchy enables you to define this type of navigation path. Figure 5-1 shows what a hierarchy looks like when used in an Excel PivotTable.

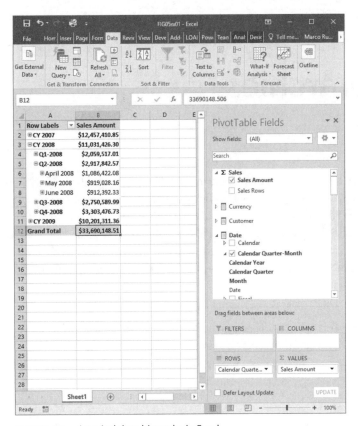

FIGURE 5-1 A typical date hierarchy in Excel.

A hierarchy like this can save your users time by helping them find what they are looking for quickly. With a hierarchy, there is only one thing to drag and drop into a PivotTable, after which users just double-click an item to drill down until they get to the level of detail they require.

Hierarchies can also prevent users from running queries that return more data than they want and that might perform badly. For example, a user might drag every date in the Date table onto the rows of a PivotTable and then filter those rows to show just the ones in which the user is interested, which would be slow because displaying every date could result in a query that returns hundreds of rows. Instead, a hierarchy encourages the user to choose a year, navigate to display just the quarters in that year, and then navigate until he or she reaches the date level, which results in much smaller, faster queries at each step.

Note Microsoft Power BI recognizes hierarchies defined in a tabular model, and it uses them to enable drill-down navigation across hierarchies' levels. However, Power View in Excel 2013/2016 does not have this capability, so Power View users cannot take advantage of this feature.

When to build hierarchies

There are several advantages to building hierarchies. That does not mean you should build hundreds of them on every table, however. The following guidelines explain when to build hierarchies and when not to:

- You should build hierarchies when one-to-many relationships exist between the columns in a single table because this usually indicates the existence of an underlying pattern in the data itself. Often, these patterns represent a natural way for users to explore the data. A hierarchy going from Year to Quarter to Month to Date has already been described; other common examples include hierarchies going from Country to State to City to ZIP Code to Customer, or from Product Category to Product Subcategory to Product.

- You can build hierarchies when one-to-many relationships do not exist between columns, but when certain columns are frequently grouped together in reports. For example, a retailer might want to drill down from Product Category to Brand to Style to Color to Product, even if there is a many-to-many relationship among Brand, Style, and Color. Just consider possible performance issues for unnatural hierarchies when using certain versions of Excel as a client, as described later in this chapter.

- Hierarchies tend to be more useful the more levels they have. There is no point in building a hierarchy with just one level in it, and hierarchies with two levels might not provide much benefit.

You can make hierarchies visible to perspectives and choose whether attributes used in hierarchies are visible for each perspective. As you will see in the "Hierarchy design best practices" section later in this chapter, you can force users to use only a hierarchy instead of its underlying columns by hiding those columns.

With the ease of use that hierarchies bring comes rigidity. If you have defined a hierarchy that goes from Product Category to Brand, and if the underlying columns are hidden, Excel users will not be able to define a report that places Brand before Product Category, nor will they be able to place Product Category and Brand on opposing axes in a report. However, other clients, such as Power BI, are more flexible and allow for the selection of data from a single level of a hierarchy, without having to previously filter higher hierarchical levels.

Building hierarchies

There are essentially two steps involved in creating a hierarchy:

1. Prepare your data appropriately.

2. Build the hierarchy on your table.

You can perform the initial data-preparation step inside the tabular model itself. This chapter discusses numerous techniques to do this. The main advantages of doing your data preparation inside the tabular model are that, as a developer, you need not switch between several tools when building a hierarchy, and you have the power of DAX at your disposal. This might make it easier and faster to write the logic involved. However, whenever possible, you should consider preparing data inside your extract, transform, load (ETL) process. You can do this either in a view or in the SQL code used to load data into the tables in your tabular model. The advantage of this approach is that it keeps relational logic in the relational database, which is better for maintainability and reuse. It also reduces the number of columns in your model and improves the compression rate so that your model has a smaller memory footprint. Additionally, if you are more comfortable writing SQL than DAX, it might be easier from an implementation point of view.

You design hierarchies in SQL Server Data Tools (SSDT) in the diagram view. To create a hierarchy on a table (it is not possible to build a hierarchy that spans more than one table), do one of the following:

- Click the **Create Hierarchy** button in the top-right corner of the table.

- Select one or more columns in the table, right-click them, and select **Create Hierarchy** to use those columns as the levels in a new hierarchy.

To add a new level to an existing hierarchy, do one of the following:

- Drag and drop a column into it at the appropriate position.

- Right-click the column, select **Add to Hierarchy**, and click the name of the hierarchy to which you wish to add it.

After a hierarchy has been created, you can move the levels in it up or down or delete them by right-clicking them and choosing the desired option from the context menu that appears. To rename a hierarchy, double-click its name, or right-click its name and choose **Rename** from the context menu.

You can create any number of hierarchies within a single table. Figure 5-2 shows what a dimension with multiple hierarchies created in SSDT looks like.

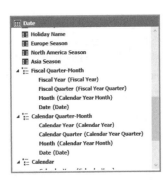

FIGURE 5-2   A hierarchy in the Diagram View of SSDT.

Hierarchy design best practices

Consider the following tips when designing hierarchies:

- After you include a column from a table as a level in a hierarchy, you can hide the column itself by right-clicking it and selecting **Hide from Client Tools**. It is then visible only to your users as a level in a hierarchy. This is usually a good idea because it stops users from becoming confused about whether they should use the original column or the hierarchy in their reports or whether there is any difference between the column and the hierarchy. Users then also have a shorter list of items to search when building their reports, making it easier to find what they want. However, in some client tools, it can make filtering on values that make up lower levels of the hierarchy (such as Month in the hierarchy shown previously in Figure 5-2) much harder.

- Levels in different hierarchies should not have the same name if they represent different things. For example, if you have Fiscal and Calendar hierarchies on your Date dimension, the top levels should be Fiscal Year and Calendar Year, respectively, and neither should be named Year. This removes a possible cause of confusion for your users.

- It can be a good idea to follow a standard naming convention for hierarchies to help your users understand what they contain. For example, you might have a hierarchy that goes from Year to Quarter to Month to Date and another that goes from Year to Week to Date. Calling the first hierarchy Year-Month-Date and the second one Year-Week-Date would make it easier for your users to find the one they need in their front-end tool.

Hierarchies spanning multiple tables

Even if it is not possible to create hierarchies that span multiple tables, you might find yourself needing to do this if you have snowflaked dimension tables. One solution is to denormalize the dimension tables in the relational data source—for example, in a view. You can achieve the same effect relatively easily by using calculated columns.

> **Note** You fill find more details about snowflake schemas in Chapter 6, "Data modeling in Tabular."

The Product dimension in the Contoso DW sample database is a good example of a snowflaked dimension. It is made up of three tables that we imported into the data model (Product Category, Product Subcategory, and Product), as shown in Figure 5-3.

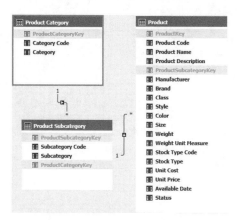

FIGURE 5-3 The Contoso DW Product dimension.

It is possible that, given a dimension like this, users would want to drill down from Product Category to Product Subcategory to Product. To enable this, you must first bring the names of the subcategory and category for each product down to the Product table by creating two calculated columns there. The DAX formulas required for this are fairly simple:

```
Product[Subcategory] = RELATED ( 'Product Subcategory'[Subcategory] )
Product[Category] = RELATED ( 'Product Category'[Category] )
```

Figure 5-4 shows what these two new calculated columns look like in the Product table.

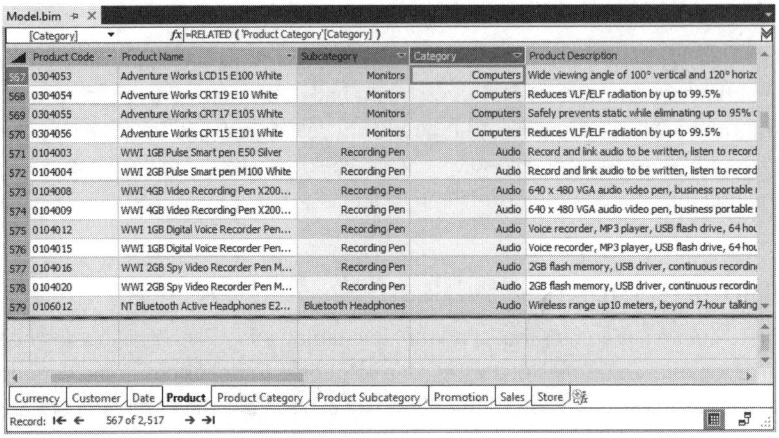

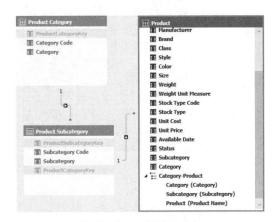

FIGURE 5-4   The two new calculated columns on the Product table.

You can then create a hierarchy on the Product table that goes from Category to Subcategory to Product, as shown in Figure 5-5. As a final step, it is advisable to completely hide the Product Category and Product Subcategory tables (right-click them and select **Hide from Client Tools**) because the new hierarchy removes the need to use any of the columns on them.

FIGURE 5-5   The Product table hierarchy.

Note Readers familiar with multidimensional models might know that it is possible to create ragged hierarchies in them, in which the user skips a level in a hierarchy in certain circumstances. One example of when this is useful is a Geography hierarchy that goes from Country to State to City, but in which the user can drill down from Country directly to City for countries that are not subdivided into states. Another example is when leaf members exist on different levels of a hierarchy.

The tabular model does not support this functionality in the model compatibility level 1200. In previous versions, it was possible to create ragged hierarchies in SSDT, leveraging the `HideMemberIf` property exposed by BIDS Helper. However, this was an unsupported feature, and it only worked using Excel as a client. We hope Microsoft provides a native implementation of ragged hierarchies in Tabular in a future update.

Natural and unnatural hierarchies

A hierarchy in a tabular model does not have any performance impact on DAX queries. This is mainly because DAX offers no way to reference a hierarchy. However, different types of hierarchies may generate different MDX queries and different corresponding query plans. In particular, there are differences between natural and unnatural hierarchies, which you will see shortly.

Note The issue described in this section does not affect a PivotTable in Excel 2016 that queries a tabular model hosted on Analysis Services 2016. However, different combinations of older versions are subject to memory and performance issues, when an MDX query includes unnatural hierarchies.

A natural hierarchy has a single parent for each unique value of a level of the hierarchy. When this is not true, then the hierarchy is said to be *unnatural*. For example, the hierarchy you saw at the beginning of this chapter, in Figure 5-1, is a natural hierarchy because every month has 12 unique values for each year, so each month has only one parent. In practice, the name is not just the month name, but is a combination of both the month name and year. In this way, the value is unique across all the branches of the hierarchy. In a multidimensional model, you can define attribute relationships, which enforces the existence of a natural hierarchy. You also get an error during processing in case the data does not respect the constraints defined. However, there is no similar setting in Tabular. Based on data coming from the data source, the engine automatically marks a hierarchy as natural or unnatural.

For example, Figure 5-6 shows an example of unnatural hierarchy. In this case, the month name does not include the year, so the value of March can have multiple parents: CY 2007, CY 2008, and other years that are not visible in the screenshot.

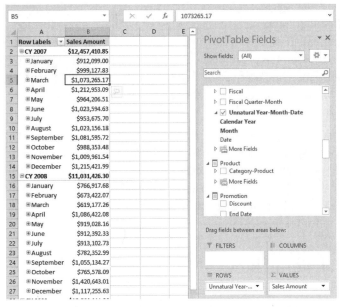

FIGURE 5-6 An unnatural hierarchy.

If you want to support previous versions of Excel and Analysis Services, you should consider creating only natural hierarchies. For more details on performance issues caused by unnatural hierarchies, see *http://www.sqlbi.com/articles/natural-hierarchies-in-power-pivot-and-tabular/*.

Parent-child hierarchies

Now that you have seen how to create a basic hierarchy, you can consider how to manage parent-child hierarchies, which require a specific data preparation.

What are parent-child hierarchies?

In dimensional modeling, a *parent-child hierarchy* is a hierarchy in which the structure is defined by a self-join on a dimension table rather than by modeling each level as a separate column, as in a regular dimension. Typical scenarios in which you might use a parent-child hierarchy include the organizational structure of a company or a chart of accounts. The main advantage of this way of modeling a dimension is that you do not need to know the maximum depth of the hierarchy at design time. If, for example, your company undergoes a reorganization, and there are suddenly 20 steps in the chain of command—from the lowliest employee up to the CEO—when previously there were only 10, you do not need to change your dimension table. Figure 5-7 shows the original Employee table from the Contoso DW sample database. (The table is imported through a view in the data model, as you can see in the examples in the companion content.)

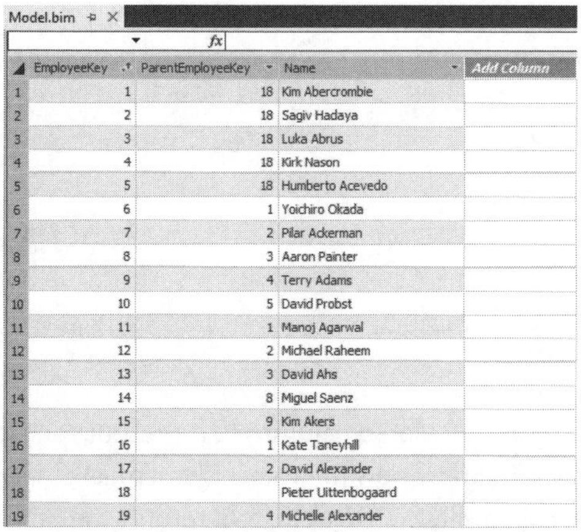
Model.bim

	EmployeeKey	ParentEmployeeKey	Name	Add Column
1	1	18	Kim Abercrombie	
2	2	18	Sagiv Hadaya	
3	3	18	Luka Abrus	
4	4	18	Kirk Nason	
5	5	18	Humberto Acevedo	
6	6	1	Yoichiro Okada	
7	7	2	Pilar Ackerman	
8	8	3	Aaron Painter	
9	9	4	Terry Adams	
10	10	5	David Probst	
11	11	1	Manoj Agarwal	
12	12	2	Michael Raheem	
13	13	3	David Ahs	
14	14	8	Miguel Saenz	
15	15	9	Kim Akers	
16	16	1	Kate Taneyhill	
17	17	2	David Alexander	
18	18		Pieter Uittenbogaard	
19	19	4	Michelle Alexander	

FIGURE 5-7 The Employee table.

In Figure 5-7, the primary key of the table is the EmployeeKey column, and each row represents an individual employee of the Contoso corporation. The employees' names are held in the Name column. The ParentEmployeeKey column holds the value of the EmployeeKey column for the employee's manager.

Configuring parent-child hierarchies

After all this explanation, it might come as something of a letdown to discover that, unlike the multidimensional model, the tabular model does not support true parent-child hierarchies. However, it does have some very useful DAX functionality for flattening parent-child hierarchies into regular, column-based hierarchies. This is good enough for most scenarios, although it means that you have to make an educated guess at design time about what the maximum depth of your hierarchy will be. In this section, you learn how to configure a simple parent-child hierarchy by using the Employee table as an example. You also find out how to handle more complex design problems.

Building a basic parent-child hierarchy

The first step in building a hierarchy on the Employee table is to create a calculated column that contains the list of values for EmployeeKey from the top of the hierarchy down to the current employee. To do this, create a calculated column called EmployeePath and use the following DAX expression:

```
Employee[EmployeePath] =
PATH ( Employee[EmployeeKey], Employee[ParentEmployeeKey] )
```

The output of the PATH function is a pipe-delimited list of values, as shown in Figure 5-8. (If your key column contains pipe characters, you might have some extra data cleaning work to do.)

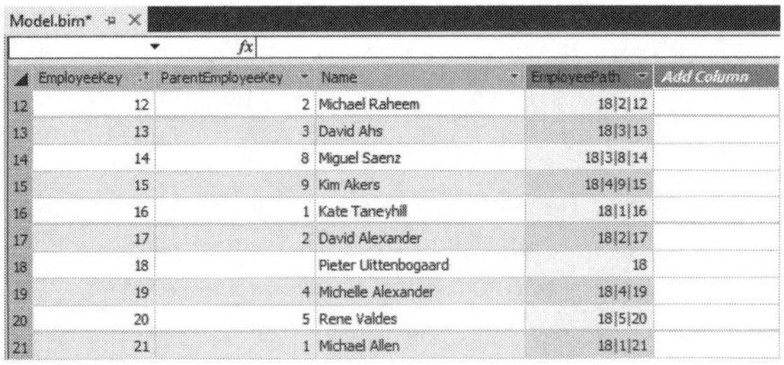

EmployeeKey	ParentEmployeeKey	Name	EmployeePath	Add Column
12	12	2 Michael Raheem	18|2|12	
13	13	3 David Ahs	18|3|13	
14	14	8 Miguel Saenz	18|3|8|14	
15	15	9 Kim Akers	18|4|9|15	
16	16	1 Kate Taneyhill	18|1|16	
17	17	2 David Alexander	18|2|17	
18	18	Pieter Uittenbogaard	18	
19	19	4 Michelle Alexander	18|4|19	
20	20	5 Rene Valdes	18|5|20	
21	21	1 Michael Allen	18|1|21	

FIGURE 5-8 The output of the PATH function.

You can use the contents of this column to create more calculated columns to represent each level in your hierarchy. Before you do that, though, you need to know how many levels you must create. You can do this by creating one more calculated column, called HierarchyDepth, that returns the number of items in the list returned in the EmployeePath column. To do so, use the following PATHLENGTH function:

```
Employee[HierarchyDepth] =
PATHLENGTH ( Employee[EmployeePath] )
```

You can then build a measure to return the maximum value in this column by using the following definition:

```
[Max Depth] :=
MAX ( Employee[HierarchyDepth] )
```

In the case of the Employee table, the maximum depth of the hierarchy is four levels, so you must create at least four new calculated columns for the levels of your new hierarchy. However, as mentioned, it might be wise to build some extra levels in case the hierarchy grows deeper over time.

To populate these new calculated columns, you must find the employee name associated with each key value in the path returned in the EmployeePath calculated column. To find the key value at each position in the path contained in the EmployeePath column, you can use the PATHITEM function, as follows:

```
PATHITEM ( Employee[EmployeePath], 1, INTEGER )
```

There are three parameters to the PATHITEM function. The first parameter takes the name of the column that contains the path. The second parameter contains the 1-based position in the path for which you want to return the value. The third parameter, which is optional, can be either TEXT (which means the value will be returned as text) or INTEGER (which means the value will be returned as an integer). You can also use 0 for TEXT and 1 for INTEGER, although we recommend using the enumeration name to make the formula easier to read.

Note The third parameter can be important for matching the value returned by PATHITEM with the value in the key column of the table. If you omit the third parameter, it will be returned as TEXT by default. In this case, however, if the value has to be compared with an integer (as in the example shown here), then the conversion from text to integer will be made implicitly at the moment of the comparison. In any case, the three following syntaxes are equivalent:

```
PATHITEM ( Employee[EmployeePath], 1, INTEGER )

INT ( PATHITEM ( Employee[EmployeePath], 1, TEXT ) )

INT ( PATHITEM ( Employee[EmployeePath], 1 ) )
```

You can make this conversion automatically when you make a comparison of this value with another value, such as when using LOOKUPVALUE. Thus, it is important to specify the third parameter only when you want to store the result of PATHITEM in a calculated column, which will be created with the data type specified by the value of the third parameter. That said, using the third parameter is a good practice because it shows other developers who might see your code what type of values you are expecting to return.

Key values on their own are not very useful, however. You must find the name of the employee associated with each key. You can do that by using the LOOKUPVALUE function. The following complete expression can be used to return the name of the employee, for the first level in the hierarchy:

```
Employee[EmployeeLevel1] =
LOOKUPVALUE (
    Employee[Name],
    Employee[EmployeeKey],
    PATHITEM ( Employee[EmployeePath], 1, INTEGER )
)
```

The following expression is for the second level in the hierarchy:

```
Employee[EmployeeLevel2] =
LOOKUPVALUE (
    Employee[Name],
    Employee[EmployeeKey],
    PATHITEM ( Employee[EmployeePath], 2, INTEGER )
)
```

With all four calculated columns created for the four levels of the hierarchy, the table will look like the screenshot in Figure 5-9.

Name	H...	EmployeePath	EmployeeLevel1	EmployeeLevel2	EmployeeLevel3	EmployeeLevel4	Add
5 Humberto Acevedo	2	18|5	Pieter Uittenbogaard	Humberto Acevedo			
6 Yoichiro Okada	3	18|1|6	Pieter Uittenbogaard	Kim Abercrombie	Yoichiro Okada		
7 Pilar Ackerman	3	18|2|7	Pieter Uittenbogaard	Sagiv Hadaya	Pilar Ackerman		
8 Aaron Painter	3	18|3|8	Pieter Uittenbogaard	Luka Abrus	Aaron Painter		
9 Terry Adams	3	18|4|9	Pieter Uittenbogaard	Kirk Nason	Terry Adams		
10 David Probst	3	18|5|10	Pieter Uittenbogaard	Humberto Acevedo	David Probst		
11 Manoj Agarwal	3	18|1|11	Pieter Uittenbogaard	Kim Abercrombie	Manoj Agarwal		
12 Michael Raheem	3	18|2|12	Pieter Uittenbogaard	Sagiv Hadaya	Michael Raheem		
13 David Ahs	3	18|3|13	Pieter Uittenbogaard	Luka Abrus	David Ahs		
14 Miguel Saenz	4	18|3|8|14	Pieter Uittenbogaard	Luka Abrus	Aaron Painter	Miguel Saenz	
15 Kim Akers	4	18|4|9|15	Pieter Uittenbogaard	Kirk Nason	Terry Adams	Kim Akers	
16 Kate Taneyhill	3	18|1|16	Pieter Uittenbogaard	Kim Abercrombie	Kate Taneyhill		
17 David Alexander	3	18|2|17	Pieter Uittenbogaard	Sagiv Hadaya	David Alexander		
18 Pieter Uittenbogaard	1	18	Pieter Uittenbogaard				
19 Michelle Alexander	3	18|4|19	Pieter Uittenbogaard	Kirk Nason	Michelle Alexander		
20 Rene Valdes	3	18|5|20	Pieter Uittenbogaard	Humberto Acevedo	Rene Valdes		

FIGURE 5-9   The result of the EmployeeLevel calculated columns.

The final step is to create a hierarchy from these columns, in the way you saw earlier in this chapter. In Excel, the result looks like the hierarchy shown in Figure 5-10.

Row Labels	Max Depth
⊟ Pieter Uittenbogaard	4
⊞	1
⊟ Humberto Acevedo	4
⊞	2
⊞ David Probst	4
⊞ Mike Nash	3
⊞ Rene Valdes	3
⊞ Kim Abercrombie	4
⊟ Kirk Nason	4
⊞	2
⊞ Christen Anderson	3
⊞ Michelle Alexander	3
⊟ Terry Adams	4
	3
Aaron Con	4
Aik Chen	4
Alice Ciccu	4
Anders Riis	4
Andreas Schou	4

FIGURE 5-10   An example of a basic parent-child hierarchy.

Handling empty items

The approach described in the previous section is sufficient for many parent-child hierarchies. However, as you can see in Figure 5-10, the hierarchy built from the Employee table contains some items that have no name. This is because not all branches of the hierarchy reach the maximum depth of four levels. Rather than show these empty values, it might be better to repeat the name of the member that is immediately above in the hierarchy. You can achieve this by using the IF function. The following example shows what the calculated column expression for the lowest level in the hierarchy looks like with this change:

```
Employee[EmployeeLevel4] =
VAR CurrentLevel = 4
VAR EmployeePreviousLevel = Employee[EmployeeLevel3]
VAR EmployeeKeyCurrentLevel =
    PATHITEM ( Employee[EmployeePath], CurrentLevel, INTEGER )
```

```
RETURN
    IF (
        Employee[HierarchyDepth] < CurrentLevel,
        EmployeePreviousLevel,
        LOOKUPVALUE ( Employee[Name], Employee[EmployeeKey], EmployeeKeyCurrentLevel )
    )
```

This makes the hierarchy a bit tidier, but it is still not an ideal situation. Instead of empty items, you now have repeating items at the bottom of the hierarchy on which the user can drill down. You can work around this by using the default behavior of tools such as Excel to filter out rows in PivotTables in which all the measures return blank values. If the user has drilled down beyond the bottom of the original hierarchy, all the measures should display a BLANK value.

To find the level in the hierarchy to which the user has drilled down, you can write the following expression to create a measure that uses the ISFILTERED function:

```
[Current Hierarchy Depth] :=
ISFILTERED ( Employee[EmployeeLevel1] )
    + ISFILTERED ( Employee[EmployeeLevel2] )
    + ISFILTERED ( Employee[EmployeeLevel3] )
    + ISFILTERED ( Employee[EmployeeLevel4] )
```

The ISFILTERED function returns True if the column it references is used as part of a direct filter. Because a True value is implicitly converted to 1, and assuming the user will not use a single level without traversing the entire hierarchy, by summing the ISFILTERED called for each level, you can add the number of levels displayed in the report for a specific calculation.

The final step is to test whether the currently displayed item is beyond the bottom of the original hierarchy. To do this, you can compare the value returned by the Current Hierarchy Depth measure with the value returned by the Max Depth measure created earlier in this chapter. (In this case, Demo Measure returns 1, but in a real model, it would return some other measure value.) The following expression defines the Demo Measure measure, and Figure 5-11 shows the result.

```
[Demo Measure] :=
IF ( [Current Hierarchy Depth] > [Max Depth], BLANK(), 1 )
```

Row Labels	Demo Measure
⊟ Pieter Uittenbogaard	1
⊟ Humberto Acevedo	1
⊞ David Probst	1
⊞ Mike Nash	1
⊞ Rene Valdes	1
⊞ Kim Abercrombie	1
⊟ Kirk Nason	1
⊞ Christen Anderson	1
⊞ Michelle Alexander	1
⊟ Terry Adams	1
Aaron Con	1
Aik Chen	1
Alice Ciccu	1
Anders Riis	1
Andreas Schou	1

FIGURE 5-11   The finished parent-child hierarchy.

Unary operators

In the multidimensional model, parent-child hierarchies are often used in conjunction with unary operators and custom rollup formulas when building financial applications. Although the tabular model does not include built-in support for unary operators, it is possible to reproduce the functionality to a certain extent in DAX, and you find out how in this section. Unfortunately, it is not possible to re-create custom rollup formulas. The only option is to write extremely long and complicated DAX expressions in measures.

How unary operators work

For full details about how unary operators work in the multidimensional model, see the SQL Server 2016 technical documentation at *http://technet.microsoft.com/en-us/library/ms175417.aspx*. Each item in the hierarchy can be associated with an operator that controls how the total for that member aggregates up to its parent. In this implementation in DAX, there is support for only the following two unary operators. (MDX in Multidimensional provides a support for more operators.)

- **+** The plus sign means that the value for the current item is added to the aggregate of its siblings (that is, all the items that have the same parent) that occur before the current item, on the same level of the hierarchy.

- **−** The minus sign means that the value for the current item is subtracted from the value of its siblings that occur before the current item, on the same level of the hierarchy.

The DAX for implementing unary operators gets more complex the more of these operators are used in a hierarchy. For the sake of clarity and simplicity, in this section only, the two most common operators used are the plus sign (+), and the minus sign (−). Table 5-1 shows a simple example of how these two operators behave when used in a hierarchy.

Table 5-1 How unary operators are calculated

Item Name	Unary Operator	Measure Value
Profit		150
- Sales	+	100
- Other Income	+	75
- Costs	−	25

In this example, the Sales, Other Income, and Costs items appear as children of the Profit item in the hierarchy. The value of Profit is calculated as follows:

```
+ [Sales Amount] + [Other Income] - [Costs]
```

Implementing unary operators by using DAX

The key to implementing unary operator functionality in DAX is to recalculate the value of your measure at each level of the hierarchy rather than calculate it at a low level and aggregate it up. This means the DAX needed can be very complicated. It is a good idea to split the calculation into multiple steps so that it can be debugged more easily. In this example, we will only implement the plus and minus sign operators.

To illustrate how to implement unary operators, you need a dimension with some unary operators on it, such as the Account view in Contoso. Figure 5-12 shows the operators applied to this hierarchy. On the left side, you see that the main logic is to subtract the Expense and Taxation branches from the Income one. All these high-level branches have only the standard plus sign in their children accounts.

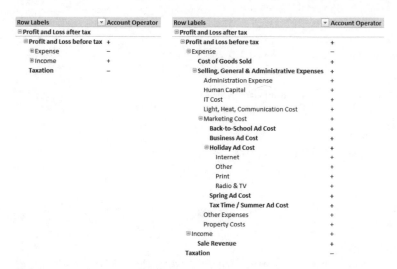

FIGURE 5-12 The parent-child hierarchy with unary operators.

The calculation of Profit and Loss Before Tax has to subtract Expense from the Income totals, which are computed by summing all their children accounts. In a similar way, the Profit and Loss After Tax must subtract the Taxation. An example of the final result is shown in Figure 5-13.

| Calendar | CY 2009 | |
| Scenario | Actual | |

Row Labels	Account Operator	PC Amount
Profit and Loss after tax		$207,057,064.28
Profit and Loss before tax	+	$396,543,540.82
Expense	−	($1,618,991,430.50)
Cost of Goods Sold	+	$873,818,107.43
Selling, General & Administrative Expenses	+	$745,173,323.07
Income	+	$2,015,534,971.32
Taxation	−	($189,486,476.54)

FIGURE 5-13 The final result of the PC Amount measure, considering unary operators.

The key point is that although each item's value can be derived from its leaves' values, the question of whether a leaf value is added or subtracted when aggregating is determined not only by its own unary operator, but also by that of all the items in the hierarchy between it and the item whose value is to be calculated. For example, the value of Selling, General & Administrative Expenses is simply the sum of all the accounts below that, because all of them have a plus sign as a unary operator. However, each of these accounts should be subtracted when aggregated in the Expense account. The same should be done for each upper level where Expense is included (such as Profit and Loss Before Tax and Profit and Loss After Tax). A smart way to obtain this result is to calculate in advance whether the final projection of an account at a certain level will keep their original value, or if it will be subtracted. You can obtain this same result by multiplying the value by –1. Thus, you can calculate for each account whether you have to multiply it by 1 or –1 for each level in the hierarchy. You can add the following calculated columns to the Account table:

```
Account[Multiplier] =
SWITCH ( Account[Operator], "+", 1, "-", -1, 1 )

Account[SignAtLevel7] =
IF ( Account[HierarchyDepth] = 7, Account[Multiplier] )

Account[SignAtLevel6] =
VAR CurrentLevel = 6
VAR SignAtPreviousLevel = Account[SignAtLevel7]
RETURN
    IF (
        Account[HierarchyDepth] = CurrentLevel,
        Account[Multiplier],
        LOOKUPVALUE (
            Account[Multiplier],
            Account[AccountKey],
            PATHITEM ( Account[HierarchyPath], CurrentLevel, INTEGER )
        ) * SignAtPreviousLevel
    )
```

The calculated column for the other levels (from 1 to 5) only changes something in the first two lines, as shown by the following template:

```
Account[SignAtLevel<N>] =
VAR CurrentLevel = <N>
VAR SignAtPreviousLevel = Account[SignAtLevel<N+1>]
RETURN ...
```

As shown in Figure 5-14, the final results of all the SignAtLevelN calculated columns are used to support the final calculation.

Account	Multiplier	SignAtLevel7	SignAtLevel6	SignAtLevel5	SignAtLevel4	SignAtLevel3	SignAtLevel2	SignAtLevel1
Profit and Loss after...	1							1
Income	1					1	1	1
Expense	-1					-1	-1	-1
Sale Revenue	1				1	1	1	1
Cost of Goods Sold	1				1	-1	-1	-1
Selling, General & Ad...	1				1	-1	-1	-1
Administration Expense	1			1	1	-1	-1	-1
IT Cost	1			1	1	-1	-1	-1
Human Capital	1			1	1	-1	-1	-1
Light, Heat, Commu...	1			1	1	-1	-1	-1
Property Costs	1			1	1	-1	-1	-1
Other Expenses	1			1	1	-1	-1	-1
Marketing Cost	1			1	1	-1	-1	-1
Holiday Ad Cost	1		1	1	1	-1	-1	-1
Spring Ad Cost	1		1	1	1	-1	-1	-1
Back-to-School Ad Cost	1		1	1	1	-1	-1	-1
Business Ad Cost	1		1	1	1	-1	-1	-1
Tax Time / Summer ...	1		1	1	1	-1	-1	-1
Taxation	-1						1	1
Radio & TV	1	1	1	1	1	-1	-1	-1
Print	1	1	1	1	1	-1	-1	-1
Internet	1	1	1	1	1	-1	-1	-1
Other	1	1	1	1	1	-1	-1	-1
Profit and Loss befor...	1						1	1

FIGURE 5-14 The calculated columns required to implement the calculation for unary operators.

The final calculation simply sums the amount of all the underlying accounts that have the same sign aggregating their value at the displayed level. You obtain this by using the PC Amount measure, based on the simple Sum of Amount, as demonstrated in the following example:

```
Account[Min Depth] :=
MIN ( Account[HierarchyDepth] )

Account[Current Hierarchy Depth] :=
ISFILTERED ( Account[AccountLevel1] )
    + ISFILTERED ( Account[AccountLevel2] )
    + ISFILTERED ( Account[AccountLevel3] )
    + ISFILTERED ( Account[AccountLevel4] )
    + ISFILTERED ( Account[AccountLevel5] )
    + ISFILTERED ( Account[AccountLevel6] )
    + ISFILTERED ( Account[AccountLevel7] )

'Strategy Plan'[Sum of Amount] :=
SUM ( 'Strategy Plan'[Amount] )

'Strategy Plan'[PC Amount] : =
IF (
    [Min Depth] >= [Current Hierarchy Depth],
    SWITCH (
        [Current Hierarchy Depth],
        1, SUMX (
            VALUES ( Account[SignAtLevel1] ),
            Account[SignAtLevel1] * [Sum of Amount]
        ),
        2, SUMX (
            VALUES ( Account[SignAtLevel2] ),
            Account[SignAtLevel2] * [Sum of Amount]
        ),
        3, SUMX (
```

```
            VALUES ( Account[SignAtLevel3] ),
            Account[SignAtLevel3] * [Sum of Amount]
        ),
        4, SUMX (
            VALUES ( Account[SignAtLevel4] ),
            Account[SignAtLevel4] * [Sum of Amount]
        ),
        5, SUMX (
            VALUES ( Account[SignAtLevel5] ),
            Account[SignAtLevel5] * [Sum of Amount]
        ),
        6, SUMX (
            VALUES ( Account[SignAtLevel6] ),
            Account[SignAtLevel6] * [Sum of Amount]
        ),
        7, SUMX (
            VALUES ( Account[SignAtLevel7] ),
            Account[SignAtLevel7] * [Sum of Amount]
        )
    )
)
```

Summary

This chapter demonstrated how many types of hierarchies can be implemented in the tabular model. Regular hierarchies are important for the usability of your model and can be built very easily. Parent-child hierarchies present more of a problem, but this can be solved with the clever use of DAX in calculated columns and measures.

CHAPTER 6

Data modeling in Tabular

Data modeling plays a very important role in tabular development. Choosing the right data model can dramatically change the performance and usability of the overall solution. Even if we cannot cover all the data-modeling techniques available to analytical database designers, we believe it is important to dedicate a full chapter to data modeling to give you some information about which techniques work best with Tabular.

In the data warehouse world, there are two main approaches to the database design of an analytical system: the school of William Inmon and the school of Ralph Kimball. Additionally, if data comes from online transaction processing (OLTP) databases, there is always the possibility that an analytical solution can be built directly on top of the OLTP system. In this chapter, you learn how to work with these different systems from the tabular point of view, which system is best, and what approach to take with each data model.

Finally, because we believe that many readers of this book already have a solid understanding of data modeling for the multidimensional model, in this chapter you learn the main differences between data modeling for the multidimensional model and data modeling for the tabular model. Because they are different systems, the two types of semantic modeling require a different approach when designing the underlying database.

 What's New in SSAS 2016 SSAS 2016 has a new type of cardinality (one-to-one) and a new type of filter propagation (bidirectional) in relationships. It also introduced calculated tables. This chapter considers the implications of these features in data-modeling choices for Tabular.

Understanding different data-modeling techniques

Before we discuss the details of how to use the tabular model over different data models, it is worth learning the different kinds of data-modeling techniques with which you are likely to work when developing a tabular solution.

Data sources for analytics usually conform to three broad categories of data modeling, as follows:

■ OLTP databases are normally composed of one or many sources of data that hold all the company information. This type of database is not specifically designed for analytical needs, but it is always present, and it is often the original source for any kind of analysis.

■ William Inmon's theory is to build a slightly denormalized version of a database that can hold all the company information, along with its historical changes—sometimes called the *corporate information factory* (*CIF*). This database should be independent from any OLTP system that is already in place and should be designed to address most (if not all) of the analytical requirements of the company. After the data warehouse is built by using Inmon's techniques, it feeds separate data marts containing the analytical databases that are exposed in a dimensional model.

■ Ralph Kimball's theory is different from Inmon's because it does not require building an initial relational data warehouse. However, using Kimball's bus technique, you build single data marts that, following the conformed dimension model, merge in a single data warehouse composed of the sum of all the data marts.

It is beyond the scope of this book to describe in detail the different techniques adopted by followers of the Inmon and Kimball schools or any of their variations. The goal of this chapter is to point out the major differences between the two.

In Inmon's view, the different OLTP systems need to be loaded inside a physical database that models all the corporate information. From there, one or more data marts are created to enable users to generate reports. In Figure 6-1, you see a sample diagram for an Inmon solution.

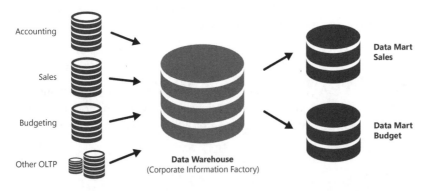

FIGURE 6-1 The Inmon vision of a BI solution, where the relational data warehouse plays a central role.

Kimball's vision is different. In Kimball's methodology, the data warehouse is nothing but the sum of all the data marts. Kimball's model is somewhat simpler in concept because there is no need to build a CIF. However, Kimball's methodology is based heavily on dimensional modeling because the dimensional model is the only model for the corporate information. There is no space for a relational data model. Figure 6-2 shows a diagram of a Kimball solution.

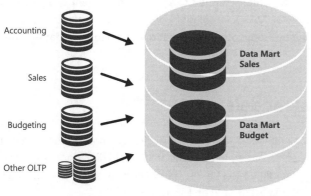

Data Warehouse = Sum of Data Marts

FIGURE 6-2 The Kimball vision of a data warehouse, where only dimensional modeling is used.

Note that in the end, both Inmon and Kimball expose a dimensional model. Inmon has an additional step with a relational data model, whereas Kimball goes directly to dimensional modeling. The OLTP database, however, is very different from a data warehouse. Thus, it requires some special considerations, which you learn about in the next section.

Using the OLTP database

The OLTP database can be a sales system, a customer relationship management (CRM) tool, an accounting manager, or—in general—any kind of database that users adopt to manage their business.

Sometimes the source is not a real database. It might consist of files generated by processes running on a host, Microsoft Excel workbooks, or other media. In this case, you can still import it into a simple Microsoft SQL Server database, which is usually your best option. Therefore, regardless of the specific media used to read the source, we refer to it as a database.

The OLTP database is not built to be easily copied in a semantic model or to answer massive reporting queries that usually involve many tables. Its main task is to answer daily queries that often touch a reduced set of information. Nevertheless, you might ask yourself whether you really need to build a data warehouse to create an analytical system. The answer is yes. You need a data warehouse.

There are very rare situations in which data can flow directly from the OLTP to the analytical data model, but these are so specific that their description is outside the scope of this book.

Building an analytical solution is complex work that starts with the correct design for the data marts. If you have a dimensional data mart, you have a database that holds dimensions and fact tables, in which you can perform cleansing and computations. We, the authors, have personally never seen an OLTP database that did not suffer from data-quality issues. Thus, you need a place to cleanse the data.

If you rely solely on the OLTP database, building complex queries upon it, you might finish your first data model in less time. However, the structure of the queries to the OLTP database will be so complex that you will lose all the time you saved at the first new implementation.

Moreover, you will not be able to create complex models to accommodate user needs and to make your solution fit the tool requirements perfectly. Tabular solutions often require a specific approach when developing a data model, which is different from both the OLTP and the dimensional data-modeling techniques.

Working with dimensional models

Whether you follow the Kimball or Inmon methodology, the final analytical database is usually a data mart. A *data mart* is a database that is modeled according to the rules of Kimball's dimensional-modeling methodology and is composed of fact and dimension tables. This section reviews the basics of dimensional modeling to ensure you have a good background on the topic.

The core of the dimensional structure of a data mart is separating the database into the following two types of entities:

- **Dimension** A *dimension* is an analytical object used to separate numbers. A dimension can be made of products, customers, time, or any other entity used to analyze your numbers. Some facts about dimensions are as follows:

  - **Dimensions have attributes** An attribute of a product can be its color, its manufacturer, or its weight. An attribute of a date might be its weekday or its month. Each dimension has a unique and specific set of attributes.

  - **Dimensions normally have both natural and surrogate keys** The natural key is the original product code, customer ID, or real date. The surrogate key is usually a new, meaningless integer number used in data marts to join facts to dimensions.

  - **Dimensions change over time** The term *slowly changing dimension* refers to a dimension that is updated over time.

  - **A dimension has relationships with facts** A dimension exists to qualify numeric information contained in facts. To perform this, it must have a relationship with facts.

  - **A dimension might reference other dimensions, correlate to other dimensions, or both** This is true even if the dimension's main purpose is to join to facts. Data models in which dimensions are related to one another are more complex to use and analyze, but these relationships are often needed.

- **Fact** A *fact* is something that has happened or has been measured. A fact can be the sale of a product to a customer, the total number of sales of a specific item during a month, the number of working hours of an employee, or any other fact expressed as a number. From the analytical point of view, a fact is a number that you want to aggregate in several forms to generate reports and get insights into your data. It is helpful to understand the following general information about facts:

- A fact is related to several dimensions, but facts are not related to other facts in any way.

- Facts are normally related to dimensions through the surrogate key.

- Facts are interesting when they are aggregated at a higher level. You are not normally interested in the details of a single sale; you want to analyze the sales of one month against the sales of another month, at a higher level of abstraction.

Both facts and dimensions are stored in tables. Fact tables contain numeric data that is to be aggregated, whereas dimension tables contain numeric and nonnumeric values that are used to slice facts.

The categories of dimensions in the following list might need some special handling in tabular modeling:

- **Type 1 slowly changing dimensions**   These are dimensions in which you are interested in only the last value of any attribute. Whenever the source changes, you update your dimension accordingly, losing the previous value of attributes.

- **Type 2 slowly changing dimensions**   These are dimensions in which the business key might be duplicated because these dimensions contain several versions of the same item to track their updates.

- **Degenerate dimensions**   These are attributes that are stored directly in the fact table. They are normally used for dimensions that have a granularity of the same order of magnitude as the fact table.

- **Junk dimensions**   These are dimensions created by merging several attributes that do not belong to any other dimension, and that you don't want to keep as separate dimensions to avoid a dimensional explosion.

There are other data structures, such as factless fact tables (also known as *bridge tables*), which are used to mimic many-to-many relationships. These tables can take advantage of the bidirectional filters that are described in the section "Relationship types" later in this chapter.

Generally speaking, dimensional models are a perfect data source for a tabular solution. In Multidimensional, the usage of dimensional modeling as a source is mandatory. This requirement is very relaxed in Tabular, however. There is no real need to divide the complete data model into facts and dimensions because after these entities are loaded in the tabular model, they become simple tables. This has both advantages and disadvantages, which are covered in the next sections of this chapter.

Working with slowly changing dimensions

Using *slowly changing dimensions* (SCD) in Tabular is straightforward. In this section's example from the AdventureWorksDW2012 database, you see in the Products table that the table identifier is ProductKey, which is the surrogate key. However, the business key is stored in the Product Code column. A new row is added to this table whenever a column changes a value. Figure 6-3 shows you an example with three products selected, each of which has two rows.

FIGURE 6-3 The SCD table, where each product might have more than one version.

In Figure 6-3, the list price and the cost of the product change over time, and the dimension table keeps track of those changes. It creates new rows to store different values in the List Price and Cost columns and uses the canonical SCD handling columns: ScdStartDate and ScdStatus. (You might also have a ScdEndDate column in certain databases, but it is not necessary in this example.)

The current price of the product is the one stored in the row with the ScdStatus column set to Current. Other rows represent old versions of the same product. If you use Excel to browse this data model, you can produce a report that shows the sales made at different prices, as shown in Figure 6-4.

FIGURE 6-4 Using SCD to analyze sales made at different prices over time.

This behavior of SCD is normal and expected, because the List Price column holds the historical price. Nevertheless, a very frequent request is to slice data by using both the current and the historical value of an attribute (the price in our example) to make comparisons. The problem is that the table does not contain the current price of the product for all the rows.

This scenario is often solved at the relational level by creating two tables: one with historical values and one with the current values. In this way, there are two keys in the fact table for the two dimensions. The drawback of this solution is that two tables are needed to hold a few columns that might be both historical and current, and, at the end, the data model exposed to the user is more complex, both to use and to understand.

In Tabular, there is an interesting alternative to the creation of the two tables. You can create some calculated columns in the dimension table that compute the current value of the attribute inside the tabular data model, without the need to modify the relational data model.

Using the Adventure Works example, you can compute the Current List Price calculated column by using the Status column and the following formula:

```
Products[Current List Price] =
LOOKUPVALUE (
    Products[List Price],
    Products[Product Code], Products[Product Code],
    Products[ScdStatus], "Current"
)
```

The LOOKUPVALUE function returns the value of the List Price column (the first argument) for the corresponding row in the Product table (which includes the List Price column). The Product Code and ScdStatus columns (the second and fourth arguments) correspond to the values provided in the third and fifth arguments, respectively. The value of the third argument corresponds to the product code of the current row for which the Current List Price calculated column is evaluated. The value of the fifth argument is the constant string Current.

Figure 6-5 shows you the result of the calculated column.

ProductKey	Product Code	Product Name	Cost	Color	List Price	ScdStatus	ScdStartDate	Current List Price
29	359 BK-M68B-38	Mountain-200 Black, 38	$1,251.98	Black	$2,294.99	Current	7/1/2007	$2,294.99
30	360 BK-M68B-42	Mountain-200 Black, 42	$1,105.81	Black	$2,049.10		7/1/2006	$2,294.99
31	361 BK-M68B-42	Mountain-200 Black, 42	$1,251.98	Black	$2,294.99	Current	7/1/2007	$2,294.99
32	362 BK-M68B-46	Mountain-200 Black, 46	$1,105.81	Black	$2,049.10		7/1/2006	$2,294.99
33	363 BK-M68B-46	Mountain-200 Black, 46	$1,251.98	Black	$2,294.99	Current	7/1/2007	$2,294.99
34	352 BK-M68S-38	Mountain-200 Silver, 38	$1,117.86	Silver	$2,071.42		7/1/2006	$2,319.99
35	353 BK-M68S-38	Mountain-200 Silver, 38	$1,265.62	Silver	$2,319.99	Current	7/1/2007	$2,319.99
	354 BK-M68S-42	Mountain-200 Silver, 42	$1,117.86	Silver	$2,071.42		7/1/2006	$2,319.99

FIGURE 6-5 The Current List Price calculated column always contains the last price of a product.

The Current List Price column is useful to calculate an Actualized Sales Amount measure, which shows all the sales made in the past as if they were made at the current price. The result of this measure compared with the simple Sales Amount measure is shown in Figure 6-6.

```
Products[Actualized Sales Amount] :=
SUMX (
    Sales,
    Sales[Line Quantity] * RELATED ( Products[Current List Price] )
)
```

Product Code	(Multiple Items)

Row Labels	Column Labels			
	2006	2007	2008	Grand Total
Mountain-200 Black, 42				
Sales Amount	$159,829.66	$627,269.94	$576,042.49	$1,363,142.09
Actualized Sales Amount	$179,009.22	$654,072.15	$576,042.49	$1,409,123.86
Mountain-200 Black, 46				
Sales Amount	$163,927.86	$679,399.00	$530,142.69	$1,373,469.55
Actualized Sales Amount	$183,599.20	$709,151.91	$530,142.69	$1,422,893.80
Total Sales Amount	$323,757.52	$1,306,668.95	$1,106,185.18	$2,736,611.64
Total Actualized Sales Amount	$362,608.42	$1,363,224.06	$1,106,185.18	$2,832,017.66

FIGURE 6-6 Comparing sales that simulate the current price for all the transactions in the Actualized Sales Amount measure.

The interesting aspect of this solution is that the calculated column is computed during the tabular database processing, when all data is in memory, and without persisting it on disk with all the inevitable locking and deadlock issues.

Before leaving this topic, note that the formula for current list price uses the presence of a column that clearly identifies the current version of the product. If you face a database in which no such column exists, you can still compute the current list price by using only the ScdStartDate column, as follows:

```
Products[Current List Price using ScdStartDate] =
VAR LastDateOfProduct =
    CALCULATE (
        MAX ( Products[ScdStartDate] ),
        ALLEXCEPT ( Products, Products[Product Code] )
    )
RETURN
    LOOKUPVALUE (
        Products[List Price],
        Products[ScdStartDate], LastDateOfProduct,
        Products[Product Code], Products[Product Code]
    )
```

You can create more complex logic using DAX, retrieving data that you do not have in a direct way in the data source. However, you should use this as a last resort whenever you cannot obtain such data through the standard extract, transform, load (ETL) process.

Working with degenerate dimensions

Another common, nonstandard dimensional modeling technique is degenerate dimensions. Degenerate dimensions are commonly used in the multidimensional model when an attribute has a granularity that is very similar to that of the fact table and when it is used to expose the metadata values that are, in effect, stored inside the fact table.

In the ContosoDW database, shown in Figure 6-7, the Order Number column in the fact table, which is a string stored in the fact table, represents the order identifier.

	OnlineSalesKey	StoreKey	ProductKey	OrderDateKey	Order Number	Order Line Number	CustomerKey
54414	25240063	306	2260	20081021	20081021BCS651	487	19058
54415	25240064	306	2260	20081021	20081021BCS651	488	19058
54416	25250023	199	72	20081022	20081022ICS667	33	18861
54417	25250024	199	72	20081022	20081022ICS667	34	18861
54418	25250025	199	72	20081022	20081022ICS667	35	18861
54419	25250026	199	72	20081022	20081022ICS667	36	18861
54420	25250028	199	72	20081022	20081022ICS667	38	18861

FIGURE 6-7 The Order Number column, stored inside the fact table.

Because Order Number is an attribute that has many values, the data modeler decided not to create a separate dimension to hold the attribute, but to store it directly inside the fact table, following the best practices for dimensional modeling.

When facing such a scenario in the multidimensional model, you are forced to create a dimension to hold the order number, and this dimension is based on the fact table. This kind of modeling often leads to long processing times because of how SQL Server Analysis Services (SSAS) queries dimensions to get the list of distinct values of each attribute.

> **Important** In Tabular mode, there is no need to create a separate dimension to hold this attribute because the very concept of a dimension is missing. Each table in Tabular mode can be used as both a dimension and a fact table, depending on the need.

Using snapshot fact tables

There are several scenarios in which a big fact table is aggregated into a smaller one, called a *snapshot fact table*, which contains periodic aggregated snapshots of the bigger fact table. A good example of this is warehouse stocking. You might have a table holding all the sales and transactions of goods, but to speed up querying, you often store a monthly snapshot of the product stock so that monthly reports do not need to traverse the complete fact table to compute the periodic stock. In this section, you learn a few considerations about how to handle scenarios such as this in a tabular model.

Consider a warehouse transactions table named Movements that contains, for each day, the number of products that entered and exited the warehouse. To get the quantity on hold at a particular date, you must implement a calculation that aggregates all the rows in Movements for the same product for all the dates that are less than or equal to the last day in the period being considered. Such a computation is so expensive that a relational database usually features an Inventory table that contains, for each day and product, the quantity available in stock. In practice, the previous calculation is consolidated in a table that usually improves the performance of a query in SQL because it reduces the amount of data that has to be read and aggregated.

Apparently, such an approach is also more efficient in DAX. This is because the formula that computes the units in stock applies a semi-additive pattern using the LASTDATE function, as shown in the following formula:

```
Inventory[Units In Stock] :=
CALCULATE (
    SUM ( Inventory[Units Balance] ),
    LASTDATE ( 'Date'[Date] )
)
```

You can obtain the same value aggregating the transactions in the Movements table by using the following measure:

```
Movements[Units In Stock Dynamic] :=
CALCULATE (
    SUM ( Movements[Quantity] ),
    FILTER (
        ALL ( 'Date' ),
        'Date'[Date] <= MAX ( 'Date'[Date] )
    )
)
```

At first sight, the simpler measure aggregating the Inventory table seems to be faster. However, in Tabular mode, you cannot assume that this outcome is true all the time. It really depends on the size of the tables and many other details about the distribution of the data and the granularity of the Inventory and Movements tables.

The snapshot fact tables are computed during an additional ETL step, aggregating the fact table that holds all the transactions and that stores the original values.

Snapshot fact tables reduce the computational effort needed to retrieve the aggregated value. There is no reason to use this modeling technique, except to get better performance, and in that respect, they are similar to the creation of other aggregate tables. However, snapshot fact tables have the unwelcome characteristic of reduced flexibility. In fact, the Inventory table holds one value, such as Unit Balance, at the end of the considered period. If, for example, you wanted to hold the minimum and maximum number of items sold in a single transaction, or the weighted average cost, you would still need to scan the transaction fact table (Movements) to compute these values.

In other words, whenever you create a snapshot fact table, you are fixing, during ETL time, the kind of analysis that can be performed by using the snapshot because you are storing data at a predefined granularity that is already aggregated by using a predefined aggregation function. Any other kind of analysis requires much greater effort, either from scanning the original fact table or from updating the snapshot table and adding the new columns.

In Tabular mode, you can use the tremendous speed of the in-memory engine to get rid of snapshots. Scanning a fact table is usually so fast that the snapshots are not needed. Based on our experience, there is no visible gain in taking a snapshot of a fact table with less than 100 million rows. When you have greater sizes—that is, in the billions range—snapshots might be useful. Nevertheless, the bar is so high that in many data warehouses, you can avoid taking any snapshots, greatly reducing the ETL effort and gaining data-model flexibility. In some cases, a snapshot table could be many times larger than the transaction table on which it is based. If you have a large number of products, you have relatively few transactions, and you take snapshots daily.

 More information For a deeper discussion about using snapshot tables or dynamic calculations in DAX, with more practical examples and benchmarks, see *https://www.sqlbi.com/articles/inventory-in-power-pivot-and-dax-snapshot-vs-dynamic-calculation/*.

Using views to decouple from the database

As discussed in Chapter 3, "Loading data inside Tabular," loading data from views is the best practice for creating a model in Analysis Services. Not following this practice will present a higher cost of maintenance later in the project lifecycle. In this section, you will find more details about this best practice.

If you load data directly from a table, you are creating a very strong dependency between the table structure in the database and your tabular solution. This is never a good idea. Databases tend to change over time due to requirements, and you do not want your solution to depend so strongly on any metadata update that might happen on the database. You may prefer to load data from SQL statements so that the dependency is weakened. If the metadata of the table changes, you can always update your SQL statements to prevent changes that might break your solution.

However, loading from a SQL statement hides from the database administrator important information about which columns you are reading and what relationships you are following. Moreover, if you must make a change, you must update the table metadata and deploy a new solution, which, in a big database, might lead to some wasted processing time.

The best option with Tabular mode, as is the case with Multidimensional mode, is to always create SQL views in the database that clearly show (to the database administrator) the data you are interested in loading. Then load the data inside the tabular model from these views, as if they were tables. (You should have already noticed that views are shown as tables when you load data inside Power Pivot from tables.)

The reasons you should import views (and not tables) in a tabular model are as follows:

- **Decoupling**   Importing views decouples the physical database structure from the tabular data model. If the database must be refactored, a column renamed, or an attribute normalized, chances are that any report tied to a physical table will run a query that is no longer valid. This is the same for a tabular model. A view defined in the database allows the DBA to alter the view at the same time that the changes are applied to the table, keeping the same output for the view, despite the changes applied to the underlying tables. As you can imagine, this decoupling should be done for any reporting and analytical system.

- **Declarative description**   The database contains a declarative description of the tables that are involved in the creation of a tabular entity. A DBA can evaluate the impact of a change in the database structure by just looking at the existing views, without having to investigate in other tools and environments that he or she might not be aware of.

- **Control performance**   Adding query hints and/or indexes can improve the speed of the query. For a tabular model, this is usually not required, because queries generated by Tabular for a data refresh are usually quite simple. (DirectQuery might require different considerations.) However, if you created a complex SQL statement to load a table, you can spend time optimizing the query plan in SQL Server Management Studio (SSMS) without having to open the .bim project file to update the SQL code.

From a practical point of view, there are a few guidelines to follow when creating views for a data model. The following list applies in particular to Microsoft SQL Server, but it could be easily adapted to any relational database that is used as a data source:

1. **Create a schema for a data model** For instance, the ContosoDW sample database used in many examples of this book has a schema called *Analytics*, which includes all the views used by tabular models. If these projects were real, and not just examples, we should have created a different schema for each tabular model.

2. **Create one view for each table you want to create in a tabular model** Keep the following points in mind:

   - The view must belong to the schema that corresponds to the tabular project.

   - The view should include only the columns that are useful and that will be used in the tabular model.

   - The names of views and of columns exposed in the views should be user friendly and identical to names exposed by the tabular model.

   - Remove any prefix/suffix from visible columns. (You might want to keep prefixes for columns that should be for internal use only and hidden to client tools, such as surrogate keys used in relationships.)

   - Use acronyms only if they are well-known by the users.

   - Use spaces to separate multiple words for visible columns, but do not use spaces in the names of hidden columns.

3. **Import the views in Tabular mode and remove the schema name** Keep the view name only in the tabular model.

The Analytics schema in the SQL Server database ContosoDW (which is part of the companion content) applies the best practices described here. For a deeper analysis of the reasons and the advantages of using views instead of tables for a tabular model, see *https://www.sqlbi.com/articles/data-import-best-practices-in-power-bi/*. Although the article was written for Power BI, all the considerations are equally valid for any tabular model.

Relationship types

The tabular model contains relationships between tables. These are a fundamental part of the semantic model because they are used to transfer filters between tables during calculation. A relationship between the Products and Sales tables automatically propagates a filter to the Sales table, applied to one or more columns of the Products table. This type of filter propagation is also possible using DAX expressions when a relationship is not available, but if a relationship is available, then the DAX code is simpler and the performances are better.

When you import tables from a SQL Server database, the Table Import wizard infers relationships from foreign-key constraints that exist in the source database. However, a foreign key is not a relationship, and you can provide more metadata to a relationship than what can be extracted from a foreign key. For this reason, it is not an issue to spend time manually creating relationships in a tabular model when you import data from views instead of tables. In reality, you might have to spend a similar amount of time reviewing the relationships that are automatically generated by the wizard.

A relationship is based on a single column. At least one of the two tables involved in a relationship should use a column that has a unique value for each row of the table. This becomes a constraint for the column on the one side of a relationship, which must be unique. Usually, the primary key of a table is used for this purpose, and this is the typical result you see in relationships inferred from foreign keys that exist in the relational data source. However, any candidate key is a valid, unique column for a relationship. For example, the Product view in the Analytics schema of the ContosoDW database has two candidate keys: ProductKey and Product Code. (Being a type 1 SCD, the surrogate key has the same cardinality as the natural key.) Thus, you might set a relationship between the Product and Sales tables by using the ProductKey surrogate key column, and another relationship between the Product and the Budget tables that is coming from another data source that uses the Product Code column, as shown in Figure 6-8. This would not be possible in a relational database because only the primary key of the Product table could be used in the foreign-key constraints of the Sales and Budget tables.

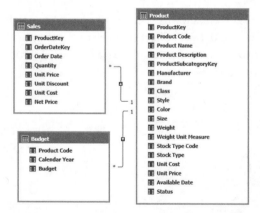

FIGURE 6-8 The different relationships using different columns in the lookup table.

If you have a logical relationship that is based on multiple columns (which are supported in foreign keys), you should consolidate them in a single column so you can create the corresponding relationship. For example, you might create a calculated column that concatenates the values of the columns involved. Separate the column values by including a character that is not used in the values of the columns being referenced. For example, if you have a primary key in a Product table that is defined using two columns, Group Code and Item Code, you should create a calculated column, as shown in the following formula:

```
Product[ItemKey] = Table[Group Code] & "|" & Table[Item Code]
```

As you saw in Chapter 2, "Getting started with the tabular model," every relationship includes attributes that define cardinality, filter direction, and active state. These are described in the following sections.

Cardinality of relationships

Most of the relationships in a tabular model have a one-to-many cardinality. For each row of a table, called a *lookup table*, there are zero, one, or more rows in the related table. For example, the relationship between the Product and Sales tables is a typical one-to-many relationship. Such a relationship is what is always inferred from a foreign-key constraint, which is always defined in the related table, referencing the lookup table. However, a relationship is not a foreign-key constraint in Tabular mode because it does not produce the same constraints on data as there are in a relational model.

The dialog box to edit a relationship in a tabular model provides you the following three options for cardinality:

- Many to One (*:1)

- One to Many (1:*)

- One to One (1:1)

The first two options are only an artifact of the dialog box shown in Figure 6-9. That is, you might have the lookup table on the right or on the left, and this does not affect your ability to define the relationship between the two tables. At the end, you always have a one-to-many relationship, and you can identify the lookup table according to the side of the "one" term.

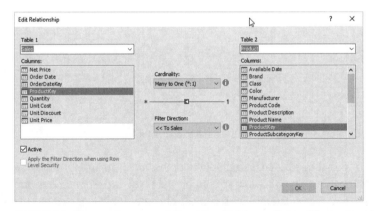

FIGURE 6-9 The one-to-many relationship, which is usually identified automatically.

If the columns selected on the two sides of a relationship are both candidate keys for the correspondent tables, then the Edit Relationship dialog box will propose the one-to-one cardinality by default. However, you can enforce any cardinality type, as shown in Figure 6-10.

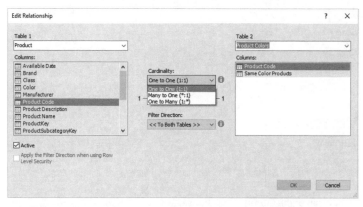

FIGURE 6-10 The one-to-one relationship, which is changed to a one-to-many type.

> **Important**   Usually, when you select the tables and the columns involved, the cardinality is automatically detected. However, when you have no rows in the workspace database for the involved tables, or if the data would be compatible with a one-to-one relationship, then the Cardinality drop-down list box will show all the possible options. The dialog box does not show the options that are not compatible with the data in the workspace database.

In terms of the side effects of the calculation engine, we only consider two types of cardinality: one-to-many and one-to-one. Regardless of the cardinality type, a relationship also propagates a filter, depending on the filter-direction settings, which will be explained in the section "Filter propagation in relationships" later in this chapter.

One-to-many relationships

In a classical one-to-many relationship, the table on the one side is the lookup table, and the table on the many side is the related table. If the data in the lookup table would invalidate the uniqueness condition of the column used in the relationship, then an operation involving a data refresh of the table will fail. As a side effect, the one-to-many relationship applies a constraint on the column that is used in the relationship, which is guaranteed to be unique in the lookup table.

The constraint of a one-to-many relationship affects only the lookup table. The related table does not have any constraint. Any value in the column of the related table that does not have a corresponding value in the lookup table will simply be mapped to a special blank row, which is automatically added to the lookup table to handle all the unmatched values in the related table.

For example, consider the Currency and Transactions tables in Figure 6-11. The Transactions table has a Total Amount measure that sums the Amount column. There are two currencies in the Transactions table that do not correspond to any row in the Currency table: CAD and GBP.

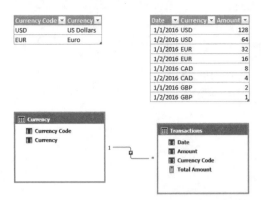

FIGURE 6-11 The content and relationship of the Currency and Transactions tables.

If you browse the model using a PivotTable in Excel, you see that the transactions for CAD and GBP are reported in a special blank row, as shown in Figure 6-12.

Row Labels	Total Amount
Euro	48
US Dollar	192
	15
Grand Total	**255**

FIGURE 6-12 The blank row sums both the CAD and GBP currencies, which are not present in the Currency table.

There is only one special blank row in the Currency table, regardless of the number of unique values in the Currency Code column of the Transactions table that do not have a corresponding value in Currency. Such a special blank row aggregates all the rows in the Transactions table that do not have a corresponding row in Currency through the relationship that exists between the two tables.

The advantage of this approach is that you can refresh the lookup table only in a data model, and all the rows of the related tables that were associated with the special blank row will be associated without the new values imported in the lookup table, without requiring you to process the related table again. For instance, if you import the GBP row in the Currency table, all the rows in the Transactions table related to GBP will now be associated with the right currency, keeping in the special blank row all the other unmatched currencies (such as CAD in this case). This will happen without any further processing of the Transactions table. You can see in Figure 6-13 the result of the PivotTable refresh after you import the GBP row into the Currency table.

Row Labels	Total Amount
British Pound	3
Euro	48
US Dollar	192
	12
Grand Total	**255**

FIGURE 6-13 Only including CAD in the blank row, once the GBP currency is included in the Currency table.

The additional row in Currency exists only if there is at least one row in Transactions with a Currency Code symbol that does not exist in the Currency table. In general, the number of rows in a lookup table can be one more than the rows in the data source because of this additional row that is automatically created after any update of any table in the data model.

In a one-to-many relationship, you can use the RELATEDTABLE function in a row-related calculation of the lookup table, and RELATED in a row-related calculation of the related table (on the many side of the relationship).

Note If you have rows in a table with keys that do not have a corresponding row in a lookup table (on the one side of a many-to-one relationship) in a corresponding foreign-key relationship of a relational database, you have what is called *broken referential integrity*. This condition is not desirable because it could confuse users and perhaps some calculations. For example, an average person would consider all the transactions of different "unknown" products as a single "empty" product. The design choice made in Tabular mode is to always import data also, in case of broken referential integrity, and this is useful for late-arriving dimensions. However, you must be aware of the consequences of missing related items in the calculations of your data model.

One-to-one relationships

Both tables involved in the one-to-one relationship get a unique constraint on the column involved in the relationship itself. However, it is not guaranteed that the two tables will have the same number of rows. In fact, every row in a table might have a corresponding row in the other table, or not. This is true for both tables. A better definition could be a (zero-or-one)-to-(zero-or-one) relationship, but for practical reasons, we use the term *one-to-one*.

When a row does not have a corresponding row in the other table, a special blank row is added to the other table to capture all the references to invalid or non-existing values. In this case, every table is both a lookup table and a related table, at the same time. For example, consider the Products and Stock tables in Figure 6-14. The Stock table has the Available measure that sums the Availability column. There are two rows in each table that do not correspond to any row in the other table. (The Bike and Laptop rows do not exist in the Stock table, whereas the Projector and Cable rows do not exist in the Products table.)

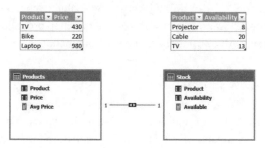

FIGURE 6-14 The content and relationship of the Products and Stock tables.

When you browse the model using a PivotTable in Excel, you can use both the Product columns of the two tables, and the products existing in both tables will produce the expected result. In Figure 6-15, you have the Product column of the Products table in the left PivotTable, and the Product column of the Stock table in the right PivotTable. The value related to the TV product is identical in the two models.

Otherwise, you see on the right the Avg Price measure populated for all the products that exist in the Products table. The two other products, Cable and Projector, in the Stock table, do not have a corresponding row in Products, so they are all aggregated in the same blank row that is added to the Products table. Similarly, the Stock table has an additional blank row that groups the products in Stock that do not exist in Products (in this case, Bike and Laptop).

Product from Products

Row Labels	Avg Price	Available
Bike	$220.00	
Laptop	$980.00	
TV	$430.00	13
		28
Grand Total	**$543.33**	**41**

Product from Stock

Row Labels	Avg Price	Available
Cable		20
Projector		8
TV	$430.00	13
	$600.00	
Grand Total	**$543.33**	**41**

FIGURE 6-15 The Product column, coming from the Products table on the left, and from the Stock table on the right.

In a one-to-one relationship, both tables can act as a lookup table and as a related table at the same time. For this reason, you can use both RELATED and RELATEDTABLE in row-related calculations for both tables.

> **Note** Any tabular model imported from Power Pivot or upgraded from a model compatibility level (that is earlier than 1200) will have only one-to-many relationships. The one-to-one relationship is available only in a model compatibility level that is greater than or equal to 1200.

Filter propagation in relationships

A filter applied to any column of a table propagates through relationships to other tables, following the filter direction defined in the relationship itself. By default, a one-to-many relationship propagates the filter from the one side of the relationship (the lookup table) to the "many" side (the related table). This propagation is called *single direction* or *one direction*. You can alter this setting by enabling a bidirectional propagation of the filter, as explained in the following sections. You define the filter-propagation settings in the data model and can modify them in DAX by using the CROSSFILTER function.

Single-direction filter

The direction of a filter propagation is visible in the diagram view. For example, the one-to-many relationship between Product and Sales in Figure 6-16 has a single arrow indicating the direction of the propagation, which is always from the one side of the relationship (in this case, Product) to the "many" side (in this case, Sales) for a single-direction filter. The relationship between Date and Sales is a single-direction filter, too.

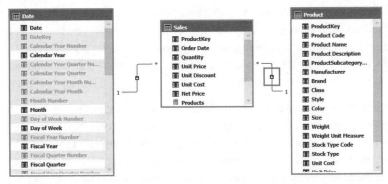

FIGURE 6-16 Single-direction filter propagation in a one-to-many relationship, between Product and Sales.

In a report that filters by year, the filter of certain dates applied to the Sales table will not propagate to the Product table. For example, consider the following distinct count measures that are defined in this data model:

```
Sales[Products] := DISTINCTCOUNT ( 'Product'[ProductKey] )
Sales[Colors] := DISTINCTCOUNT ( 'Product'[Color] )
Sales[Products Sales] := DISTINCTCOUNT ( Sales[ProductKey] )
```

A PivotTable in Excel that filters data by the Calendar Year column propagates the filter only to the Sales table, affecting only the Products Sales measure, which aggregates the ProductKey column of the Sales table. The other two measures consider all the rows in the Product table, not only those belonging to at least one of the transactions filtered in the Sales table. For this reason, the Colors and Products Sales measures show the same amount regardless of the row in the PivotTable, as shown in Figure 6-17. In other words, the filter made over Calendar Year does not propagate to the Product table.

Row Labels	Products Sales	Products	Colors
⊞ CY 2005		2,517	16
⊞ CY 2006		2,517	16
⊞ CY 2007	1,258	2,517	16
⊟ CY 2008	1,478	2,517	16
⊞ January 2008	173	2,517	16
⊞ February 2008	172	2,517	16
⊞ March 2008	189	2,517	16
⊞ April 2008	208	2,517	16
⊞ May 2008	213	2,517	16
⊞ June 2008	183	2,517	16
⊞ July 2008	200	2,517	16
⊞ August 2008	171	2,517	16
⊞ September 2008	219	2,517	16
⊞ October 2008	178	2,517	16
⊞ November 2008	232	2,517	16
⊞ December 2008	205	2,517	16
⊞ CY 2009	1,513	2,517	16
⊞ CY 2010		2,517	16
⊞ CY 2011		2,517	16
Grand Total	**2,235**	**2,517**	**16**

FIGURE 6-17 The results of measures that use single-direction filters.

The value displayed for the Products Sales measure represents the unique number of products sold by year and month, regardless of how many products exist in the Products dimension table. The grand total counts how many unique products have been sold at least once over all the available years. This number is lower than the Products measure because only the products that have been sold at least once are considered in the Products Sales measure.

You might think that it is enough to use the Products Sales measure for such a requirement, and in part this could be correct. However, this is not possible when you want to count how many unique colors have been used in the products sold in a certain period, or when the Product table is a slowly changing dimension with different ProductKey values for the same product code. The Colors measure always shows 16, which is the number of unique colors in the table, regardless of whether they have been used at least once in any transaction being considered.

DAX provides several approaches to compute the expected value for the Products and Colors measures. For example, you might use the following definitions for the previous measures, obtaining the result you will see later in Figure 6-20:

```
Sales[Products] :=
CALCULATE (
    DISTINCTCOUNT ( 'Product'[ProductKey] ),
    Sales
)

Sales[Colors] :=
CALCULATE (
    DISTINCTCOUNT ( 'Product'[Color] ),
    Sales
)
```

However, this technique requires that you apply the same pattern to every other single measure you want to include in this type of calculation. A simpler and better way to obtain the same result with minimal effort is by using the bidirectional filter propagation, as explained in the next section.

Bidirectional filter

The Edit Relationship dialog box has a Filter Direction drop-down list box that controls the direction of the filter propagation in a relationship. The single direction that is available by default in a one-to-many relationship can be To Table 1 or To Table 2, corresponding to the cardinality Many to One or One to Many, respectively. (The names Table 1 and Table 2 are replaced by the corresponding names of the tables that are referenced by the relationship.)

Figure 6-18 shows how the dialog box appears after you choose To Both Tables in the Filter Direction drop-down list box, which means that the relationship now has a propagation of the filter in both directions. This is called a *bidirectional filter*.

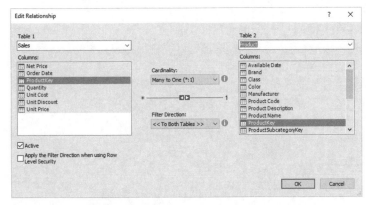

FIGURE 6-18 A bidirectional filter in the Sales–Product relationship that is set as To Both Tables in the Filter Direction drop-down list box.

The bidirectional filter propagation is also represented in the Diagram view through a pair of arrows along the relationship line, pointing to opposite directions. This graphical representation is shown in Figure 6-19.

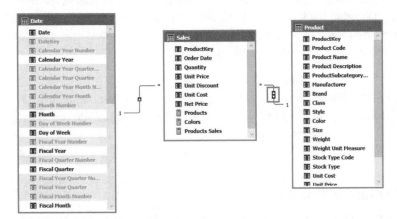

FIGURE 6-19 A bidirectional filter propagation in a one-to-many relationship between the Product and Sales tables.

Using this setting, the original measures (shown previously in Figure 6-17) now exhibit a different behavior. Any filter applied to the Sales table propagates to the Product table, and vice versa. Therefore, the Products and Colors measures now consider the rows in the Product table to have at least one related row in the Sales table, within the filter considered. In Figure 6-20, the Products measure shows how many unique products have been sold in every period, and the Colors measure conveys how many unique colors appear in those products.

Row Labels	Products Sales	Products	Colors
⊞ CY 2007	1,258	1,258	16
⊟ CY 2008	1,478	1,478	16
⊞ January 2008	173	173	14
⊞ February 2008	172	172	15
⊞ March 2008	189	189	13
⊞ April 2008	208	208	14
⊞ May 2008	213	213	16
⊞ June 2008	183	183	13
⊞ July 2008	200	200	15
⊞ August 2008	171	171	14
⊞ September 2008	219	219	14
⊞ October 2008	178	178	14
⊞ November 2008	232	232	14
⊞ December 2008	205	205	15
⊞ CY 2009	1,513	1,513	16
Grand Total	2,235	2,517	16

FIGURE 6-20 The results of measures that use a bidirectional filter.

The Products measure corresponds to the Products Sales measure, with one exception: The Grand Total row is different. This is because the Products measure still returns the number of all the unique products in the Products table, whereas Products Sales returns the number of unique products with sales. The reason for that is that the bidirectional filter applies a filter from Sales to Product only if there is at least one filter that is active on the Sales table, either direct (on one or more columns of the Sales table) or indirect (on one or more columns of any table that could propagate the filter to the Sales table). This seems like a small detail, but it could have important performance implications in complex models with many relationships. You can find more details about this topic at *http://www.sqlbi.com/ articles/many-to-many-relationships-in-power-bi-and-excel-2016/.*

> **Important**   A one-to-one relationship always has a bidirectional filter propagation, and you cannot modify that. To control the filter-direction setting of a relationship, you must revert the relationship to a one-to-many type.

Active state of relationships

By default, every relationship in the data model is active. You can disable a relationship by deselecting the **Active** checkbox in the Edit Relationship dialog box. However, you can have only one active relationship between two tables in the data model, and you cannot have circular references through relationships. For this reason, SQL Server Data Tools (SSDT) for Visual Studio automatically deactivates new relationships in case they conflict with previously existing ones.

For example, in Figure 6-21 you can see the following multiple relationships created between the Date and Sales tables:

- **Sales[Order Date] to 'Date'[Date]**   This is active and is represented by a solid line.

- **Sales[Due Date] to 'Date'[Date]**   This is inactive and is represented by a dotted line.

- **Sales[Delivery Date] to 'Date'[Date]**   This is inactive and is represented by a dotted line.

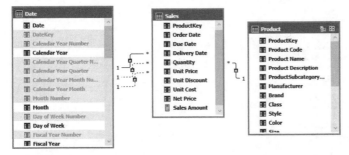

FIGURE 6-21 Multiple relationships between the Date and Sales tables, with only one that is active.

You can activate an inactive relationship by selecting the **Active** check box in the Edit Relationship dialog box. When you do that, the relationship that was previously active is automatically deactivated because you can have only one active relationship between two tables.

An inactive relationship creates the same internal structures that optimize the filter propagation. However, an inactive relationship is not automatically used in a DAX expression unless it is activated by using the USERELATIONSHIP function. This function activates the relationship in the context of a single DAX expression without altering the state of the relationships for other calculations and without modifying the underlying data model.

The three relationships existing between Date and Sales can be used in three different measures, showing the sales by order date (Sales Amount), by due date (Due Sales), and by delivery date (Delivered Sales). Figure 6-22 shows the result of the following three measures, where Due Sales and Delivered Sales call the USERELATIONSHIP function to change the active relationship within the calculation of Sales Amount:

```
Sales[Sales Amount] :=
SUMX ( Sales, Sales[Quantity] * Sales[Net Price] )

Sales[Due Sales] :=
CALCULATE (
    [Sales Amount],
    USERELATIONSHIP ( Sales[Due Date], 'Date'[Date] )
)

Sales[Delivered Sales] :=
CALCULATE (
    [Sales Amount],
    USERELATIONSHIP ( Sales[Delivery Date], 'Date'[Date] )
)
```

Row Labels	Sales Amount	Due Sales	Delivered Sales
⊟ CY 2007	$11,309,946.12	$11,022,672.25	$11,034,860.44
⊞ January 2007	$794,248.24	$610,978.36	$624,650.61
⊞ February 2007	$891,135.91	$771,214.11	$790,981.53
⊞ March 2007	$961,289.24	$1,013,632.16	$992,760.62
⊞ April 2007	$1,128,104.82	$1,125,747.85	$1,140,575.75
⊞ May 2007	$936,192.74	$846,178.91	$839,658.92
⊞ June 2007	$982,304.46	$997,252.08	$991,050.56
⊞ July 2007	$922,542.98	$1,080,708.75	$1,078,819.68
⊞ August 2007	$952,834.59	$772,026.24	$776,586.75
⊞ September 2007	$1,009,868.98	$1,074,371.03	$1,082,690.27
⊞ October 2007	$914,273.54	$899,246.33	$901,968.98
⊞ November 2007	$825,601.87	$876,555.02	$872,217.70
⊞ December 2007	$991,548.75	$954,761.43	$942,899.08
⊞ CY 2008	$9,927,582.99	$9,877,155.20	$9,901,407.94
⊞ CY 2009	$9,353,814.87	$9,442,986.38	$9,442,286.09
⊞ CY 2010		$248,530.15	$212,789.51
Grand Total	$30,591,343.98	$30,591,343.98	$30,591,343.98

FIGURE 6-22 The result of three measures, showing Sales Amount applying different relationships.

Note The CROSSFILTER function is not a replacement of USERELATIONSHIP. You can disable a relationship using the None argument in CROSSFILTER, but the only way you can activate an inactive relationship is by using the USERELATIONSHIP function.

Implementing relationships in DAX

The main effect of a relationship is the propagation of the filter context, according to its filter-direction settings. If a relationship is not defined in the data model, because it was not designed up front or because it was not possible to define, you can always create an equivalent behavior in a DAX expression by using a technique that transfers a filter from one table to another table. For an example, see Figure 6-23.

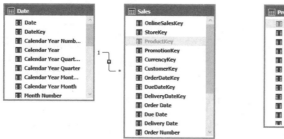

FIGURE 6-23 Showing how no relationship is defined between the Product and Sales tables.

For example, if you want to transfer a relationship from the Product table to the Sales table without a relationship defined in the data model (as shown in Figure 6-23), you can write the following filter argument in a CALCULATE function, obtaining the same effect of the filter propagation that is produced by a relationship by using the ProductKey column:

```
Sales[Sales Amount] :=
CALCULATE (
    SUMX ( Sales, Sales[Quantity] * Sales[Net Price] ),
```

```
INTERSECT (
    ALL ( Sales[ProductKey] ),
    VALUES ( 'Product'[ProductKey] )
)
)
```

The advantage of this technique is that it can also be applied when the column used to transfer the filter is not a candidate key, as when you need a relationship at a different granularity than the one of the table that propagates the filter. You can find DAX examples of this technique applied at *http://www.daxpatterns.com/handling-different-granularities/.* However, by using bidirectional filters, you can now use the technique described in the next section of this chapter: using standard relationships with bidirectional filters, through a hidden table that has the granularity required. Thus, the relationship implemented through DAX filters is useful when the data model does not contain such a definition.

Normalization versus denormalization

A tabular model can easily import every table and relationship that exists in a relational model. However, this is not necessarily a good idea because the data-modeling requirements for a relational database are very different, depending on the primary goal of the database itself. At the beginning of this chapter, you learned that a data mart is the best starting point for a tabular model rather than an OLTP database. This section discusses pros and cons of different levels of normalization in a tabular model, suggesting a few best practices for shaping the tables that are imported from a data mart.

When you consider the spectrum of options in data modeling, you can go between two extremes for a single analytical model. At one side, you can design a fully normalized database, with numerous tables and relationships. At the other extreme, you can completely denormalize a model in a single flattened table, which contains all the attributes and measures of a data mart. Because a tabular model is based on a columnar database, querying columns in two tables requires a join that leverages a relationship, and this is more expensive (in terms of storage memory and query time) than querying two columns on the same table. Nevertheless, a completely denormalized model is not practical because it has the following negative side effects:

- **A longer processing time** This is because the amount of raw data read during the refresh operation includes more columns in an uncompressed form, which generates a longer process that also requires more memory.

- **A worse user experience** This is because all the columns are part of the same table and because navigation through them is more difficult, even if you organize attributes in folders.

- **An inability to represent measures at different granularities** This is because this requires different tables.

- **Complex DAX code** For some calculations, the DAX code may become complex. For example, time intelligence is hard to use without a properly designed date table.

In a model with multiple tables, relationships are the more efficient way to transfer the filter context from one table to another. They simplify the DAX code and make the entire process extremely efficient and automated. However, transferring a filter through a relationship has a higher cost (it takes longer) than transferring a filter between columns of the same table. Thus, a fully normalized model has these negative side effects:

- **A slower query execution** This is because more tables requires more relationships, which adds the cost of several relationships involved also in relatively simple queries.

- **The inability to create user hierarchies** A hierarchy can only use columns that are part of the same table, so it is not possible to create hierarchies using columns from different tables.

For these reasons, the best data-modeling technique for a tabular model is the star schema, using shared dimensions when there are two or more fact tables. The star schema is a better choice over the snowflake schema, which "normalizes" certain attributes of an entity. For example, Figure 6-24 shows the Product entity modeled through a star schema, whereas Figure 6-25 models the same entity in a snowflake schema. The Subcategory and Category columns are included in the single table for the products in the star schema, whereas they are in different tables in the snowflake schema.

FIGURE 6-24 The Product entity, modeled as a single table in a star schema.

Important The examples of this book often use a snowflake schema to represent the Product entity, but only because it enables us to show features that otherwise would be hard to explain in a simple star schema. Moreover, a snowflake schema makes some filters very complex in DAX, as described in Chapter 10, "Advanced evaluation context," of *The Definitive Guide to DAX*. A single Product table, which denormalizes all the columns of the related table example, is usually the best practice for a tabular model.

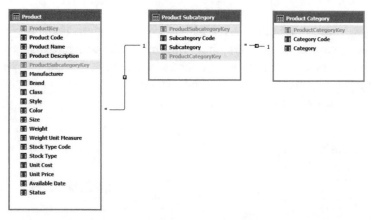

FIGURE 6-25 The Product entity, modeled with multiple tables in a snowflake schema.

It is worth mentioning that a snowflake schema could appear to be the more natural way to create relationships between fact tables with different granularities. For example, consider the schema shown in Figure 6-26, where the Strategy Plan table has a relationship with the Product Category table, and the Sales table has a relationship with the Product table. Relationships between entities correspond to the physical relationships in the data model, each with a proper granularity.

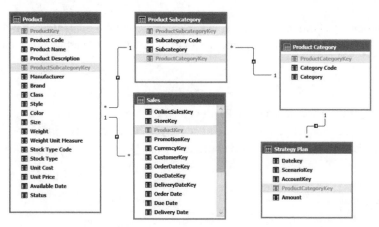

FIGURE 6-26 Showing the Strategy Plan fact table reference the Product Category table, and the Sales table reference the Product table.

Because the inability to create a user hierarchy negatively affects the user experience, you can denormalize the product attributes in a single table, which is named Product – Star Schema in the companion content and in Figure 6-27. This propagates the filter through a hidden ProductCategory table, thanks to a bidirectional filter, as shown in Figure 6-27.

Note The use of names in Pascal case, without space between words, is intentional when that name should be hidden to the user. That way, if the data model does not have the right property set, the user might complain about the ugly names. Alternatively, you might spot the issue during testing. You can then hide the table and column names in the data model or rename them if they should be visible.

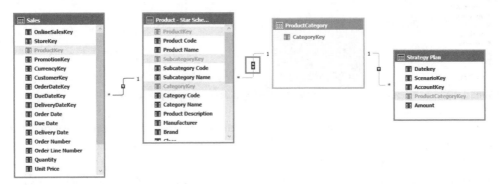

FIGURE 6-27 The hidden ProductCategory table and its relationship with the Product – Star Schema table, which has a bidirectional filter.

The bidirectional filter between Product – Star Schema and ProductCategory guarantees that the selection made in the Product – Star Schema table propagates to the Strategy Plan table, as you can see in Figure 6-28.

Note In a real project, you should rename the Product – Star Schema table to simply Product. We keep the longer name in this example because you have both versions in the Contoso database that is part of the companion content.

Row Labels	Sales Amount	Budget
Audio	$384,518.16	$471,055.19
Cameras and camcorders	$7,192,581.95	$8,062,649.19
Cell phones	$1,604,610.26	$2,865,483.53
Computers	$6,741,548.73	$10,294,422.64
Games and Toys	$360,652.81	$434,510.10
Home Appliances	$9,600,457.04	$12,455,756.30
Music, Movies and Audio Books	$314,206.74	$523,377.13
TV and Video	$4,392,768.29	$4,365,378.66
Grand Total	**$30,591,343.98**	**$39,472,632.74**

FIGURE 6-28 The Category Name rows, filtering both the Sales Amount and Budget measures from the Sales and Strategy Plan tables, respectively.

Important Even if bidirectional filters are natively supported in the data model and in DAX expressions, the propagation of a filter in a single-direction, one-to-many relationship is faster than in a bidirectional filter, where the propagation also follows the many-to-one direction of the same relationship. You should consider this in the data-model design, especially for single relationships with a high cardinality (more than 100,000 unique values in the column that is used by the relationship).

Calculated tables versus an external ETL

In Chapter 2, you saw that a tabular model can include calculated tables, which are obtained by automatically evaluating a DAX table expression whenever any table in the data model changes. In this way, you can denormalize data in other tables, and the consistency of the model is guaranteed by the engine.

Calculated tables are not strictly necessary in a tabular model. Instead of using calculated tables, you might be able to prepare the data before loading the tabular model. This usually results in more control over the calculation process. For example, if you prepare the data beforehand, you can skip individual rows that fail a particular calculation. In contrast, a calculated table is an all-or-nothing option. If any row generates a calculation error, the entire calculated table refresh operation fails.

As a general rule, you should try to prepare data before loading it in a tabular model. That being said, there are certain situations in which a calculated table might be a better option:

- **You have source tables that come from different data sources** When you prepare data for a tabular model, normally you write tables in a data mart or implement a transformation logic in a view. In the former case, if you use ETL tools that can gather data from different data sources in a single transformation, such as SQL Server Integration Services (SSIS), then you have a certain level of flexibility in collecting data from different data sources. However, when the ETL is implemented directly in procedures that extract the data, then joining tables coming from different sources becomes really hard. In the latter case, a single view can get data from different data sources by using technologies (such as linked servers in Microsoft SQL Server) that generate a certain overhead and impact on performances. Thus, if you connect a tabular model directly to different data sources (not a best practice, but it could be necessary sometimes), then you might consider calculated tables as the easiest way to process data from different sources.

- **Creating a derived table is too expensive outside of a tabular model** If you have to aggregate or transform millions of rows, processing and transferring data to a tabular model could take longer than evaluating such a calculation by using data that is already loaded in the tabular model. However, you should consider that the evaluation of a calculated table always happens entirely in a tabular model, whereas a table persisted in SQL Server could be updated incrementally if the business logic allows that.

For example, consider the requirement for a table that classifies customers on a monthly basis, based on their historical sales, summing all the transactions made in the past. Figure 6-29 shows the tabular data model, including the Sales and Customer tables that are imported from the Contoso relational database.

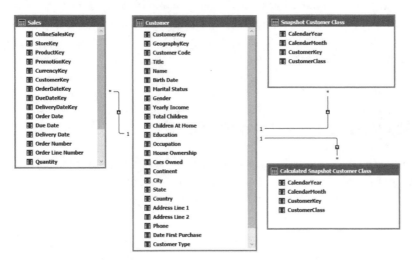

FIGURE 6-29 The Sales fact table and two snapshot tables with customer classification referencing the Customer table.

The Snapshot Customer Class table contains the historical classification of customers. You can write the following query in SQL to obtain such a result:

```
WITH    SalesRunningTotal
        AS ( SELECT   d.CalendarYear,
                      d.CalendarMonth,
                      s.CustomerKey,
                      Sales = ( SELECT   SUM(hs.Quantity * hs.[Net Price])
                                FROM     Analytics.Sales hs
                                WHERE    hs.[Order Date] <= MAX(s.[Order Date])
                                         AND hs.CustomerKey = s.CustomerKey
                              )
             FROM     Analytics.Sales s
             LEFT JOIN dbo.DimDate d
                      ON s.[Order Date] = d.Datekey
             GROUP BY d.CalendarYear,
                      d.CalendarMonth,
                      s.CustomerKey
           )
    SELECT  rt.CalendarYear,
            rt.CalendarMonth,
            rt.CustomerKey,
            rt.Sales,
            CustomerClass = CASE WHEN rt.Sales < 1000 THEN 'Retail'
                                 WHEN rt.Sales < 10000 THEN 'Affluent'
                                 ELSE 'Vip'
                            END
    FROM    SalesRunningTotal rt;
```

The preceding SQL query, which corresponds to the Analytics.[Snapshot Customer Class] view in the Contoso database, runs in around 35 seconds on a development server that we used to test it. Instead of importing this view in a table in the tabular model, you can create a calculated table that completes the execution three times faster (11 seconds faster on the same test hardware) by using the following DAX expression, which is stored in the Calculated Snapshot Customer Class calculated table:

```
=SELECTCOLUMNS (
    SUMMARIZECOLUMNS (
        'Date'[Calendar Year],
        'Date'[Calendar Year Month Number],
        Customer[CustomerKey],
        Sales,
        "Cumulated Sales", CALCULATE (
            SUMX ( Sales, Sales[Net Price] * Sales[Quantity] ),
            FILTER ( ALL ( 'Date' ), 'Date'[Date] <= MAX ( 'Date'[Date] ) )
        )
    ),
    "CalendarYear", 'Date'[Calendar Year],
    "CalendarMonth", 'Date'[Calendar Year Month Number],
    "CustomerKey", Customer[CustomerKey],
    "CustomerClass", SWITCH (
        TRUE,
        [Cumulated Sales] < 1000, "Retail",
        [Cumulated Sales] < 10000, "Affluent",
        "Vip"
    )
)
```

The calculated table is a powerful tool for a tabular data model. You can denormalize data without worrying about consistency because the table is automatically refreshed if the data in the underlying table changes. As you saw in Figure 6-29, you can also create relationships with calculated tables, but there could be restrictions in their DAX expressions, as described in the following section.

Circular reference using calculated tables

If you create a relationship with a calculated table, you must ensure that the DAX expression used in the calculated table does not depend on the other tables in the data model. Otherwise, you might have a circular-reference problem, which blocks the creation of the relationship itself.

For example, consider the following DAX expression, which generates the Customer Yearly Sales calculated table:

```
=CALCULATETABLE (
    ADDCOLUMNS (
        CROSSJOIN (
            ALL ( Customer[CustomerKey] ),
            VALUES ( 'Date'[Calendar Year] )
        ),
        "Sales 2007", CALCULATE ( SUMX ( Sales, Sales[Net Price] * Sales[Quantity] ) )
    ),
```

```
        'Date'[Calendar Year] = "CY 2007"
            || 'Date'[Calendar Year] = "CY 2008"
)
```

The expression ALL (Customer[CustomerKey]) depends on the Customer table, which depends on all the tables on the "many" side of a relationship. If you try to create a relationship between Customer and the calculated table created in the preceding code, you get the error shown in Figure 6-30.

FIGURE 6-30   The message for a circular reference when creating a relationship with a calculated table.

The reason is that the Customer table could have an additional blank row depending on the content of the tables on the "many" side of each relationship that connects to Customer. Thus, Customer depends on the Customer Yearly Sales table, because any unreferenced customer in the latter would produce a blank in the former. But Customer Yearly Sales also depends on Customer because it uses the ALL function, which depends on the content of Customer, including the special blank row.

In this case, you can avoid the circular reference by using the ALLNOBLANKROW function instead of ALL. This always produces the same result, ignoring the additional blank row created automatically by the engine when it is needed. Thus, the following DAX expression creates a calculated table that can reference the Customer table:

```
=CALCULATETABLE (
    ADDCOLUMNS (
        CROSSJOIN (
            ALLNOBLANKROW ( Customer[CustomerKey] ),
            VALUES ( 'Date'[Calendar Year] )
        ),
        "Sales 2007", CALCULATE ( SUMX ( Sales, Sales[Net Price] * Sales[Quantity] ) )
    ),
    'Date'[Calendar Year] = "CY 2007"
        || 'Date'[Calendar Year] = "CY 2008"
)
```

For the same reasons, you might want to use the DISTINCT function instead of VALUES to avoid generating a circular dependency. This is not the case for the preceding expression because it references the Date table, which is not connected to the new calculated table. However, you should consider using DISTINCT to avoid any future issue in case you will create new relationships in the tabular model.

Summary

In this chapter, you have seen the best practices in data modeling for Tabular. The star schema in a relational model is the optimal starting point, even if surrogate keys are not required and could be avoided when a model is created specifically for Tabular. You also learned the following:

- Slowly changing dimensions do not require special handling.

- Degenerate dimensions do not require a specific dimension entity, as in the case of a multi-dimensional model.

- When using views, it is important to decouple the tabular model from the physical data source structure of a relational database.

- Relationships in a tabular model can have different cardinality types and filter-propagation settings.

- Calculated tables are a tool that can replace part of ETL in specific cases.

Tabular Model Scripting Language (TMSL)

The Model.bim file in a compatibility level 1200 tabular project contains the definition of the objects of the data model in a JSON format called Tabular Model Scripting Language (TMSL). The TMSL specifications include the description of the objects in a tabular model (such as tables, partitions, relationships, and so on) and the commands you can send to Analysis Services to manipulate (such as create, alter, and delete) and manage (such as back up, restore, and synchronize) a tabular model. This chapter describes the TMSL, particularly for the object's definition. It also provides a short introduction to the TMSL commands, which are described in more detail in Chapter 13, "Interfacing with Tabular." You can also find several TMSL examples in Chapter 11, "Processing and partitioning tabular models."

Note All the names of object classes, such as `Database` and `Model`, have the first letter in uppercase in the text. However, in JSON the first letter of an attribute name is always lowercase. For example, `database` in the JSON code corresponds to the `Database` object in the textual description.

What's new in SSAS 2016 TMSL is a new feature in SSAS 2016. Therefore, this chapter is new to this edition of the book.

Defining objects in TMSL

The Model.bim file is a text file in the JSON format that contains the definition of a tabular object model. From a technical point of view, this JSON file is the serialization of objects of the tabular object model (TOM), which is a programming library described in Chapter 13, "Interfacing with Tabular." However, it is useful to introduce this structure looking at the JSON format directly because it allows you to understand (and sometimes to directly manipulate) the raw content of a Model.bim file.

To explain this structure, consider the following content of the Model.bim file of a new tabular project, as soon as it is created by Visual Studio:

```
{
  "name": "SemanticModel",
  "compatibilityLevel": 1200,
  "model": {
    "culture": "en-US",
    "annotations": [
      {
        "name": "ClientCompatibilityLevel",
        "value": "400"
      }
    ]
  },
  "id": "SemanticModel"
}
```

This JSON structure corresponds to the content of a Database object in TMSL, as described at *https://msdn.microsoft.com/en-us/library/mt716020.aspx*. However, the properties' names and IDs are replaced and removed, respectively, when you deploy the database to the server. The following command (whose syntax is described in the final section of this chapter) includes the previous JSON as content of the database property, assigning the name *TabularProject1* to the database and removing the id property:

```
{
  "createOrReplace": {
    "object": {
      "database": "TabularProject1"
    },
    "database": {
      "name": "TabularProject1",
      "compatibilityLevel": 1200,
      "model": {
        "culture": "en-US",
        "annotations": [
          {
            "name": "ClientCompatibilityLevel",
            "value": "400"
          }
        ]
      }
    }
  }
}
```

The Database object is the only special type managed in the Model.bim file. The most important part is its model property, which contains the definition of the tabular model and includes all the changes applied to the tabular model by Visual Studio. In the previous empty example, the model contains only two properties: culture and annotations. As you will see, most of the objects in a tabular model, including the model itself, can have annotations. These are defined as an array of name/value properties.

These annotations are kept in the data model but are ignored by Analysis Services because they are used to store additional metadata information used by client tools or maintenance scripts. We will ignore annotations in this book and will remove them from the following examples to improve code readability.

> **Note** TMSL contains properties that are not exposed or cannot be edited in the Visual Studio user interface. When you modify these properties, Visual Studio usually respects the change applied, exposing to the Visual Studio user interface only the known properties. However, editing certain objects (such as relationships) might override any existing property of the previous version of the object. Therefore, if you apply manual changes to the Model. bim file, make sure your changes are still there after you modify in Visual Studio an object containing the settings you manually applied.

The Model object

The Model object is the most important object in a Model.bim file. It contains a limited number of properties that can be assigned with a string. These are as follows:

- **name** This is the name of the model. This property is not used by Visual Studio.

- **description** This is a description of the model. This property is not used by Visual Studio.

- **defaultMode** This can be either directQuery or import. It is set to directQuery when the DirectQuery Mode property in Visual Studio is set to On.

- **defaultDataView** You can set this to full or sample, but you do not set it in Visual Studio. Instead, you modify it in SQL Server Management Studio (SSMS). It defines the default behavior of the dataView property of partitions. (For more details on this, see Chapter 9, "Using Direct-Query.")

- **culture** This defines the culture used by the data model. (Translations of the data model in other cultures are available in the cultures collection.)

- **collation** This defines the collation used by the data mode, which controls the behaviors of sorting and comparison of values. Visual Studio shows the collation as a read-only property, and if it is not defined, it uses the Analysis Services default. By setting this property, you can override the default behavior of the Analysis Services instance. (For details on language and collation, see Chapter 8, "The tabular presentation layer.")

The larger part of a Model object is defined by collections of other objects, as follows:

- **dataSources** This is a list of the DataSource objects that describe the existing connections. Every table in the model has one or more partitions, and each partition can reference a different data source.

- **tables** This is a list of Table objects. Each one contains collections of columns, measures, partitions, and hierarchies.

- **relationships** This is a list of Relationship objects, where each one connects two tables of the same model.

- **perspectives** This is a list of Perspective objects, each one containing a list of PerspectiveTable objects. A PerspectiveTable object includes collections of PerspectiveColumn, PerspectiveMeasure, and PerspectiveHierarchy objects.

- **cultures** This is a list of Culture objects, each one containing collections of ObjectTranslation and LinguisticMetadata objects.

- **roles** This is a list of Role objects, each one containing collections of RoleMembership and TablePermission objects.

Figure 7-1 shows the dependencies of the collections included in the Model object.

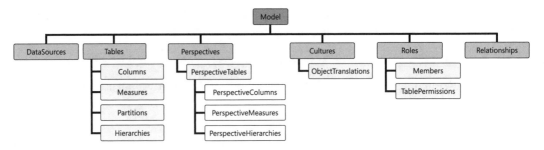

FIGURE 7-1 A dependency chart of collections that are used by the Model object.

The following is an example of a simple model containing two tables read from a single data source and connected by one relationship. (Internal collections of columns of Table objects are not expanded for readability.)

```
{
  "name": "SemanticModel",
  "compatibilityLevel": 1200,
  "model": {
    "culture": "en-US",
    "dataSources": [
      {
        "name": "SqlServer Demo ContosoDW",
        "connectionString": "Provider=SQLNCLI11;Data Source=Demo;Initial
Catalog=ContosoDW;Integrated Security=SSPI;Persist Security Info=false",
        "impersonationMode": "impersonateServiceAccount"
      }
    ],
```

```
    "tables": [
      {
        "name": "Product",
        "columns": [...],
        "partitions": [
          {
            "name": "Product",
            "dataView": "full",
            "source": {
              "query": " SELECT [Analytics].[Product].[ProductKey],[Analytics].[Product].
[Product Name],[Analytics].[Product].[Color] FROM [Analytics].[Product] ",
              "dataSource": "SqlServer Demo ContosoDW"
            }
          }
        ]
      },
      {
        "name": "Sales",
        "columns": [...],
        "partitions": [
          {
            "name": "Sales",
            "dataView": "full",
            "source": {
              "query": " SELECT [Analytics].[Sales].[ProductKey],[Analytics].[Sales].
[Order Date],[Analytics].[Sales].[Quantity],[Analytics].[Sales].[Net Price] FROM
[Analytics].[Sales] ",
              "dataSource": "SqlServer Demo ContosoDW"
            }
          }
        "measures": [
          {
            "name": "Sales Amount",
            "expression": " SUMX ( Sales, Sales[Quantity] * Sales[Net Price] )",
            "formatString": "\\$#,0.00;(\\$#,0.00);\\$#,0.00"
          }
        ]
      }
    ],
    "relationships": [
      {
        "name": "f587ad3d-a92b-444f-8ee2-42f4d3b38e51",
        "fromTable": "Sales",
        "fromColumn": "ProductKey",
        "toTable": "Product",
        "toColumn": "ProductKey"
      }
    ]
  },
  "id": "SemanticModel"
}
```

The DataSource object

The DataSource object defines a connection to a data source used by a partition. Visual Studio usually assigns only the name, connectionString, and impersonationMode properties. From SSDT, however, you cannot assign a value to other properties, such as maxConnections, isolation, and timeout. The following is a more complete list of the properties available:

- **name** This is the name of the data source. It corresponds to the Friendly Name for This Connection text box in the Edit Connection dialog box in Visual Studio.

- **connectionString** This is the connection string that must be recognized by the provider used.

- **impersonationMode** This specifies the following Windows credentials provided by Analysis Services when connecting to the data source:

  - **default** The server uses the appropriate impersonation method for the context used.

  - **impersonateAccount** The server impersonates the user account specified in the account property. (The property can be set by Visual Studio.)

  - **impersonateAnonymous** The server uses the anonymous user account. This setting is not recommended, although it is sometimes used in HTTP access scenarios by custom applications that handle authentication.

  - **impersonateCurrentUser** The server employs the user account that the client is using to connect. It should be used only in DirectQuery mode when Analysis Services is configured for trusted delegation in Kerberos.

  - **impersonateServiceAccount** The server uses the user account that the server is running as.

  - **impersonateUnattendedAccount** The server uses an unattended user account. This is used for Power Pivot or tabular models that run in a SharePoint environment.

- **account** This is the account name used for impersonation.

- **password** This is the encrypted string that provides the password of the account.

- **maxConnections** This is the maximum number of connections to be opened concurrently to the data source. You might want to apply this property when a data source experiences performance degradation due to serving too many concurrent requests.

- **isolation** This is reserved for future use. It is not implemented yet in Analysis Services Tabular mode.

- **timeout** This is the timeout in seconds (as an integer value) for executing a command.

- **provider** This optional string identifies the name of the managed data provider that is used on the connection to the relational database (if it is not otherwise specified on the connection string).

In the following example, the `DataSource` object has a limit of two connections and a timeout of 120 seconds:

```
"dataSources": [
  {
    "name": "SqlServer Demo ContosoDW",
    "connectionString": "Provider=SQLNCLI11;Data Source=Demo;Initial
Catalog=ContosoDW;Persist Security Info=false;Integrated Security=SSPI",
    "impersonationMode": "impersonateServiceAccount",
    "maxConnections": 2,
    "timeout": 120
  }
],
```

The Table object

The `Table` object contains the following properties that can be assigned with a string:

- **name** This is the name of the table. It corresponds to the Table Name property in Visual Studio.

- **description** This is a description of the table. It corresponds to the Table Description property in Visual Studio.

- **dataCategory** This is a string describing the category of data included in the table. Visual Studio sets this property to `Time` if the table is marked as a date table. This is the only value that affects calculations made by Analysis Services. The other values are used only as metadata for client tools. The possible values are `Unknown`, `Time`, `Measure`, `Other`, `Quantitative`, `Accounts`, `Customers`, `Products`, `Scenario`, `Utility`, `Currency`, `Rates`, `Channel`, `Promotion`, `Organization`, `Bill of Materials`, and `Geography`.

- **isHidden** This is `true` when the column is hidden from the client tool. It corresponds to the Hidden property in Visual Studio.

Every table has the following collection of other objects defining columns, measures, hierarchies, and partitions:

- **columns** This lists columns in the table. Every table requires at least one column.

- **measures** This lists measures in the table. It could be omitted if the table does not have any measures.

- **hierarchies** This lists hierarchies in the table. It could be omitted if the table does not have any hierarchies.

- **partitions** This lists partitions in the table. Every table requires at least one partition.

The Column object

Every column in a table can be either a `DataColumn` (imported from a data source), a `CalculatedColumn` (calculated in a table imported from a data source), or a `CalculatedTableColumn` (a column of a calculated table). All these columns have the following common properties:

- **name**   This is the name of the column. It corresponds to the Column Name property in Visual Studio.

- **description**   This is a description of the column. It corresponds to the Description property in Visual Studio.

- **alignment**   This can be `default`, `left`, `right`, or `center`. It is not used by Visual Studio.

- **dataCategory**   This defines the category of data for the column. It can be `Address`, `City`, `Continent`, `CountryRegion`, `County`, `Latitude`, `Longitude`, `Place`, `PostalCode`, `StateOrProvince`, `WebUrl`, `ImageUrl`, `Barcode`, `PaddedDateTableDates`, `Years`, `MonthOfYear`, `Months`, `QuarterOfYear`, `Quarters`, or `DayOfMonth`. The list of values could grow in the future, adding values listed as possible attribute types for multidimensional models (see *https://msdn.microsoft.com/en-us/library/ms175662.aspx*). It is not used by Visual Studio, but it is used by Power BI.

- **dataType**   This is the data type of the column. It can be `automatic`, `string`, `int64`, `double`, `dateTime`, `decimal`, `boolean`, `binary`, `unknown`, or `variant`. It corresponds to the Data Type property in Visual Studio, where `int64` corresponds to Whole Number setting, `double` corresponds to Decimal Number, `decimal` corresponds to Currency, and `boolean` corresponds to True/False.

- **displayFolder**   This corresponds to the Display Folder property in Visual Studio.

- **displayOrdinal**   This is reserved for future use.

- **formatString**   This is the format string of the column. It is generated by Visual Studio according to the Data Format property and related properties. However, this string is always the corresponding setting of the Format String property for a Custom setting of Data Format. The settings defined in Visual Studio are saved in the annotations; only the final result in `formatString` is considered by Analysis Services. If you set this property directly in the JSON file, you should remove the related annotations to avoid an inconsistent representation in Visual Studio.

- **isAvailableInMDX**   This is reserved for future use. It is not yet implemented in Analysis Services Tabular. When set to `false`, this property disables the creation of the attribute hierarchy for MDX usage. This would be useful for numeric columns with a high number of unique values that are used only in measures and not as filters in MDX clients (such as in Excel PivotTables).

- **isDefaultImage**   This can be either `true` or `false` (the default is `false`). It corresponds to the Default Image property in Visual Studio.

- **isDefaultLabel**   This can be either `true` or `false` (default is `false`), and corresponds to the Default Label property in Visual Studio.

- **isHidden** This can be either `true` or `false` the (default is `false`). It corresponds to the Hidden property in Visual Studio.

- **isKey** This can be either `true` or `false` (the default is `false`). It corresponds to the Row Identifier property in Visual Studio. It is also set to `true` for the date column used to mark a table that is marked as a date table.

- **isNullable** This can be either `true` or `false` (the default is `false`). It corresponds to the Nullable property in Visual Studio. Analysis Services can optimize storage engine queries using this property, especially for DirectQuery models.

- **isUnique** This can be either `true` or `false` (the default is `false`). It specifies whether the values of the columns are unique for each row of the table. It is not displayed by Visual Studio. Analysis Services can optimize storage engine queries using this property, especially for DirectQuery models.

- **keepUniqueRows** This can be either `true` or `false` (the default is `false`). It corresponds to the Keep Unique Rows property in Visual Studio. It can be set to `true`, but only if there is a column with `isKey` set to `true` in the same table.

- **sortByColumn** This is the name of the column to use as the sort order. It corresponds to the Sort by Column property in Visual Studio.

- **summarizeBy** This is the default aggregation applied to the column in Power BI and Power View. It can be one of the following values: `default`, `none`, `sum`, `min`, `max`, `count`, `average`, and `distinctcount`.

- **tableDetailPosition** This is the integer value corresponding to the position of the Detail record in the table. It is set by Visual Studio according to the choices made in the Default Field Set dialog box, as displayed in the Table Detail Position property of the column, or in the Default Field Set property of the table.

- **type** This is the column's type. It can be `data` (corresponding to DataColumn), `calculated` (corresponding to CalculatedColumn), or `calculatedTableColumn` (corresponding to CalculatedTableColumn). The default value is `data`.

For data columns, you can specify the following properties:

- **sourceProviderType** This is the data type of the column in the external data source. It is assigned by Visual Studio, even if it is not visible in its user interface.

- **sourceColumn** This is the name of the column in the external data source. It is assigned by Visual Studio when the data is imported. It is visible only in the Table Properties dialog box, by selecting Source in the Column Names From options.

For calculated columns, you can specify the following properties:

- **isDataTypeInferred** This can be either `true` or `false` (the default is `false`). Specify `true` if the data type is inferred from the source or `false` if the data type has been enforced in the calculated table or calculated column.

- **expression**   This is a string containing the DAX expression that defines the content of the calculated column.

For calculated tables, you can specify the following properties:

- **sourceColumn**   This is the name of the column in the calculated table expression that this column represents.

- **isNameInferred**   This can be either `true` or `false` (the default is `false`). Specify `true` if the name is inferred from the DAX expression that defines the calculated table or `false` if the column has been renamed in the calculated table.

- **columnOriginTable**   This is a read-only property that should not be used when creating or altering a tabular model. If the calculated table expression returns a column whose lineage can be determined, then this property indicates the table from which the values are computed.

- **columnOriginColumn**   This is a read-only property that should not be used when creating or altering a tabular model. If the calculated table expression returns a column whose lineage can be determined, then this property indicates the column from which the values are computed.

The Measure object

Every measure in a table has the following properties:

- **name**   This is the name of the measure. It corresponds to the Measure Name property in Visual Studio.

- **description**   This is a description of the measure. It corresponds to the Description property in Visual Studio.

- **expression**   This is a string that contains the DAX expression that defines the content of the measure.

- **formatString**   This is the measure's format string, which is generated by Visual Studio according to the Data Format and related properties. However, this string always corresponds to the Format String property for a Custom setting of the Format property in the Visual Studio user interface. The complete settings defined in Visual Studio to format a measure are saved in annotations, even if they are there for Visual Studio only. Analysis Services ignores them, considering them only for the final result in `formatString`. If you set this property directly in the JSON file, you should remove the related annotations to avoid an inconsistent representation in Visual Studio.

- **isHidden**   This can be either `true` or `false` (the default is `false`). You can change it in Visual Studio by selecting **Hide from Client Tools** or **Unhide from Client Tools** from the context menu.

- **isSimpleMeasure**   This property is `true` for implicit measures that are automatically created by the client tools. It is not used by Visual Studio.

- **displayFolder**   This corresponds to the Display Folder property in Visual Studio.

- **kpi**   This property defines the key performance indicator (KPI) associated to a measure. It has the following internal properties:

  - **description**   This is a description of the KPI. It is not used in Visual Studio.

  - **targetDescription**   This is a description of the KPI target. It is not used in Visual Studio.

  - **targetExpression**   This is a string containing the DAX expression that defines the target value for the KPI.

  - **targetFormatString**   This is the KPI target format string, which is generated by Visual Studio according to the Data Format and related properties. However, this string always corresponds to the Format String property for a Custom setting of the Format property in the Visual Studio user interface. The complete settings defined in Visual Studio to format a KPI target are saved in annotations, even if they are there for Visual Studio only. Analysis Services ignores them, considering them only for the final result in targetFormatString. If you set this property directly in the JSON file, you should remove the related annotations to avoid an inconsistent representation in Visual Studio.

  - **statusGraphic**   This is a string with the name of a visual element that is associated with the status for the KPI.

  - **statusDescription**   This is a description of the KPI status. It is not used in Visual Studio.

  - **statusExpression**   This is a string containing the DAX expression that defines the value of the KPI status.

  - **trendGraphic**   This is a string with the name of a visual element that is associated with the trend for the KPI.

  - **trendDescription**   This is a description of the KPI trend. It is not used in Visual Studio.

  - **trendExpression**   This is a string containing the DAX expression that defines the value of the KPI trend. It is not used by Visual Studio.

The following example shows a measure with a KPI assigned to the measures collection of a table with just one measure:

```
"measures": [
  {
    "name": "Sales Amount",
    "expression": " SUMX ( Sales, Sales[Quantity] * Sales[Net Price] )",
    "formatString": "\\$#,0.00;(\\$#,0.00);\\$#,0.00",
    "kpi": {
      "targetExpression": "100",
      "targetFormatString": "\\$#,0.00;(\\$#,0.00);\\$#,0.00",
      "statusGraphic": "Traffic Light - Single",
      "statusExpression": [
```

```
                    "VAR x='Sales'[Sales Amount] RETURN",
                    "        IF ( ISBLANK ( x ), BLANK(),",
                    "                IF ( x<40,-1,",
                    "                IF ( x<80,0,1 )",
                    "           )",
                    "        )",
                    "           "
                ]
            }
        }
    ],
```

The Hierarchy object

Every hierarchy in a table has the following properties:

- **name**   This is the name of the hierarchy. It corresponds to the Name property in Visual Studio.

- **description**   This is a description of the hierarchy. It is not used in Visual Studio.

- **isHidden**   This can be either `true` or `false` (the default is `false`). You can change it in Visual Studio by selecting **Hide from Client Tools** or **Unhide from Client Tools** from the context menu.

- **displayFolder**   This corresponds to the Display Folder property in Visual Studio.

- **levels**   This property defines the levels of the hierarchy associated with a measure. It is an array of objects. Each object has the following internal properties:

  - **name**   This is the name of the hierarchy level. It corresponds to the Name property in Visual Studio.

  - **description**   This is a description of the hierarchy level. It is not used in Visual Studio.

  - **ordinal**   This is the integer value defining the ordinal position of the level in the hierarchy. (The first level sets the ordinal property equal to zero).

  - **column**   This is a string containing the name of the column in the table that is used in this hierarchy level. It corresponds to the Source Column property in Visual Studio.

The Partition object

Every table needs at least one `Partition` object in its Partitions property. Every `Partition` object has the following properties:

- **name**   This is the name of the partition. It corresponds to the Partition Name property in the Partition Manager dialog box in Visual Studio.

- **description**   This is a description of the partition. It is not used in Visual Studio.

- **mode**   This defines the type of partition. It can be `default`, `import`, or `directQuery`. In Visual Studio, you can change the state of this property by clicking the **Set as Sample** or **Set as DirectQuery** button in the Partition Manager dialog box.

- **dataView**   This defines the type of data view that defines the partition slice. It can be `default`, `full`, or `sample`. When a model has DirectQuery mode active, Visual Studio automatically sets this property to `sample` for the partitions in import mode. It sets this property to `full` for all the other cases.

- **source**   This property defines the data source of the partition. It has the following internal properties:

  - **type**   This is the type of partition. It can be `query`, `calculated`, or `none`. Visual Studio assigns `query` to all the partitions of a table imported from a data source and `calculated` to the partitions of calculated tables. (Only one partition is allowed for each calculated table.)

  - **query**   This is a string containing the command for the data source to read any data for the partition (for example, a SQL statement for a relational database). This property is available only when the type is `query`.

  - **dataSource**   This is the name of the data source that is used to load the data in the partition. This property is available only when the type is `query`.

  - **expression**   This is a string containing the DAX expression that defines the content of the calculated table. This property is available only when the type is `calculated`.

In this chapter, you have seen examples of partitions in imported tables. In the following sample code, the definition of the partition of a calculated table is highlighted:

```
{
  "name": "DailySales",
  "columns": [
    {
      "type": "calculatedTableColumn",
      "name": "Order Date",
      "dataType": "dateTime",
      "isNameInferred": true,
      "isDataTypeInferred": true,
      "sourceColumn": "Sales[Order Date]",
      "formatString": "General Date"
    },
    {
      "type": "calculatedTableColumn",
      "name": "Day Sales",
      "dataType": "decimal",
      "isNameInferred": true,
      "isDataTypeInferred": true,
      "sourceColumn": "[Day Sales]",
      "formatString": "\\$#,0.00;(\\$#,0.00);\\$#,0.00"
    }
  ],
  "partitions": [
    {
      "name": "Day Sales",
      "source": {
        "type": "calculated",
```

```
          "expression": "SUMMARIZECOLUMNS ( Sales[Order Date], \"Day Sales\", SUMX (
Sales, Sales[Quantity] * Sales[Net Price] ) )"
            }
          }
        ]
      }
```

The Relationship object

Each relationship connects two tables in the data model and has the following properties:

- **name**   This is the name of the relationship. Usually it is a globally unique identifier (GUID) defined by Visual Studio that is not shown in its user interface.

- **fromTable**   This is the name of the starting table in a relationship, which should be the many side of a one-to-many relationship.

- **fromColumn**   This is the name of the column in the starting table in a relationship, which should be the many side of a one-to-many relationship.

- **fromCardinality**   This represents the cardinality of the starting table in a relationship. It can have the values many, none, or one.

- **toTable**   This is the name of the destination table in a relationship, which should be the one side of a one-to-many relationship.

- **toColumn**   This is the name of the column in the destination table in a relationship, which should be the one side of a one-to-many relationship.

- **toCardinality**   This represents the cardinality of the destination table in a relationship. It can have the values many, none, or one, but the current implementation only supports the value one.

- **isActive**   This is set to `false` if the relationship is inactive. The default is `true`.

- **crossFilteringBehavior**   This specifies the cross-filter direction of the relationship. It can be set to oneDirection, bothDirections, or automatic. By default, it is set to oneDirection, applying a filter to the from end of the relationship. This propagates the filter that exists in the to end of the relationship. The bothDirections setting propagates the filter context in both directions. With the automatic behavior, the engine analyzes the relationships and chooses one of the behaviors by using heuristics (such a setting is not used by SSDT). This property corresponds to the Filter Direction setting in the Edit Relationship dialog box in SSDT. It must be set to bothDirections when fromCardinality is set to one.

- **joinOnDateBehavior**   When a relationship connects two columns of the DateTime data type, this property specifies whether the join should use just the date part (datePartOnly) or the complete date and time information (dateAndTime). The default setting is dateAndTime, and Visual Studio does not expose it. You can modify this setting only by editing the Model.bim file with a text editor.

- **relyOnReferentialIntegrity**   This is set to `true` if Analysis Services can assume that the relationships have referential integrity. Any value on the from end of the relationship has a corresponding value in the to end of the relationship. This assumption generates a more efficient SQL expression in DirectQuery mode. The default of this setting is `false`, and Visual Studio does not show a user interface to edit it. (As of October 2016, this setting is available in Power BI and should appear in the Edit Relationship dialog box in a future release of SSDT.)

- **securityFilteringBehavior**   This defines the filtering behavior for security. It can have the value `oneDirection` or `bothDirections`. By default, it is set to `oneDirection`. You should change this setting to `bothDirections` only if the `crossFilteringBehavior` setting is set to `bothDirections`, too.

The Perspective object

Every perspective has a name and a list of tables. Each table includes a list of columns and measures. Only the elements that are visible in the perspective are referenced by the perspective itself. The following properties are for a `Perspective` object:

- **name**   This is the name of the perspective.

- **tables**   This is a list of tables. Each table has the following properties:

  - **name**   This is the name of the table that is visible in the perspective.

  - **columns**   This is a list of columns in the table that are visible in the perspective. The list has objects with a single property, name, which corresponds to the name of the column that is visible in the table.

  - **hierarchies**   This is a list of hierarchies in the table that are visible in the perspective. The list has objects with a single property, name, which corresponds to the name of the hierarchy that is visible in the table.

  - **measures**   This is a list of measures in the table that are visible in the perspective. The list has objects with a single property, name, which corresponds to the name of the measure that is visible in the table.

The following is an example of the definition of a perspective named *SamplePerspective*:

```
"perspectives": [
  {
    "name": "SamplePerspective",
    "tables": [
      {
        "name": "Product",
        "columns": [
          {
            "name": "Product Name"
          },
          {
```

```
            "name": "ProductKey"
          }
        ],
        "hierarchies": [
          {
            "name": "Colors"
          }
        ]
      },
      {
        "name": "Sales",
        "columns": [
          {
            "name": "Net Price"
          },
          {
            "name": "Order Date"
          },
          {
            "name": "ProductKey"
          },
          {
            "name": "Quantity"
          }
        ],
        "measures": [
          {
            "name": "Sales Amount"
          }
        ]
      }
    ]
  }
],
```

The Culture object

When you enable translations in the data model, the culture's property contains a list of `Culture` objects. Each object includes several lists of objects that describe the translation for a specific culture. You will find a more complete explanation of how to manage translations in a tabular model in Chapter 8, "The tabular presentation layer."

Each object for the translations has the following standard properties:

- **name** This is the name of the object that is translated. It must exist in the data model.

- **translatedCaption** This is the translated string for the caption of the object. It usually corresponds to the `name` property of the original object.

- **translatedDescription** This is the translated string for the description of the object. It usually corresponds to the `description` property of the original object.

- **translatedDisplayFolder**   This is the translated string for the display folder of the object. It is defined only for those entities that support the display folder.

The properties of a `Culture` object are as follows:

- **name**   This specifies the culture. It is a string, such as en-US (for US English), it-IT (for Italian in Italy), and so on.

- **translations**   This is an array of objects that are structured in the same way as the objects of a model. In fact, every object has a single property or **model**, which contains the following properties:

  - **name**   This is the name of the model (by default, it is Model).

  - **tables**   This is an array of objects that is used to translate tables in the data model. It includes the standard properties and the following lists: columns, measures, and hierarchies. Each object in these lists contains the standard translation properties.

  - **perspectives**   This is an array of objects used to translate perspectives in the data model. It includes the standard properties and the following lists: perspectiveColumns, perspectiveMeasures, and perspectiveHierarchies. Each object in these lists contains the standard translation properties.

The following is an example of the definition of an Italian translation for a simple data model:

```
"cultures": [
  {
    "name": "it-IT",
    "translations": {
      "model": {
        "name": "Model",
        "translatedCaption": "Model",
        "tables": [
          {
            "name": "Product",
            "translatedCaption": "Prodotto",
            "columns": [
              {
                "name": "ProductKey",
                "translatedCaption": "ProdottoKey"
              },
              {
                "name": "Product Name",
                "translatedCaption": "Nome prodotto"
              },
              {
                "name": "Color",
                "translatedCaption": "Colore"
              }
            ]
          },
          {
```

```
              "name": "Sales",
              "translatedCaption": "Vendite",
              "columns": [
                {
                  "name": "ProductKey",
                  "translatedCaption": "ProdottoKey"
                },
                {
                  "name": "Order Date",
                  "translatedCaption": "Data ordine"
                },
                {
                  "name": "Quantity",
                  "translatedCaption": "Quantità"
                },
                {
                  "name": "Net Price",
                  "translatedCaption": "Prezzo netto"
                }
              ],
              "measures": [
                {
                  "name": "Sales Amount",
                  "translatedCaption": "Totale vendite"
                }
              ]
            }
          ]
        }
      }
    }
  ],
```

The Role object

Security settings are defined in a data model that uses an array of Role objects. The properties of each Role object are as follows:

- **name**   This is the name of the role in the data model.

- **modelPermission**   This is the level of access for the role. It can have one of the following values: none (no access to the model), read (it can read the metadata and data of the model), readRefresh (it can read and refresh data), refresh (it can only refresh the data and calculations in the model), and administrator (it can administer the model).

- **members**   This is a list of objects with members and/or groups assigned to the role. Each object for one member or group contains the following properties:

  - **memberName**   This is the name of the user or group.

  - **memberId**   This is a string that uniquely identifies the member. It is not used by Visual Studio yet.

- **identityProvider** This is a string that defines which identity provider to use to authenticate the user.

- **memberType** This indicates whether the particular member of a security role is an individual user or a group of users, or if the member is automatically detected. It can have one of the following values: auto, user, or group.

■ **tablePermissions** This is a list of objects representing the permissions associated with each table. It uses the following properties:

- **name** This is the name of the table to which the permissions are applied.

- **filterExpression** This is a string that contains the DAX expression with the logical condition that makes it visible or invisible, in each single row of the table that is specified by the name property.

The following is an example of the definition of two roles (Red Products and Blue Products) that are used to demonstrate the use of translations in a simple data model:

```
"roles": [
  {
    "name": "Red Products",
    "modelPermission": "read",
    "members": [
      {
        "memberName": "Marco",
        "memberId": "S-1-5-23-1253425662-234762666-7545327646-4321"
      },
      {
        "memberName": "Users",
        "memberId": "S-1-5-32-545"
      }
    ],
    "tablePermissions": [
      {
        "name": "Product",
        "filterExpression": " 'Product'[Color] = \"Red\""
      }
    ]
  },
  {
    "name": "Blue Products",
    "modelPermission": "read",
    "tablePermissions": [
      {
        "name": "Product",
        "filterExpression": " 'Product'[Color] = \"Blue\""
      }
    ]
  }
],
```

TMSL commands

There are several commands available in TMSL. They are divided in the following categories (each including one or more commands):

- **Object operations**   This category has the following commands: Alter, Create, CreateOrReplace, and Delete.

- **Data refresh operations**   This category has the following commands: MergePartitions and Refresh.

- **Scripting**   This category has just one command: Sequence.

- **Database management**   This category has the following commands: Attach, Detach, Backup, Restore, and Synchronize.

You can execute these commands with one of the following techniques, which are described in more detail (and with more examples) in Chapter 13:

- Using an XMLA window in SSMS

- Invoking the Execute method of the Microsoft.AnalysisServices.Tabular.Server class in the AMO library

- Using the invoke-ascmd cmdlet in PowerShell

- Using the Analysis Services Execute DDL task in SQL Server Integration Services (SSIS)

The following sections highlight some aspects of these commands that could be useful to know in general. The complete syntax for these TMSL commands is available online at *https://msdn.microsoft.com/en-us/library/mt637139.aspx*.

Object operations in TMSL

You can manipulate objects in a tabular database by using one of the object operations commands available in TMSL. For example, you can create a database named *SingleTableDatabase* by using the following TMSL code, which includes a complete database object. The following code is an abbreviated version that does not include the complete details of the table columns and partitions:

```
{
    "create": {
        "database": {
            "name": "SingleTableDatabase",
            "compatibilityLevel": 1200,
            "model": {
                "description": "This is a sample model",
                "culture": "en-US",
                "dataSources": [
```

```
                {
                    "name": "SqlServer Demo ContosoDW",
                    "connectionString": "<...>"
                    "impersonationMode": "impersonateServiceAccount",
                }
            ],
            "tables": [
                {
                    "name": "Currency",
                    "columns": [ <...> ],
                    "partitions": [ <...> ]
                }
            ]
        },
        "id": "SemanticModel"
    }
  }
}
```

If you create an entire database, you must provide all the details about the data model. If you add an object to an existing data model or replace an existing one, you must specify the parent object in the TMSL script. For example, you can add a partition to a table using the following TMSL code (the query for the partition is abbreviated):

```
{
  "createOrReplace": {
    "object": {
      "database": "SingleTableDatabase",
      "table": "Currency"
      "partition": "Currency - others"
    },
    "partition": {
      "name": "Currencies no longer used",
      "mode": "import",
      "dataView": "full",
      "source": {
        "query": [ <...> ],
        "dataSource": "SqlServer Demo ContosoDW"
      }
    }
  }
}
```

As you see, it is necessary to specify the position in the object hierarchy of the data model where the object must be added.

> **Note** Certain objects cannot be added or modified in TMSL because they can only be part of the object containing them. For example, a measure belongs to a table, so the table contains the measure. The only way to modify these objects not supported in TMSL as independent entities is to replace the object containing them. This might change in future updates, however. We suggest you check the updated documentation to see whether a certain operation is available or not. For example, as of October 2016, you cannot add a measure to a tabular model without including a description of the entire table in TMSL. A workaround for this type of problem is described in an article at the following URL: *http://www.sqlbi.com/articles/adding-a-measure-to-a-tabular-model/*.

Data-refresh and database-management operations in TMSL

Data-refresh and database-management operations require a reference to the affected object(s). For example, you refresh a single table with the following TMSL script:

```
{
  "refresh": {
    "type": "automatic",
    "objects": [
      {
        "database": "SingleTableDatabase",
        "table": "Currency"
      }
    ]
  }
}
```

In this case, the `objects` property identifies the element to manage because the command could be applied to different entities (database, table, or partition). Other commands might have other specific properties that directly identify the objects involved in the operation (partitions or databases).

Scripting in TMSL

You can create a list of commands sent to Analysis Services that are executed sequentially in a single transaction by using the `sequence` command. Only the objects specified in the `refresh` command are executed in parallel to one another. The `sequence` command also provides a property to control the parallelism level of the operation. For example, the following script executes the `refresh` operation on all the tables of the database, but it only processes one partition at a time:

```
{
    "sequence":  {
        "maxParallelism": 1,
        "operations": [
            {
                "refresh": {
                    "type": "automatic",
                    "objects": [
                        {
                            "database": "Contoso"
                        }
                    ]
                }
            }
        ]
    }
}
```

By default, Analysis Services executes, in parallel, the refresh of all the objects that are involved in the request (within the maximum parallelism possible with the hardware available). You can specify an explicit integer value to maxParallelism to optimize the process for the available resources. (Refreshing more objects in parallel increases the workload on the data sources and the memory pressure on Analysis Services.)

Note   The value for maxParallelism is an integer value rather than a string.

Summary

This chapter discussed the internal representation of the data model using the JSON format adopted by the Model.bim file in compatibility version 1200. It showed the difference between objects and commands in TMSL as well as several examples of the building blocks that are required to create and modify a tabular data model.

CHAPTER 8

The tabular presentation layer

One important consideration that is often ignored when designing tabular models is usability. You should think of a tabular model as a user interface for the data it contains. To a large degree, the success or failure of your project depends on whether your end users find that interface intuitive and easy to use.

This chapter covers several features that the tabular model provides to improve usability, such as the ability to sort data in a column and control how the measure values are formatted. It also covers perspectives, translations, and key performance indicators (KPIs). Although these features might seem less important than the ability to query vast amounts of data and perform complex calculations, you should not dismiss them or view them as having only secondary importance. The functionality they provide is vital to helping your users make the most effective use of your tabular model.

 What's new in SSAS 2016 This chapter includes a description of the new translations feature. In addition, several parts of the chapter are new or have been partially rewritten because of the new compatibility model (1200), the JSON format to save the tabular model, and the new Power BI Desktop client tool.

Setting metadata for a Date table

When you have a table containing calendar dates in a tabular model, it is important to set the right metadata so the engine can take advantage of them and enable you to use all the time intelligence functions available in DAX. In this section, you will see how to set these metadata correctly in the tabular model.

Many DAX functions that operate over dates (such as TOTALYTD, SAMEPERIODLASTYEAR, and many others) require a Date table to exist and assume that a column of the date data type exists. To specify the column to use for date calculations in date tables, you must use the Mark as Data Table dialog box in SSDT to select the Date column, as shown in Figure 8-1. (In this figure, the Date table in the Contoso database has been selected.) To open this dialog box, open the **Table** menu, choose **Date**, and select **Mark as Date Table**.

FIGURE 8-1 The Mark as Date Table dialog box, which requires the selection of a Date column.

After you mark a table as a Date table, you can change the Date column by opening the Mark as Date Table dialog box again—this time by opening the **Table** menu, choosing **Date**, and selecting **Date Table Settings**.

Side effects of Mark as Date Table to DAX expressions

Marking a table as a Date table in a tabular model has several side effects on any DAX expression—and not only on time intelligence functions. The presence of this metadata modifies any CALCULATE or CALCULATETABLE statement, including the Date column used in the Mark as Date Table dialog box, in its filter arguments. In such a case, an ALL function over the entire Date table is automatically applied to the CALCULATE or CALCULATETABLE function. For example, consider the following expression:

```
CALCULATE ( [measure], 'Date'[Date] <= DATE ( 2016, 12, 15 ) )
```

If the 'Date'[Date] column is used in the Mark as Date Table dialog box, the engine interprets the previous DAX expression as follows:

```
CALCULATE ( [measure], 'Date'[Date] <= DATE ( 2016, 12, 15 ), ALL ( 'Date' ) )
```

If this were not the case, existing filters over year, month, and other columns in the Date table would still be active in the filter context when measure was evaluated. The same behavior happens if a column of the date type is used in a relationship, making the Mark as Date Table setting unnecessary as explained in this article: *http://www.sqlbi.com/articles/time-intelligence-in-power-bi-desktop/*.

Naming, sorting, and formatting

The first (and probably most important) aspect of the tabular presentation layer to be considered is the naming, sorting, and formatting of objects.

Naming objects

The naming of tables, columns, measures, and hierarchies is one area in which business intelligence (BI) professionals—especially if they come from a traditional database background—often make serious mistakes with regard to usability. When developing a tabular model to import data from various data sources, it is all too easy to start without first thinking about naming. As the development process continues, it becomes more difficult to change the names of objects because doing so breaks existing calculations and queries (including Microsoft Excel PivotTables and Power View reports). However, from an end user's point of view, naming objects is extremely important. It helps them not only to understand what each object represents, but also to produce professional-looking reports that are easy for their colleagues to understand.

As an example, consider the section of a field list shown in the Microsoft Excel PivotTable Fields pane in Figure 8-2.

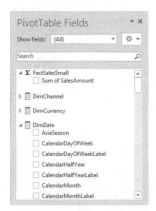

FIGURE 8-2 An example of poor object naming.

Now ask yourself the following questions:

- Do your users know what a fact table is? If not, will they understand what the Fact prefix in the FactSalesSmall table name means? Most likely, it would be clearer to call the table Sales.

- Your users might know what a dimension is. Still, will they want all their dimension table names to be prefixed with Dim, as in DimDate and DimProduct? Date and Product might look better.

- Technical naming conventions often remove spaces from names, but what purpose does this achieve in a tabular model? Putting spaces in names might be more professional and help readability.

- Even if the Sum of SalesAmount measure does return the sum of values in the SalesAmount column, will your users want to build reports with Sum of SalesAmount as a column header and then show that report to their colleagues? Wouldn't using Sales Amount as a measure name be a better option?

> **Note** Measures and table columns share the same namespace. This can present a dilemma when you want to build a measure from a column, such as SalesAmount, and expose the column so it can be used on the rows or columns of a query. In this case, calling the measure Sales Amount and the underlying column Sales Amount Values might be appropriate. But in cases like this, you should always let your end users make the final decision.

Figure 8-3 shows what the same PivotTable field list looks like after these issues have been fixed.

FIGURE 8-3 An example of user-friendly object naming.

It is important to discuss the names of tables, columns, measures, and hierarchies with your users at a very early stage in the project life cycle. As mentioned, this saves you many hours of tedious work in fixing calculations and queries at the end of your project. Sometimes users decide they cannot work with the names you have given them, so you should prepare for that. A strict naming convention is usually not necessary (and, indeed, can be counterproductive) as long as you follow the following two rules:

- Use names that help users understand what the data means in business terms. For example, if users always talk about *volume* rather than *units sold*, use the term *volume* in your measure names.

- Use names that a user could place unaltered on a report shown to the CEO. Again, think about which names work best from a business standpoint rather than an IT standpoint. For example, the object names in Figure 8-2 might not be clear to most people, including top executives.

Hiding columns and measures

As noted several times in this book, if a column in your data warehouse will not be useful to your end users, you should not import it into your model because it will use up memory and increase the processing time. Useless columns also hurt usability because the more columns there are to choose from, the harder it is for your end users to find the columns they want to use in their reports. Some columns, however, are necessary for properties such as Row Identifier (described in the section "Table behavior properties" later in this chapter) and for use in calculations, so they must be present even if the user does not want to use them in a report. In these cases, the Hidden property of the column should be set to True because the smaller the number of columns that are displayed to the end user, the easier the model is to use. The Hidden property is also available for all the measures, so you can hide those measures that are for internal use only—for example, measures used only by other measures.

Organizing measures and columns

One useful piece of functionality is the ability to group multiple measures and table columns into display folders so that users can find what they are looking for more easily. The Display Folder property, which is available for columns and measures, controls the folder hierarchy used to arrange their visualization to the users. The string you write in the Display Folder property corresponds to the name of the folder that contains the column or measure. If you want to use nested folders, you simply type the complete path from the root folder to the leave folder, separating names by a backslash (\). For example, Figure 8-4 shows the columns of the Product table displayed to users when the values for the Display Folder property (shown in Table 8-1) are used.

TABLE 8-1 The values of the Display Folder property

Column	Display Folder Property
Product Code	
Product Description	
Product Name	
Brand	Info
Class	Info
Color	Info
Manufacturer	Info
Style	Info
Available Date	Info\Stock
Status	Info\Stock
Stock Type	Info\Stock
Size Info	Info\Volume
Weight	Info\Volume
Weight Unit Measure	Info\Volume
Unit Cost	Pricing
Unit Price	Pricing

FIGURE 8-4 The columns arranged by using the Display Folder property.

Sorting column data

In many cases, the order in which values appear in a column is irrelevant. By default, Tabular does not apply any sorting to data in columns, and this usually causes no problems. The most common situations when alphabetical ordering for data is not suitable occur on Date dimension tables. Days of the week and months of the year have their own inherent order, which must be used in any reports built on your model. You can sort data in columns by using the Sort by Column property of a column, or through the Sort by Column dialog box shown in Figure 8-5. (To open this dialog box, open the **Column** menu, choose **Sort**, and select **Sort by Column**.)

FIGURE 8-5 The Sort by Column dialog box.

The Sort by Column property is fairly straightforward. For any column in a table, it enables you to specify another column in the same table to control the sort order. However, there are three important things to know about this property:

■ It is possible to sort only in ascending order, according to the data in the Sort by Column property.

- The data in the column to be sorted and the data in Sort by Column property must be of the same granularity. So, for each distinct value in the column, there must be a single, equivalent value in Sort by Column.

- For MDX client tools, this property affects how members are ordered in a hierarchy, but it does not directly affect DAX queries. Client tools, such as Power BI, should read this property value from the model metadata and then generate an appropriate `ORDER BY` clause in the queries they generate.

For the Month column shown in Figure 8-5, there is another column already in the Date table that can be used for sorting: Month Number. This contains the month numbers from 1 to 12, with 1 corresponding to January and 12 to December. Setting the Sort by Column property for Month to Month Number means that the Month column will be displayed in PivotTables, as shown in Figure 8-6.

Sales Amount	Column Labels			
Row Labels	CY 2007	CY 2008	CY 2009	Grand Total
January	$794,248.24	$656,766.69	$580,901.05	$2,031,915.98
February	$891,135.91	$600,080.00	$622,581.14	$2,113,797.05
March	$961,289.24	$559,538.52	$496,137.87	$2,016,965.62
April	$1,128,104.82	$999,667.17	$678,893.22	$2,806,665.20
May	$936,192.74	$893,231.96	$1,067,165.23	$2,896,589.93
June	$982,304.46	$845,141.60	$872,586.20	$2,700,032.26
July	$922,542.98	$890,547.41	$1,068,396.58	$2,881,486.97
August	$952,834.59	$721,560.95	$835,707.46	$2,510,103.00
September	$1,009,868.98	$963,437.23	$709,610.40	$2,682,916.61
October	$914,273.54	$719,792.99	$806,738.22	$2,440,804.75
November	$825,601.87	$1,156,109.32	$868,164.01	$2,849,875.20
December	$991,548.75	$921,709.14	$746,933.50	$2,660,191.40
Grand Total	$11,309,946.12	$9,927,582.99	$9,353,814.87	$30,591,343.98

FIGURE 8-6 Sorted month names.

What happens if there is not an obvious candidate for a column to use for sorting? Consider the Calendar Year Month column shown in Figure 8-7, which contains the month name concatenated with the year. For example, it returns values such as February 2006 or April 2007.

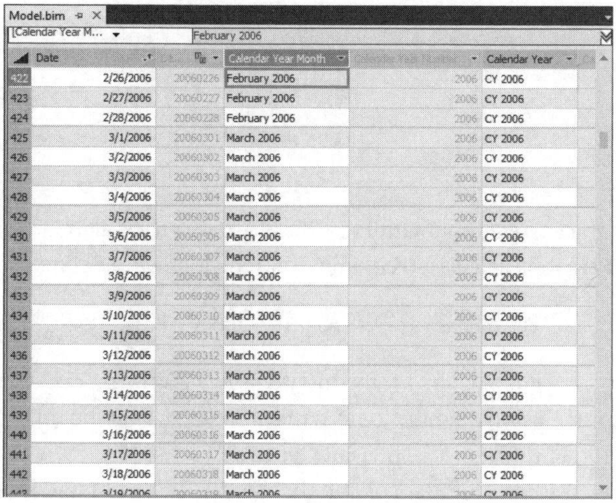

	Date		Calendar Year Month		Calendar Year
422	2/26/2006	20060226	February 2006	2006	CY 2006
423	2/27/2006	20060227	February 2006	2006	CY 2006
424	2/28/2006	20060228	February 2006	2006	CY 2006
425	3/1/2006	20060301	March 2006	2006	CY 2006
426	3/2/2006	20060302	March 2006	2006	CY 2006
427	3/3/2006	20060303	March 2006	2006	CY 2006
428	3/4/2006	20060304	March 2006	2006	CY 2006
429	3/5/2006	20060305	March 2006	2006	CY 2006
430	3/6/2006	20060306	March 2006	2006	CY 2006
431	3/7/2006	20060307	March 2006	2006	CY 2006
432	3/8/2006	20060308	March 2006	2006	CY 2006
433	3/9/2006	20060309	March 2006	2006	CY 2006
434	3/10/2006	20060310	March 2006	2006	CY 2006
435	3/11/2006	20060311	March 2006	2006	CY 2006
436	3/12/2006	20060312	March 2006	2006	CY 2006
437	3/13/2006	20060313	March 2006	2006	CY 2006
438	3/14/2006	20060314	March 2006	2006	CY 2006
439	3/15/2006	20060315	March 2006	2006	CY 2006
440	3/16/2006	20060316	March 2006	2006	CY 2006
441	3/17/2006	20060317	March 2006	2006	CY 2006
442	3/18/2006	20060318	March 2006	2006	CY 2006

FIGURE 8-7 The Calendar Year Month column.

If there is no column with the same granularity (which means you need a column with one distinct value for each distinct value in Calendar Year Month) by which to sort, you could try to sort by using a column with a different granularity. However, if you choose a column with a larger number of distinct values, such as the Date column, you get the error shown in Figure 8-8. The error message is as follows:

Cannot sort Calendar Year Month by Date because at least one value in Calendar Year Month has multiple distinct values in Date. For example, you can sort [City] by [Region] because there is only one region for each city, but you cannot sort [Region] by [City] because there are multiple cities for each region.

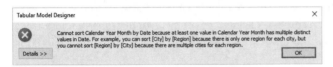

FIGURE 8-8 The Sort by Column error message.

If you sort by a column that has a smaller number of distinct values, such as Calendar Year Number, you will not get an error, but the values in the column will not be sorted correctly, either. Instead, you will see each month sorted by year, but you cannot guarantee the order within the year, as shown in Figure 8-9.

Row Labels	Sales Amount
July 2007	$922,542.98
February 2007	$891,135.91
March 2007	$961,289.24
April 2007	$1,128,104.82
May 2007	$936,192.74
June 2007	$982,304.46
January 2007	$794,248.24
August 2007	$952,834.59
September 2007	$1,009,868.98
October 2007	$914,273.54
November 2007	$825,601.87
December 2007	$991,548.75
July 2008	$890,547.41
January 2008	$656,766.69
February 2008	$600,080.00
March 2008	$559,538.52
April 2008	$999,667.17
May 2008	$893,231.96
June 2008	$845,141.60

FIGURE 8-9 An incorrect sorting by year.

One solution is to get a column with the correct granularity specifically to sort the Calendar Year Month column. For example, you might create a calculated column using the following definition:

```
Date[Calendar Year Month Number] = 'Date'[Calendar Year Number] * 100 + 'Date'[Month Number]
```

This expression, for example, returns the value 200707 for the month of July 2007. You can also create the column in your relational data source using a similar logic in the view you use in the relational database. (Using views to retrieve data for a tabular model is always a good practice.) In Figure 8-10, you can see the value of the Calendar Year Month Number column that has the same granularity as the Calendar Year Month column.

FIGURE 8-10 The Calendar Year Month Number column.

In Figure 8-11, you see that the Calendar Year Month content is now sorted properly in the Pivot-Table after the Calendar Year Month Number column is used in the Sort by Column property.

Row Labels	Sales Amount
January 2007	$794,248.24
February 2007	$891,135.91
March 2007	$961,289.24
April 2007	$1,128,104.82
May 2007	$936,192.74
June 2007	$982,304.46
July 2007	$922,542.98
August 2007	$952,834.59
September 2007	$1,009,868.98
October 2007	$914,273.54
November 2007	$825,601.87
December 2007	$991,548.75
January 2008	$656,766.69
February 2008	$600,080.00
March 2008	$559,538.52
April 2008	$999,667.17

FIGURE 8-11 The Calendar Year Month column, sorted correctly.

> **Note** Analysis Services checks that a column of appropriate granularity is used for Sort by Column only when that property is first set. Therefore, new data can be loaded into the table that breaks the sorting, with no errors raised. You must be careful that this does not happen. Including a check for this in your extract, transform, and load (ETL) process might be a good idea.

Formatting

You can apply formatting to numeric values in columns and measures. It is important to do this because unformatted, or raw, values can be extremely difficult to read and interpret.

Formatting columns

You can set number formats for numeric data in both normal columns and calculated columns with the Data Format property. The values available for this property are determined by the value of the Data Type property, discussed in Chapter 3, "Loading data inside Tabular," and the type is set for the values held in the column. Depending on the value selected for Data Format, other properties might become enabled that further control formatting. As with the Sort by Column property, number formatting is applied automatically only when connecting through an MDX client tool. DAX queries do not display formatted values. They display only the raw data. If you are running DAX queries, you must read the metadata to determine the appropriate format and then apply it to your results yourself.

The available Data Format property values for each data type (excluding Text) are as follows:

■ For the Date type, a General format shows the date and time in the default format for the locale of the client that is querying the model. (See the following for more details about how language affects formatting.) There is also a long list of built-in formats for showing dates, times and dates, and times together in different formats. In addition, you can enter your own formats.

■ For the Whole Number and Decimal Number types, the following formats are available:

- **General** This shows the number in the default format for the client tool.

- **Decimal Number** This shows the value formatted as a decimal number. When this format is selected, two further properties are enabled:

  - **Decimal Places** This sets the number of decimal places displayed.

  - **Show Thousand Separator** This sets whether the thousand separator that is appropriate for the language of the client is displayed.

- **Whole Number** This formats the value as a whole number. The Show Thousand Separator property is enabled when this format is selected.

- **Currency** This formats the value as a monetary value. When this format is selected, two further properties are enabled:

  - **Decimal Places** By default, this is set to 2.

  - **Currency Symbol** This sets the currency symbol used in the format. The default symbol used is the symbol associated with the language of the model.

- **Percentage** This formats the value as a percentage. Note that the formatted value appears to be multiplied by 100, so a raw value of 0.96 will be displayed as 96%. The Decimal Places and Show Thousand Separator properties are enabled when this format is selected.

- **Scientific** This formats the value in scientific form using exponential (e) notation. (For more details on scientific form, see *http://en.wikipedia.org/wiki/Scientific_notation*.) The Decimal Places property is enabled when this format is selected.

- **Custom** This allows the introduction of any custom format string in the Format String property. However, any format string that corresponds to one of the patterns described by other formats is automatically converted in said format description in the SSDT user interface.

■ For the True/False type, values can be formatted as TRUE or FALSE only.

Note Number formats in the tabular model are designed to be consistent with PowerPivot, which is designed to be consistent with Excel.

Formatting measures

You can format measures in much the same way as columns. However, in the case of measures, the property used is Format. The property values available for Format are the same as the values available for the Data Format property of a column.

> ## Formatting internals
>
> The information provided to the Data Format and Format properties of calculated columns and measures is different from the one stored in the tabular model. If you look into the settings of the Unit Cost column in the Product table, you'll see that the formatString property has a single string with all the details about the format of the column. You store settings defined in the SSDT user interface in the annotations by using an XML structure that is embedded in a single string for the Format annotation. See the following example:
>
> ```
> {
>   "name": "Unit Cost",
>   "dataType": "decimal",
>   "sourceColumn": "Unit Cost",
>   "formatString": "\\$#,0.00;(\\$#,0.00);\\$#,0.00",
>   "sourceProviderType": "Currency",
>   "displayFolder": "Pricing",
>   "annotations": [
>     {
>       "name": "Format",
>       "value": "<Format Format=\"Currency\" Accuracy=\"2\"ThousandSepa
> rator=\"True\"><Currency LCID=\"1033\" DisplayName=\"$ English (United States)\"
> Symbol=\"$\" PositivePattern=\"0\" NegativePattern=\"0\" /></Format>
>     }
>   ]
> },
> ```
>
> If you manually edit the text of the model file (or create the JSON file from scratch), you obtain a valid model by just defining the formatString property in the JSON file. The lack of annotations will only affect SSDT, which will display the Data Format as Custom. You will see the formatString property in JSON represented in the Format String property in SSDT.

Language and Collation properties

A tabular model has both a Language property and a Collation property (visible in the Property pane when the BIM file of your model is selected in Solution Explorer in SSDT). Both are fixed when the model is created, and they cannot be changed. The collation of a model controls how the sorting and comparison of values behave. The Language of a model influences how formatting takes place for the General formats for dates and numeric values (for example, it controls the default currency symbol used), but you can and should override these defaults when configuring the Data Format and Format properties. The locale of the machine that is querying the tabular model also plays an important role.

For example, the date of the 4th of August, 2012, when formatted using the General format, will be displayed as 8/4/2012 00:00:00 on a machine that uses the English (US) locale, but it will be displayed as 04/08/2012 00:00:00 on a machine that uses the English (UK) locale. In a similar case, the thousands and decimal separators vary by locale. A value that is displayed as 123,456.789 in the English (US) locale will be displayed as 123.456,789 in the Italian locale.

The following links describe in more detail how languages and collations work and how they are set when a model is created:

- *https://msdn.microsoft.com/en-us/library/ms174872(v=sql.130).aspx*

- *https://blogs.msdn.microsoft.com/cathyk/2011/10/21/collation-and-language-settings-in-tabular-models/*

Perspectives

Most tabular models that work on large and complex data sources contain many tables, each with many columns in it. Although hiding tables and columns that should never be used in queries or reports will go a long way toward improving the usability of a model, it may still be the case that some groups of users will never want to see or use some parts of the model. For example, if a single model contains data from the HR, Marketing, and Finance departments, some users want to see and use all this data. However, it is equally possible that some users in the HR department want to use only the HR data, while some users in Marketing will want to use only the Marketing data, and so on. Perspectives enable you to meet this requirement by creating something like a view in a relational database. You can create what looks like a new model for specific groups of users by hiding the parts of the underlying model that these users do not want to see.

To create a new perspective, follow these steps:

1. Open the **Model** menu in SSDT, choose **Perspectives**, and select **Create and Manage**. This opens the Perspectives dialog box, which displays all perspectives in the model.

2. Click the **New Perspective** button.

3. Enter a name for the new perspective at the top of the new column that appears.

4. Select all the fields and measures in the dialog box under the new perspective's name to add them to the perspective, as shown in Figure 8-12. Then click **OK**.

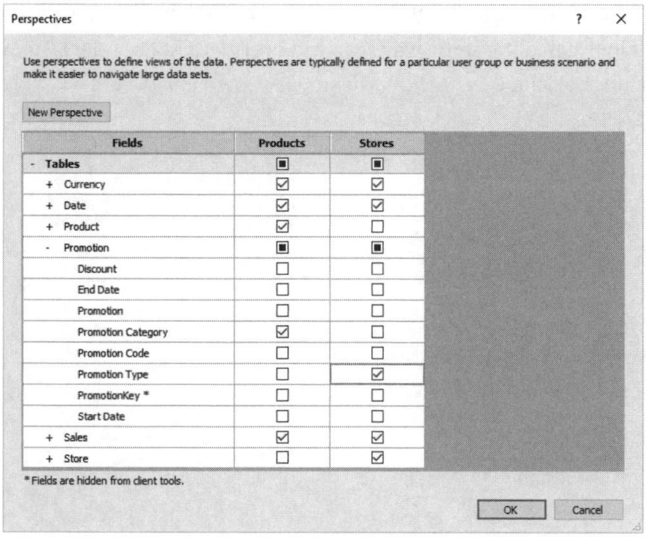

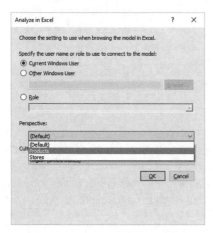

FIGURE 8-12 The Perspectives dialog box.

You can use the perspective in SSDT. To do so, open the **Model** menu, select **Perspectives**, choose **Select**, and select the perspective's name. This hides tables and columns not included in the perspective from the SSDT user interface. This could be useful to reduce the number of tables you operate with when editing a large data model. To test a perspective from the user point of view, click the **Analyze in Excel** button on the toolbar in SSDT. Then, in the Analyze in Excel dialog box, open the **Perspective** drop-down menu and choose the name of the desired perspective, as shown in Figure 8-13.

FIGURE 8-13 Choosing a perspective to test.

This opens Excel with a new PivotTable connected to the perspective. As an alternative, if you want to create a new connection yourself in Excel in the same way that end users would do, select the perspective name from the list of cubes in the Data Connection Wizard, as shown in Figure 8-14.

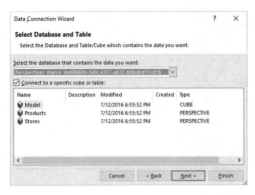

FIGURE 8-14 Connecting to a perspective by using Excel.

Note that in the PivotTable field list, you can see only the tables, measures, and columns that you added to the perspective. In all other respects, however, the experience is the same as querying the whole model. You will have a similar user experience in Power BI when you connect live to a tabular model. After selecting the server, you can select one of the available perspectives to use in the list under the database name. The default name of the data model is *Model*, but it could be modified in the Cube Name property of the project property dialog box in SSDT.

> **Important** Perspectives are not a substitute for security and cannot be secured as objects. Even if a user cannot see an object in a perspective, that user can still write DAX or MDX queries that return data from those objects if he or she knows the object's name.

Power View–related properties

Several properties in the tabular model act as metadata for Power View (or any other client tools that want to read them), influencing how the model is displayed in a client tool. However, the PivotTable in Excel does not directly use the metadata that is specific for Tabular, nor does Power BI support many of these properties (as of January 2017). Thus, you must pay attention to which clients support each of these properties.

Default field set

The default field set for a table is a set of columns and measures that is displayed automatically in a Power View canvas when a user double-clicks that table in the field list. As of January 2017, a similar feature is not available in Power BI, but it could be implemented in future releases. Setting up a default field set makes it faster for Power View users to create a report because it reduces the amount of dragging and dropping needed.

To set up a default field set, follow these steps:

1. Select the table in SSDT and click the **Default Field Set** property or select a measure or column in a table and click the **Table Detail Position** property. This opens the Default Field Set dialog box, shown in Figure 8-15.

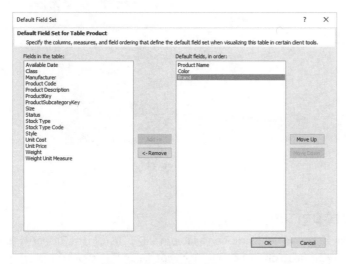

FIGURE 8-15   The Default Field Set dialog box.

2. Specify which columns and measures are to be displayed in the default field set and the order in which they should appear. This information is stored as a 1-based index in the Table Detail Position property for a column or measure.

3. After the model has been saved and deployed, connect to the model in a Power View report in Excel. Then double-click the name of the table in the field list to create a table on the canvas that contains the selected columns and measures, as shown in Figure 8-16.

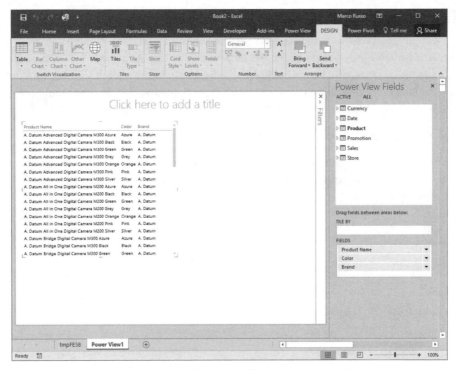

FIGURE 8-16 A sample report obtained by double-clicking the Product table.

Table behavior properties

You can find the table behavior properties by clicking a table in SSDT. Then, in the Properties pane, click the **Table Behavior** property group to open the Table Behavior dialog box, shown in Figure 8-17. (Do not try to expand the property group in the pane and edit the properties outside the dialog box. It is not possible to do this, except for the Keep Unique Rows property, but there is a specific dialog box for that.)

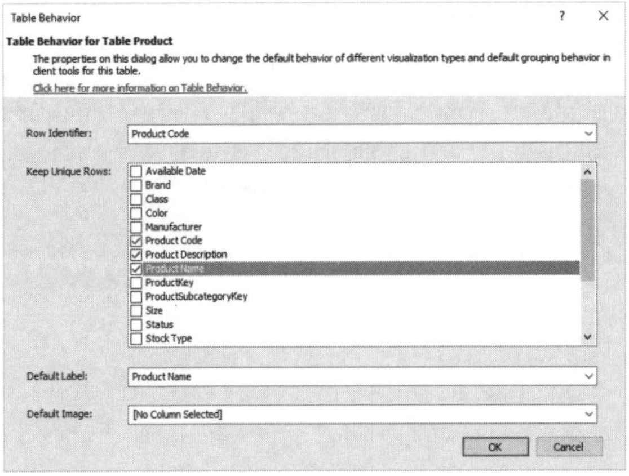

FIGURE 8-17 The Table Behavior dialog box.

The properties that can be set in this dialog box are as follows:

- **Row Identifier** This property enables you to specify a single column to act like the primary key of the table. (Note that it must have a unique value for each row.) You can also modify the corresponding Row Identifier property on a column. Just be aware that setting a column to True will set all the other columns to False. Setting a Row Identifier property also enables the Keep Unique Rows, Default Label, and Default Image properties. It also affects where subtotals are displayed in Matrix controls in reports. The process of marking a table as a Date table, which you saw at the beginning of this chapter, involves setting the Row Identifier property. After this is done, you cannot change the Row Identifier property manually. Finally, the Row Identifier property can be useful to avoid circular dependencies in a calculated column if a table does not have relationships with other related tables, as explained in *https://www.sqlbi.com/articles/understanding-circular-dependencies/*.

- **Keep Unique Rows** This property enables you to select columns whose uniqueness is determined by the column specified in the Row Identifier property when used in a Power BI or Power View report. For example, this would be important on a Customer dimension table in which some customers might have the same name. If there were a Customer Key column with a numeric key that identified individual customers, as well as a Customer Name column, you could set the Row Identifier property of the table to Customer Key and specify Customer Name in Keep Unique Rows. That way, when you use the Customer Name column alone in a table in a Power BI report, there is one row for each unique customer, not for each unique name. That is, if there were two customers with the name John Smith, there would be two rows with that name. This property does not have any automatic effect on DAX queries. It simply informs Power BI (and any other clients that look at this property in the metadata, such as Power View) that it should include the column specified in Row Identifier in any queries that use any of the columns selected in the Keep Unique Rows property. Note that the PivotTable in Excel does not use this property.

- **Default Label** This property sets the column that contains the name or label that should be used for each unique row in the table. For example, consider the Customer dimension table example used in the previous bullet. If each row in the table represents a customer, the Customer Name column should be used as the Default Label. This property is used as the default label for a card or a chart in a Power View report. Power BI ignores this property.

- **Default Image** This property sets the column that contains either binary data that contains an image or text data that can be interpreted as the URL of an image. (For a text column to be selectable in this case, it must have its Image URL property set to True.) This image is then used by Power View either in the navigation pane of a tile report or on the front of a card. Power BI ignores this property.

As noted, many of these properties are not used by Power BI. They exist only for compatibility with Power View reports. Because the most important property (Row Identifier) is also available in the columns' properties, you can create a data model in Tabular and ignore the settings in the Table Behavior dialog box if your users do not use Power View as a client.

Key performance indicators

A *key performance indicator* (*KPI*) is a way of comparing the value of one measure with another. For example, you might want to analyze profitability by comparing the cost of goods used to make a product with the value at which the product is sold, or to see whether the time taken to deal with support calls on a help desk is within the acceptable thresholds.

To create a KPI in a tabular model, you must start with an existing measure. In this case, we will use the Sales table in Contoso. Follow these steps:

1. Create the following measures: Sales Amount, Cost, Margin, and Margin %. (These are also shown in Figure 8-18.)

   ```
   Sales[Sales Amount] := SUMX ( Sales, Sales[Net Price] * Sales[Quantity] )
   ```

   ```
   Sales[Cost] := SUMX ( Sales, Sales[Unit Cost] * Sales[Quantity] )
   ```

   ```
   Sales[Margin] := [Sales Amount] - [Cost]
   ```

   ```
   Sales[Margin%] := [Margin] / [Sales Amount]
   ```

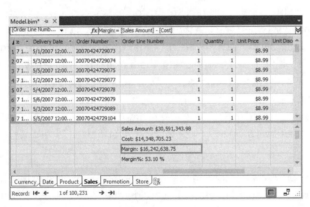

FIGURE 8-18   The measures used in the KPI example.

2. Select the Margin measure and click the **Create KPI** button in the toolbar. Alternatively, right-click the measure and choose **Create KPI** from the context menu. This opens the Key Performance Indicator (KPI) dialog box, shown in Figure 8-19. The disabled KPI Base Measure (Value) drop-down list displays the name of the measure you have just selected.

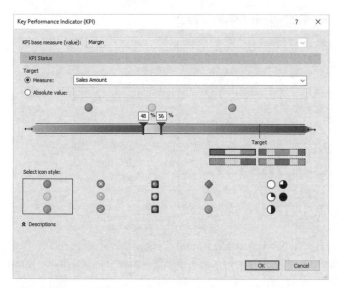

FIGURE 8-19 The Key Performance Indicator (KPI) dialog box.

3. Define a target value. This can be either another measure in the model or an absolute value, which you must enter. In this example, select the Sales Amount measure. The ratio of the base measure to the target is compared to a set of thresholds that determine the status: good, intermediate, or bad.

4. Click one of the four rectangular boxes in the center-right portion of the dialog box to choose a threshold type. For example, the top-left threshold type defines a low ratio value as bad (red), a middling ratio value as intermediate (yellow), and a high ratio value as good (green). In contrast, the bottom-left threshold type defines a low ratio value as good, a middling ratio value as intermediate, and a high ratio value as bad. In this case, select the top-left box.

5. Use the slider in the center of the screen, above the boxes, to set the threshold values as percentages. In this example, set a value of 48% for the lower threshold and 56% for the higher threshold.

6. Select an icon style for your client tools to use. (Note that the client tool will not necessarily use the icons shown in the dialog box; this is just a guide to the *style* of icon to use.)

7. Click the **Descriptions** arrow in the bottom-left corner of the dialog box to display a series of text boxes. Here, you can enter a description for the KPI, the value, the status, and the target.

8. Click **OK**. The KPI appears in the measure grid in SSDT in the same place as the base measure, as shown in Figure 8-20. You can edit the KPI by right-clicking that cell.

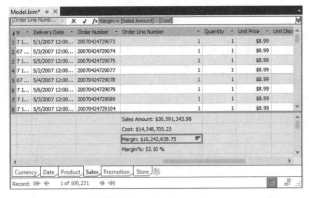

FIGURE 8-20 A KPI in the measure grid.

After the KPI has been created, it can be used in several clients, such as an Excel PivotTable or a Power BI report, as shown in Figure 8-21. It appears as a special semaphore icon in the list of fields, which contains three measures:

- **Value** This is the value of the measure.

- **Goal** This corresponds to the value of the target measure.

- **Status** This is the KPI icon.

These last two names are displayed in the report as suffixes of the original measure name, so you can include multiple KPIs in the same report.

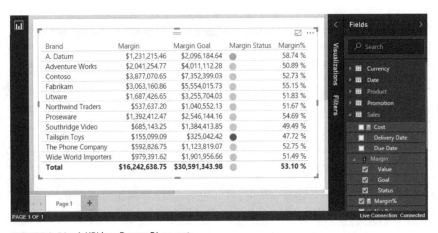

FIGURE 8-21 A KPI in a Power BI report.

Translations

The entities of the semantic model defined by Analysis Services Tabular can be translated in other languages and cultures. Such a feature is available in models created at the 1200 compatibility level, but it is not supported in previous compatibility levels. The feature available for tabular models translates only object metadata, such as column, table, and measure names. However, it does not support loading translated data, such as the translation of product names or descriptions. That feature is available in a multidimensional model, even in previous versions of Analysis Services.

Translations using BIDS Helper and upgrade issues

Translations were not supported in previous versions of Analysis Services Tabular. However, the model compatibility level 110*x* does allow for the creation of translations for metadata, by using the same technique employed for multidimensional models. Such a translation is available only for MDX clients, such as a PivotTable in Excel. For this reason, it was used by several developers even though it was not supported by Microsoft. To make it easier to insert the translations in the XMLA content, a community tool named BIDS Helper (*https://bidshelper.codeplex.com/*) provides a user interface to insert translated names into the data model. If you use such a feature, you will lose all the translations when migrating the model to the 1200 compatibility level. Also, you must create translations from scratch by using the procedure described in this section. Alternatively, you can migrate the existing translations using the procedure described by Daniel Otykier at *http://www.kapacity.dk/migrating-ssas-tabular-models-to-sql-server-2016-translations-and-display-folders/*.

The translated metadata is included in the JSON file that contains the definition of the tabular data model. These translations are in a specific section of the data model: `cultures`. Every object has a reference to the original element in the data model, and properties such as `translatedCaption`, `translatedDescription`, and `translatedDisplayFolder` contain the corresponding translated strings, as shown in Figure 8-22.

```
 1    ⊟{
 2        "name": "SemanticModel",
 3        "compatibilityLevel": 1200,
 4    ⊟    "model": {
 5            "culture": "en-US",
 6    ⊞      "dataSources": [...],
19    ⊞      "tables": [...],
650   ⊞      "relationships": [...],
673   ⊟      "cultures": [
674            {
675                "name": "it-IT",
676   ⊟            "translations": {
677   ⊟                "model": {
678                        "name": "Model",
679   ⊟                    "tables": [
680   ⊞                      [...],
698   ⊞                      [...],
808   ⊟                        {
809                            "name": "Product",
810                            "translatedCaption": "Prodotto",
811   ⊟                        "columns": [
812   ⊞                          [...],
816   ⊞                          [...],
820   ⊞                          [...],
824   ⊞                          [...],
828   ⊞                          [...],
832   ⊟                            {
833                                "name": "Manufacturer",
834                                "translatedCaption": "Produttore",
835                                "translatedDisplayFolder": "Info"
836                            },
```

FIGURE 8-22 The Italian translation included in a BIM model file.

SSDT does not provide a user interface to directly manipulate the translations in the tabular model. Instead, you can export a file that contains only the translations in one or more languages. You can then import this file back into the model. The idea is that you initially export an empty translation file, which you pass to someone who can insert the translated names in the proper places. Once the translation file contains the translated names, you import this file in the data model. SSDT provides tools to export and import translation files, requiring you to complete the following steps:

1. Create a translation file.

2. Write translated names in translation file.

3. Import a translation file.

4. Test translations using a client tool.

In the following sections, you will see a description of these steps and a few best practices to avoid common mistakes.

Creating a translation file

You export a translation file from a data model by using the Manage Translations dialog box in SSDT. Follow these steps:

1. Open the **Model** menu, choose **Translations**, and select **Manage Translations** to open the Manage Translations dialog box. The first time you open this dialog box, you can choose the languages you want to add as translations in your data model, as shown in Figure 8-23.

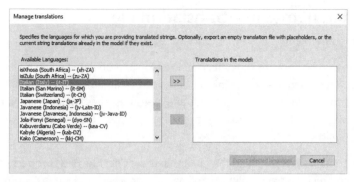

FIGURE 8-23 The Manage Translations dialog box.

2. Select one or more languages on the left side of the dialog box and click the **>>** button to add the selected languages to the list on the right, as shown in Figure 8-24.

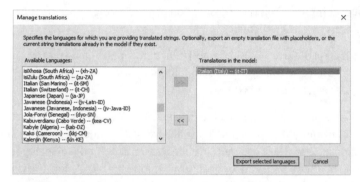

FIGURE 8-24 The selection that is required to export the file for Italian translation.

3. Select one or more languages in the list on the right side and click the **Export Selected Languages** button. This creates a single JSON file that contains placeholders to insert the translations for all the languages selected.

> **Tip** Even If you can export more languages in the same file, it is probably better to have only one file for each language.

4. Name and save the file. Then give it to someone who can translate the names from your tabular data model into the selected language.

Writing translated names in a translation file

The JSON file that contains translations has two important sections:

- **referenceCulture**   This contains the objects of the tabular model that could be translated, such as tables, columns, and measures. This is where you can find the original names, the descriptions, and the display folders of columns and measures. These names should not be changed—if they are, the changes will be ignored during import. They simply provide a reference for the translation.

- **cultures**   This contains a reference to the objects in the model (the name property of tables, columns, and measures). It also contains the following properties for the translations, which are initially empty strings:

  - **translatedCaption**   This is the name of the table, column, or measure that is displayed to the users.

  - **translatedDescription**   This is the description of a table, column, or measure that can be displayed to users by certain clients.

  - **translatedDisplayFolder**   This is the translation of the folder name that is used to group columns and measures. In the case of nested folders, it includes the path of the folders separated by backslash characters (\).

The file created by the Manage Translations dialog box initially contains empty strings for translated names. If imported, an empty string will not define any translation, and the original name will be displayed in the translation instead. Thus, you must include a string only for the objects you need to translate. Because it could be useful to see the original string during the translation, the structure of the file requires you to keep two copies of the file open or to split the editor window in two parts.

Figure 8-25 shows an empty translation file opened in Visual Studio using the JSON editor. The upper part of the JSON editor in Visual Studio 2015 contains information about the original value of displayFolder and its description properties (the latter is not included in this example). The lower part shows the same tables and columns in the cultures section. If you consider the Manufacturer column of the Product table, you probably need to know the original value of displayFolder (Info) to write the translated version in the translatedDisplayFolder property. This round trip is usually not necessary for the translatedCaption property because the name property is also the original caption in the data model.

FIGURE 8-25 The translation file that contains the original model and the translated properties in two different sections.

> **Note** The JSON editor is available only if you installed a complete version of Visual Studio 2015, not just the shell that is required by SSDT. The Visual Studio Community edition includes the JSON editor. It is a free tool, and you can download it from *https://www.visualstudio.com/downloads/download-visual-studio-vs.aspx*.

Choosing an editor for translation files

You do not need Visual Studio to edit translation files. You can use any text editor for that. One alternative to Visual Studio is Notepad++ (*https://notepad-plus-plus.org/*), which correctly manages the encoding of the files that are required for translations. Because several languages use non-ANSI characters, however, you must make sure that the file is saved in Unicode UTF-8. This is the file type generated by the export language feature you saw earlier. It is also the encoding expected by the import feature discussed in the next section.

If you do use Visual Studio, be aware that by default, JSON files that contain no ANSI characters higher than 127 are saved as a standard ANSI file, without using Unicode. Visual Studio controls this behavior via the Save with Encoding option of the Save File As dialog box, which displays the Advanced Save Options dialog box shown in Figure 8-26. Be sure you have the same Encoding settings for your translation file when you save it from Visual Studio. Otherwise, many special characters used in specific languages will be converted incorrectly.

FIGURE 8-26 The correct encoding setting for JSON translation files that are saved by Visual Studio.

 Important If you create the initial model in the English language, chances are the translation file does not contain any special character. Therefore, if you open it in Visual Studio, it will not be saved as Unicode, even if you create strings that use special characters. If you see strange characters in the resulting data model, reopen the translation file in Visual Studio and save it using the encoding settings shown in Figure 8-26. Then import the translation again.

The JSON format is not very user-friendly, but at least it is a text file. However, it is relatively easy to load a JSON file in a program that provides a better user experience. You might want to write your own script to transform the JSON format into a simpler file to edit. Or you could use some specific editor to manipulate such a file format. Kasper De Jonge has created an initial release of a tool named *Tabular Translator*, which receives updates from other contributors. You will find links to download the executable and source code at *https://www.sqlbi.com/tools/ssas-tabular-translator/*. The user interface of this tool is shown in Figure 8-27. Such a system displays the original and translated names of each entity in a single row, making it easier to manage the translation files. Tabular Translator also manages more languages that are included in the same translation file.

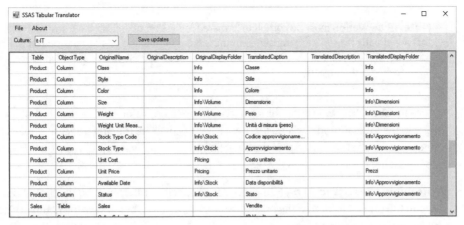

FIGURE 8-27   SSAS Tabular Translator, which edits the contents of a JSON translation file.

Importing a translation file

After you obtain the translated file, you must import it in the tabular model. Follow these steps:

1. Open the **Model** menu, choose **Translations**, and select **Import Translations**. This opens the Import Translations dialog box shown in Figure 8-28.

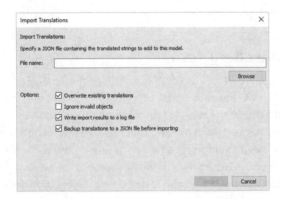

FIGURE 8-28   The Import Translations dialog box.

2. Choose the file to import.

3. Select any of the following options, according to your needs:

   - **Overwrite Existing Translations**   When this option is unchecked, only languages that are not already defined in the tabular model are imported. When it is checked, languages already defined in the tabular model are overwritten.

> **Note** A translation must be complete. If there are missing objects in the translation file that are already present and translated in the tabular model, the existing translation will be removed, and only the translations included in the imported file will be stored in the tabular model after the import.

- **Ignore Invalid Objects** When this option is checked, any reference to objects that are no longer in the tabular model will be ignored. If it is unchecked, then references to objects no longer in the model will cause the import action to stop and will display a dialog box with an error message.

- **Write Import Results to a Log File** This option specifies whether a log file should be saved in the project folder. At the end of the import, a dialog box shows the complete path and file name of the log file saved.

- **Backup Translations to a JSON** If this option is checked, a JSON file is created with the backup of the translations for only the languages that are imported. It is useful when you select the Overwrite Existing Translations check box and you want to be able to recover the previous version of the translation if something goes wrong. The backup is created in the project folder with a name that includes the date and time of the operation.

4. Click the **Import** button. If there are no errors, your model will include the new translations.

5. Save the model file. If you do not do so, the previous version of the translations will remain.

Testing translations using a client tool

To test the translations, you must use a client tool that can display translated metadata. For example, the PivotTable in Excel supports translations of the data model, and you can connect the PivotTable by enforcing a particular culture setting in the connection string, overriding the default culture that is inherited by default user settings. Thanks to the default behavior, Tabular users will typically get their favorite language automatically, but you need to enforce a different culture in case you want to test the translations. The easiest way to do that is to use the Analyze in Excel dialog box, shown in figure 8-29. (To open it, click the **Analyze in Excel** button in Visual Studio.) The Culture setting provides a list of the available translations, and you can choose the one you want to use.

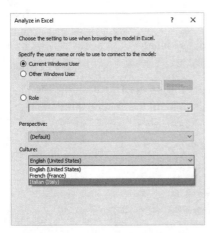

FIGURE 8-29 The Analyze in Excel dialog box, with the available Culture settings shown.

When you're finished, you can navigate in a PivotTable that displays the translated names of tables, columns, hierarchies, folders, measures, and KPIs, as shown in Figure 8-30. This way, you can verify that at least all the visible objects have been translated.

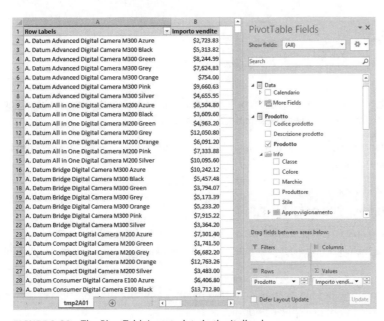

FIGURE 8-30 The PivotTable's metadata in the Italian language.

Note The translation file contains all the objects, regardless of their visibility state. When you navigate in the PivotTable, you can see only the visible objects, not the hidden ones. Although it is a good idea to also translate invisible objects, it is not strictly required for the user interface because they will never be displayed to the user.

Removing a translation

You can remove a translation from a tabular model by using the Manage Translations dialog box in SSDT. Follow these steps:

1. Open the **Model** menu, choose **Translations**, and select **Manage Translations**. The Manage Translations dialog box opens. The right pane contains a list of the existing translations, as shown in Figure 8-31.

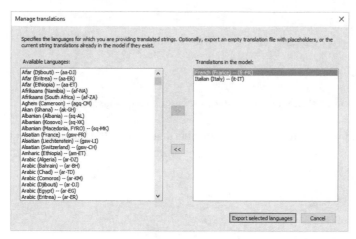

FIGURE 8-31 The selection that is required to remove the French translation.

2. Select one or more languages in the right pane and click the << button to remove the selected languages from the model. This removes all the translated strings.

3. A dialog box appears to confirm the removal, which is irreversible. Click **Export Selected Languages** to complete the operation.

Best practices using translations

When you manage translations, you export and import parts of the tabular model in JSON format. Therefore, you should use the following best practices to avoid problems during project development and maintenance:

- Export only one language per file. Managing different languages in the same file can be complex, especially if you do not use specific editors.

- After you export the translation file, do not rename any object in the tabular model. If the translation references an object that you later rename in the model, subsequent import operations will fail. To complete the import, you must rename the same object in the translation file before importing it or restore the original name of the object in the model.

- If you create new objects in the data model after you export a translation file, these objects will not be translated after you import the translation. You must export a new file. Note, however, that the translation file contains all the objects, so you cannot merge partial translations and/or export only the new strings that require a translation. Due to these limitations, you should start the translation at the very end of the project lifecycle.

- If you use the JSON editor in Visual Studio to edit the translation files, remember to save them using the Unicode UTF-8 encoding.

- Consider using specific editors for translation files, such as the SSAS Tabular Translator (*https://www.sqlbi.com/tools/ssas-tabular-translator/*).

Selecting culture and collation in a tabular model

Every tabular model has two settings that affect the formatting, sort order, and string comparisons: Language and Collation. These settings appear as read-only properties of the model, and they cannot be changed in the Visual Studio user interface. You must change them in the JSON file, following the instructions described later in this section.

The Language property defines the character set to use for strings. By default, it corresponds to the current Windows language identifier when you create a new tabular project. For example, Figure 8-32 shows the Language property set to English (United States).

FIGURE 8-32 The properties of the Model.bim file, which include the Language setting.

The Language property corresponds to the `culture` property in the JSON file, which you can open by using the **View Code** context menu in the Solution Explorer window. Figure 8-33 shows an excerpt of the JSON file.

```
1   {
2       "name": "SemanticModel",
3       "compatibilityLevel": 1200,
4       "model": {
5           "culture": "en-US",
6           "dataSources": [
7               {
```

FIGURE 8-33 The `culture` property in the model section that corresponds to the Language property.

The Collation property defines the ordering of characters and their equivalence, which affects the way string comparisons are made. Every instance of SQL Server Analysis Services (SSAS) has a default collation that is defined during setup. Every model that does not specify a particular collation will inherit the behavior defined by the default collation of the SSAS instance. By default, Visual Studio does not set the Collation property for a new empty tabular project. The Collation property corresponds to the `collation` property in the JSON file. Figure 8-34 shows a JSON file where both the `culture` and `collation` properties are explicitly set to specific values.

```
1  ⊟{
2      "name": "SemanticModel",
3      "compatibilityLevel": 1200,
4  ⊟  "model": {
5          "culture": "it-IT",
6          "collation": "Latin1_General_CS_AS",
```

FIGURE 8-34 The `culture` and `collation` properties, which are explicitly set in a Model.bim file.

As a quick reference, the following are commonly used values of the `collation` property, which use different styles of the `Latin1_General` collation designer:

- **Latin1_General_CS_AS** Case-sensitive, accent-sensitive

- **Latin1_General_CS_AI** Case-sensitive, accent-insensitive

- **Latin1_General_CI_AS** Case insensitive, accent sensitive

- **Latin1_General_CI_AI** Case insensitive, accent insensitive

The values available for the collation are the same for SQL Server. You can find a complete description of these values at *https://msdn.microsoft.com/en-us/library/ff848763.aspx* and a detailed explanation of the collation options at *https://msdn.microsoft.com/en-us/library/ms143726.aspx#Collation_Defn*.

If you want to modify the `culture` and/or `collation` properties in the JSON file, the deployment of the model must happen on a server where such a database does not exist. That means you must remove the workspace database to apply the change in Visual Studio, and you must delete an existing deployed database before deploying such a change. If you try to modify one of these properties, you will get the following error message when you try to deploy the database or try to open the designer window in Visual Studio:

> Culture and Collation properties of the Model object may be changed only before any other object has been created.

Removing a workspace database in Visual Studio to apply these changes is not intuitive. You can find a step-by-step description of this procedure in the following sections, depending on the type of workspace database you have: integrated workspace or workspace server.

Changing culture and collation using an integrated workspace

If you have an integrated workspace, you must close Visual Studio before removing the directory that contains the files of the workspace database. When you reopen Visual Studio, the workspace database is created from scratch using the new settings. Follow these steps:

1. Open the context menu in the Solution Explorer and choose **View Code** to open the JSON file in Visual Studio.

2. Modify or add the `culture` and/or `collation` settings in the model object using the same syntax you saw in Figure 8-34.

3. Save and close the Model.bim file in Visual Studio.

4. Select the Model.bim file in the Solution Explorer window and take note of the file's `Full Path` property. You need to know the directory where the Model.bim file is stored. (We will refer to this directory as <path> in the following steps.)

5. Close Visual Studio.

6. Open Windows Explorer and point to the <path>\bin folder.

7. Remove the Data folder in <path>\bin.

8. Open Visual Studio and use the designer to open the tabular model. Visual Studio automatically creates a new version of the data model in the integrated workspace.

9. Open the **Model** menu, choose **Process**, and select **Process All** to process the model.

At the end of these steps, you will have a tabular model in the integrated workspace that uses the Language and Collation settings that correspond to the `culture` and `collation` properties you specified in the Model.bim file.

Changing culture and collation using a workspace server

If you have a workspace server, you need not close Visual Studio before removing the workspace database form the workspace server. Instead, you close the designer window. Follow these steps:

1. Open the context menu in the Solution Explorer and choose **View Code** to open the JSON file in Visual Studio. When you do, Visual Studio also checks that you do not have a designer window open on the same file.

2. Modify or add the `culture` and/or `collation` settings in the model object using the same syntax you saw in Figure 8-34.

3. Save and close the Model.bim file in Visual Studio.

4. Select the Model.bim file in the Solution Explorer window and take note of the file's Workspace Database and Workspace Server properties.

5. Open SQL Server Management Studio (SSMS) and connect to the Tabular instance specified by the Workspace Server property of the tabular model.

6. In SSMS, select and delete the tabular database that corresponds to the name specified in the Workspace Server property of the tabular model.

7. Switch to Visual Studio and use the designer to open the tabular model. Visual Studio automatically creates a new version of the data model in the workspace server.

8. Open the **Model** menu, choose **Process**, and select **Process All** to process the model.

At the end of these steps, you have a tabular model in the workspace server that uses the Language and Collation settings that correspond to the `culture` and `collation` properties that you specified in the Model.bim file.

Summary

In this chapter, you learned how important usability and a professional presentation is to tabular models, as well as the various features available to improve the experience of your end users. Naming, hiding or showing, sorting, and formatting columns and measures, as well as providing translations and creating perspectives and KPIs, can make the difference between your model being rejected or embraced by your users. Therefore, they determine the success of your project. If you are using Power View on your project, configuring the Default Field Set and Table Behavior properties can make creating reports much easier for users.

Using DirectQuery

As you saw in Chapter 1, "Introducing the tabular model," you can deploy a tabular model using either in-memory mode (VertiPaq) or pass-through SQL queries to relational sources (DirectQuery). This chapter covers the DirectQuery storage mode. You will learn how to configure DirectQuery, what are the limitations in a data model with regard to supporting DirectQuery, and what to consider before deciding whether to adopt DirectQuery.

You can apply DirectQuery to a model that was originally defined using VertiPaq. However, this is possible only if the model does not have any of the unsupported features. Therefore, it is important to be aware of the features that would disallow a switch to DirectQuery mode if you want to keep this option available at a later stage.

DirectQuery has very different behavior and configuration settings between the model-compatibility levels 110x and 1200 (or later). This book focuses only on DirectQuery for model-compatibility levels greater than or equal to 1200. It ignores the previous version, which had a completely different (and more complex) configuration. The previous version of DirectQuery also offered limited support of data sources, had more limitations in data modeling and DAX, and had very serious performance issues that limited the adoption of such a solution.

If you have a legacy data model using DirectQuery, consider migrating it to the 1200 compatibility level. In the new model, table partitions that are not defined for DirectQuery are considered sample data, removing the formal definition of hybrid models. In practice, you can still have data in memory for a DirectQuery model, but the purpose of it is to offer a quick preview of the data rather than act as a real on-demand choice between DirectQuery and VertiPaq (as hybrid modes were conceived in previous versions of Analysis Services).

What's new in SSAS 2016 DirectQuery has undergone a complete overhaul in Analysis Services 2016. This chapter reflects the new design and user interface of this feature.

Configuring DirectQuery

Enabling DirectQuery involves a single setting at the data-model level, which affects the entire tabular model. When a model is in DirectQuery mode, VertiPaq does not persist any data in memory (unless you define sample partitions). The process operation simply updates the metadata, mapping the entities of the tabular model to the tables in the data source. When DirectQuery is enabled, any DAX or MDX query is translated into one or more SQL queries, always getting data that is up to date.

You can switch a model to DirectQuery in one of the following two ways:

- During development, use SQL Server Data Tools (SSDT) to activate the DirectQuery Mode setting in the model properties.

- After deployment, use SQL Server Management Studio (SSMS) to set the model's Default Mode property to DirectQuery or apply an equivalent change using PowerShell, TMSL, or XMLA.

Setting DirectQuery in a development environment

When you create a new data model using SSDT, the DirectQuery Mode setting shown in Figure 9-1 is set to Off by default. This means the data in all the tables is imported into VertiPaq. You can see a preview of the data in the grid view.

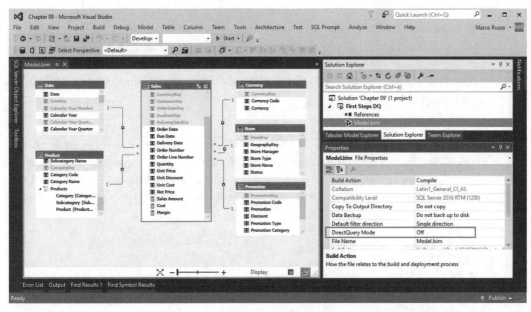

FIGURE 9-1 The DirectQuery Mode property, which is available at the model level in Visual Studio.

Switching the data model to DirectQuery is simple: just set the **DirectQuery Mode** property to **On** (see Figure 9-2). The tables do not show any row in the grid view. In addition, all the measures are blank in the data grid preview. This is because the model has no data in memory.

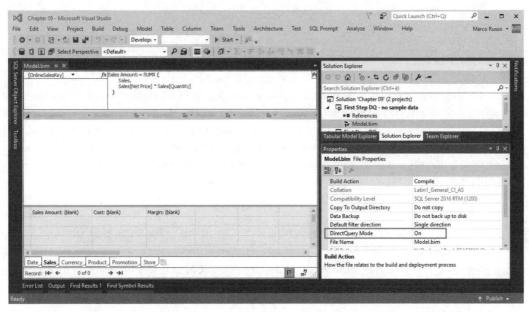

FIGURE 9-2 Switching the DirectQuery Mode property to On. Note that you no longer see the data preview in the grid view.

Tip If you import the tables in a tabular model when the DirectQuery Mode property is set to Off, you also import the content of the tables in memory, losing that content when you switch DirectQuery Mode to On. To avoid the processing time required to read the table in memory, you should switch DirectQuery Mode to On before importing the tables in the data model.

To browse the data through the workspace database, open the **Model** menu and select **Analyze in Excel**. Then choose the **Full Data View** option in the DirectQuery Connection Mode setting in the Analyze in Excel dialog box, as shown in Figure 9-3. (By default, Sample Data View is selected, but as you will see shortly, you do not have a defined sample data at this point.)

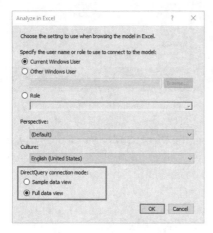

FIGURE 9-3 Switching the DirectQuery Connection Mode to Full Data View so you can see the data using Direct-Query in Excel.

Once in Excel, you can browse the data model with a PivotTable. Notice that performance is probably slower than what you are used to for the same data model. We assume you are using the same Contoso database we used in the previous example, which has not been optimized for DirectQuery. For example, the PivotTable shown in Figure 9-4 might require several seconds to refresh. (Around 30 seconds is normal, but you might need to wait more than one minute depending on your SQL Server configuration.)

 Note One reason for this response time is that we mapped the Sales table through a view that does a number of calculations, which SQL Server repeats for every query. If you design the table and indexes in SQL Server to avoid calculations at query time, you can improve performance, too.

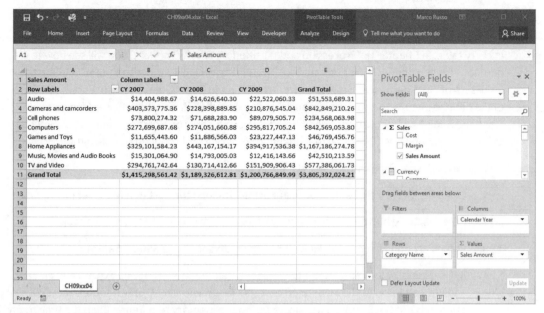

FIGURE 9-4 The PivotTable using the full data view of the DirectQuery connection mode.

The slow speed of this first example is normal and intentional. We wanted to show that the Analysis Services engine requires most of the calculations to be done by SQL Server. Optimizing the calculation becomes a problem of optimizing the SQL Server database for the typical workload that is produced by a tabular model in DirectQuery. This is very different from the type of queries sent by VertiPaq to process an in-memory database. Generally, a columnstore index is a good solution for optimizing a Microsoft SQL Server database for DirectQuery, but you will find more details on this topic in the white-paper mentioned at the beginning of this chapter.

You will also notice that there are no user hierarchies in DirectQuery. For example, the original tabular model we used in this example had a Products hierarchy in the Product table. Such a hierarchy is not avail-able when you browse the data in DirectQuery using Excel because of the limitations of the DirectQuery mode (described later in this chapter in the section "Limitations in tabular models for DirectQuery").

Using DirectQuery in the development environment could be harder if you do not have a preview of the data and all the queries you execute to test the model are particularly slow. For example, you might have a data source for development that does not have the same performance as the production envi-ronment. For this reason, you might define additional partitions in the data model to use as sample data. The logic is as follows: If you provide sample data, Analysis Services will use the partitions loaded in mem-ory with sample data, and will show only this content to the user. It is up to you to define what content to use as sample data in every table. By default all the tables of a tabular model do not have sample data. Thus, if you open the Analyze in Excel dialog box shown in Figure 9-3 (open the **Model** menu and choose **Analyze In Excel**), and you choose **Sample Data View** instead of Full Data View under DirectQuery Connection Mode, you will obtain a PivotTable with just a list of measures, table, and columns, without any content. No products, no customers, no dates, and no values will be provided by a measure. In the following section, you will learn how to add sample data for DirectQuery to your tables.

Creating sample data for DirectQuery

In a tabular model enabled for DirectQuery, you can define one or more partitions with sample data in every table. In Chapter 11, "Processing and partitioning tabular models," you will see how to create partitions for large tables. Partitions are usually useful for reducing processing time, and the table data is the sum of all its partitions. However, a model running in DirectQuery mode uses only one partition of the table to identify the corresponding table object in the relational database, used as a data source. This table is marked DirectQuery. In addition, there can be only one partition marked DirectQuery. In a model enabled for DirectQuery, all the other partitions of a table contain sample data.

You can add a partition with sample data by following these steps:

1. Open the **Table** menu and choose **Partitions** to open the Partition Manager dialog box.

2. Click the **Copy** button to create a copy of the only partition you have in the table.

3. In the Partition Name field, delete the existing text and type **Sales - Sample**.

4. If the table is large, apply a filter to the SQL statement by clicking the **SQL** button and applying a WHERE condition to the SQL statement. This way, you will load only a subset of the rows of the entire table in the Sample partition, reducing the memory requirement and the time to process the data.

In our example, we copied the data of all the tables into a new Sample partition by following the first three steps above. For the Sales table we added a WHERE condition to filter only the first day of each month, as shown in Figure 9-5.

> **Note** If you disable DirectQuery mode in a tabular model that has partitions with sample data, SSDT requires you to remove all the sample partitions before moving forward. Otherwise, it cancels your request.

After you define the sample partitions, you must populate them by processing the tables of the workspace database. To do so, open the **Model** menu, choose **Process**, and select **Process All**. After you have processed the tables, you can open the Analyze in Excel dialog box and choose the **Sample Data View** option under DirectQuery Connection Mode. (Refer to Figure 9-3.) You can browse data using a PivotTable with a very good response time. As shown in Figure 9-6, the numbers are smaller than those you saw with the Full Data View option because you are only querying the partitions with sample data and you are not using DirectQuery in this PivotTable.

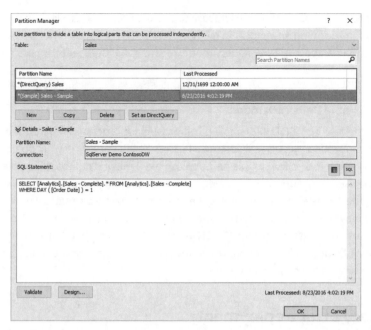

FIGURE 9-5 The Partition Manager dialog box with one sample partition in a model that is enabled for DirectQuery.

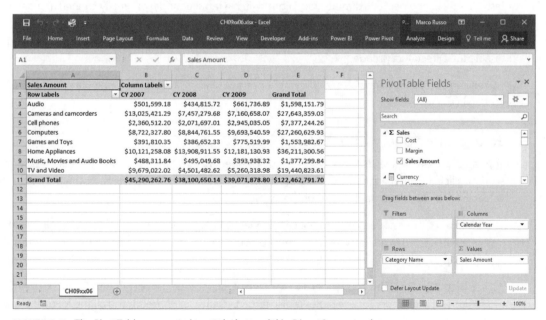

FIGURE 9-6 The PivotTable connected to a tabular model in DirectQuery mode.

After you complete your test, you can deploy the database to a tabular server. This will simply update the metadata without performing any import in memory. A process operation is not necessary in this case. All users will use the database in DirectQuery mode, regardless of the client they use (Excel, Power BI, or others).

Processing partitions for Sample Data View mode

When you deploy a tabular model from SSDT, the sample partitions are not processed regardless of the project's Processing Option setting. However, if you run a Process Default or Process Full operation at the database level, you will also process the sample partitions on the deployed database. Sample partitions are designed to be used only during development, and you should not process a database deployed in DirectQuery mode. However, you can enforce the process of sample partitions if you need them for test reasons. The `DataView=Sample` property in the connection string enables a client to use the data in the sample partitions instead of in the DirectQuery mode. (Remember that even with sample partitions that are mainly for development purposes, any user who can access the model can use the `DataView=Sample` setting in the connection string.)

Setting DirectQuery after deployment

If you have only one partition per table in your data model, you can enable and disable the DirectQuery mode after deployment. This is an alternative to using sample partitions to test your data with the faster VertiPaq engine. For example, you might switch a tabular model originally created as a default in-memory model to DirectQuery, or you could switch a model originally created for DirectQuery to VertiPaq. In the latter case, you must not have sample partitions. If you do, they must be removed to disable the DirectQuery mode.

You can apply this change after deployment using SSMS interactively or running a script, as described in the following sections.

Setting DirectQuery with SSMS

You can change a database's DirectQuery mode by opening the Database Properties dialog box. To do so, right-click the database name in the Object Explorer and choose **Properties**. Figure 9-7 shows the values available for the Default Mode property:

- **Import**   This corresponds to the DirectQuery Mode property set to Off in SSDT. All the tables are imported in memory, and you must process the database to see data after you set this property.

- **DirectQuery**   This corresponds to the DirectQuery Mode property set to On in SSDT. Any data loaded in memory for the tables is discharged, its memory is freed, and all the following queries run in DirectQuery mode. There is no need to process the database after you set its DirectQuery property to On.

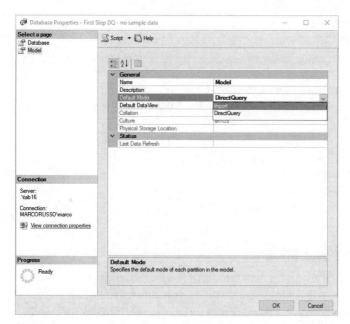

FIGURE 9-7 The Default Mode options available in Database Properties dialog box.

> **Note** Notice the Default DataView property in Figure 9-7. This setting defines a default for the partitions' DataView property. Changing this property is not useful if you created partitions with SSDT because as of this writing, those partitions always have the DataView option set to Full or Sample. (This could change in future updates.)

Setting DirectQuery with XMLA

To change the DirectQuery Mode setting through an XMLA script, you can use the code described in the following example, where the DefaultMode node can have one of the following values:

- **0** This corresponds to the Default Mode property set to Import, with the DirectQuery Mode property set to Off.

- **1** This corresponds to the Default Mode property set to DirectQuery, with the DirectQuery Mode property set to On.

```
<Alter xmlns="http://schemas.microsoft.com/analysisservices/2014/engine">
    <DatabaseID>First Step DQ - no sample data</DatabaseID>
    <Model>
        <xs:schema xmlns:xs="http://www.w3.org/2001/XMLSchema"
                   xmlns:sql="urn:schemas-microsoft-com:xml-sql">
            <xs:element>
                <xs:complexType>
                    <xs:sequence>
                        <xs:element type="row"/>
```

```
                    </xs:sequence>
                </xs:complexType>
            </xs:element>
            <xs:complexType name="row">
                <xs:sequence>
                    <xs:element name="DefaultMode" type="xs:long"
                                sql:field="DefaultMode" minOccurs="0"/>
                </xs:sequence>
            </xs:complexType>
        </xs:schema>
        <row xmlns="urn:schemas-microsoft-com:xml-analysis:rowset">
            <DefaultMode>1</DefaultMode>
        </row>
    </Model>
</Alter>
```

Setting DirectQuery with PowerShell

If you want to change the DirectQuery Mode setting through a PowerShell script, you can use the code described in the following example, which corresponds with the Set-DirectQueryMode.ps1 file in the PowerShell folder of the companion content. You must pass three parameters that correspond to the SSAS instance name, the database name, and the desired Default Mode setting, which can be either Import or DirectQuery, as follows:

```
param (
    [ValidateNotNullOrEmpty()][string]$ssasInstanceName,
    [ValidateNotNullOrEmpty()][string]$databaseName,
    [ValidateSet('Import','DirectQuery')][string]$defaultMode="" )
[System.Reflection.Assembly]::LoadWithPartialName("Microsoft.AnalysisServices.Tabular")
$svr = new-Object Microsoft.AnalysisServices.Tabular.Server
$svr.Connect($ssasInstanceName)
$database = $svr.databases
$db = $database.GetByName($databaseName)
$db.Model.DefaultMode = $defaultMode
$db.Model.SaveChanges()
```

For example, you can set the DirectQuery mode of the First Step DQ database on the Tabular instance of the local server using the following command:

```
.\Set-DirectQueryMode.ps1 $ssasInstanceName'LOCALHOST\TABULAR' $databaseName'First Step
DQ' $defaultMode'DirectQuery'
```

To revert to the in-memory mode using VertiPaq, you just change the last parameter to Import, as follows:

```
.\Set-DirectQueryMode.ps1 $ssasInstanceName'LOCALHOST\TABULAR' $databaseName'First Step
DQ' $defaultMode'Import'
```

Setting DirectQuery with TMSL

As of this writing (January 2017), there was no syntax available in Tabular Modeling Scripting Language (TMSL) to change just the defaultMode property of a model using an alter command. When you change this setting from SSDT, the entire model is deployed with the new value, so you can do the same with a large TMSL script that deploys the entire data model using a createOrReplace command. You can find more details about TMSL in Chapter 7, "Tabular Model Scripting Language (TMSL)," and Chapter 13, "Interfacing with Tabular."

Limitations in tabular models for DirectQuery

When you define a tabular model in DirectQuery mode, there are some restrictions limiting the features that you can use and/or that are available from a user point of view. Certain features, such as calculated tables, are removed from the development environment. Others, such as user hierarchies, are not available even if defined in the data model.

This section describes the existing restrictions, the supported data sources, and specific properties for tabular models in DirectQuery mode. You can find an updated list of restrictions and supported data sources at *https://msdn.microsoft.com/en-us/library/hh230898.aspx*. (This chapter is updated as of September 2016.)

Supported data sources

The DirectQuery mode supports the following relational databases:

- Microsoft SQL Server 2008 and later

- Microsoft Azure SQL Database

- Microsoft Azure SQL Data Warehouse

- Microsoft Azure SQL Analytics Platform System (APS)

- Oracle 9i and later

- Teradata V2R6 and later

> **Note** Only specific providers are supported for the DirectQuery mode. You can check the list of supported providers for each data source at *https://msdn.microsoft.com/en-us/library/hh230898.aspx#Anchor_2*.

Restrictions for data sources

All the tables of a tabular model in DirectQuery mode must be from a single relational database of the supported data sources. You cannot have multiple data sources for the same model in DirectQuery. All the tables must be connected to a SQL statement, which cannot be a stored procedure. In T-SQL you can use table, views, and table-valued functions.

Restrictions for data modeling

A tabular model in DirectQuery cannot have calculated tables. In addition, there are a number of limitations in the DAX expression that you can use in calculated columns and in expressions for row-level security (RLS).

Generally, in calculated columns and RLS, you can use DAX functions, returning a scalar value and operating in a row context. However, you cannot use aggregation functions, table functions, or iterators. The idea is that the DAX expression of a calculated table or an RLS filter should be translated in a correspondent SQL expression. This is not possible—or at least not efficient—when the function depends on concepts that are specific to the DAX language, such as filter context and context transition.

Even for DirectQuery, it is a good practice to create views in the relational database to decouple the tabular model from the physical structure of the database. In these views, you should be able to create the same calculation that you might write in a calculated column in DAX. This gives you more control over the SQL code generated. At the same time, you do not risk trying an unsupported feature. However, if you try to write a DAX expression that is not supported in DirectQuery, you receive an error in SSDT and you cannot save or deploy a model that would not work.

As mentioned, user hierarchies are not supported in MDX queries sent to a model in DirectQuery mode. Thus, you can always create user hierarchies in the tabular model. However, these hierarchies are not visible for a client using MDX (such as Excel), whereas they are available for a client using DAX (such as Power BI).

Restrictions for DAX formulas

As mentioned in the previous section, only a limited number of DAX functions are supported in calculated columns and RLS filters. These functions correspond to the DAX functions that are optimized for DirectQuery and are supported in all DAX formulas. As of September 2016, this list includes the formulas shown in Table 9-1.

TABLE 9-1 DAX functions supported in calculated columns and RLS filters

ABS	DATE	HOUR	MAX	QUOTIENT	SIN	UNICODE
ACOS	DATEDIFF	IF	MID	RADIANS	SQRT	UPPER
ACOT	DATEVALUE	INT	MIN	RAND	SQRTPI	USERNAME
AND	DAY	ISBLANK	MINUTE	RELATED	SUBSTITUTE	USERELATIONSHIP
ASIN	DEGREES	ISO.CEILING	MOD	REPT	SWITCH	VALUE
ATAN	DIVIDE	KEEPFILTERS	MONTH	RIGHT	TAN	WEEKDAY
BLANK	EDATE	LEFT	MROUND	ROUND	TIME	WEEKNUM
CEILING	EOMONTH	LEN	NOT	ROUNDDOWN	TIMEVALUE	YEAR
CONCATENATE	EXACT	LN	NOW	ROUNDUP	TODAY	
COS	EXP	LOG	OR	SEARCH	TRIM	
COT	FALSE	LOG10	PI	SECOND	TRUE	
CURRENCY	FIND	LOWER	POWER	SIGN	TRUNC	

Other DAX functions are optimized for DirectQuery and supported only in measures and query formulas, but they cannot be used in calculated columns and RLS filters. These are shown in Table 9-2. (An updated list of this group of functions is available at *https://msdn.microsoft.com/en-us/library/mt723603.aspx#Anchor_0.*)

TABLE 9-2 DAX functions supported only in measures and query formulas

ALL	CALCULATE	DISTINCT	ISFILTERED	STDEV.P	VAR.P
ALLEXCEPT	CALCULATETABLE	DISTINCTCOUNT	MAXA	STDEV.S	VAR.S
ALLNOBLANKROW	COUNT	FILTER	MAXX	STDEVX.P	VARX.P
ALLSELECTED	COUNTA	FILTERS	MIN	STDEVX.S	VARX.S
AVERAGE	COUNTAX	HASONEFILTER	MINA	SUM	
AVERAGEA	COUNTROWS	HASONEVALUE	MINX	SUMX	
AVERAGEX	COUNTX	ISCROSSFILTERED	RELATEDTABLE	VALUES	

All the other DAX functions not included in these two lists are available for DirectQuery only in measures and query formulas. However, they are not optimized. As a consequence, the calculation could be implemented in the formula engine on Analysis Services, which will retrieve the required granularity from SQL Server to perform the calculation. Apart from the slower performance, this could require the materialization of a large result, coming from a SQL query in the memory of Analysis Services, to complete the execution of a query. Also for this reason, if you have complex calculations over large tables, you should carefully consider the setting MaxIntermediateRowSize, described later in this chapter in the section "Tuning query limit."

Finally, you must be aware that there are conditions when the same DAX expression might produce different results between DirectQuery and in-memory models. This is caused by the different semantic between DAX and SQL in comparisons (string and numbers, text with Boolean, and nulls), casts (string to Boolean, string to date/time, and number to string), math functions and arithmetic operations (order of addition, use of the POWER function, numerical overflow, LOG functions with blanks, and division by zero), numeric and date-time ranges, currency, and text functions. A detailed and updated documentation of these differences is available at *https://msdn.microsoft.com/en-us/library/mt723603.aspx*.

Restrictions for MDX formulas

In a tabular model, you must use DAX to define measures and calculated columns, but the queries can be written using both DAX and MDX. In this way, a tabular model is compatible with any existing MDX client, such as a PivotTable in Excel, and any DAX client, such as Power BI. In DirectQuery mode, there are limitations to the MDX features available. As a rule of thumb, the MDX generated by Excel works in DirectQuery, but the following limitations might affect other client products or MDX queries created manually in reports or other tools:

- You cannot use relative object names. All object names must be fully qualified.

- There are no session-scope MDX statements (named sets, calculated members, calculated cells, visual totals, default members, and so forth), but you can use query-scope constructs, such as the WITH clause.

- There are no tuples with members from different levels in MDX subselect clauses.

- There are no user-defined hierarchies. (This limitation was mentioned previously in this chapter because it is the only one that also affects the PivotTable in Excel.)

- There are no native SQL queries to the tabular model. Normally, Analysis Services supports a T-SQL subset, but not for DirectQuery models.

You can find an updated list of these limitations at *https://msdn.microsoft.com/en-us/library/hh230898.aspx#Anchor_1*.

Tuning query limit

Every time DirectQuery generates a query to SQL Server, it retrieves only a predefined maximum number of rows from SQL Server, which is 1,000,000 by default (such a default could change in future updates). This is to limit queries that could run too long, requesting too much memory on Analysis Services to store an intermediate result during a more complex query.

For example, consider the following DAX query:

```
EVALUATE
ROW ( "rows", COUNTROWS ( Sales ) )
```

It generates a corresponding SQL query that returns only one row, as follows:

```
SELECT   COUNT_BIG(*) AS [a0]
FROM     ( SELECT  [Analytics].[Sales - Complete].*
             FROM     [Analytics].[Sales - Complete]
         ) AS [t1];
```

However, other DAX queries might transfer numerous rows to Analysis Services for an evaluation. For example, consider the following DAX query:

```
EVALUATE
ROW ( "orders", COUNTROWS ( ALL ( Sales[Order Number], Sales[Order Line Number] ) ) )
```

The SQL query that is generated does not execute the COUNT operation on SQL Server, and it transfers the list of the existing combination of the Order Number and Order Line Number values to Analysis Services. However, a TOP clause, shown as follows, limits the number of rows that could be returned by this query to 1,000,000:

```
SELECT TOP ( 1000001 )
        [t1].[Order Number],
        [t1].[Order Line Number]
FROM     ( SELECT  [Analytics].[Sales - Complete].*
             FROM     [Analytics].[Sales - Complete]
         ) AS [t1]
GROUP BY [t1].[Order Number],
        [t1].[Order Line Number];
```

If the result is greater than 1,000,000 rows, the number of rows transferred is exactly 1,000,001. When this happens, SSAS assumes that there are other rows that have not been transferred, and the result based on this incomplete result would be incorrect. Thus, it returns the following error:

```
The resultset of a query to external data source has exceeded the maximum allowed size of
'1000000' rows.
```

This default limit of 1,000,000 rows is the same limit used for models created by the Power BI Desktop. However, you might want to increase this setting on your SSAS instance. To do that, you must manually edit the msmdsrv.ini configuration file, specifying a different limit for the MaxIntermediateRowSize setting. You must add this to the file, using the following syntax, because it is not present by default:

```
<ConfigurationSettings>
. . .
<DAX>
  <DQ>
     <MaxIntermediateRowsetSize>1000000
     </MaxIntermediateRowsetSize>
  </DQ>
</DAX>
. . .
```

You can find more details about this and other settings for DAX in the MSDN documentation at *https://msdn.microsoft.com/en-us/library/mt761855.aspx*.

Tip If you have an SSAS tabular server with a good amount of memory and good bandwidth for connecting to the data source in DirectQuery mode, you probably want to increase this number to a higher value. As a rule of thumb, this setting should be higher than the larger dimension of a star schema model. For example, if you have 4,000,000 products and 8,000,000 customers, you should increase the `MaxIntermediateRowSize` setting to 10,000,000. In this way, any query that aggregates the data at the customer level would continue to work. Using a value that is too high (such as 100,000,000) could exhaust the memory and/or timeout the query before the limit is reached, so a lower limit helps avoid such a critical condition.

Choosing between DirectQuery and VertiPaq

In a perfect world, the relational database would be fast enough to provide a result to any query in less than one second, making the choice very easy. There would be no need to copy and process data on another engine (such as VertiPaq), Analysis Services would be just a semantic layer on top of the relational database, and the performance would be guaranteed by the server running the only copy of data. This would lead to zero processing time, zero latency, data that is always up to date, and less memory requirements for Analysis Services.

Unfortunately, even if we live in the best of worlds, it is far from perfect. Even using a columnstore index on SQL Server, which is based on the same technology used to build the VertiPaq engine, you would not achieve the same performance that you could get with an in-memory model in Analysis Services. Thus, choosing between DirectQuery and VertiPaq is a question of tradeoffs and priorities.

The main reason to use DirectQuery is to reduce the latency between updates on the relational database and the availability of the same data in the tabular model. DirectQuery removes this latency, but it uses the same relational engine used to update the data. This means the same relational database will manage concurrent updates and queries in such conditions, so you must figure out whether the server will be able to support the concurrent workload or not. Using VertiPaq is also a way to reduce the pressure on a relational database, because an increasing number of users does not change the workload on the data source. If you import data on VertiPaq, you read data only once, regardless of the following queries run by the users.

Another possible scenario for using DirectQuery is when you have a database that is too large to fit in the memory of a single Analysis Services server. As you will see in Chapter 15, "Optimizing tabular models," tables with more than 100,000,000,000 rows might be hard to manage with VertiPaq. Therefore, if you cannot reduce the cardinality of data loaded in memory, you might use particular architectures to handle such a volume—for example, by using Microsoft SQL Server Analytics Platform System (APS) or SQL Data Warehouse on Microsoft Azure. In these conditions, you can use an Analysis Services tabular model in DirectQuery mode to create a semantic layer to access a very large database. You might not expect the same level of performance you are used to in such an interactive scenario, but this approach could be faster than any other available option. Even certain queries will still require many seconds, if not minutes.

We can recap the following two main scenarios where you might consider using DirectQuery:

- **A small database that is updated frequently** What is considered "small" really depends on the performance and optimization of the relational database. For example, a SQL Server database using a columnstore index can handle much more data than a database based on classical indexes.

- **A large database that would not fit in memory** Even if this scenario does not guarantee an interactive user experience navigating the data (as you might expect by most of the VertiPaq models you can create in Tabular), it could be good enough to support scenarios where a query can run in seconds, if not minutes, and the semantic value provided by Tabular is an important added value for the analytical solution.

At the moment, a hybrid approach is not possible. Therefore, the choice between these two engines is all or nothing. If this feature is enhanced in the future, making it possible to mix tables (if not partitions) with different storage types, it will open up new possibilities and scenarios where the two technologies could be combined—for example, by keeping data for the current day in DirectQuery and other historical data in VertiPaq.

Summary

DirectQuery is a technology alternative to VertiPaq that can transform any MDX or DAX query sent to a tabular model into one or more SQL queries made to the relational database that is used as a data source. DirectQuery has a number of limitations that restrict certain features of the tabular model and the DAX language. Choosing between DirectQuery and VertiPaq requires you to evaluate the tradeoffs between latency, performance, and features. In this chapter, you learned how to configure DirectQuery in your development environment and on a production server, and the evaluations required before adopting DirectQuery in a tabular model.

If you want more details about DirectQuery, including insights and performance hints, read the whitepaper "DirectQuery in 2016 Analysis Services," available at *http://www.sqlbi.com/articles/ directquery-in-analysis-services-2016/.*

CHAPTER 10

Security

On many business intelligence (BI) projects, you will find yourself working with some of the most valuable and sensitive data that your organization possesses. It is no surprise, then, that implementing some form of security is almost always a top priority when working with Analysis Services. Of course, that means ensuring that only certain people have access to the model. However, it may also mean ensuring that certain people can see only some of the data and that different groups of users can see different slices of data. Fortunately, the tabular model has some comprehensive features for securing the data in your tables, as you will see in this chapter.

> **What's new in SSAS 2016**   The security roles in SSAS 2016 are not different from previous versions. Nevertheless, this chapter has been updated to include sections about testing roles using DAX Studio, visual totals and security in calculated columns and calculated tables, and security in DirectQuery.

User authentication

Analysis Services does not have a custom authentication service. It relies entirely on Windows authentication or on Azure Active Directory, which is available on Azure Analysis Services. In general, a user belonging to a Windows domain should have access to an SSAS instance within the same domain. If a user belongs to a different domain or is not connecting within the enterprise network (for example, the user is employing a VPN), then a workaround is possible—for example, connecting through HTTP/HTTPS access. Power BI also provides an alternative way to access SSAS databases on premises through the Data Gateway, mapping the Power BI user to the internal Windows users.

In this section, you will see some of the most common scenarios that require certain settings to establish a connection with Analysis Services. Alternatively, a connection within the corporate network is usually straightforward and does not require particular insights. A detailed description of the options for obtaining Windows authentication connecting to Analysis Services is also available at *https://msdn.microsoft.com/en-us/library/dn141154.aspx*.

Connecting to Analysis Services from outside a domain

Because Analysis Services relies on Windows authentication, enabling users from outside a domain to access Analysis Services can represent a challenge. Additionally, it can be a problem for users to connect to Analysis Services when a firewall blocks the ports on which it listens for client connections. The solution is to configure Analysis Services to use HTTP access through Internet Information Server (IIS), as shown in Figure 10-1.

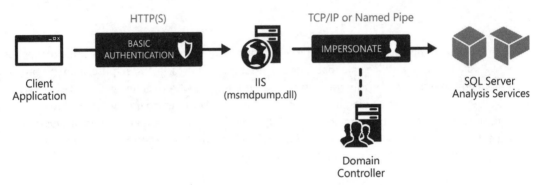

FIGURE 10-1   How HTTP connectivity works.

In this scenario, a DLL called msmdpump.dll inside IIS acts as a bridge between the client machine and Analysis Services. When the client connects to IIS, IIS handles the authentication; msmdpump.dll then opens a connection to Analysis Services by using the end user's credentials. You should use integrated Windows authentication with IIS whenever possible. If you cannot do so—for example, because users are accessing from outside a trusted Windows domain—use anonymous access or basic authentication with IIS. If you are using basic authentication, you should always use HTTPS connections. Otherwise, user credentials will be transmitted without encryption over the wire, making the system more vulnerable to unauthorized access.

Describing how to configure HTTP connectivity for Analysis Services is outside the scope of this book, but plenty of resources are available on the Internet that cover how to do this for Analysis Services Multidimensional, and the steps are the same for the tabular model. You can find a detailed description of how to configure HTTP access to Analysis Services on MSDN at *http://msdn.microsoft.com/en-us/library/gg492140.aspx*.

Kerberos and the double-hop problem

Figure 10-2 shows another common problem you might encounter when designing an Analysis Services solution: a scenario in which a client connects to a web-based reporting tool, and the web-based reporting tool must then connect to a separate Analysis Services server by using the end user's credentials to run a query. This is called the *double-hop problem*.

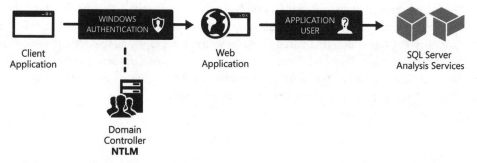

FIGURE 10-2 The double-hop problem.

By default, this situation is not possible with standard Windows authentication. But in cases in which it does occur, it can be solved in one of the following three ways:

- **By setting up constrained delegation and Kerberos**   With this approach, you obtain the architecture shown in Figure 10-3. This is probably the best option, although setting up Kerberos is notoriously difficult, and many consultants and their customers would like to avoid it. A good starting point on enabling Kerberos for Analysis Services is the article from the Microsoft knowledge base at *https://msdn.microsoft.com/en-us/library/dn194199.aspx*.

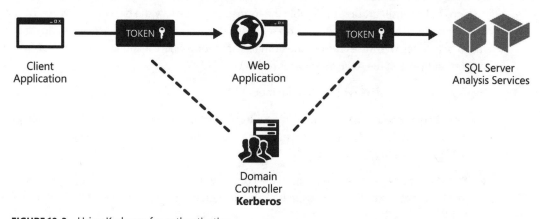

FIGURE 10-3 Using Kerberos for authentication.

- **By using dynamic security and the CUSTOMDATA function**   This requires you to configure your web application to open a connection. You do this by using the CustomData connection string property and passing an appropriate value through it. This is described later in this chapter in the section "Creating dynamic security." This technique would not be possible in many cases, but the SQL Server Reporting Services expression-based connection strings can be used to do this. (See *http://msdn.microsoft.com/en-us/library/ms156450.aspx* for more details.)

- **By using the EffectiveUserName connection string property**   To use the connection string property, the user connecting to Analysis Services must be an Analysis Services administrator.

Therefore, this technique represents a significant security concern. Nevertheless, this is the approach Microsoft uses in the Data Gateway for Power BI, also providing a user interface to change the UPN property. Then, users in Azure Active Directory map to existing Windows users in the domain where Analysis Services is installed. For a detailed guide to the configuration of the Data Gateway for Analysis Services connections, see *https://powerbi.microsoft.com/en-us/documentation/powerbi-gateway-enterprise-manage-ssas/*.

Roles

Like the multidimensional model, the tabular model uses roles to manage security. A role is a grouping of users who all perform the same tasks and therefore share the same permissions. When you grant a role the permission to do something, you are granting that permission to all users who are members of that role.

Users are either Microsoft Windows domain user accounts or local user accounts from the machine on which Analysis Services is installed. All Analysis Services security relies on Windows integrated security, and there is no way to set up your own user accounts with passwords in the way that you can in the Microsoft SQL Server relational engine (by using SQL Server authentication). Instead of adding individual user accounts to a role, it is possible to add Windows user groups to a role—either domain user groups or local user groups, preferably the former. This is usually the best option. Note that only security groups work; distribution groups do not work. If you create a domain user group for each role, you need only to remove the user from the domain user group when an individual user's permissions change rather than edit the Analysis Services role.

There are two types of roles in the tabular model:

- **The server administrator role** This controls administrative permissions at the server level. This role is built into Analysis Services and cannot be deleted. It can be managed only by using SQL Server Management Studio (SSMS).

- **Database roles** These control both the administrative and data permissions at the database level. The database roles can be created and deleted by using SQL Server Data Tools (SSDT) and SSMS.

Creating database roles

Database roles can grant permissions only at the database level. You can create and edit them in SSDT. Follow these steps:

1. Open the **Model** menu and select **Roles**. This opens the Role Manager dialog box, shown in Figure 10-4.

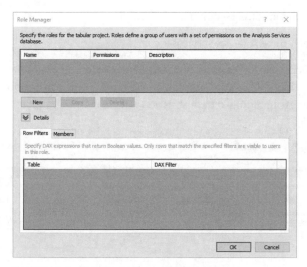

FIGURE 10-4   The Role Manager dialog box.

2.   To create a new role, click the **New** button. This creates a new role with a default name in the list box at the top of the dialog box.

3.   Rename the role, enter a description, and set its permissions, as shown in Figure 10-5.

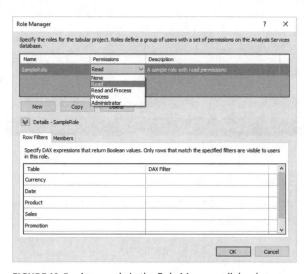

FIGURE 10-5   A new role in the Role Manager dialog box.

4.   To add Windows users and groups to this role, click the **Members** tab in the bottom half of the dialog box.

You can also create database roles in SSMS by doing the following:

1. In Object Explorer, connect to the Analysis Services instance.

2. Expand a database, right-click the **Roles** node, and select **New Role**. This opens the Create Role dialog box, shown in Figure 10-6. Here, you can do the same things you can do in SSDT. However, some of the names are slightly different, as you will see in the next section.

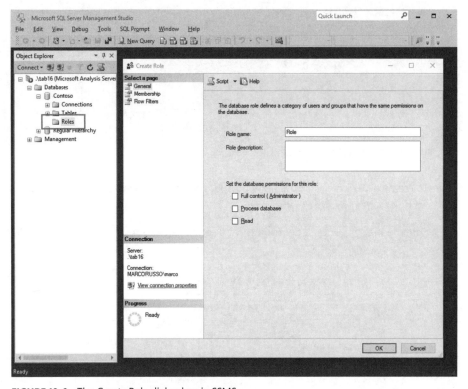

FIGURE 10-6 The Create Role dialog box in SSMS.

> **Note** A role name must not include the comma character, because it interferes with the Roles connection string property (described later in this chapter).

Membership of multiple roles

In some cases, users might be members of more than one role. In this case, the user has the permission of each individual role of which he or she is a member. If one role grants the user permission to do or see something, then he or she retains that permission, no matter what other roles he or she is a member of. For example, if a user is a member of multiple roles, one of which grants him or her administrative permissions on a database, that user is an administrator on that database even if other roles grant more restrictive permissions. In a similar way, if a user is a member of two roles, one granting permission to query only some of the data in a table and the other to query all the data in a table, the user will be able to query all the data in the table. There is no concept of "deny wins over grant," as in the SQL Server relational engine. In fact, all security in Analysis Services is concerned with granting permissions, and there is no way of specifically denying permission to do or see something.

Administrative security

Administrative security permissions can be granted in two ways: through the server administrator role and through database roles.

Granting permission through the server administrator role

The server administrator role is very straightforward. Any user who is a member of this role has administrator privileges over the whole Analysis Services instance. This means server administrators can see all the data in the tables in every database, and create, delete, and process any objects.

By default, any members of the local administrator group on the server on which Analysis Services is running are also administrators of Analysis Services. The Analysis Services server property that controls this behavior is BuiltinAdminsAreServerAdmins. You can set it in SQL Server Management Studio in the Analysis Server Properties dialog box (see Figure 10-7) and in the msmdsrv.ini file. By default, it is set to True. If you set it to False, only users or groups you add to the role have administrator privileges on your Analysis Services instance. Likewise, the Windows account that the Analysis Services service is running as is also an Analysis Services administrator. You can turn this off by setting the ServiceAccountIsServerAdmin server property to False.

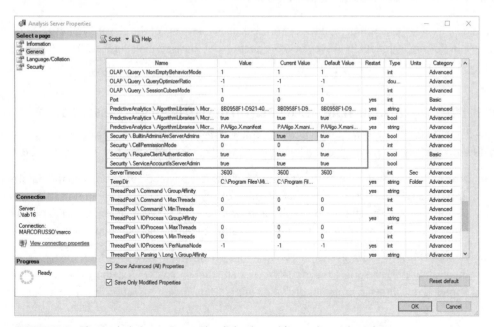

FIGURE 10-7 The Analysis Server Properties dialog box with security settings shown.

You must add at least one user to the server administrator role during installation, on the Analysis Services Configuration step of the installation wizard. After that, you can add users and groups in SSMS by right-clicking the instance name, selecting **Properties**, and, in the Analysis Server Properties dialog box, selecting the **Security** page, as shown in Figure 10-8. Then click **Add** and follow the prompts to add a new user or group.

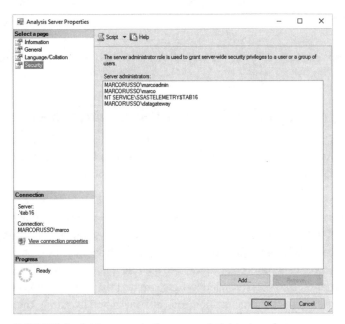

FIGURE 10-8   Adding users to the server administrator role.

In a development environment, developers are usually members of the server administrator role. In a production environment, however, only production database administrators (DBAs) should be members of this role.

Granting database roles and administrative permissions

At the database level, only a very limited set of administrative permissions can be granted. (These are also listed in the Permissions drop-down list in the SSDT Role Manager dialog box, shown in Figure 10-5.)

- **None**   This is the default setting. Members of this role have no permissions on this database. Because a Windows user who is not a member of any role and is not an administrator has no permissions anyway, this option might seem unnecessary. However, it forces you to explicitly grant permissions to a role for it to be useful rather than blindly accepting any defaults.

- **Read**   This setting grants members of the role permission to read data from the tables, which means that they can query the model. You can further control what data can be queried by applying row filters to tables, as discussed in the "Data security" section later in this chapter.

- **Process**   This setting grants members of the role permission to process any object within the database, but not to query it. This permission would be appropriate for applications, such as SQL Server Integration Services (SSIS), that automate processing tasks. Note that a user with process permissions would not be able to process an object from SSMS because he or she would not have sufficient permissions to connect to Analysis Services in the Object Explorer pane.

- **Read and process**   This setting grants members of the role permission to both query the model and process the objects.

- **Administrator**   This setting grants members of the role permission to query, process, create, alter, and delete any object. Developers and DBAs must be administrators of a database to do their jobs properly.

A slightly different set of options is presented when creating a role in SSMS. As Figure 10-6 shows, three check boxes control the following administrative permissions:

- **Full control (administrator)**   This is equivalent to the administrator permission in SSDT.

- **Process database**   This is equivalent to the process permission in SSDT.

- **Read**   This is equivalent to the read permission in SSDT.

Selecting both the Process Database and the Read check boxes is equivalent to setting the Read and Process permission shown in SSDT. Checking any combination of boxes that includes Full Control (Administrator) is equivalent to the administrator permission.

Data security

It is an extremely common requirement on an Analysis Services project to make sure that some users can see only some of the data in a table. For example, in a multinational company, you might want to allow users at the head office to see the sales data for the entire company, but to enable staff at each of the local offices in each country to see the sales for just that country. You can achieve this by using DAX expressions in roles that act as filters on the tables. This is referred to as data security (as opposed to administrative security).

Basic data security

To set up data security on a role in SSDT, open the Role Manager dialog box and enter DAX filter expressions for one or more tables on the Row Filters tab, as shown in Figure 10-9. You can also set up data security in roles in SSMS after selecting the Read check box on the Row Filters page in the Create Role or Role Properties dialog box. The user interface is almost identical to the one described here for SSDT.

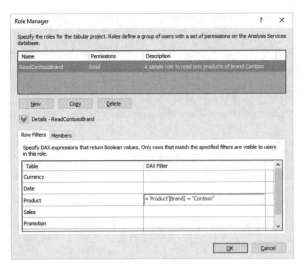

FIGURE 10-9 Configuring row filters in the Role Manager dialog box.

The DAX expression used to filter a table must return a Boolean value. For example, the following expression would result in the user being able to access only the data for the rows in the Product table where the Brand column is equal to the value Contoso:

```
= Product[Brand] = "Contoso"
```

It is important to understand that data security can be applied only to the rows of tables. It is not possible to secure entire tables, columns on a table, or perspectives. Thus, it is not possible to secure the individual measures in a model. A user can see all the measures in a model if he or she has read permissions on a database. (In contrast, in the multidimensional model, it is possible to secure individual measures—although security on calculated measures is problematic.) However, as you will see later, it is possible to apply a row filter that prevents the user from accessing any rows in a table. This gives a result similar to that of denying access to an entire table.

After row filters have been applied to a table, a user can see only subtotals and grand totals in his or her queries based on the rows he or she is allowed to see. Additionally, DAX calculations are based on the rows for which the user has permission, not all the rows in a table. This contrasts with the multidimensional model in which, when using dimension security, the Visual Totals property controls whether subtotals and grand totals are based on all the members of an attribute or just the members of the attribute that the user has permission to see.

> **Note** If you use MDX to query a tabular model, the VisualTotals() MDX function still works. The VisualTotals() function has nothing to do with the Visual Totals property controls for roles.

If you change the data security permissions of a role, those changes come into force immediately. There is no need to wait for a user to close and reopen a connection before they take effect.

Testing security roles

When writing row-filter expressions for data security, it is important that you test whether they work properly. However, as a developer, you have administrative rights over the database on which you are working, so you can see all the data in all the tables. Before any further discussion of data security, it is necessary to examine how to test the roles you develop.

Using Excel to test roles

The easiest way to test whether the row filters you have created work properly is to use Microsoft Excel. After you have created a role and clicked OK to close the Role Manager dialog box, open the **Model** menu and choose **Analyze in Excel** to browse your model as you normally would. Then, in the Analyze in Excel dialog box (shown in Figure 10-10), you can choose to test the security by browsing your model in one of two ways:

- **As if you have logged in as a specific Windows user**   To do so, select either **Current Windows User** or **Other Windows User**. If you choose the latter, enter the desired user name in the corresponding text box.

- **As if you were a member of one or more roles**   To do so, select the **Role** option and choose the desired role name(s) in the corresponding drop-down list.

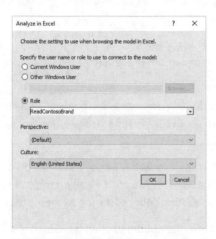

FIGURE 10-10   Testing roles through the Analyze in Excel dialog box.

Click **OK** to open Excel with the permissions of that user or that role(s) applied. You can then browse the model as you normally would. To illustrate what querying a model through a role looks like, Figure 10-11 shows a Microsoft PivotTable with a query on a Contoso model run by a user with administrative permissions. Figure 10-12 shows the same PivotTable with the row filter on Contoso, applied to the Product table that was shown in the preceding section, "Basic data security." Notice how the PivotTable shows data only for Contoso and how the Grand Total row, at the bottom of the PivotTable, is the same as the subtotal shown for Contoso in the previous example.

Row Labels	Sales Amount
⊞ A. Datum	$2,096,184.64
⊟ Adventure Works	$4,011,112.28
Adventure Works	$4,011,112.28
⊟ Contoso	$7,352,399.03
Contoso, Ltd	$7,352,399.03
⊞ Fabrikam	$5,554,015.73
⊞ Litware	$3,255,704.03
⊞ Northwind Traders	$1,040,552.13
⊞ Proseware	$2,546,144.16
⊞ Southridge Video	$1,384,413.85
⊞ Tailspin Toys	$325,042.42
⊞ The Phone Company	$1,123,819.07
⊞ Wide World Importers	$1,901,956.66
Grand Total	$30,591,343.98

FIGURE 10-11   The data in a model when browsing as an administrator.

Row Labels	Sales Amount
⊟ Contoso	$7,352,399.03
Contoso, Ltd	$7,352,399.03
Grand Total	$7,352,399.03

FIGURE 10-12   The data in the same model when browsing by using a role with data security.

Testing roles by using connection string properties

When you choose a user or a role in the Analyze in Excel dialog box, SSDT opens Excel in the background and creates a connection to the workspace database with one of the following connection string properties set:

- **Roles**   This takes a comma-delimited list of role names as its input and forces the connection to behave as if the user connecting is a member of these roles—for example, Roles=RoleName1,RoleName2 and so on.

- **EffectiveUserName**   This takes a Windows domain user name and applies the security permissions that user would have—for example, EffectiveUserName=MyDomain\MyUserName. (Note the local machine accounts are not supported.)

The Roles and EffectiveUserName connection string properties can be used only by Analysis Services administrators. You can apply both properties directly in Excel by editing the connection string properties of a connection in a workbook. To edit an existing connection, follow these steps:

1. Click the **Connections** button (on the Data tab in the ribbon) to open the Workbook Connections dialog box.

2. Select the connection you wish to edit.

3. Click the **Properties** button to open the Connection Properties dialog box.

4. Click the **Definition** tab and edit the connection string, as shown in Figure 10-13.

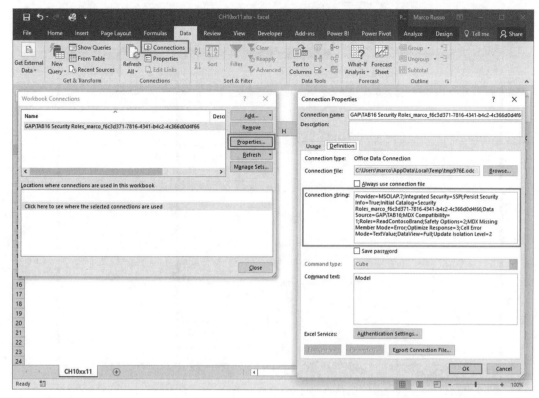

FIGURE 10-13 Editing a connection string in Excel.

If you want to see how a DAX query is affected by security, you can also use these connection string properties in SQL Server Management Studio. To do so, enter the connection string properties in the Connect to Analysis Services dialog box, which appears when you open a new MDX query window. (Click the **Options** button in the bottom-right corner of the dialog box to display the advanced options, and then choose the **Additional Connection Parameters** tab, as shown in Figure 10-14.) The appropriate roles will be applied to the connection, which are used to run queries from the MDX pane. These connection string properties are not, however, applied to the connection that is used to populate the metadata pane to the left of the query window, so you will see all the MDX dimensions and hierarchies listed there.

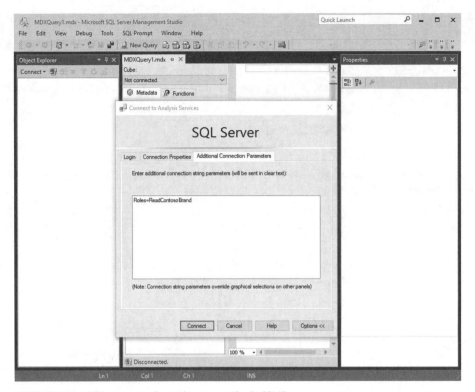

FIGURE 10-14 Editing connection string properties in SSMS.

Using DAX Studio to test roles

You can also test roles using DAX Studio, affecting both the metadata and the data that will be visible in the connection. To do so, expand the **Advanced Options** section in the Connect dialog box and enter the role's name in the **Roles** text box, as shown in Figure 10-15. (If you have more than one role, use commas to separate them.)

> **Note** When you test roles or an effective user name in DAX Studio, the buttons in the Traces section are grayed out. You must log on as an administrator to activate these features.

You can specify other parameters in the Additional Options section that will be added to the connection string. For example, you might specify the CustomData property (discussed later in the section "Creating dynamic security") by entering the following definition in the **Additional Options** text box:

```
CustomData = "Hello World"
```

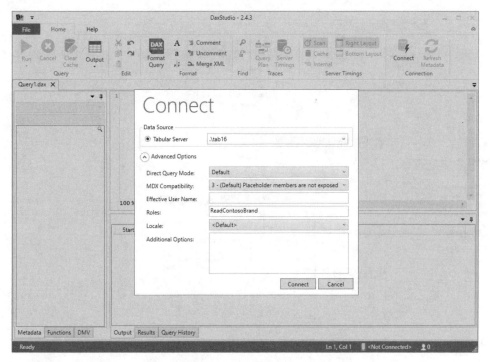

FIGURE 10-15 Editing connection string properties in DAX Studio.

Impersonating users to test roles

The third and final way to test a role is to log on to a machine or run an application using a specific user's credentials to see how security behaves. Although logging off and logging on as someone else can be time-consuming, it is relatively easy to run an application as another user. All you have to do is press the **Shift** key while right-clicking the executable file or shortcut, select the **Run as Different User** option, and enter the user name and the password of the user whose security you wish to test.

Advanced row-filter expressions

In many cases, some complex DAX is necessary to implement your security requirements. You can expand the limited amount of space in the Role Manager dialog box available for entering row-filter expressions by clicking the edge of the text box and dragging it outward. This section covers examples of row filters that address commonly encountered requirements. For all these examples, the Product, Sales, and Store tables in the Contoso database are used. The relationships among these tables are shown in Figure 10-16. Notice the bidirectional filter propagation defined between Store and Sales.

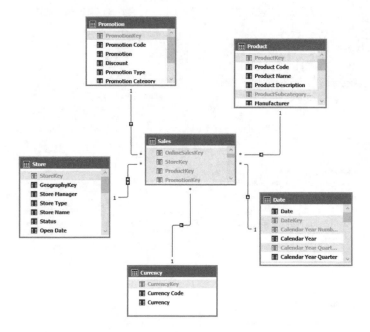

FIGURE 10-16 The relationships among the tables used for the Security Roles examples.

Filtering on multiple columns

When applying filters to multiple columns in a table, you usually use a mixture of And and Or logic. For example, if you want to filter the Product table to show only the products whose color is black and list price is greater than 3,000, you can use the following expression:

```
= Product[Color] = "Black" && Product[ListPrice] > 3000
```

If you want to change the logic so that you show the products whose color is black or list price is greater than 3,000, you can use the following expression:

```
= Product[Color] = "Black" || Product[ListPrice] > 3000
```

To get all the products whose color is anything other than black, you can use the following expression:

```
= [Color] <> "Black"
```

Finally, to deny access to every row in the product table, you can use the following expression:

```
= FALSE()
```

In this last example, although the table and all its columns remain visible in client tools, no data is returned.

Filtering and table relationships

Filters applied on one table can also have an indirect impact on other tables in the model. For example, you can use a filter such as the following one on the Product table:

```
= Product[Brand] = "Contoso"
```

This indirectly filters all the tables with which it has a one-to-many relationship—in this case, the Sales table. As a result, only the rows in Sales that are related to the product brand Contoso are returned in any query.

By default, filtering on a table does not result in a filter being applied to tables with which it has a many-to-one relationship. For example, after you filtered the Contoso brand in the Product table, the list of values visible in the CountryRegion column of the Store table always contains all the names available in the Store table, including the names for which there are no sales for the Contoso brand. This happens regardless of the filter propagation you have defined in the relationship between the Sales and Store tables (which in this case is bidirectional). In fact, the filter propagation affects only the DAX calculation, not the security, unless you enable a particular flag available in the relationship configuration.

Consider the list of values in CountryRegion that you see in the PivotTable in Excel. The list contains all the values of that column, regardless of whether there are visible rows in the Sales table for the active roles of the connected user. (In this case, the user belongs to the ReadContosoBrand role.) Because there is a measure in the PivotTable, you must change the **Show Items with No Data on Rows** setting (in the PivotTable Options dialog box) to show all the names, as shown in Figure 10-17.

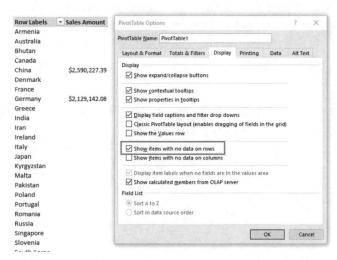

FIGURE 10-17 The PivotTable showing all the values in CountryRegion.

Figure 10-18 shows the Apply the Filter Direction When Using Row Level Security check box in the Edit Relationship dialog box. You can select this check box after you enable the bidirectional filter of the relationship. By enabling this setting, the filter propagates from Sales to Store, so each user of the role (who can see only the Contoso branded products) will see only those stores where there is data available.

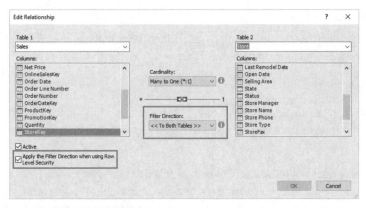

FIGURE 10-18 The Edit Relationship dialog box.

 Important You cannot enable the Apply the Filter Direction When Using Row Level Security setting when the table on the *many* side of the relationship has a filter applied in any role. Similarly, if you apply this setting, you cannot later apply any filter to the table on the *many* side of the relationship. You would get an error, such as *"Table 'Sales' is configured for row-level security, introducing constraints on how security filters are specified. The setting for Security Filter Behavior on relationship [...] cannot be Both."*

After you apply the setting shown in Figure 10-18, the same PivotTable with the same options will show only the values in the CountryRegion column, for which there is at least one related row in the Sales table for the active security roles. This result is shown in Figure 10-19. Notice that the Show Items with No Data on Rows check box is now unchecked.

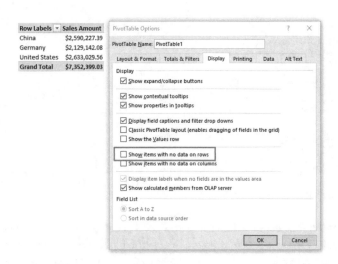

FIGURE 10-19 The PivotTable showing only the values in CountryRegion that have rows in Sales.

In some cases, you might need to filter specific combinations of keys in your fact table. For example, suppose you want to display only the sales values for black products in the year 2007 and for silver products in the year 2008. If you apply a filter on the Product attribute to return only the rows in which the Color value is Black or Silver and another filter on the Date column to return only rows in which the year is 2007 or 2008, then you see sales for all the combinations of those years and colors. To allow access to the sales values for only the black products from 2007 and the silver products from 2008—in other words, to disallow access to the sales values for the black products in 2008 or for the silver products in 2007, you can apply the filter to the Sales table itself instead of filtering by Product or Date at all. As noted, you cannot enable a filter on the Sales table if any of the relationships from this table to the other tables enable the bidirectional filter with row-level security. The following is the row-filter expression to use on Sales:

```
= ( RELATED ( 'Date'[Calendar Year Number] ) = 2007
        && RELATED ( 'Product'[Color] ) = "Black"
  )
||
  ( RELATED ( 'Date'[Calendar Year Number] ) = 2008
        && RELATED ( 'Product'[Color] ) = "Silver"
  )
```

Figure 10-20 shows a PivotTable containing data for the years 2007 and 2008 and the colors black and silver with no security applied. Figure 10-21 shows the same PivotTable when used with a role that applies the preceding filter to Sales.

Sales Amount	Column Labels		
Row Labels	CY 2007	CY 2008	Grand Total
Black	$1,988,875.64	$1,955,354.25	$3,944,229.89
Silver	$3,377,312.96	$1,783,697.39	$5,161,010.35
Grand Total	$5,366,188.60	$3,739,051.64	$9,105,240.24

FIGURE 10-20   A PivotTable with no security applied.

Sales Amount	Column Labels		
Row Labels	CY 2007	CY 2008	Grand Total
Black	$1,988,875.64		$1,988,875.64
Silver		$1,783,697.39	$1,783,697.39
Grand Total	$1,988,875.64	$1,783,697.39	$3,772,573.03

FIGURE 10-21   A PivotTable with security on Sales applied.

> **Note**   This last technique enables you to implement something like cell security in the multidimensional model. However, by using cell security, it is also possible to secure by using measures—and, as mentioned, this is not possible in the tabular model. That said, cell security in the multidimensional model often results in very poor query performance. It is usually best avoided, so the tabular model is not at a disadvantage to the multidimensional model because it does not have cell security.

Security in calculated columns and calculated tables

The values in calculated columns and calculated tables are evaluated at processing time. This is worth considering before you apply security as you decide where to apply row filters and where to create calculated columns and calculated tables. This behavior can be useful to create the non-visual totals in a tabular model.

For example, consider the requirement of a measure returning the percentage of the sales for a certain selection of products compared to the sales of all the products, including also those that are not visible to the user. A DAX measure used to compute such a percentage by default would use only the visible products in the ALL condition, as shown in the following formula:

```
Sales[% Sales] :=
DIVIDE ( [Sales Amount], CALCULATE ( [Sales Amount], ALL( 'Product' ) ) )
```

To retrieve the total of the sales while also considering the products hidden by security roles, you can create a DailySales calculated table (hidden to the user) that stores the total of sales day by day as follows. (In this example, we support browsing the model using only the Data and Product tables.)

```
DailySales =
ADDCOLUMNS (
    ALLNOBLANKROW ( 'Date'[DateKey] ),
    "Total Daily Sales", [Sales Amount]
)
```

You define a relationship between the DailySales table and the Date table and you create the following measure to compute the percentage against all the products, including those that are not visible to the user:

```
Sales[% All Sales] :=
DIVIDE ( [Sales Amount], SUM ( DailySales[Total Daily Sales] ) )
```

In Figure 10-22, you see the result of the two measures using the ReadContosoBrand role, defined previously in this chapter. The user can see only the products of the brand Contoso, so the first percentage represents the allocation of the sales by class in each year for the Contoso products (so the sum is always 100 percent at the year level). The second percentage represents the ratio between products visible to the user and the total of all the products, regardless of class and visibility. In this case, the value at the year level represents the ratio between the Contoso products and all the products in that year.

Row Labels	Sales Amount	% Sales	% All Sales
⊟ CY 2007	$2,729,818.54	100.00 %	24.14 %
Deluxe	$1,165,701.72	42.70 %	10.31 %
Economy	$230,399.79	8.44 %	2.04 %
Regular	$1,333,717.02	48.86 %	11.79 %
⊟ CY 2008	$2,369,167.68	100.00 %	23.86 %
Deluxe	$564,400.11	23.82 %	5.69 %
Economy	$360,547.96	15.22 %	3.63 %
Regular	$1,444,219.62	60.96 %	14.55 %
⊟ CY 2009	$2,253,412.80	100.00 %	24.09 %
Deluxe	$568,072.59	25.21 %	6.07 %
Economy	$619,606.69	27.50 %	6.62 %
Regular	$1,065,733.53	47.29 %	11.39 %
Grand Total	$7,352,399.03	100.00 %	24.03 %

FIGURE 10-22 A PivotTable showing the percentages against visual and non-visual totals.

You must take care to avoid disclosing sensitive data because of calculated tables and calculated columns, considering that these tables are evaluated without using security roles. However, you can use this behavior to build the tables and columns supporting the calculation related to the non-visual totals.

> **More info** You can find a more complete implementation of non-visual totals leveraging calculated tables in this article: *http://www.sqlbi.com/articles/implement-non-visual-totals-with-power-bi-security-roles/.*

Using a permissions table

As your row filters become more complicated, you might find that it becomes more and more difficult to write and maintain the DAX expressions needed for them. Additionally, security permissions might become difficult for a developer to maintain because they change frequently and each change requires a deployment to production. This is a time-consuming task. You can use a data-driven approach instead, by which security permissions are stored in a new table in your model and your row-filter expression queries this table.

Recall the example at the end of the "Filtering and table relationships" section earlier in this chapter. Now suppose that, instead of hard-coding the combinations of 2007 and Black and 2008 and Silver in your DAX, you created a new table in your relational data source like the one shown in Figure 10-23 and imported it into your model with the PermissionsYearColor name.

RoleName	CalendarYear	Color
1 MyRole	2002	Black
2 MyRole	2003	Silver

FIGURE 10-23 The PermissionsYearColor table.

A permissions table like this enables you to store the unique combinations of Calendar Year and Color, that you must secure, and the RoleName column enables you to store permissions for multiple roles in the same table. Inside your role definition, your row-filter expression on Sales can then use an expression like the following to check whether a row exists in the PermissionsYearColor table for the current role, the current CalendarYear column, or the current Color column:

```
= CONTAINS (
    PermissionsYearColor,
    PermissionsYearColor [RoleName], "MyRole",
    PermissionsYearColor [CalendarYear], RELATED ( 'Date'[Calendar Year Number] ),
    PermissionsYearColor [Color], RELATED ( 'Product'[Color] )
)
```

Adding new permissions or updating existing permissions for the role can then be done by adding, updating, or deleting rows in the PermissionsYearColor table, and then reprocessing that table. No alterations to the role itself are necessary.

As a final step, you should not only hide the Permissions table from end users by setting its Hidden property to True. You should also make sure the end users cannot query it by using the following row filter in the security role:

```
= FALSE()
```

Securing the Permissions table would not prevent the data in it from being queried when the role is evaluated. The row filter on the preceding Sales table is evaluated before the row filter on the Permissions table is applied.

Evaluating the impact of data security on performance

The existence of table filters in security roles can affect the performance of all the users belonging to that role. In general, you might experience performance issues with large tables, even when you apply the filters only to small tables.

The only rule of thumb is that you should measure performance of security roles before deploying the model in production. Do not wait for the user to experience poor performance accessing the data. When you connect to the model as an administrator, the security roles are not applied, so any performance issue related to table filters is not visible. Moreover, if you work in a development environment with a reduced set of data, you should test security roles using the full set of data because certain performance issues might arise with only a certain number of rows.

It is not easy to provide a more detailed list of best practices to avoid performance issues using security. This is because it depends on the specific data model and calculations of your solution and requires the ability to evaluate and optimize DAX query plans. However, you can find specific chapters that relate to this topic in our book *The Definitive Guide to DAX*, published by Microsoft Press. You can also find a more detailed explanation of the performance impact of data security in this article: *https://www.sqlbi.com/articles/security-cost-in-analysis-services-tabular/*.

Creating dynamic security

Dynamic security is a technique that enables a single role to apply different permissions for different users. It is useful when you would otherwise be forced to create and maintain numerous individual roles. For example, if you had a sales force of 1,000 people and you wanted to grant each salesperson access to only the sales in which he or she was involved, a non-dynamic approach would force you to create a thousand individual roles.

DAX functions for dynamic security

Two DAX functions can be used to implement dynamic security:

- **USERNAME**   This returns the Windows user name of the user who is currently connected.

- **CUSTOMDATA**   This returns the string value that has been passed to the CustomData connection string property.

The following query shows how these functions can be used:

```
CustomData = "Hello World"
```

Figure 10-24 shows the results of the query when the connection string property has been set. Refer to the section "Testing security roles" for details on how to do this in SSMS or DAX Studio. The functions are used as follows:

```
EVALUATE
ROW(
    "Results from Username", USERNAME(),
    "Results from CustomData", CUSTOMDATA()
)
```

FIGURE 10-24 The output from the USERNAME and CUSTOMDATA functions.

The key point is that these functions are useful because they can return different values for different users. So, the same DAX expression that is used for a row filter in a role can return different rows for different users.

> **Note** In a multidimensional model, it is also possible to implement dynamic security by creating a custom MDX function (also known as an *Analysis Services stored procedure*) in a .NET dynamic link library (DLL) by uploading the DLL to Analysis Services and then calling the new function from inside the role definition. This approach is not possible in the tabular model because Tabular does not support the creation of custom DAX functions.

Implementing dynamic security by using CUSTOMDATA

The CUSTOMDATA function is used for dynamic security when a front-end application handles the authentication of users itself but you must push the job of applying data security back to Analysis Services. For instance, an Internet-facing reporting tool might not want to rely on Windows authentication. Instead it might have its own system for authenticating end users. It would then open a connection to Analysis Services (as a single Windows user) for each query that was run. Each time it opened a connection, it would pass a different value through the CUSTOMDATA connection string property to indicate the end user for whom the query was being run. Analysis Services would then use the value passed through the CUSTOMDATA property as part of a row-filter expression.

CUSTOMDATA is not suitable for dynamic security when end users connect to the tabular model directly. In those situations, an end user might be able to edit the connection string property in whatever client tool he or she is using and, therefore, see data he or she is not meant to see.

The use of CUSTOMDATA in a dynamic role can be demonstrated by creating a new role, called CustomDataRole, with read permissions, and by adding the following row-filter expression to the Product table:

```
=
IF (
    CUSTOMDATA () = "",
    FALSE (),
    Product[Brand] = CUSTOMDATA ()
)
```

You can then connect to the model in SSMS by using the following connection string properties:

```
Roles=CustomDataRole; CustomData=Contoso
```

Alternatively, in DAX Studio, you can type **CustomDataRole** in the **Roles** text box and **CustomData=Contoso** in the **Additional Options** text box, as shown in Figure 10-25.

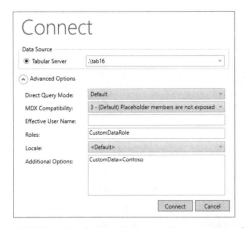

FIGURE 10-25 Setting the connection properties for testing CustomData in DAX Studio.

Then run the following DAX query:

```
EVALUATE ALL ( Product[Brand] )
```

You see that only one row is returned from the Brand column of the Product table—the row for the Contoso brand, as shown in Figure 10-26.

FIGURE 10-26 The output of a query demonstrating the use of CUSTOMDATA in a role.

Implementing dynamic security by using USERNAME

The USERNAME function is used to implement dynamic security when end users connect to a tabular model directly, which means they will be opening connections to the model by using their own Windows identities. Because one user is likely to need access to many rows on the same table, and one row on a table is likely to be accessible by more than one user, a variation on the Permissions table approach (previously described) is usually necessary when this flavor of dynamic security is used. To illustrate this, use the UserPermissions values shown in Figure 10-27 as a starting point.

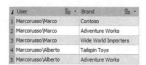

FIGURE 10-27   The UserPermissions table.

> **Important**   Marcorusso is the domain name in this example. To make this work on your own machine, you must use the names of users that exist in your own domain.

Next, create a new role called UserNameDataRole, give it read permissions, and add the users Marcorusso\Marco and Marcorusso\Alberto to it. Use the following row-filter expression on the Product table:

```
= CONTAINS (
    UserPermissions,
    UserPermissions[User], USERNAME(),
    UserPermissions[Brand], Product [Brand]
)
```

Then, in SQL Server Management Studio, open a new MDX query window with the following connection string properties set:

```
Roles=UserNameDataRole; EffectiveUserName=Marcorusso\Marco
```

Run the following DAX query again:

```
EVALUATE ALL ( Product[Brand] )
```

You see that the three rows associated with the Marcorusso\Marco user are returned from the Brand column of the Product table as shown in Figure 10-28.

FIGURE 10-28   The output of a query demonstrating the use of USERNAME in a role.

If you have multiple tables you want to control with dynamic security, you might prefer an approach based on the propagation of the security filters through the relationships instead of using a DAX expression for every table you want to filter. This technique requires you to create more tables and relationships, but it simplifies the DAX code required. For example, consider how to implement the same dynamic security model for product brands with a model-based approach. Using the UserPermissions table you have seen before, you can create two other calculated tables, Brands and Users, using the following DAX expressions:

```
Brands =
DISTINCT ( 'Product'[Brand] )

Users =
DISTINCT ( UserPermissions[User] )
```

Then, you can hide the new tables and create the following relationships that are represented in Figure 10-29:

- Product[Brand] → Brands[Brand]

- UserPermissions[Brand] → Brands[Brand]

> **Note** This relationship is bidirectional and has the Apply the Filter Direction When Using Row Level Security setting enabled, as shown previously in Figure 10-18.

- UserPermissions[User] → User[User]

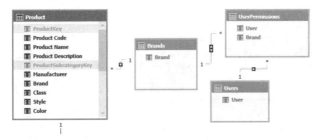

FIGURE 10-29 The diagram of hidden tables that is used to implement the security.

At this point, create or replace the UserNameDataRole by specifying only this filter in the Users table and by removing any other filter from other tables. Use the following formula:

```
= Users[User] = USERNAME()
```

You can repeat the same test performed in the text that precedes Figure 10-28, obtaining the same result. The advantage of this approach is that you must implement other permissions for other tables. You will apply the security filter to only one hidden Users table in the data model. You can find further information about this technique in the whitepaper available at *https://blogs.msdn.microsoft.com/analysisservices/2016/06/24/bidirectional-cross-filtering-whitepaper/*.

Security in DirectQuery

When you have a tabular model in DirectQuery mode, you can define the security in two ways:

- By using the security roles defined in Analysis Services, just as you do in other models using in-memory mode

- By applying the security on the relational data source by instructing Analysis Services to impersonate the current user when it sends the necessary SQL queries to the data source

Usually, you choose either one technique or the other, but there is nothing that stops you from combining both together, even if it is usually unnecessary to do so.

If you want to rely on the standard role-based security provided by Analysis Services, be aware that all the SQL queries will include the necessary predicates and will only join to retrieve the required data. When you use DirectQuery, there are restrictions to the DAX expressions you can use in the filters of the role. These are the same restrictions applied to the calculated columns in DirectQuery mode. For more details about these limitations, refer to Chapter 9, "Using DirectQuery."

If you have already implemented row-level security in the relational database and are supporting Windows integrated security, you must configure Analysis Services to impersonate the current user to use it, as described in the next section.

Security and impersonation with DirectQuery

A tabular model in DirectQuery mode can connect to SQL Server in two ways:

- By always using the same user (defined in the connection)

- By impersonating the user that is querying Analysis Services

The latter option requires Analysis Services to be configured for the Kerberos constrained delegation, as explained at *https://msdn.microsoft.com/en-us/library/dn194199.aspx*. This section focuses on configuring the desired behavior on Analysis Services.

When you use DirectQuery, the tabular model has only a single connection, which has a particular configuration for impersonation. (This is the `impersonationMode` property in the JSON file, but it is called *Impersonation Info* in SSMS and simply *Impersonation* in SSDT). This security setting specifies which user must be impersonated by Analysis Services when connecting to the data source. Such impersonation determines which Windows user will execute the code in Analysis Services connecting to the data source. If the source database supports the Windows integrated security, this user will be flagged as the user consuming the data on the relational data source. If the source database does not support the Windows integrated security, then this setting is usually not relevant for DirectQuery.

Suppose the source database was a SQL Server database using integrated security. In this case, if Analysis Services were to impersonate the current user, SQL Server could receive queries from different users and could provide different results to the same requests depending on the user itself.

If you have SQL Server 2016, this feature is available with the row-level security on the relational database, as described at *https://msdn.microsoft.com/en-us/library/dn765131.aspx*.

If your relational database can produce different results depending on the Windows user connected, then you might be interested in impersonating the current Analysis Services user in DirectQuery mode instead of using a fixed user. (Using a fixed user connecting to the data source is common when you create a tabular model that imports data in memory.) For example, you can edit the properties of the connection in SSMS in the Connection Properties dialog box, as shown in Figure 10-30. (To open this dialog box, right-click the connection of the database in the Object Explorer pane and choose **Properties**.)

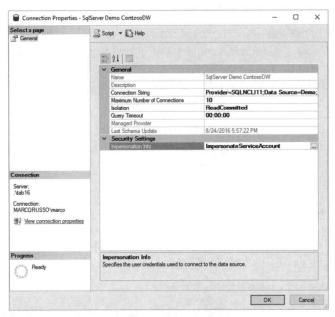

FIGURE 10-30   The Impersonation Info in the Security Settings section of the Connection Properties dialog box in SSMS.

By clicking the button marked with an ellipsis (...) to the right of the Impersonation Info entry in the Security Settings section, open the Impersonation Information dialog box shown in Figure 10-31. There, you can choose the **Use the Credentials of the Current User** option instead of the fixed user that is available in the other two options (the service account or another specific one).

FIGURE 10-31   The Impersonation Information dialog box.

Click **OK** twice to close the two dialog boxes. Your Analysis Services instance will start to use a different user for every connection made to Analysis Services, impersonating the user connected to Analysis Services for each query. You can verify this behavior by checking the NTUserName column in SQL Profiler when monitoring the SQL queries received by SQL Server. You can also set impersonation options using the same Impersonation Information dialog box in SSDT, when you define the connection to the data source.

Row-level security on SQL Server earlier than 2016

If you are using a version of SQL Server earlier than SQL Server 2016, you can use an alternative technique to implement row-level security. This technique is based on permissions assigned to schemas and involves creating the same views on different schemas that are used as default by different users. You can implement it with the following steps:

1. Assume you have the original table of the model created in the dbo schema. (If you do not, replace the dbo with the schema name in the following steps.) The user used in the data source connection in Analysis Services must use the dbo schema as a default schema.

2. Define a schema on SQL Server for every group of users.

3. Define a user on SQL Server for every user you will also enable on Analysis Services to access the tabular model that is published in DirectQuery mode.

4. Assign to each user you create in SQL Server the corresponding schema (of the group to which he or she belongs) as a default schema.

5. Grant SELECT permission on each schema to all the users belonging to the same group (that is, users who see the same rows of data).

6. For every table in the dbo schema that you reference in the tabular model, create a SQL view with the same name in each schema. This view must include a WHERE condition that filters only the rows that should be visible to that group of users.

7. In the tabular model, assign to every DirectQuery partition a SQL statement instead of a direct table binding and remove any reference to schema in the SQL query you use.

After you complete these steps, when the user queries the Analysis Services model, his or her credentials will be used by Analysis Services to connect to SQL Server. That user has a default schema that uses views with the same name as the original tables. Alternatively, they use views with an additional WHERE condition that filters only the rows he or she can see. Therefore, the SQL query generated by Analysis Services will use these views and return only the rows that the user can see. You can find another implementation of row-level security that is based on a more dynamic (data-based) approach at *http://sqlserverlst.codeplex.com*.

Monitoring security

One final subject that must be addressed regarding security is monitoring. When you are trying to debug a security implementation, it is useful to see all the connections open on a server and find out which permissions they have. This is possible by running a trace in SQL Server Profiler and looking for the events shown in Figure 10-32.

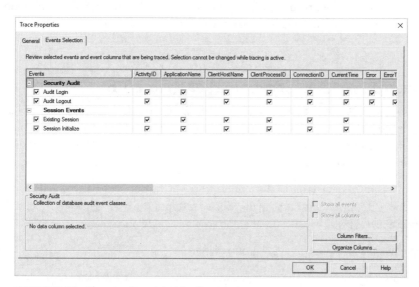

FIGURE 10-32 The security-related Profiler events.

The following events can be selected in the Events Selection tab:

- **Audit Login/Logout** These events are fired every time a user logs on and logs out of Analysis Services.

- **Existing Session** This event lists all the sessions that are currently active when the trace starts.

- **Session Initialize** These events are fired every time a new session is created, which usually happens every time a user connects to Analysis Services.

The last two of these events contain a lot of useful information, such as the user who is connecting to the model, the database to which he or she is connecting, all the properties from the connection string, and, crucially, the security roles applied to this session. It also shows the application from which the user is connecting, if the Application Name connection string property has been set. Some Microsoft client tools do this, and you might want to set it in your own applications to make debugging easier. When an administrator opens a session, you see a comma-delimited list of all the roles in the Analysis Services database, plus an asterisk at the beginning to show administrator rights in the TextData pane in Profiler, as shown in Figure 10-33. When a user who is not an administrator connects, you will see a list of the roles of which that user is a member instead.

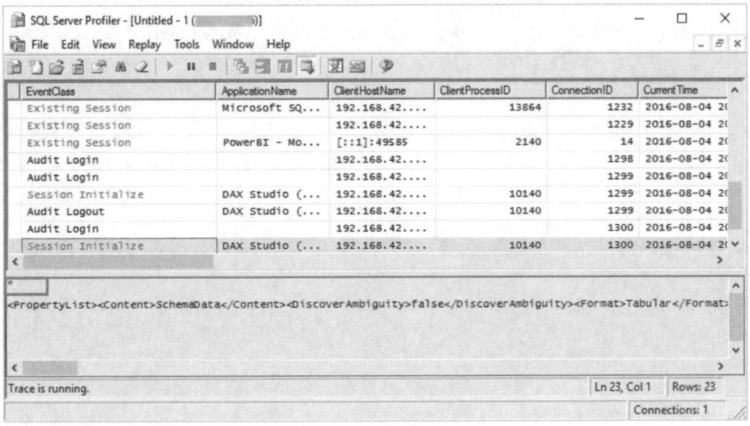

FIGURE 10-33   The Existing Session event and roles used for an administrator.

The name of the user who is connecting is always shown in the NTUserName column. When the EffectiveUserName property is used, the value that was passed to that property is shown in the Text-Data pane, along with the other connection string properties used, as shown in Figure 10-34.

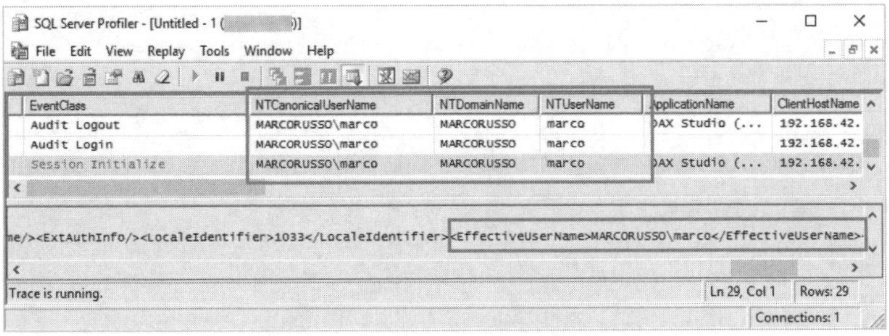

FIGURE 10-34   The actual user name and the effective user name.

Summary

In this chapter, you saw how to implement security in the tabular model. Administrative security can be configured at the instance level, through the server administrator role and at the database level. This configuration is done by creating database roles with the administrator permission. Data security can also be implemented through database roles by applying DAX row filters to tables to filter the data in each table where the role allows access. Dynamic security can be used to make a single role apply different filters for different users. DirectQuery might take advantage of impersonating the current user to leverage data security filters already implemented in the relational database. Finally, this chapter describes more advanced security configurations, such as HTTP authentication and Kerberos, and how SQL Server Profiler can be used to monitor which roles are applied when a user connects to Analysis Services.

Processing and partitioning tabular models

After you create a tabular model, you should deploy it in a production environment. This requires you to plan how you will partition and process the data. This chapter has extensive coverage of these topics, with particular attention given to design considerations that give you the knowledge to make the right decisions based on your specific requirements. You will also find step-by-step guides to introduce you to the use of certain functions that you will see for the first time in this chapter.

> **What's new in SSAS 2016**   The concepts behind process and partitioning are the same as in previous versions, but SSAS 2016 has new scripts, libraries, and tools to manage processing, deployment, and partitioning for models with compatibility level 1200 or higher.

Automating deployment to a production server

You can deploy a tabular model to a production server in the following ways:

- **By deploying it directly from SQL Server Data Tools (SSDT)**   This deploys the model according to the deployment server configuration of your project. Visual Studio 2015 configurations support tabular projects (which were not supported in previous versions of Visual Studio). You can create different configurations with different deployment server properties such as the server and database name. For example, you can create different configurations for development, a user acceptance test, and the production environments.

- **By using the Analysis Services Deployment Wizard**   This can generate a deployment script that you can forward to an administrator. The administrator can then execute the script directly in SSMS by using the ASCmd cmdlet in PowerShell (*https://msdn.microsoft.com/en-us/library/hh479579.aspx*) or by scheduling it in SQL Server Agent, provided he or she has the required administrative rights. For further information about the wizard, refer to the documentation available on MSDN at *https://msdn.microsoft.com/en-us/library/ms176121(v=sql.130).aspx*.

- **By using the Synchronize Database Wizard or by executing the script that this wizard can generate**   This wizard copies the contents of a database from a source server that you select to a target server. The server on which the wizard has been selected is the target server and will receive the Synchronize command in a script. This option can be useful to move a database that is deployed on a development or test server to a production server. It is also useful when you want to duplicate the tabular database in a server farm that is part of a scale-out architecture. You can find more information about synchronizing databases in Analysis Services at *https://msdn.microsoft.com/en-us/library/ms174928(v=sql.130).aspx.*

You can also automate the deployment from SSDT by using a custom post-build task that performs the deployment by using the MSBuild tool. Follow the instructions at *https://blogs.msdn.microsoft.com/cathyk/2011/08/10/deploying-tabular-projects-using-a-custom-msbuild-task/.*

Backup and restore operations

You can also back up and restore an Analysis Services database by using a procedure that is identical to the one used for a multidimensional database. In fact, many of the management operations (such as synchronization, deployment, backup, and restore) use the same commands and procedures for both multidimensional and tabular models. Note that the backup of an Analysis Services database is just the copy of all the files in all the directories that are contained in the database folder, including metadata and data. For this reason, the granularity of synchronize, backup, and restore operations is throughout the whole database. You can find more information about the backup and restore of an Analysis Services database at *https://msdn.microsoft.com/en-us/library/ms174874(v=sql.130).aspx.*

Table partitioning

An important design decision in a tabular model using in-memory mode is the partitioning strategy. Every table in Tabular can be partitioned, and the reason for partitioning is related exclusively to table processing. As you will see in Chapter 12, "Inside VertiPaq," partitions do not give query performance benefits in Tabular. They are useful only to reduce the time required to refresh data because you can update just the parts of a table that have been updated since the previous refresh. In this section, you learn when and how to define a partitioning strategy for your tabular model.

Defining a partitioning strategy

Every table in Tabular has one or more partitions. Every partition defines a set of rows that are read from the source table. Every partition can be processed independently and in parallel with others, so you can use partitions to accelerate the processing of a single table. Parallel processing of partitions was not possible in previous versions of Analysis Services, but it is available with Analysis Services 2016 for any compatibility level (including the 110x ones).

You define partitions related to the source table, but from the Tabular point of view, every table is made of several columns, and every column is a different object. Some columns are calculated and based on the data of other columns belonging to the same or different tables. The engine knows the dependencies of each calculated column and calculated table. When you process a partition of a table, every dependent calculated table must be completely recalculated. Moreover, every calculated column in the same or other tables must be completely recalculated for the entire table to which it belongs.

Calculated tables cannot have more than one partition. Even if they are calculated according to the dependency order that is automatically recognized by the engine, the evaluation and compression of the calculated table could be faster than the time required to evaluate a correspondent number of calculated columns in a table that has the same number of rows.

Finally, other indexing structures exist for storing column dictionaries and relationships between tables. These structures are not partitioned and require recalculation for the whole table to which they belong if a column on which they depend has been refreshed (even if only for one partition).

> **Note**   In a multidimensional model, only measure groups can be partitioned, and you can-not create partitions over dimensions. When a measure group partition is processed, all the aggregations must be refreshed, but only for the partition. However, when a dimension is refreshed, it might invalidate aggregations of a related measure group. Dependencies be-tween partitions and related structures, such as indexes and aggregations, in a multidimen-sional model might seem familiar. In reality, however, they are completely different, and the partitioning strategy can be very different between multidimensional and tabular models that use the same data source. For example, processing a table in Tabular that is a dimension in a star schema does not require you to rebuild indexes and aggregations on the measure group that corresponds to the fact table in the same star schema. Relationships and calcu-lated columns are dependent structures that must be refreshed in Tabular, but their impact is usually lower than that incurred in a multidimensional model.

The following are reasons for creating more partitions for a table:

- **Reducing processing time**   When the time required for processing the whole table is too long for the available processing window, you can obtain significant reduction by processing only the partitions that contain new or modified data.

- **Easily removing data from a table**   You can easily remove a partition from a table. This can be useful when you want to keep the last *n* months in your tabular model. By using monthly partitions, every time you add a new month, you create a new partition, removing the older month by deleting the corresponding partition.

- **Consolidating data from different source tables**   Your source data is divided into several tables, and you want to see all the data in a single table in Tabular. For example, suppose you have a different physical table in the source database for each year of your orders. In that case, you could have one partition in Tabular for every table in your data source.

The most common reason is the need to reduce processing time. Suppose you can identify only the rows that were added to the source table since the last refresh. In that case, you might use the Process Add operation. This operation reads from the data source only the rows to add, implicitly creates a new partition, and merges it with an existing one, as you will see later in this chapter in the section "Managing partitions for a table." The processing time is faster because it only reads the new rows from the data source. However, Process Add can be used only when the existing data in the partition will be never modified. If you know that a row that was already loaded has changed in the data source, you should reprocess the corresponding partition containing that row.

> **Note** An alternative approach to handling data change is to use Process Add to insert a compensating transaction. This is very common in a multidimensional model. However, because a table can be queried in Tabular without aggregating data, this approach would result in showing all the compensating transactions to the end user.

Partitions do not give you a benefit at query time, and a very high number of partitions (100 or more) can be counterproductive because all the partitions are considered during queries. VertiPaq cannot ignore a partition based on its metadata, as Analysis Services does with a multidimensional model that contains partitions with a slice definition. A partition should merely define a set of data that can be easily refreshed or removed from a table in a tabular model.

You can merge partitions—for example, by merging all the days into one month or all the months into one year. Merging partitions does not process data and therefore does not require you to access the data source. This can be important when data access is an expensive operation that occupies a larger part of the process operation. Other activities, such as refreshing internal structures, might still be required in a merge, but they are done without accessing the data sources.

Finally, carefully consider the cost of refreshing indexing structures after you process one or more partitions. (See the "Process Recalc" section later in this chapter). With complex models, this could be an important part of the process, and you must lower the object dependencies to reduce the time required to execute a Process Recalc operation. Moreover, if you remove partitions or data changes in existing partitions that are refreshed, you must plan a Process Defrag operation to optimize the table dictionary, reduce memory consumption, and improve query performance. Thus, implementing a partitioning strategy requires you to make a plan for maintenance operations. This maintenance is not required when you use the Process Full operation on a table because this operation completely rebuilds the table.

> **Important** Do not underestimate the importance of Process Defrag if you have a partitioned table where you never run a full process over the entire table. Over time, the dictionary might continue to grow with values that are never used. When this happens, you have two undesirable side effects: The dictionary becomes unwieldy and the compression decreases in efficiency because the index to the dictionary might require more bits. This can result in higher memory pressure and lower performance. A periodic Process Defrag might be very useful in these scenarios.

Defining partitions for a table in a tabular model

After you define your partition strategy, the first place in which you can create table partitions is the project of the tabular model. This option is useful mainly if you have a fixed number of partitions—because, for example, data comes from different tables or the partitioning key is not based on time. If you have a more dynamic structure of partitions, you can change them by using SSMS or scripts, as you will see in the following sections. In this section, you learn how to create partitions by using SSDT. Follow these steps:

1. Open the **Table** menu and choose **Partitions** to open the Partition Manager dialog box, shown in Figure 11-1. Here, you can edit the partitions for a table. In this example, the Customer table has just one partition (Customer) with 18,484 rows.

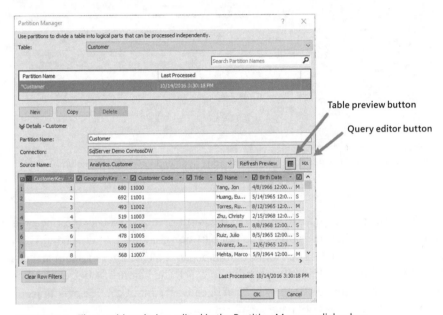

FIGURE 11-1   The partitions being edited in the Partition Manager dialog box.

2. The Table Preview and Query Editor buttons enable you to choose the content shown in the Details area below the Source Name drop-down list. Figure 11-1 shows Table Preview mode, which displays the columns and rows that can be read from the table selected in the Source Name drop-down list (in this case, Analytics.Customer). Select values for one column to filter data in the table preview and implicitly define a query that applies the same filter when processing the partition. Figure 11-2 shows how to select just a few values for the *Education* column.

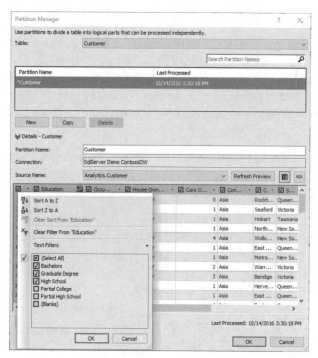

FIGURE 11-2 Filters for partitions, which you define by selecting values for a column.

> **Note** This is just an example to show you the Partition Manager user interface. It is not a best practice. This is because you should not partition columns that will change over time. This is not the case with the Education column because a customer might in fact change her education over time, changing the partition to which she belongs. A better partitioning column for Customer could be *Country of Birth* because it cannot change over time. However, the sample database does not have such a column.

3. Click the **Query Editor** button to view and edit the query in the Customer partition. The query that is generated depends on the sequence of operations you perform through the user interface. For example, if you start from the default setting (all items selected) and clear the Partial College, Partial High School, and (blanks) items, you obtain the query shown in Figure 11-3. This includes all future values, excluding those you cleared in the list.

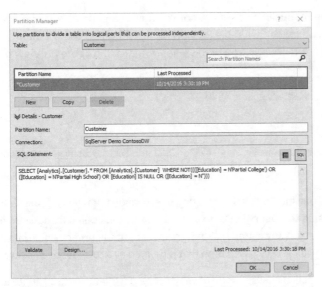

FIGURE 11-3 The Partition query obtained by clearing values in the list, which contains a NOT in the WHERE condition.

4. Clear the **Select All** check box and then manually select the Bachelor, Graduate Degree, and High School columns to obtain a SQL statement that includes only the values you explicitly selected in the list, as shown in Figure 11-4.

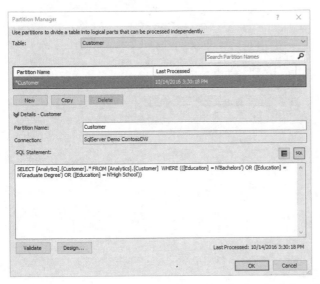

FIGURE 11-4 The Partition query obtained by clearing the Select All check box and selecting values in the list. The query includes only the selected items in the WHERE condition.

5. Edit the SQL statement manually by creating more complex conditions. Note, however, that when you do, you can no longer use Table Preview mode without losing your query. The message shown in Figure 11-5 warns you of this when you click the **Table Preview** button.

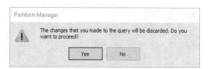

FIGURE 11-5 Showing how the manual changes to the SQL statement are lost by going back to the Table Preview mode.

6. After you create a new partition or copy an existing one, change the filters in Table Preview mode or in the SQL statement in the Query Editor to avoid the same data being loaded into more than one partition. You do not get any warning at design time about the potential for data duplication. The process operation will fail only if a column that is defined as a row identifier is duplicated.

7. Often, you will need to select a large range of values for a partition. To do so, write a SQL statement that is like the one you see in the examples shown in Figure 11-6.

Note After you modify the query's SQL statement, you cannot switch back to the Table Preview mode. If you do, the SQL statement will be replaced by a standard SELECT statement applied to the table or view that is specified in the Source Name property.

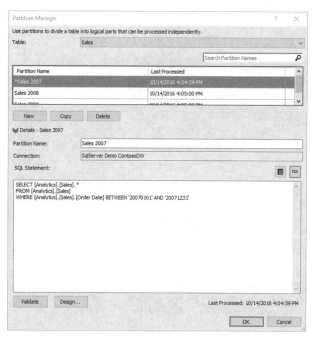

FIGURE 11-6 How the Table Preview mode cannot be used when a partition is defined by using a SQL statement.

8. **Check the SQL query performance and optimize it if necessary.** Remember, one of the goals of creating a partition is to lessen the time required to process the data. Therefore, the SQL statement you write should also run quickly on the source database.

Managing partitions for a table

After you deploy a tabular model on Analysis Services, you can create, edit, merge, and remove partitions by directly modifying the published database without deploying a new version of the model itself. This section shows you how to manage partitions by using SSMS. Follow these steps:

1. Use SSMS to browse the tables available in a tabular model. Then right-click a table name and select **Partitions** in the context menu, as shown in Figure 11-7.

FIGURE 11-7   Opening the Partitions dialog box through the context menu in SSMS.

2. The Partitions dialog box opens. You can use this dialog box to manage the partitions of any table. Open the **Table** drop-down list and choose the table that contains the partition(s) you want to manage. As shown in Figure 11-8, a list of the partitions in that table appears, including the number of rows and the size and date of the last process for each partition.

FIGURE 11-8   Editing the partitions of a table in the Partitions dialog box.

3. Select the partition(s) you want to manage. Then click one of the buttons above the list of partitions. As shown in Figure 11-8, the buttons are as follows:

- **New** Click this button to create a new partition by using a default SQL statement that gets all the rows from the underlying table in the data source. You must edit this statement to avoid loading duplicated data in the tabular table.

- **Edit** Click this button to edit the selected partition. This button is enabled only when a single partition is selected.

- **Delete** Click this button to remove the selected partition(s).

- **Copy** Click this button to create a new partition using the same SQL statement of the selected partition. (You must edit the statement to avoid loading duplicated data in the tabular table.)

- **Merge** Click this button to merge two or more partitions. The first partition selected will be the destination of the merge operation. The other partition(s) selected will be removed after being merged into the first partition.

- **Process** Click this button to process the selected partition(s).

- **Properties** Click this button to view the properties of the selected partition. (This button is enabled only when a single partition is selected.)

Clicking the New, Edit, or Copy button displays the dialog box shown in Figure 11-9, except when you click New or Copy, the name of the dialog box changes to New Partition. Note that unlike with SSDT, there is no table preview or a query designer in SSMS for editing a partition.

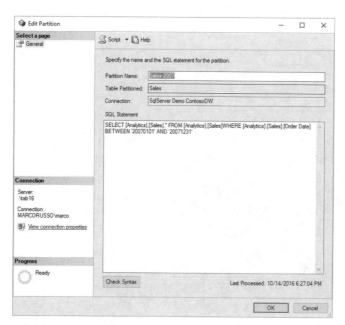

FIGURE 11-9 The dialog box shown after you click the New, Edit, or Copy button.

4. Return to the Partitions dialog box shown in Figure 11-8 and select the following partitions: Sales 2007, Sales 2008, and Sales 2009. (To select all three, hold down the **Ctrl** key as you click each partition.) Then click the **Merge** button. The Merge Partition dialog box appears, as shown in Figure 11-10.

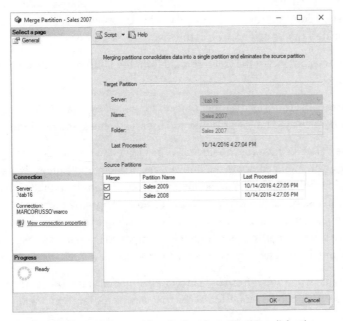

FIGURE 11-10 Merging partitions in the Merge Partition dialog box.

5. In the Source Partitions list, select the partitions you want to merge and click **OK**. The first partition you select will be the only partition that remains after the Merge operation. The other partitions selected in the Source Partitions list will be merged into the target partition and will be removed from the table (and deleted from disk) after the merge.

> **Note** For any operation you complete by using SSMS, you can generate a script (TMSL for compatibility level 1200, XMLA for compatibility levels 110x) that can be executed without any user interface. (Chapter 13, "Interfacing with Tabular," covers this in more detail.) You can use such a script to schedule an operation or as a template for creating your own script, as you'll learn in the "Processing automation" section later in this chapter.

Processing options

Regardless of whether you define partitions in your tabular model, when you deploy the model by using the in-memory mode, you should define how the data is refreshed from the data source. In this section, you learn how to define and implement a processing strategy for a tabular model.

Before describing the process operations, it is useful to quickly introduce the possible targets of a process. A tabular database contains one or more tables, and it might have relationships between tables. Each table has one or more partitions, which are populated with the data read from the data source, plus additional internal structures that are global to the table: calculated columns, column dictionaries, and attribute and user hierarchies. When you process an entire database, you process all the objects at any level, but you might control in more detail which objects you want to update. The type of objects that can be updated can be categorized in the following two groups:

- **Raw data**   This is the contents of the columns read from the data source, including the column dictionaries.

- **Derived structures**   These are all the other objects computed by Analysis Services, including calculated columns, calculated tables, attribute and user hierarchies, and relationships.

In a tabular model, the derived structures should always be aligned to the raw data. Depending on the processing strategy, you might compute the derived structures multiple times. Therefore, a good strategy is to try to lower the time spent in redundant operations, ensuring that all the derived structures are updated to make the tabular model fully query-able. Chapter 12 discusses in detail what happens during processing, which will give you a better understanding of the implications of certain processing operations. We suggest that you read both this chapter and the one that follows before designing and implementing the partitioning scheme for a large tabular model.

A first consideration is that when you refresh data in a tabular model, you process one or more partitions. The process operation can be requested at the following three levels of granularity:

- **Database**   The process operation can affect all the partitions of all the tables of the selected database.

- **Table**   The process operation can affect all the partitions of the selected table.

- **Partition**   The process operation can only affect the selected partition.

> **Note**   Certain process operations might have a side effect of rebuilding calculated columns, calculated tables, and internal structures in other tables of the same database.

You can execute a process operation by employing the user interface in SSMS or using other programming or scripting techniques discussed later in this chapter in the section "Processing automation."

Available processing options

You have several processing options, and not all of them can be applied to all the granularity levels. Table 11-1 shows you the possible combinations, when using Available for operations that can also be used in the SSMS user interface and Not in UI for operations that can be executed only by using other programming or scripting techniques. The following sections describe what each operation does and what its side effects are.

TABLE 11-1 Processing options available on entities of tabular models

Processing Option	Database	Table	Partition
Process Add			Available
Process Clear	Available	Available	Available
Process Data		Available	Available
Process Default	Available	Available	Available
Process Defrag	Not in UI	Available	
Process Full	Available	Available	Available
Process Recalc	Available		

Process Add

The Process Add operation adds new rows to a partition. It should be used only in a programmatic way. You should specify the query returning only new rows that must be added to the partition. After the rows resulting from the query are added to the partitions, only the dictionaries are incrementally updated in derived structures. All the other derived structures (calculated columns, calculated tables, hierarchies, and relationships) are automatically recalculated. The tabular model can be queried during and after a Process Add operation.

> **Important**   Consider using Process Add only in a manually created script or in other programmatic ways. If you use Process Add directly in the SSMS user interface, it repeats the same query defined in the partition and adds all the resulting rows to the existing ones. If you want to avoid duplicated data, you should modify the partition so that its query will read only the new rows in subsequent executions.

Process Clear

Process Clear drops all the data in the selected object (Database, Table, or Partition). The affected objects are no longer query-able after this command.

Process Data

Process Data loads raw data in the selected object (Table or Partition), also updating the columns' dictionaries, whereas derived structures are not updated. The affected objects are no longer query-able after this command. After Process Data, you should execute Process Recalc or Process Default to make the data query-able.

Process Default

Process Default performs the necessary operations to make the target object query-able (except when it is done at the partition level). If the database, table, or partition does not have data (that is, if it has just been deployed or cleared), it performs a Process Data operation first, but it does not perform

Process Data again if it already has data. (This is true even if data in your data source has changed because Analysis Services has no way of knowing it has changed.) If dependent structures are not valid because a Process Data operation has been executed implicitly or before the Process Default operation, it applies a partial Process Recalc to only those invalid derived structures (calculated columns, calculated tables, hierarchies, and relationships). In other words, Process Default can be run on a table or partition, resulting in only Process Recalc on those specific objects, whereas Process Recalc can be run only on the database.

A Process Default operation completed at the database level is the only operation that guarantees that the table will be query-able after the operation. If you request Process Default at the table level, you should include all the tables in the same transaction. If you request Process Default for every table in separate transactions, be careful of the order of the tables because lookup tables should be updated after tables pointing to them.

Processing tables in separate transactions

Processing tables in separate transactions can be order-dependent because of calculated columns, calculated tables, and relationships existing between tables. For example, suppose you have an Orders table and a Products table. Each order row is related to a product and the Products table contains a column that is calculated by using the Orders table. In that case, you should process the Orders table before the Products table. Otherwise, you will find that the Products table cannot be queried until it runs a Process Default after this operation has been done on the Orders table. If you use separate transactions, a better option is to perform the following sequence of operations:

1. Execute Process Data on the Orders table.

2. Execute Process Data on the Products table.

3. Execute Process Default on the Orders table.

4. Execute Process Default on the Products table.

5. Execute Process Recalc on the database.

You should execute a Process Recalc operation after Process Default because Process Recalc recalculates only those structures that have been invalidated by a Process Data operation, and it does not consume resources if the calculated columns and other structures have already been updated. Thus, unless you want Orders-related columns to be available before those related to the Products table, you can use the following simpler sequence of operations because Process Recalc implies that all the Process Default operations are made on single tables:

1. Execute Process Data on the Orders table.

2. Execute Process Data on the Products table.

3. Execute Process Recalc on the database.

Including all these operations in a single transaction is also a best practice.

The easiest way to execute commands in separate transactions is to execute each command individually. Using XMLA, you can control the transaction of multiple commands that are executed in a single batch. Using TMSL, grouping more operations in a sequence command implicitly executes a single transaction that includes all the requests, as described in Chapter 7, "The Tabular Model Scripting Language (TMSL)."

A Process Default operation made at the partition level does a Process Data operation only if the partition is empty, but it does not refresh any dependent structure. In other words, executing Process Default on a partition corresponds to a conditional Process Data operation, which is executed only if the partition has never been processed. To make the table query-able, you must still run either Process Default at the database or table level or a Process Recalc operation. Using Process Recalc in the same transaction is a best practice.

Process Defrag

The Process Defrag operation rebuilds the column dictionaries without the need to access the data source to read the data again. It is exposed in the SSMS user interface for tables only. This operation is useful only when you remove partitions from your table or you refresh some partitions and, as a result, some values in columns are no longer used. These values are not removed from the dictionary, which will grow over time. If you execute a Process Data or a Process Full operation on the whole table (the latter is covered next), then Process Defrag is useless because these operations rebuild the dictionary.

Tip A common example is a table that has monthly partitions and keeps the last 36 months. Every time a new month is added, the oldest partition is removed. As a result, in the long term, the dictionary might contain values that will never be used. In these conditions, you might want to schedule a Process Defrag operation after one or more months have been added and removed. You can monitor the size of the dictionary by using VertiPaq Analyzer (*http:// www.sqlbi.com/tools/vertipaq-analyzer/*), which is described in more detail in Chapter 12.

If you use Process Defrag at the database level, data for the unprocessed tables is also loaded. This does not happen when Process Defrag is run on a single table. If the table is unprocessed, it is kept as is.

Process Full

The Process Full operation at a database level is the easiest way to refresh all the tables and the related structures of a tabular model inside a transaction. This is so that the existing data is query-able during the whole process, and new data will not be visible until the process completes. All the existing data from all partitions are thrown away, every partition is loaded, all the tables are loaded, and then Process Recalc is executed over all the tables.

When Process Full is executed on a table, all the partitions of the table are thrown away, every parti-tion is loaded, and a partial Process Recalc operation is applied to all the derived structures (calculated columns, calculated tables, hierarchies, and relationships). However, if a calculated column depends on a table that is unprocessed, the calculation is performed by considering the unprocessed table as an empty table. Only after the unprocessed table is populated will a new Process Recalc operation compute the calculated column again, this time with the correct value. A Process Full operation of the unprocessed table automatically refreshes this calculated column.

> **Note** The Process Recalc operation that is performed within a table's Process Full operation will automatically refresh all the calculated columns in the other tables that depend on the table that has been processed. For this reason, Process Full over tables does not depend on the order in which it is executed in different transactions. This distinguishes it from the Process Defrag operation.

If Process Full is applied to a partition, the existing content of the partition is deleted, the partition is loaded, and a partial Process Recalc operation of the whole table is applied to all the derived structures (calculated columns, calculated tables, hierarchies, and relationships). If you run Process Full on multiple partitions in the same command, only one Process Recalc operation will be performed. If, however, Process Full commands are executed in separate commands, every partition's Process Full will execute another Process Recalc over the same table. Therefore, it is better to include in one transaction multiple Process Full operations of different partitions of the same table. The only side effect to consider is that a larger transaction requires more memory on the server because data processed in a transaction is loaded twice in memory (the old version and the new one) at the same time until the process transac-tion ends. Insufficient memory can stop the process or slow it down due to paging activity, depending on the Memory\VertiPaqPagingPolicy server setting, as discussed in *http://www.sqlbi.com/articles/memory-settings-in-tabular-instances-of-analysis-services*.

Process Recalc

The Process Recalc operation can be requested only at the database level. It recalculates all the derived structures (calculated columns, calculated tables, hierarchies, and relationships) that must be refreshed because the underlying data in the partition or tables is changed. It is a good idea to include Process Recalc in the same transaction as one or more Process Data operations to get better performance and consistency.

> **Tip** Because Process Recalc performs actions only if needed, if you execute two consecutive Process Recalc operations over a database, the second one will perform no actions. However, when Process Recalc is executed over unprocessed tables, it makes these tables query-able and handles them as empty tables. This can be useful during development to make your smaller tables query-able without processing your large tables.

Defining a processing strategy

After you have seen all the available Process commands, you might wonder what the best combinations to use for common scenarios are. Here you learn a few best practices and how transactions are an important factor in defining a processing strategy for your tabular model.

Transactions

Every time you execute a process operation in SSMS by selecting multiple objects, you obtain a sequence of commands that are executed within the same transaction. If any error occurs during these process steps, your tabular model will maintain its previous state (and data). If using SSMS, you cannot create a single transaction, including different process commands, such as with Process Data and Process Recalc. However, by using a script (which you can obtain from the user interface of existing process operations in SSMS), you can combine different operations in one transaction, as you will learn later in this chapter.

You might want to separate process operations into different transactions to save memory usage. During process operations, the Tabular engine must keep in memory two versions of the objects that are part of the transaction. When the transaction finishes, the engine removes the old version and keeps only the new one. If necessary, it can page out data if there is not enough RAM, but this slows the overall process and might affect query performance if there is concurrent query activity during processing. When choosing the processing strategy, you should consider the memory required and the availability of the tabular model during processing. The following scenarios illustrate the pros and cons of different approaches, helping you define the best strategy for your needs.

Process Full of a database

Executing a Process Full operation over the whole database is the simpler way to obtain a working updated tabular model. All the tables are loaded from the data source, and all the calculated columns, relationships, and other indexes are rebuilt.

This option requires a peak of memory consumption that is more than double the space required for a complete processed model, granting you complete availability of the previous data until the process finishes. To save memory, you can execute Process Clear over the database before Process Full. That way, you will not store two copies of the same database in memory. However, the data will not be available to query until Process Full finishes.

> **Tip** You can consider using Process Clear before Process Full if you can afford out-of-service periods. However, be aware that in the case of any error during processing, no data will be available to the user. If you choose this path, consider creating a backup of the database before the Process Clear operation and automatically restoring the backup in case of any failure during the subsequent Process Full operation.

Process Full of selected partitions and tables

If the time required to perform a Process Full operation of the whole database is too long, you might consider processing only changed tables or partitions. The following two approaches are available:

- **Include several Process Full operations of partitions and tables in the same transaction** This way, your tabular model will always be query-able during processing. The memory required will be approximately more than double the space required to store processed objects.

- **Execute each Process Full operation in a separate transaction** This way, your tabular model will always be query-able during processing, but you lower the memory required to something more than double the space required to store the largest of the processed objects. This option requires a longer execution time.

Process Data or Process Default of selected partitions and tables

Instead of using Process Full, which implies a Process Recalc at the end of each operation, you may want to control when Process Recalc is performed. It could be a long operation on a large database, and you want to minimize the processing-time window. You can use one of the following approaches:

- **Include Process Data of selected partitions and tables followed by a single Process Recalc operation of the database in the same transaction** This way, your tabular model will always be query-able during processing. The memory required will be approximately more than double the space required to store the processed objects.

- **Execute Process Clear of partitions and tables to be processed in a first transaction and then Process Default of the database in a second transaction** This way, you remove from memory all the data in the partitions and tables that will be processed, so the memory pressure will not be much higher than the memory that is originally used to store the objects to be processed. (Processing might require more memory than that required just to store the result, also depending on parallelism you enable in the process operation.) If you use this approach, the data will be not query-able after Process Clear until Process Default finishes. The time required to complete the operation is optimized because only one implicit Process Recalc operation will be required for all the calculated columns, relationships, and other indexes.

- **Execute Process Data of partitions and tables to be processed in separate transactions and then Process Recalc in the last transaction** This way, you minimize the memory required to handle the processing to more than double the size of the largest object to be processed. With this approach, data will not be query-able after the first Process Data until the Process Recalc operation finishes. However, in case of an error during one of the Process Data operations, you can still make the database query-able by executing the final Process Recalc, even if one or more tables contain old data and other tables show refreshed data.

- **Execute Process Clear of partitions and tables to be processed in a first transaction, then Process Data of partitions and tables in separate transactions and Process Recalc in the last transaction** Consider this approach when you have severe constraints on memory.

Data will be not query-able after Process Clear until Process Recalc executes. Because you immediately remove from memory all the tables that will be processed, the first table to be processed will have the larger amount of memory available. Thus, you should process the remaining objects by following a descendent sort order by object size. You can also consider using Process Full instead of Process Recalc to anticipate the calculation of larger objects that do not depend on tables that will be processed near the end. You should consider this approach only in extreme conditions of memory requirements.

Process Add of selected partitions

If you can identify new rows that must be added to an existing partition, you can use the Process Add operation. It can be executed in a separate transaction or included in a transaction with other commands. However, consider that Process Add implies an automatic partial Process Recalc of related structures. Thus, you should consider the following two scenarios for using it:

- **Execute one or more Process Add operations in a single transaction**   This way, your tabular model will be always query-able during processing. You should consider including more than one Process Add operation in the same transaction when the rows added in a table are referenced by rows that are added in another table. You do not want to worry about the order of these operations, and you do not want to make data visible until it is consistent.

- **Execute Process Add in the same transaction with Process Data commands on other partitions and tables, including a Process Recalc at the end**   You might want to do this when the added rows reference or are referenced from other tables. Enclosing operations in a single transaction will show new data only when the process completes and the result is consistent.

Choosing the right processing strategy

As discussed, you must consider the following factors to choose the processing strategy for your tabular model:

- **Available processing window**   How much time can you dedicate to process data?

- **Availability of data during processing**   The database should be query-able during processing.

- **Rollback in case of errors**   Which version of data do you want to see in case of an error during processing? Is it OK to update only a few tables? You can always do a database backup.

- **Available memory during processing**   The simplest and most secure processing options are those that require more physical memory on the server.

You should always favor the simplest and most secure strategy that is compatible with your requirements and constraints.

Executing processing

After you define a processing strategy, you must implement it, and you probably want to automate operations. In this section, you will learn how to perform manual process operations. Then, in the "Processing automation" section of the chapter, you will learn the techniques to automate the processing.

Processing a database

To process a database, follow these steps:

1. In SSMS, right-click the name of the database you want to process in the Object Explorer pane and choose **Process Database** in the context menu shown in Figure 11-11. The Process Database dialog box opens.

FIGURE 11-11   Opening the Process Database dialog box.

2. Open the **Mode** drop-down list and select the processing mode. In this example, the default mode, **Process Default**, is selected, as shown in Figure 11-12.

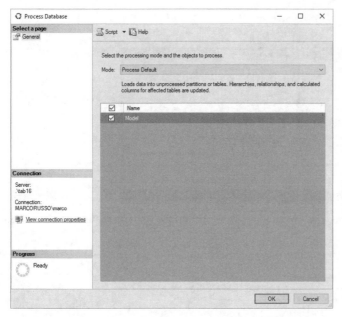

FIGURE 11-12   Using the Process Database dialog box to process the database.

3.   Click **OK** to process the database.

You can generate a corresponding script by using the Script menu in the Process Database dialog box. You'll see examples of scripts in the "Sample processing scripts" section later in this chapter.

> **Note**   Even if you process a database without including the operation in a transaction, all the tables and partitions of the database will be processed within the same transaction and the existing database will continue to be available during processing. In other words, a single Process command includes an implicit transaction.

Processing table(s)

Using SSMS, you can manually request to process one or more tables. Follow these steps:

1.   Select the tables in the Object Explorer Details pane, right-click one of the selections, and choose **Process Table** in the context menu, as shown in Figure 11-13. The Process Table(s) dialog box opens, with the same tables you chose in the Object Explorer Details pane selected, as shown in Figure 11-14.

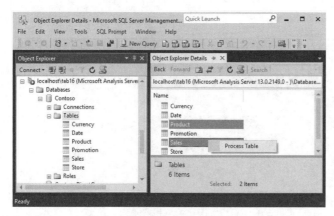

FIGURE 11-13   Opening the Process Table(s) dialog box using the table context menu in SSMS.

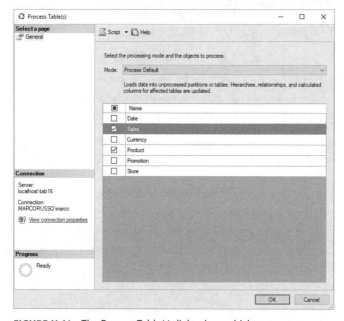

FIGURE 11-14   The Process Table(s) dialog box, which can process one or more tables.

Note   You can also open the Process Table(s) dialog box by right-clicking a table in the
Object Explorer pane and choosing **Process Table**. However, when you go that route, you
can select only one table—although you can select additional tables in the Process Table(s)
dialog box.

2.   Click the **OK** button to start the process operation. In this case, the selected tables will be processed in separate batches (and therefore in different transactions) using the process selected
in the Mode drop-down list.

Note The script generated by the Process Table(s) dialog box includes all the operations within a single transaction. This is true of the script generated through the Script menu. In contrast, the direct command uses a separate transaction for every table.

Processing partition(s)

You can process one or more partitions. Follow these steps:

1. Click the **Process** button in the Partitions dialog box (refer to Figure 11-8). This opens the Process Partition(s) dialog box, shown in Figure 11-15.

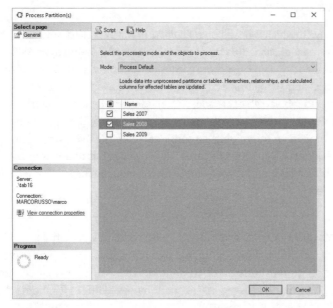

FIGURE 11-15 The Process Partition(s) dialog box, which can process one or more partitions.

2. Click the **OK** button to process all the selected partitions as part of the same batch within a single transaction using the process mode you selected in the Mode drop-down list.

Note The script generated through the Script menu will also execute the process in a single transaction, regardless of the number of partitions that have been selected.

If you want to implement Process Add on a partition, you cannot rely on the SSMS user interface because it will execute the same query that exists for the partition, adding its result to existing rows. Usually, a query will return the same result, and therefore you will obtain duplicated rows. You should manually write a script or a program that performs the required incremental update of the partition. You can find an example of a Process Add implementation in the article at *http://www.sqlbi.com/articles/using-process-add-in-tabular-models/*.

Processing automation

After you define partitioning and processing strategies, you must implement and, most likely, automate them. To do so, the following options are available:

- Tabular Model Scripting Language (TMSL)

- PowerShell

- Analysis Management Objects (AMO) and Tabular Object Model (TOM) libraries (.NET languages)

- SQL Server Agent

- SQL Server Integration Services (SSIS)

We suggest that you use TMSL (which is based on a JSON format) to create simple batches that you can execute interactively. Alternatively, schedule them in a SQL Server Agent job or an SSIS task. If you want to create a more complex and dynamic procedure, consider using PowerShell or a programming language. Both access the AMO and TOM libraries. (You will see some examples in the "Using Analysis Management Objects (AMO) and Tabular Object Model (TOM)" section later in this chapter, and a more detailed explanation in Chapter 13.) In this case, the library generates the required script dynamically, sending and executing it on the server. You might also consider creating a TMSL script using your own code, which generates the required JSON syntax dynamically. However, this option is usually more error-prone, and you should consider it only if you want to use a language for which the AMO and TOM libraries are not available.

> **Note** All the statements and examples in this section are valid only for tabular models that are created at the 1200 compatibility level or higher. If you must process a tabular model in earlier compatibility levels, you must rely on documentation available for Analysis Services 2012/2014. Also, the XMLA format discussed in this section uses a different schema than the XMLA used for compatibility levels 1100 and 1103.

Using TMSL commands

Tabular Model Scripting Language (TMSL) is discussed in Chapter 7. To automate processing activities, you use only a few of the commands available in TMSL. Every time you use SSMS to execute an administrative operation—for example, processing an object or editing partitions—you can obtain a TMSL script that corresponds to the operation you intend to do.

You can execute such a script in several ways. One is to use SSMS to execute a TMSL script in an XMLA query pane. Follow these steps:

1. Open the **File** menu, choose **New**, and select **Analysis Services XMLA Query**, as shown in Figure 11-16. Alternatively, by right-click a database, choose **New Query** from the context menu, and select **XMLA** from the context menu.

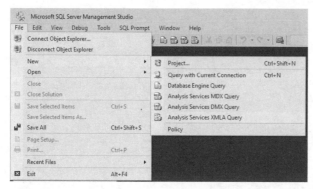

FIGURE 11-16 Opening the Analysis Services XMLA Query pane.

2. In the XMLA query pane, write a TMSL command.

3. Open the **Query** menu and choose **Execute** to execute the command. Even if the editor does not recognize the JSON syntax, you can see the result of a Process Default command on the Contoso database, as shown in Figure 11-17.

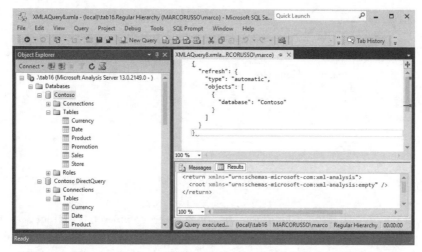

FIGURE 11-17 The execution of a TMSL script to process a database, with the result shown in the Results pane on the lower right.

You can use the `sequence` command to group several TMSL commands into a single batch. This implicitly specifies that all the commands included should be part of the same transaction. This can be an important decision, as you saw in the "Processing options" section earlier in this chapter. For example, the TMSL `sequence` command in Listing 11-1 executes within the same transaction the Process Data of two tables (Product and Sales) and the Process Recalc of the database:

LISTING 11-1 Script TMSL\Process Sequence Tables.xmla

```
{
  "sequence": {
    "maxParallelism": 10,
    "operations": [
      {
        "refresh": {
          "type": "dataOnly",
          "objects": [
            {
              "database": "Contoso",
              "table": "Sales"
            },
            {
              "database": "Contoso",
              "table": "Product"
            }
          ]
        }
      },
      {
        "refresh": {
          "type": "calculate",
          "objects": [
            {
              "database": "Contoso"
            }
          ]
        }
      }
    ]
  }
}
```

The sequence command can include more than one process command. The target of each process operation is defined by the objects element in each refresh command. This identifies a table or database. If you want to group several commands in different transactions, you must create different sequence commands, which must be executed separately. For example, to run Process Clear on two tables and then a single Process Default on the database, without keeping in memory the previous versions of the tables cleared during the database process, you must run the two refresh commands shown in Listing 11-2 separately:

LISTING 11-2 Script TMSL\Process Clear and Refresh.xmla

```
{
  "refresh": {
    "type": "clearValues",
    "objects": [
```

```
        {
            "database": "Contoso",
            "table": "Sales"
        },
        {
            "database": "Contoso",
            "table": "Product"
        }
        ]
    }
}
{
    "refresh": {
        "type": "automatic",
        "objects": [
            {
                "database": "Contoso"
            }
        ]
    }
}
```

All the partitions of a table are processed in parallel by default. In addition, all the tables involved in a refresh command are processed in parallel, too. Parallel processing can reduce the processing-time window, but it requires more RAM to complete. If you want to reduce the parallelism, you can specify the maxParallelism setting in a sequence command, even if you run a single refresh operation involving more tables and/or partitions. Listing 11-3 shows an example in which the maximum parallelism of a full database process is limited to 2.

LISTING 11-3   Script TMSL\Process Database Limited Parallelism.xmla

```
{
    "sequence": {
        "maxParallelism": 2,
        "operations": [
            {
                "refresh": {
                    "type": "full",
                    "objects": [
                        {
                            "database": "Contoso"
                        }
                    ]
                }
            }
        ]
    }
}
```

It is beyond the scope of this section to provide a complete reference to TMSL commands. You can find a description of TMSL in Chapter 7 and a complete reference at *https://msdn.microsoft.com/en-us/library/mt614797.aspx*. A more detailed documentation of the JSON schema for TMSL is available at *https://msdn.microsoft.com/en-us/library/mt719282.aspx*.

The best way to learn TMSL is by starting from the scripts you can generate from the SSMS user interface and then looking in the documentation for the syntax that is required to access other properties and commands that are not available in the user interface. You can generate a TMSL command dynamically from a language of your choice and then send the request by using the AMO and TOM libraries that we introduce later in this chapter. (These are described in more detail in Chapter 13.)

XMLA-based tabular metadata commands

The Tabular engine can receive commands in two formats: XMLA and JSON. The current implementation of Analysis Services 2016 (RTM) transforms any JSON request into an internal XMLA request. However, this implementation might change in the future. Using JSON is the recommended way to write a commands batch for a tabular model because its syntax is simpler and more readable and the overhead required by the internal translation to XMLA is negligible. Moreover, the XMLA syntax is very context-dependent; the same script might not work even on a different deployment of the same logical schema.

For example, consider the following TMSL script to process a table:

```
{
  "refresh": {
    "type": "full",
    "objects": [
      {
        "database": "Contoso",
        "table": "Currency"
      }
    ]
  }
}
```

Internally, it is converted in the following XMLA command, which has several numeric references to internal IDs that are not immediately recognizable in the high-level definition of the data model that you create in Visual Studio:

```
<Batch Transaction="true"
       xmlns="http://schemas.microsoft.com/analysisservices/2003/engine">
  <Refresh xmlns="http://schemas.microsoft.com/analysisservices/2014/engine">
    <DatabaseID>Contoso</DatabaseID>
    <Tables>
      <xs:schema xmlns:xs="http://www.w3.org/2001/XMLSchema"
                 xmlns:sql="urn:schemas-microsoft-com:xml-sql">
        <xs:element>
          <xs:complexType>
            <xs:sequence>
```

```
                <xs:element type="row"/>
              </xs:sequence>
            </xs:complexType>
          </xs:element>
          <xs:complexType name="row">
            <xs:sequence>
              <xs:element name="ID" type="xs:unsignedLong" sql:field="ID" minOccurs="0"/>
              <xs:element name="ID.Table" type="xs:string" sql:field="ID.Table"
                        minOccurs="0"/>
              <xs:element name="RefreshType" type="xs:long" sql:field="RefreshType"
                        minOccurs="0"/>
            </xs:sequence>
          </xs:complexType>
        </xs:schema>
        <row xmlns="urn:schemas-microsoft-com:xml-analysis:rowset">
          <ID>16</ID>
          <RefreshType>1</RefreshType>
        </row>
      </Tables>
      <Bindings>
        <Binding>
          <ObjectID>1</ObjectID>
        </Binding>
      </Bindings>
    </Refresh>
    <SequencePoint xmlns="http://schemas.microsoft.com/analysisservices/2014/engine">
      <DatabaseID>Contoso</DatabaseID>
    </SequencePoint>
</Batch>
```

You might encounter the XMLA-based syntax when you capture profiler or extended events from Analysis Services. This syntax could be displayed as an internal command that is generated by a TMSL syntax. Alternatively, it could be sent by SSMS when you process an object from its user interface, without generating a script first.

If you are interested in the syntax of XMLA-based tabular metadata commands, see the documentation at *https://msdn.microsoft.com/en-us/library/mt719151.aspx*. However, this could be useful only for debugging purposes, not for directly manipulating this syntax. For the purposes of this book, we consider the use of XMLA (made by the Tabular engine and SSMS) for a model in compatibility level 1200 as an internal implementation detail that could change in the future.

Executing from PowerShell

You can execute a TMSL command by using the `Invoke-ASCmd` cmdlet in PowerShell. You can provide the TMSL command straight in the `Query` parameter of the cmdlet, in an external input file. If you want to dynamically modify the process operation to execute, you should consider using the SQLAS provider for PowerShell, which provides access to the features that are available in the AMO and TOM libraries, as described later in this chapter.

For example, you can run a full process of the Contoso database by using the following PowerShell command. (Note that all the double quotes have been duplicated because they are defined within a string that is passed as an argument to the cmdlet.)

```
Invoke-ASCmd -server "localhost\tab16" -query "{""refresh"": {""type"":
""full"",""objects"": [{""database"": ""Contoso""}]}}"
```

If you have a file containing the TMSL command, you can run a simpler version:

```
Invoke-ASCmd -Server "localhost\tab16" -InputFile "c:\scripts\process.json"
```

The content of the process.json file could be what appears in Listing 11-4.

LISTING 11-4   Script TMSL\Process Contoso Database.xmla

```
{
  "refresh": {
    "type": "full",
    "objects": [
      {
        "database": "Contoso"
      }
    ]
  }
}
```

More details about the Invoke-ASCmd cmdlet are available at *https://msdn.microsoft.com/en-us/library/hh479579.aspx*.

Executing from SQL Server Agent

You can schedule an execution of a TMSL script in a SQL Server Agent job. Open the Job Step Properties dialog box and follow these steps:

1. Open the **Type** drop-down list and select **SQL Server Analysis Services Command**.

2. Open the **Run As** drop-down list and choose a proxy user (in this example, **SQL Server Agent Service Account**). The proxy user must have the necessary rights to execute the specified script.

3. In the **Server** field, specify the Analysis Services instance name.

4. Write the script in the **Command** text box (Figure 11-18 shows an example) and click **OK**.

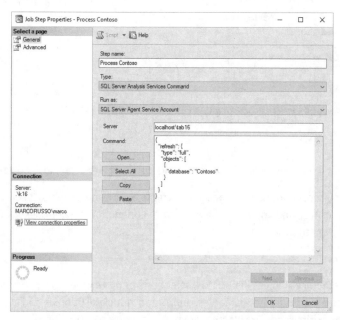

FIGURE 11-18 A TMSL command, which can be executed in a SQL Server Agent job step.

> **Tip** When SQL Server Agent runs a job, it does so by using the SQL Server Agent account. This account might not have sufficient privileges to run the process command on Analysis Services. To use a different account to run the job step, you must define a proxy account in SQL Server so that you can choose that account in the Run As combo box in the Job Step Properties dialog box. For detailed instructions on how to do this, see *http://msdn.microsoft. com/en-us/library/ms175834.aspx.*

Executing from SQL Server Integration Services

You can use SSIS to execute a TMSL script into an Analysis Services Execute DDL task. This approach is described in the next section, which also describes the Analysis Services Processing task that you can use for simpler process operations.

Using SQL Server Integration Services

SSIS 2016 supports Tabular in both the Analysis Services Processing task and the Analysis Services Execute DDL task controls. (Previous versions of SSIS supported only multidimensional models.) To help with this, you can add an Analysis Services Processing task control to the control flow of your package, as shown in Figure 11-19.

FIGURE 11-19 Inserting an Analysis Services Processing task control in an SSIS package.

Next, follow these steps:

1. Open the Analysis Services Processing Task Editor and display the Processing Settings page.

2. Select an Analysis Services connection manager or create a new one. (You must select a specific database with this control, and you must use a different connection in your package for each database that you want to process.)

3. Click the **Add** button.

4. In the Add Analysis Services Object dialog box, select one or more objects to process in the database—the entire model, individual tables, and/or individual partitions—and click **OK**. (In this example, the entire model is selected, as shown in Figure 11-20.)

5. Run a full process of the entire model.

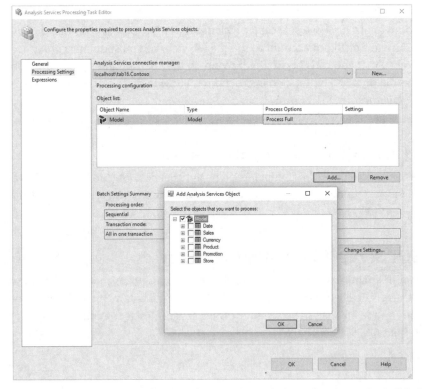

FIGURE 11-20 Scheduling a full process by using the Analysis Services Processing task in SSIS.

The Processing Order and Transaction Mode properties are not relevant when you process a tabular model. They are relevant only when the target is a multidimensional model. The TMSL generated by this task is always a single sequence command containing several refresh operations that are executed in parallel in a single transaction. If you need a more granular control of transactions and an order of operation, you should use several tasks, arranging their order using the Integration Services precedence constraints.

If you want more control over the TMSL code sent to Analysis Services, you can use the Analysis Services Execute DDL task, which accepts a TMSL script in its DDL Statements property, as shown in Figure 11-21.

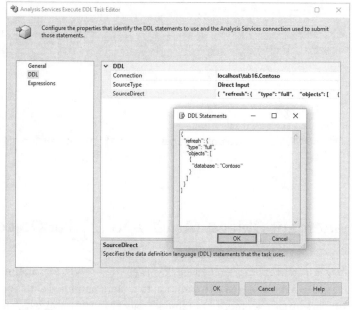

FIGURE 11-21 Scheduling a full process by using the Analysis Services Execute DDL task in SSIS.

> **Tip** It is better to prepare the TMSL command by using the XMLA query pane in SSMS (so you have a minimal editor available) than to try to modify the SourceDirect property directly in the DDL Statements editor (which is the basic text box shown in Figure 11-21).

If you want to parameterize the content of the TMSL command, you must manipulate the SourceDirect property as a string. For example, you can build the TMSL string in a script task by assigning it to a package variable and then using an expression to set the Source property of the task. There is no built-in parameterization feature for the TMSL script in this component.

Using versions of Integration Services earlier than 2016

If you use Integration Services on a version of SQL Server earlier than 2016, you cannot use the Analysis Services Processing task. It supports commands for multidimensional models only and lacks the specific processing commands for a tabular model. Moreover, in previous versions of Integration Services, the TMSL script is not recognized as a valid syntax of an Analysis Services Execute DDL task. In this case, you can specify a TMSL script by wrapping it in an XMLA Statement node, as in the following example:

```
<Statement xmlns="urn:schemas-microsoft-com:xml-analysis">
    {
        "refresh": {
            "type": "calculate",
            "objects": [
                {
                    "database": "Contoso"
                }
            ]
        }
    }
</Statement>
```

The TMSL script wrapped in an XMLA `Statement` node can also run on the latest version of Integration Services (2016).

Using Analysis Management Objects (AMO) and Tabular Object Model (TOM)

You can administer Analysis Services instances programmatically by using the Analysis Management Objects (AMO) API. AMO includes several features that are common to multidimensional and tabular deployments. Specific tabular APIs are usually referenced as Tabular Object Model (TOM), which is an extension of the original AMO client library. Today, however, you could consider TOM a subset of AMO. You might find both terms in the SSAS documentation. You can use AMO and TOM libraries from managed code (such as C# or Visual Basic) or by using PowerShell.

These libraries support the creation of XMLA scripts, or the direct execution of commands on Analysis Services. In this section, you will find a few examples of these capabilities applied to the processing of objects in a tabular model. You will find a more detailed explanation of these libraries in Chapter 13. For a complete example of how to manage rolling partitions, see the "Sample processing scripts" section later in this chapter.

Listing 11-5 shows how you can execute Process Data in C# on the Product and Sales tables, followed by Process Recalc in the same transaction, applying a max parallelism of 5.

Models\Chapter 11\AmoProcessTables\Program.cs

```csharp
using Microsoft.AnalysisServices.Tabular;

namespace AmoProcessTables {
    class Program {
        static void Main(string[] args) {
            Server server = new Server();
            server.Connect(@"localhost\tab16");
            Database db = server.Databases["Contoso"];
            Model model = db.Model;
            Table tableProduct = model.Tables["Product"];
            Table tableSales = model.Tables["Sales"];
            tableProduct.RequestRefresh(RefreshType.DataOnly);
            tableSales.RequestRefresh(RefreshType.DataOnly);
            model.RequestRefresh(RefreshType.Calculate);
            model.SaveChanges(new SaveOptions() { MaxParallelism = 5 });
            server.Disconnect();
        }
    }
}
```

The SaveChanges method called on the Model object is the point where the activities are executed. In practice, all the previous calls to RequestRefresh are simply preparing the list of commands to be sent to Analysis Services. When you call SaveChanges, all the refresh operations are executed in parallel, even if the Process Recalc operation that is applied to the data model always follows the process of other tables and partitions. If you prefer to execute the process commands sequentially, you must call SaveChanges after each RequestRefresh. In other words, SaveChanges executes all the operations requested up to that time.

You can execute the same operations by using PowerShell with script shown in Listing 11-6. You will find more details about these libraries and their use in Chapter 13.

LISTING 11-6 Script PowerShell\AmoProcessTables.ps1

```powershell
[System.Reflection.Assembly]::LoadWithPartialName("Microsoft.AnalysisServices.Tabular")

$server = New-Object Microsoft.AnalysisServices.Tabular.Server
$server.Connect("localhost\tab16")
$db = $server.Databases["Contoso"]
$model = $db.Model
$tableProduct = $model.Tables["Product"]
$tableSales = $model.Tables["Sales"]
$tableProduct.RequestRefresh("DataOnly")
$tableSales.RequestRefresh("DataOnly")
$model.RequestRefresh("Calculate")
$saveOptions = New-Object Microsoft.AnalysisServices.Tabular.SaveOptions
$saveOptions.MaxParallelism = 5
$model.SaveChanges( $saveOptions )using Microsoft.AnalysisServices.Tabular;
```

As discussed in the "Using TMSL commands" section, the engine internally converts TMSL into an XMLA script that is specific for Tabular. The AMO library directly generates the XMLA script and sends it to the server, but if you prefer, you can capture this XMLA code instead. You might use this approach to generate valid scripts that you will execute later, even if TMSL would be more compact and readable. (In Chapter 13, you will see a separate helper class in AMO to generate TMSL scripts in JSON.) To capture the XMLA script, enable and disable the CaptureXml property before and after calling the SaveChanges method. Then iterate the CaptureLog property to retrieve the script, as shown in the C# example in Listing 11-7.

LISTING 11-7   Models\Chapter 11\ AmoProcessTablesScript\Program.cs

```
using System;
using Microsoft.AnalysisServices.Tabular;

namespace AmoProcessTables {
    class Program {
        static void Main(string[] args) {
            Server server = new Server();
            server.Connect(@"localhost\tab16");
            Database db = server.Databases["Contoso"];
            Model model = db.Model;
            Table tableProduct = model.Tables["Product"];
            Table tableSales = model.Tables["Sales"];
            tableProduct.RequestRefresh(RefreshType.DataOnly);
            tableSales.RequestRefresh(RefreshType.DataOnly);
            model.RequestRefresh(RefreshType.Calculate);
            server.CaptureXml = true;
            model.SaveChanges(new SaveOptions() { MaxParallelism = 5 });
            server.CaptureXml = false;

            // Write the XMLA script on the console
            Console.WriteLine("------ XMLA script ------");
            foreach (var s in server.CaptureLog) Console.WriteLine(s);
            Console.WriteLine("----- End of script -----");
            server.Disconnect();
        }
    }
}
```

Every call to SaveChanges executes one transaction that includes all the requests made up to that point. If you want to split an operation into multiple transactions, simply call SaveChanges to generate the script or execute the command for every transaction.

Using PowerShell

In addition to using the AMO libraries from PowerShell, you can also use task-specific cmdlets that simplify the code required to perform common operations such as backup, restore, and process. Before starting, you must make sure that specific PowerShell components are installed on the computer where you want to run PowerShell. The simplest way to get these modules is by downloading and installing the latest version of SSMS. The following modules are available:

- **SQLAS**   This is for accessing the AMO libraries.

- **SQLASCMDLETS**   This is for accessing the cmdlets for Analysis Services.

For a step-by-step guide on installing these components, see *https://msdn.microsoft.com/en-us/library/hh213141.aspx.*

The following cmdlets are useful for a tabular model:

- **Add-RoleMember**   This adds a member to a database role.

- **Backup-ASDatabase**   This backs up an Analysis Services database.

- **Invoke-ASCmd**   This executes a query or script in the XMLA or TMSL (JSON) format.

- **Invoke-ProcessASDatabase**   This processes a database.

- **Invoke-ProcessTable**   This processes a table.

- **Invoke-ProcessPartition**   This processes a partition.

- **Merge-Partition**   This merges a partition.

- **Remove-RoleMember**   This removes a member from a database role.

- **Restore-ASDatabase**   This restores a database on a server instance.

For a more complete list of available cmdlets and related documentation, see *https://msdn.microsoft.com/en-us/library/hh758425.aspx.*

Listing 11-8 shows an example of a cmdlet-based PowerShell script that processes the data of two partitions (Sales 2008 and Sales 2009). It then executes a Process Default at the database level, making sure that the database can be queried immediately after that:

LISTING 11-8   Script PowerShell\Cmdlet Process Partitions.ps1

```
Invoke-ProcessPartition -Server "localhost\tab16" -Database "Partitions" -TableName
"Sales"
-PartitionName "Sales 2008" -RefreshType DataOnly


Invoke-ProcessPartition -Server "localhost\tab16" -Database "Partitions" -TableName
"Sales"
-PartitionName "Sales 2009" -RefreshType DataOnly


Invoke-ProcessASDatabase -Server "localhost\tab16" -DatabaseName "Partitions"
-RefreshType Automatic
```

Sample processing scripts

This section contains a few examples of processing scripts that you can use as a starting point to create your own versions.

Processing a database

You can process a single database by using a TMSL script. By using the `full` type in the `refresh` command, users can query the model just after the process operation. You identify the database by specifying just the database name. The script in Listing 11-9 processes all the tables and partitions of the Static Partitions database.

LISTING 11-9   Script TMSL\Process Database.xmla

```
{
  "refresh": {
    "type": "full",
    "objects": [
      {
        "database": "Static Partitions",
      }
    ]
  }
}
```

You can obtain the same result using the PowerShell script shown in Listing 11-10. In this case, the script contains the name of the server to which you want to connect (here, `localhost\tab16`).

LISTING 11-10   Script PowerShell\Process Database.ps1

```
[System.Reflection.Assembly]::LoadWithPartialName("Microsoft.AnalysisServices.
Tabular")

$server = New-Object Microsoft.AnalysisServices.Tabular.Server
$server.Connect("localhost\tab16")
$db = $server.Databases["Static Partitions"]
$model = $db.Model
$model.RequestRefresh("Full")
$model.SaveChanges()
```

The PowerShell script retrieves the model object that corresponds to the database to process. (This is identical to the previous TMSL script.) It also executes the RequestRefresh method on it. The call to SaveChanges executes the operation. All the previous lines are required only to retrieve information and to prepare the internal batch that is executed on the server by this method.

Processing tables

You can process one or more tables by using a TMSL script. By using the `full` type in the `refresh` command in TMSL, users can query the model just after the process operation. You identify a table by specifying the database and the table name. The script shown in Listing 11-11 processes two tables, Product and Sales, of the Static Partitions database.

LISTING 11-11   Script TMSL\Process Tables.xmla

```
{
  "refresh": {
    "type": "full",
    "objects": [
      {
        "database": "Static Partitions",
        "table": "Product"
      },
      {
        "database": "Static Partitions",
        "table": "Sales"
      }
    ]
  }
}
```

You can obtain the same result by using the PowerShell script shown in Listing 11-12. In this case, the script contains the name of the server to which you want to connect (`localhost\tab16`).

LISTING 11-12   Script PowerShell\Process Tables.ps1

```
[System.Reflection.Assembly]::LoadWithPartialName("Microsoft.AnalysisServices.
Tabular")

$server = New-Object Microsoft.AnalysisServices.Tabular.Server
$server.Connect("localhost\tab16")
$db = $server.Databases["Static Partitions"]
$model = $db.Model
$tableSales = $model.Tables["Sales"]
$tableProduct = $model.Tables["Product"]
$tableSales.RequestRefresh("Full")
$tableProduct.RequestRefresh("Full")
$model.SaveChanges()
```

The PowerShell script retrieves the table objects that correspond to the tables to process. (This is identical to the previous TMSL script.) It then executes the `RequestRefresh` method on each one of them. The call to `SaveChanges` executes the operation. All the previous lines are required only to retrieve information and to prepare the internal batch that is executed on the server by this method.

Processing partitions

You can process a single partition by using a TMSL script. By using the `full` type in the `refresh` command in TMSL, users can query the model just after the process operation. You identify a partition by specifying the database, table, and partition properties. The script in Listing 11-13 processes the Sales 2009 partition in the Sales table of the Static Partitions database.

LISTING 11-13   Script TMSL\Process Partition.xmla

```
{
  "refresh": {
    "type": "full",
    "objects": [
      {
        "database": "Static Partitions",
        "table": "Sales",
        "partition": "Sales 2009"
      }
    ]
  }
}
```

You can obtain the same result by using the PowerShell script shown in Listing 11-14. In this case, the script contains the name of the server to which you want to connect (`localhost\tab16`).

LISTING 11-14   Script PowerShell\Process Partition.ps1

```
[System.Reflection.Assembly]::LoadWithPartialName("Microsoft.AnalysisServices.
Tabular")

$server = New-Object Microsoft.AnalysisServices.Tabular.Server
$server.Connect("localhost\tab16")
$db = $server.Databases["Static Partitions"]
$model = $db.Model
$tableSales = $model.Tables["Sales"]
$partitionSales2009 = $tableSales.Partitions["Sales 2009"]
$partitionSales2009.RequestRefresh("Full")
$model.SaveChanges()
```

The PowerShell script retrieves the partition object that corresponds to the partition to process. (This is identical to the previous TMSL script.) It then executes the `RequestRefresh` method on it. The call to SaveChanges executes the operation. All the previous lines are required only to retrieve information and to prepare the internal batch that is executed on the server by this method.

Rolling partitions

A common requirement is to create monthly partitions in large fact tables, keeping in memory a certain number of years or months. To meet this requirement, the best approach is to create a procedure that automatically generates new partitions, removes old partitions, and processes the last one or two partitions. In this case, you cannot use a simple TMSL script, and you must use PowerShell or some equivalent tool that enables you to analyze existing partitions and to implement a logic based on the current date and the range of months that you want to keep in the tabular model.

The PowerShell script shown in Listing 11-15 implements a rolling partition system for a table with monthly partitions. The script has several functions before the main body of the script. These remove partitions outside of the months that should be online, add missing partitions, and process the last two partitions. The current date implicitly defines the last partition of the interval.

Before the main body of the script, you can customize the behavior of the script by manipulating the following variables:

- **$serverName**   This lists the name of the server, including the instance name.

- **$databaseName**   This lists the name of the database.

- **$tableName**   This lists the name of the table containing the partitions to manage.

- **$partitionReferenceName**   This lists the name of the partition reference.

- **$monthsOnline**   This lists the number of months/partitions to keep in memory.

The data model should be defined with a single partition, called the *partition reference*. This should include a (1=0) condition in the query's WHERE predicate. The script then copies the partition reference; clones the partition reference to create one partition for each month; renames the partition with a *YYYYMM* name (where *YYYY* is the year and *MM* the month number); and replaces the (1=0) condition with a SQL predicate that contains only the dates included in the partition (in this example, these are found in the Order Date column). All the partitions are added, removed, and processed in parallel within the same transaction, which corresponds to the execution of the SaveChanges method in the model object.

LISTING 11-15   Script PowerShell\Rolling Partitions.ps1

```
[System.Reflection.Assembly]::LoadWithPartialName("Microsoft.AnalysisServices.
Tabular")
# Set Verbose to 0 if you do not want to see verbose log
$verbose = 1

function GetPartitionNumber ( [int]$year, [int]$month ) {
    $year * 12 - 1 + $month
}

function GetPartitionYear ( $partitionNumber ) {
    [int][math]::floor( $partitionNumber / 12)
}
```

```
function GetPartitionMonth ( $partitionNumber ) {
    [int]( ($partitionNumber ) % 12 + 1)
}

function GetPartitionStart ( $partitionNumber ) {
    $year = GetPartitionYear ($partitionNumber )
    $month = GetPartitionMonth ($partitionNumber )
    (New-Object DateTime( $year, $month, 1 ))
}

function GetPartitionEnd ( $partitionNumber ) {
    $year = GetPartitionYear ($partitionNumber )
    $month = GetPartitionMonth ($partitionNumber )
    (New-Object DateTime( $year, $month, 1 )).AddMonths(1).AddDays(-1)
}

function GetPartitionName ( $partitionNumber ) {
    $year = GetPartitionYear ($partitionNumber )
    $month = GetPartitionMonth ($partitionNumber )
    (New-Object DateTime( $year, $month, 1 )).ToString( "yyyyMM" )
}

function AddPartition( $table, $referencePartition, [int]$partitionNumber ) {
    $partitionStart = GetPartitionStart ( $partitionNumber )
    $partitionEnd = GetPartitionEnd ( $partitionNumber )
    $partitionName = GetPartitionName ( $partitionNumber )
    $existingPartition = $table.Partitions.Find($partitionName)
    if (!$existingPartition) {
        if ($verbose) {
            "Add Partition " + $partitionName
        }
        $placeHolder = "(1=0)"
        $newPartitionFilter = '
            "([Order Date] BETWEEN '" '
            + $partitionStart.ToString( "yyyyMMdd" ) '
            + "' AND '" + $partitionEnd.ToString( "yyyyMMdd" ) + "')"

        $newPartition = $referencePartition.Clone()
        $newPartition.Source.Query = $referencePartition.Source.Query.
Replace($placeHolder, $newPartitionFilter )
        # $newPartition.Source.Query
        $newPartition.Name = $partitionName
        $table.Partitions.Add( $newPartition )
    }
    else {
        if ($verbose) {
            "Existing Partition=" + $partitionName
        }
    }
}
```

```
function ProcessPartition( $table, [int]$partitionNumber ) {
    $partitionName = GetPartitionName ( $partitionNumber )
    $existingPartition = $table.Partitions.Find($partitionName)
    if (!$existingPartition) {
        if ($verbose) {
            "Partition not found: " + $partitionName
        }
    }
    else {
        if ($verbose) {
            "Process table " + $table.Name + " partition " + $partitionName
        }
        $existingPartition.RequestRefresh("DataOnly")
    }
}

function RemovePartition( $table, [int]$partitionNumber ) {
    $partitionName = GetPartitionName ( $partitionNumber )
    $existingPartition = $table.Partitions.Find($partitionName)
    if (!$existingPartition) {
        if ($verbose) {
            "Partition not found: " + $partitionName
        }
    }
    else {
        if ($table.Partitions.Remove($existingPartition)) {
            if ($verbose) {
                "Removing partition: " + $partitionName
            }
        }
        else {
            if ($verbose) {
                "Failed remove partition: " + $partitionName
            }
        }
    }
}


# ----------------------------------------------------
#   Parameters to process monthly partitions
# ----------------------------------------------------

# Name of the server (including instance name)
$serverName = "localhost\tab16"
# Name of the database
$databaseName = "Dynamic Partitions"
#Name of the table containing partitions
$tableName = "Sales"
# Name of partition reference, should contain (1=0) in WHERE condition
$partitionReferenceName = "Sales"
# Number of months/partitions to keep in memory
$monthsOnline = 18
```

```
# ---------------------------------------------------
#   Script to process monthly partitions
# ---------------------------------------------------

$server = New-Object Microsoft.AnalysisServices.Tabular.Server
$server.Connect( $serverName )
$db = $server.Databases[$databaseName]
$model = $db.Model
$table = $model.Tables[$tableName]
$referencePartition = $table.Partitions[$partitionReferenceName]


# Generate range of partitions to process
$today = Get-Date
# NOTE: The sample database has data between 2007 and 2009.
#       By subtracting 8 years, any date in 2017 corresponds
#       to dates in 2009. For this reason, we normalize the current
#       year so that it corresponds to the last year in the sample database.
#       You should remove the AddYears function for your database.
$currentDay = $today.AddYears(2009 - $today.Year)
$lastPartition = $currentDay.Year * 12 - 1 + $currentDay.Month
$firstPartition = $lastPartition - $monthsOnline

# Remove older partitions
ForEach ( $partitionScan in $table.Partitions) {
    if ($partitionScan.Name -ne $partitionReferenceName) {
        $year = [math]::Floor([int]($partitionScan.Name) / 100)
        $month = [int]($partitionScan.Name) % 100
        $partitionNumber = GetPartitionNumber $year $month
        if ( ($partitionNumber -lt $firstPartition) '
            -or ($partitionNumber -gt $lastPartition) ) {
            RemovePartition $table $partitionNumber
        }
    }
}

# Add missing partitions
For ($partitionNumber = $firstPartition; $partitionNumber -le $lastPartition;
$partitionNumber++) {
    AddPartition $table $referencePartition $partitionNumber
}

# Process last two partitions
ProcessPartition $table ($lastPartition - 1)
ProcessPartition $table $lastPartition

# Complete refresh at database level (also process new partitions)
$model.RequestRefresh("Automatic")
$model.SaveChanges()
```

Summary

This chapter discussed how to define and implement partitioning and processing strategies for tabular models. Various APIs and tools can help you in the implementation of your strategy, such as TMSL, AMO, SSIS, and PowerShell. The chapter contained several practical examples for common processing and partitioning operations using TMSL and PowerShell scripts. For more details about the API used by PowerShell scripts, see Chapter 13.

Inside VertiPaq

I n Chapter 1, "Introducing the tabular model," you saw that the tabular model can execute a query by using an in-memory analytics engine or by translating the MDX or DAX query into one or more SQL queries. The former uses a storage engine called *VertiPaq*, whereas the latter uses DirectQuery. This chapter is dedicated to the internal architecture of the VertiPaq engine, which is the in-memory columnar database that stores and hosts tabular models.

Before reading this chapter, you need to be aware of the following two facts:

- Implementation details change often. We did our best to show information at a level that is not likely to change soon. We carefully balanced the detail level and usefulness with consistency over time. The most up-to-date information will always be available in blog posts and articles on the web.

- All the considerations about the engine are useful if you rely on the VertiPaq engine, but they are not relevant if you are using DirectQuery. However, we suggest you read and understand it anyway because it shows many details that will help you choose the best engine for your analytical scenario.

> **What's new in SSAS 2016** The VertiPaq engine has been improved in SSAS 2016, but this does not affect the general concepts behind how it works. However, this chapter has been reviewed and updated to include sections about internal metadata, memory usage, and tools to analyze VertiPaq structures.

Understanding VertiPaq structures

In this first part of the chapter, you learn how VertiPaq stores data in memory. This knowledge is fundamental in understanding how to improve compression and performance of both processing and querying a tabular model.

Understanding column storage

VertiPaq is an in-memory columnar database. This means all the data handled by a model resides in RAM, making it an easy concept to grasp. We think of a table as a list of rows, where each row is divided into columns—for example, the Product table shown in Figure 12-1.

Product

ID	Name	Color	Unit Price
1	Camcorder	Red	112.25
2	Camera	Red	97.50
3	Smartphone	White	100.00
4	Console	Black	112.25
5	TV	Blue	1,240.85
6	CD	Red	39.99
7	Touch screen	Blue	45.12
8	PDA	Black	120.25
9	Keyboard	Black	120.50

FIGURE 12-1 The Product table, with four columns and nine rows.

If you think of a table as a set of rows, then you are using the most natural visualization of a table structure, also known as a *row store*. In a row store, data is organized in rows. Using the values in the table shown in Figure 12-1 as an example, when data is stored in memory, the value in the Name column in the first row is adjacent to the values in the ID and Color columns in the same row. That means the value in the Name column in the second row is not adjacent to the value of the Name column in the first row. Between them are values in the Color and Unit Price columns in the first row and in the ID column in the second row.

Suppose you need to compute the sum of the values in the Unit Price column. If you were to read the data in the table sequentially in the way we just described, you would have to scan the entire table, reading many values that you are not interested in seeing. In other words, when scanning the memory of the database sequentially, to read the first value of Unit Price, you must read (and skip) ID, Name, and Color from the first row. Only then will you find an interesting value. The same process repeats for all the rows. You need to read and ignore many columns to find the interesting values to sum.

Reading and ignoring values takes time. In fact, if you were asked to compute the sum of the values in the Unit Price column, you would not follow that algorithm. Instead, as a human being, you would probably scan the first row and search for the position of Unit Price. You would then move your eyes vertically, reading only the values in the Unit Price column one at a time and mentally accumulating their values to produce the sum. The reason for this very natural behavior is that you save time by reading vertically instead of on a row-by-row basis.

In a columnar database, data is organized in such a way to optimize vertical scanning. To obtain this result, you need a way to make the different values of a column adjacent one to the other. Figure 12-2 shows the same Product table organized as a columnar database.

Product Columns

ID	Name	Color	Unit Price
1	Camcorder	Red	112.25
2	Camera	Red	97.50
3	Smartphone	White	100.00
4	Console	Black	112.25
5	TV	Blue	1,240.85
6	CD	Red	39.99
7	Touch screen	Blue	45.12
8	PDA	Black	120.25
9	Keyboard	Black	120.50

FIGURE 12-2 The Product table organized on a column-by-column basis.

When stored in a columnar database, each column has its own data structure, and is physically separated from the others. Thus, the different values of Unit Price are adjacent to each other and are distant from the values in the Color, Name, and ID tables.

On this data structure, computing the sum of the values in the Unit Price column is much easier because you immediately go to the table that contains the Unit Price column, where you can find all the values you need to perform the computation. In other words, you need not read and ignore other column values. In a single scan, you obtain only the useful numbers, and you can quickly aggregate them.

Now imagine that instead of asking you for the sum of the values in the Unit Price column, we asked you to compute the sum of the values in the Unit Price column for only those products that contain a value of Red in the Color column. Try this before you continue reading. It will help you better understand the algorithm.

Computing the sum is more difficult now because you cannot obtain the sum by simply scanning the Unit Price column. Instead, you might scan the Color column and, whenever it contains the value Red, note the corresponding value in the Unit Price column. Then you would sum up all those values to compute the result. This algorithm, although very natural, would require you to constantly move your eyes from one column to another, possibly guiding your finger to keep the last scanned position. It is definitely not an optimized way of computing the value! A better way—one that only computers use— is to first scan the Color column, find the row numbers where the value is Red, and then, once you know the row numbers, scan the Unit Price column and sum only the rows you identified in the previous step.

This last algorithm is much better because it lets you perform one scan of the first column and one scan of the second column, always accessing the memory locations that are adjacent to each other (apart from the jump between the scan of the first and second column).

Things are even worse for a more complex expression, such as the sum of all the products that contain either Blue or Black in the Color column and a value higher than USD 50 in the Unit Price column. This time, you have no chance of scanning the column one at a time because the condition depends on many columns. (As usual, if you try it on paper, it helps you understand it better.) The simplest algorithm to produce such a result is to scan the table, not on a column basis, but on a row basis. You probably scanned the table row by row, even if the storage organization is column by column. Although it is a very simple operation when executed on paper by a human, the same operation is extremely expensive if executed by a computer in RAM because it requires a lot of random reads of memory, leading to a worse performance than if computed by doing a sequential scan.

> **Note** You might know that RAM is short for *random-access memory*, which allows data to be read at the same speed and latency, irrespective of the physical location of data inside the memory. While true in theory, this statement is no longer valid in modern hardware. Because RAM's access time is high compared to the CPU clock speed, there are different levels of caches for the CPU to improve performance. Data is transferred in pages to the cache, so reading a contiguous area of memory is faster than accessing the same amount of data scattered in different non-contiguous memory addresses. You can find more information about the role of CPU cache at *https://en.wikipedia.org/wiki/CPU_cache*.

Columnar databases provide very quick access to a single column. If you need a calculation that involves many columns, they need to spend some time reorganizing the information in such a way that the final expression can be computed. Even though this example was very simple, it is already very useful to highlight the most important characteristics of column stores:

- Single-column access is very fast because it reads a single block of memory and then computes whatever aggregation you need on that memory block.

- If an expression uses many columns, the algorithm requires the engine to access different memory areas at different times, while keeping track of the progress in a temporary area.

- The more columns you need to compute an expression, the harder it becomes to produce a final value. Eventually, it is easier to rebuild the row storage out of the column store to compute the expression.

Column stores aim to reduce the read time. However, they spend more CPU cycles to rearrange the data when many columns from the same table are used. Row stores, on the other hand, have a more linear algorithm to scan data, but they result in many useless reads. As a rule, reducing reads and increasing CPU usage is a good exchange because with modern computers it is always easier (and cheaper) to increase the CPU speed than to reduce the I/O (or memory access) time. Moreover, columnar databases can reduce the amount of time spent scanning data, via compression. VertiPaq compression algorithms aim to reduce the memory footprint of your data model. This is very important for two reasons:

- **A smaller model makes a better use of your hardware**   Why spend money on 1 TB of RAM when the same model, once compressed, can be hosted in 256 GB? Saving RAM is always a good option, if feasible.

- **A smaller model is faster to scan**   As simple as this rule is, it is very important when speaking about performance. If a column is compressed, the engine will scan less RAM to read its content, resulting in better performance.

> **Important**   The actual details of VertiPaq's compression algorithm are proprietary. Naturally, we cannot publish them in a book. What we explain in this chapter is simply a good approximation of what happens in the engine. You can use this information to understand how the VertiPaq engine stores data.

Value encoding versus hash encoding

The first compression technique concerns how VertiPaq stores column values in memory. Each column can be encoded using either one of these techniques: value encoding or hash encoding.

Value encoding

Value encoding stores data by applying both an offset and a reduction of the bits required to store the value, based on the range of values that are available in the column. Suppose you have a column that contains the price of products, stored as integer values. There are many different values, and to represent them all, you need a defined number of bits.

Let's use the values in Figure 12-3 as an example. The maximum value in the Unit Price column is 216. Therefore, you need at least 8 bits to store each value. However, by using a simple mathematical operation, you can reduce the storage to 5 bits. In this case, by subtracting the minimum value (194) from all the values in the Unit Price column, VertiPaq reduces the range of the column to a range from 0 to 22. Storing numbers up to 22 requires fewer bits than storing numbers up to 216. While 3 bits might seem like a very small saving, when you multiply this over a few billion rows, it is easy to see that the difference can be important.

Reducing the number of bits needed

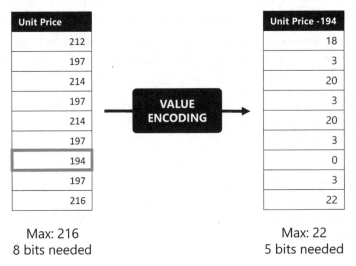

Unit Price
212
197
214
197
214
197
194
197
216

Max: 216
8 bits needed

Unit Price -194
18
3
20
3
20
3
0
3
22

Max: 22
5 bits needed

FIGURE 12-3 Using VertiPaq to reduce the number of bits needed for a column.

The VertiPaq engine is even much more sophisticated than that. It can discover mathematical relationships between the values of a column. When it finds them, it can use them to modify the storage, reducing its memory footprint. Obviously, when using the column, it must re-apply the transformation in the opposite direction to obtain the original value. Depending on the transformation, this can happen before or after aggregating the values. Again, this will increase the CPU usage and reduce the number of reads, which, as discussed, is a very good option.

Value encoding happens only for numeric columns. Obviously, it cannot be applied on strings, as there are no values to encode. Note that VertiPaq stores the currency data type of DAX in an integer value. However, value encoding can also be applied to floating-point values, when the used values can be stored as a series of sequential integers with simple arithmetical transformations. For example, sequences compressed as value encoding might include 1, 2, 3, 4; or 0.01, 0.02, 0.03, 0.04; or 10, 20, 30, 40; or 120, 130, 140.

Hash encoding

Hash encoding (also known as *dictionary encoding*) is another technique used by VertiPaq to reduce the number of bits required to store a column. Hash encoding builds a dictionary of the distinct values of a column and then it replaces the column values with indexes to the dictionary. Let's see this with an example. In Figure 12-4, you can see the Color column, which uses strings and, thus, cannot be value-encoded.

Replacing datatypes with dictionary and indexes

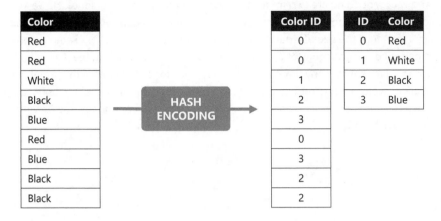

FIGURE 12-4 Creating the dictionary and replacing the values with indexes.

When VertiPaq encodes a column with hash encoding, it does the following:

- It builds a dictionary, containing the distinct values of the column.

- It replaces the column values with integer numbers, where each number is the dictionary index of the original value.

There are some advantages to using hash encoding:

- Columns contain only integer values, making it simpler to optimize the internal code of the engine. Moreover, it basically means that VertiPaq is data-type independent.

- The number of bits used to store a single value is the minimum number of bits necessary to store an index entry. In the example provided, having only four different values, 2 bits are sufficient.

These two aspects are of paramount importance for VertiPaq. When you leverage hash encoding, it does not matter whether you use a string, a 64-bit integer, or a floating point to represent a value. All these data types can be hash-encoded, providing the same performance in terms of both speed of scanning and storage space. The only difference might be in the size of the dictionary, which is typically very small when compared to the size of the column itself.

The primary factor to determine the column size is not the data type, but the number of distinct values of the column. We refer to these numbers as the column's *cardinality*. Of all the various factors of an individual column, the most important one when designing a data model is its cardinality. The lower the cardinality, the smaller the number of bits required to store a single value and, consequently, the smaller the memory footprint of the column. If a column is smaller, not only will it be possible to store more data in the same amount of RAM, it will also be much faster to scan it whenever you need to aggregate its values in a DAX expression.

Run-length encoding

Hash encoding and value encoding are two mutually exclusive compression techniques. However, there is a third complementary compression technique used by VertiPaq: *run-length encoding* (*RLE*). This technique aims to reduce the size of a dataset by avoiding repeated values. For example, consider a column that contains the calendar quarter of a sale, which is stored in the Sales table. This column might have the string Q1 repeated many times in contiguous rows, for all the sales in the same quarter. In such a case, VertiPaq avoids storing repeated values and replaces them with a slightly more complex structure. The structure contains the value only once, with the number of contiguous rows having the same value, as shown in Figure 12-5.

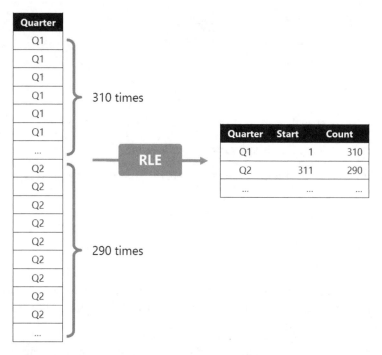

FIGURE 12-5   Using RLE to replace repeated values with the number of contiguous rows that contain the same value.

    Note   The table on the right side of Figure 12-5 contains the Quarter, Start, and Count columns. In reality, Start is not required because VertiPaq can compute it by summing all the previous values of Count, which again saves precious bytes of RAM.

RLE's efficiency strongly depends on the repetition pattern of the column. Some columns will have the same value repeated for many rows, which results in a higher compression ratio. Others, with quickly changing values, will produce a lower compression ratio. Data sorting is extremely important to improve the compression ratio of RLE, as you will see later in this chapter.

You might have a column in which the content changes so often that, if you try to compress it using RLE, you end up using *more* space. Think, for example, of a table's primary key. It has a different value for each row, resulting in an RLE version that is larger than the original column itself. In such a case, VertiPaq skips the RLE compression and stores the column as it is. Thus, the VertiPaq column storage will never exceed the original column size.

The previous example showed RLE applied to the Quarter column's strings. In this case, RLE processed the already hash-encoded version of the column. In fact, each column can use RLE with either hash or value encoding. VertiPaq's column storage, compressed with hash encoding, consists of two distinct entities: the dictionary and the data rows. The latter is the RLE-encoded result of the hash-encoded version of the original column, as shown in Figure 12-6.

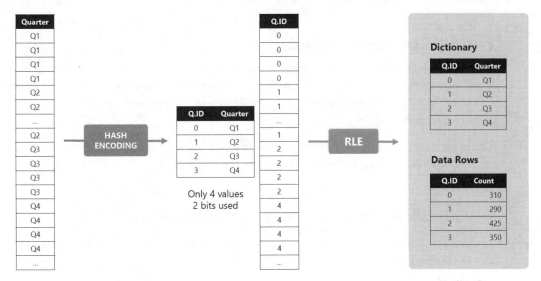

FIGURE 12-6 RLE applied to the hash-encoded version of a column.

VertiPaq also applies RLE to value-encoded columns. In this case, the dictionary is missing because the column already contains value-encoded integers.

When working with a tabular model, the factors to consider regarding its compression ratio are as follows, in order of importance:

- **The cardinality of the column**   This defines the number of bits used to store values.

- **The distribution of data in a column**   A column with repeated values will be compressed more than a column with frequently changing values.

- **The number of rows in the table**   Note that this is less important than cardinality and the distribution of data in columns.

- **The data type of the column**   This affects only the dictionary size.

Given these considerations, it is nearly impossible to predict the compression ratio of a table. Moreover, you can limit the number of rows and change the data types, but these are the least important aspects of the table.

Finally, it is worth noting that if you reduce the cardinality of a column, you are also increasing the chances of repetition. For example, if you store a column containing time values with a granularity of seconds, then you have up to 86,400 distinct values in the column. If, on the other hand, you store the same column with time values with a granularity of hours, then you have not only reduced the cardinality, but you have also introduced repeating values (3,600 seconds converts to the same hour), resulting in a much better compression ratio. Also consider that changing the data type from date to integer or string has an irrelevant impact on the column size because it affects only the dictionary size, not the number of unique values and the consequent compression rate.

Controlling column encoding

SQL Server Analysis Services (SSAS) must decide which algorithm to use to encode each column. In general, it needs to decide whether to use a value or hash encoding. However, the patented algorithms used by SSAS are much more complex. This description is a simplification of them, yet it is enough to give you a solid understanding.

To determine the best algorithm to use, SSAS reads a sampling of rows during the first scan of the source. It then selects the algorithm based on the following conditions:

- If the data type of the column is a string, hash encoding is used.

- For numeric values, SSAS uses the following additional heuristics:

  - If the column numbers increase linearly, it is probably a primary key, and value encoding is the best option.

  - If the numbers are in a defined range of values, then value encoding is the way to go.

  - If the numbers have a wide range of values, then dictionary encoding is the best choice.

Once the decision is made, SSAS starts to compress the column using the chosen algorithm. Occasionally, values that were not in the original sampling can cause the process to require reevaluation. For example, SSAS might read a few million rows in which the values are in the range 100–201, making value encoding the best choice. However, after those millions of rows, an outlier might suddenly appear—for example, a large number like 60,000,000. Cleary, value encoding cannot continue because the number of bits needed to store such a large number is larger than the bits available. Instead of continuing with the wrong choice, SSAS can decide to re-encode the column. This means the whole column is re-encoded using, in this case, hash encoding. This process might take a long time because it needs to reprocess the entire column.

For very large datasets, where processing time is important, a best practice is to provide SSAS with a good sample of data distribution in the first set of rows it reads. This reduces re-encoding risks to a minimum. This technique can also be useful to "suggest" the type of encoding you want to use.

For example, if the first partition read in a table has a small number of rows, and the interval of values is wide, then dictionary encoding might seem the best option for VertiPaq. However, you cannot apply a real constraint to the encoding choice made by the engine, and re-encoding is always possible later.

Hierarchies and relationships

As you saw in Chapter 11, "Processing and partitioning tabular models," SSAS builds two additional data structures after table processing:

- **Hierarchies** There are of two types of hierarchies: attribute hierarchies and user hierarchies. Both are data structures used to improve the performance of MDX queries. Because DAX does not have the concept of hierarchy in the language, user hierarchies are not used in DAX calculations. They are required only if you want to make a column visible to MDX. Attribute hierarchies are used internally by the engine for certain optimizations, such as looking for a certain value in an attribute. If a column is hidden from the client and used only in particular DAX calculations (such as aggregation) and not to filter or group values, then these structures are of limited use in your data model, but you still must pay the price to store them in memory.

- **Relationships** A relationship is a data structure that maps IDs in one table to row numbers in another table.

> **Note** Relationships play an important role in the VertiPaq engine, and, for some extreme optimizations, it is important to understand how they work.

With regard to relationships, consider two related tables—Sales and Products—both containing a ProductKey column. Products[ProductKey] is a primary key. You know that VertiPaq used value encoding and no compression at all on Products[ProductKey] because RLE could not reduce the size of a column without duplicated values. However, Sales[ProductKey] is likely hash-encoded and compressed because it probably contains many repetitions. In other words, the data structures of the two columns are completely different.

Moreover, because you created the relationship, VertiPaq knows that you are likely to use it often, thus placing a filter on Products and expecting to filter Sales, too. If every time it needed to move a filter from Products to Sales, VertiPaq had to retrieve values from Products[ProductKey], search them in the Sales[ProductKey] dictionary, and retrieve the Sales[ProductKey] IDs to place the filter, then it would result in slow queries.

To improve query performance, VertiPaq stores relationships as pairs of IDs and row numbers. Given the ID of a Sales[ProductKey], it can immediately find the corresponding rows in the Products table that match the relationship. Relationships are stored in memory, as any other data structure of VertiPaq. Figure 12-7 shows you how the relationship between Sales and Products is stored.

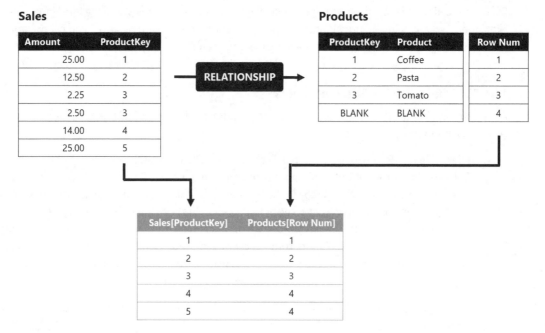

Sales

Amount	ProductKey
25.00	1
12.50	2
2.25	3
2.50	3
14.00	4
25.00	5

RELATIONSHIP

Products

ProductKey	Product	Row Num
1	Coffee	1
2	Pasta	2
3	Tomato	3
BLANK	BLANK	4

Sales[ProductKey]	Products[Row Num]
1	1
2	2
3	3
4	4
5	4

FIGURE 12-7   The Sales and Products relationship.

Segmentation and partitioning

As you might imagine, compressing a table of several billion rows in a single step would be extremely memory-intensive and time-consuming. However, the table is not processed as a whole. Instead, SSAS reads it into segments during processing. By default, these segments contain 8 million rows each. When a segment is completely read, the engine starts to compress it, and at the same time reads the next segment.

You can configure the segment size by using the DefaultSegmentRowCount entry in the Management Studio server properties of a SSAS instance. You can change this property without restarting the service, which would affect all the associated process operations (as shown in Figure 12-8). A value of 0 uses the default value of 8,000,000 rows in Analysis Services. If you import a model from a Power Pivot workbook, consider that the segments in Power Pivot are limited to 1,000,000 rows each. Thus, reprocessing such a database in Analysis Services usually reduces the number of segments.

> **Note**   A future release of Analysis Services might introduce a setting for this column that is local to a single process operation, without requiring you to change the server settings to affect a single process.

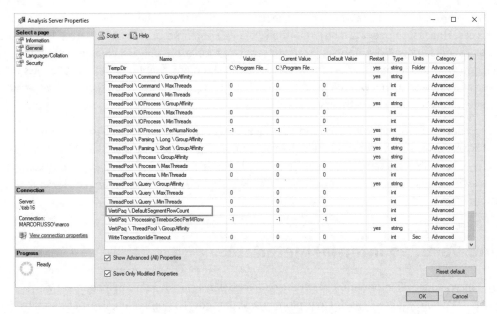

FIGURE 12-8 DefaultSegmentRowCount setting in the Analysis Services Properties dialog box.

Segmentation is important for the following reasons:

- When querying a table, VertiPaq uses the segments as the basis for parallelism, using one core per segment when scanning a column. By default, SSAS always uses one single thread to scan a table with 8,000,000 rows or less. You start seeing parallelism in action only on much larger tables.

- The larger the segment, the better the compression. VertiPaq can achieve better compression levels by analyzing more rows in a single compression step. On very large tables, it is important to test different segment sizes and measure the memory usage to achieve optimal compression. Keep in mind that increasing the segment size can negatively affect processing time; the larger the segment, the slower the processing.

- Although the dictionary is global to the table, bit-sizing can be further reduced at the segment level. Thus, if a column has 1,000 distinct values but, in a specific segment, only two of them are used, then that column might be compressed up to a single bit for that segment. The actual number of bits used in a segment depends on the range of internal indexes that reference the dictionary. For this reason, the sort order of a partition could be important in large tables to reduce the number of distinct values per segment. For optimal compression, the values used in a partition must be adjacent in the dictionary if the column has hash encoding. Parallel processing of multiple partitions might affect this optimal result.

- If segments are too small, then the parallelism at query time is increased. This is not always a good thing. In fact, while scanning the column is faster, VertiPaq needs more time at the end of the scan to aggregate partial results that are computed by the different threads. If a partition is too small, then the time required to manage task switching and final aggregation is more than the time needed to scan the data, with a negative impact to the overall query performance.

During processing, if the table has only one partition, the first segment receives a special treatment. In this case, the first segment can be larger than DefaultSegmentRowCount. VertiPaq reads twice the size of DefaultSegmentRowCount and starts to segment a table, but only if it contains more rows. (This does not apply to a table with more than one partition.) Therefore, a table with 10,000,000 rows will be stored as a single segment, whereas a table with 20,000,000 rows will use three segments: two containing 8,000,000 rows and one with only 4,000,000 rows.

Segments cannot exceed the partition size. If you have a partitioning schema on your model that creates partitions of only 1,000,000 rows, then all your segments will be smaller than 1,000,000 rows (namely, they will be the same as the partition size). The over-partitioning of tables is a very common mistake for new VertiPaq users. Remember that creating too many small partitions can lower the performance.

Reading VertiPaq internal metadata

SSAS lets you discover information about the data model by using dynamic management views (DMVs). DMVs are extremely useful to explore how your model is compressed, the space used by different columns and tables, the number of segments in a table, or the number of bits used by columns in different segments.

You can run DMVs from inside SQL Server Management Studio (SSMS) or, even better, by using DAX Studio. DAX Studio offers you the list of all DMVs in a simpler way, without requiring you to remember them. This chapter describes how to interpret the information coming from DMVs using another free tool, VertiPaq Analyzer (*http://www.sqlbi.com/tools/vertipaq-analyzer/*), which automatically retrieves data from DMVs and shows them in useful reports.

Using DMVs for VertiPaq memory usage

Although DMVs use a SQL-like syntax, you cannot use full SQL syntaxes to query them because they do not run inside SQL Server. They are a convenient way to discover the status of SSAS and to gather information about data models. Moreover, even if a new set of DMVs specific for tabular models is introduced in SSAS 2016, certain data (such as memory used by columns) is available only using other DMVs that were created when SSAS supported only Multidimensional. The information provided there is not optimized for Tabular. Therefore, certain views get column information provided as a CUBE_NAME, MEASURE_GROUP_NAME, or DIMENSION_NAME, although in VertiPaq there is no concept of a cube, measure group, or dimension. For this reason, a tool like VertiPaq Analyzer is useful to read high-level information without having to manage these details.

There are different DMVs, divided in the following two main categories:

- **SCHEMA views**   These views return information about SSAS metadata, such as database names, tables, and individual columns. They do not provide statistical information. Instead, they are used to gather information about data types, names, and similar data. There are two groups of DMVs with schema information, with the following prefixes:

  - **TMSCHEMA**   The views with this prefix are new in SSAS 2016 for Tabular databases with 1200 compatibility level and higher, and are not available in earlier compatibility levels. They describe the metadata structure of a tabular model. The structure of each view is described in corresponding "Messages in the Protocol Details" section of the SQL Server Analysis Services Tabular protocol documentation, which is available at *https://msdn.microsoft.com/en-us/library/mt719260.aspx*.

  - **MDSCHEMA**   The views with this prefix describe entities seen from a multidimensional perspective, even if the model is tabular. These views are available in any version of Analysis Services Tabular, and the documentation is available at *https://msdn.microsoft.com/en-us/library/ms126079.aspx*.

- **DISCOVER views**   These views are intended to gather information about the SSAS engine and/or discover statistics information about objects in a database. For example, you can use views in the discover area to enumerate the DAX keywords, the number of connections and sessions that are currently open, or the traces running. There are views containing information about the memory used to store segment data, for both multidimensional and tabular databases. (A specific view for Tabular with the same information is not available yet.) For example, DISCOVER_STORAGE_TABLE_COLUMN_SEGMENTS provides data using the multidimensional nomenclature (cube, measure group, dimension, and so on) even for tabular databases. The documentation about these views is available at *https://technet.microsoft.com/en-us/library/ms126221.aspx*.

This book does not describe the details of these views. Instead, it analyzes the meaning of the information for a tabular model, using the reports provided by VertiPaq Analyzer. We focus on the meaning of the data and not on how to retrieve it from DMVs. If you need more information about DMV views, follow the preceding links to find the Microsoft documentation on the web.

Interpreting VertiPaq Analyzer reports

VertiPaq Analyzer is a Power Pivot model that you can open in Excel 2013 or Excel 2016. It contains numerous tables and gets data from several DMVs. To use VertiPaq Analyzer, open the workbook available at *http://www.sqlbi.com/tools/vertipaq-analyzer/*, click the **Download** link on the right, and then follow the instructions at *http://www.sqlbi.com/articles/data-model-size-with-vertipaq-analyzer/* to collect the data from the specific tabular database that you want to analyze. After you have connected VertiPaq Analyzer to the SSAS database to analyze, you can refresh the data model and analyze the content of the PivotTables, as shown in Figure 12-9.

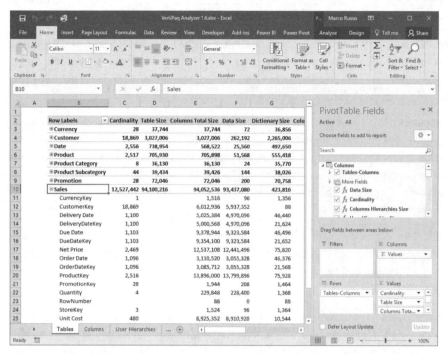

FIGURE 12-9 The VertiPaq Analyzer PivotTable, showing the table and columns size.

VertiPaq Analyzer shows data in one PivotTable for each of the following worksheets:

- **Tables**   This displays the size of columns and tables. It also provides a summary of segments and partitions used by the columns of the table. This is the first and most important summary to analyze when you want to get a complete overview of the data volume and distribution in a tabular model.

- **Columns**   This provides the same information as the Tables worksheet but without grouping the columns by table. This report is useful to look for the most expensive columns in the entire data model. It can also be used to determine the columns with the highest memory cost or cardinality.

- **User Hierarchies**   This shows the structure size used for the user hierarchies defined in the tabular model. This cost is usually a fraction of the cost of the attributes hierarchies (one for each column), which is available in the Tables and Columns worksheets.

- **Relationships**   This displays the cost of the relationships defined in the data model and the granularity of the columns involved. The memory cost of each relationship is usually a fraction of the data model.

- **Compression**   This offers a complete overview of the bits used in compressing segments of the data. You can add table and columns names to this PivotTable to analyze the compression applied to specific objects. This information can be useful to check whether there is space for improving compression in very large data models.

- **Columns Data Types** This groups the columns by their data type so you can quickly verify whether the data type of columns is what you expected. For example, using this report, you can quickly identify floating-point columns that could or should be stored as currency, as you will learn later in this section.

- **Encoding** This groups the columns by their encoding type, which is useful when you want to verify whether columns that are critical for certain DAX expressions use the encoding (hash or value) that works best for that specific task.

- **Measures** This displays a list of all the measures defined in the model, including their DAX expressions.

- **Calc. Columns** This displays a list of all the calculated columns defined in the model, including their DAX expressions.

- **Calc. Tables** This displays a list of all the calculated tables defined in the model, including their DAX expressions.

The data model in VertiPaq Analyzer provides a limited number of Columns entities, which contain the table and column names and type, and Columns Segments entities, which contain attributes related to compression, partitions, and segments. The measures are defined in the Columns table, so they are easily reachable in the PivotTable fields list. These measures include the following:

- **Data Size** This includes the bytes for all the compressed data in segments and partitions. It does not include dictionary and attribute hierarchies. This number is the amount of memory read by VertiPaq when doing a complete column scan. Different columns in the same table have different data sizes, resulting in varying performance for aggregation functions.

- **Cardinality** This is the object's number of rows in a table or number of unique values within a column. The cardinality of a column is the number of entries in the dictionary. The number of unique values used in the column could be smaller if the dictionary has unused entries. We consider a cardinality of 1,000,000 or more to be large. However, a table can have 100,000,000 rows without experiencing performance issues. The cardinality of a column is more important than the cardinality of a table from a performance point of view.

- **Rows** This is the number of rows in a table, partition, or segment.

- **Columns Hierarchies Size** This is the number of bytes of automatically generated hierarchies for columns (used by MDX), also called *attribute hierarchies*.

- **User Hierarchies Size** This is the number of bytes of user-defined hierarchies.

- **Relationship Size** This is the number of bytes of relationships between tables.

- **Columns Total Size** This is the number of bytes of all the structures related to a column (that is, the sum of Data Size, Dictionary Size, and Columns Hierarchies Size).

- **Dictionary Size**   This is the number of bytes of dictionary structures. The dictionary size is related strictly to the number of unique values in the column. The dictionary might include values no longer used in the column, in case single partitions are removed or reprocessed. (You can use Process Defrag to shrink the dictionary size in these cases.) The dictionary size is minimal (less than 100 bytes) for columns stored using value encoding, whereas a larger size usually indicates a hash encoding of the column.

- **Table Size**   This is the number of bytes of a table (in other words, the sum of Columns Total Size, User Hierarchies Size, and Relationships Size).

- **Table Size %**   This is the ratio of Columns Total Size versus Table Size.

- **Database Size %**   This is the ratio of Table Size versus Database Size (that is, the sum of Table Size of all the tables). You can use this measure to quickly identify columns that have a big impact on the overall database size.

- **Segments #**   This is the number of segments. There is always at least one segment for each partition, and all the columns in a table have the same number of segments.

- **Partitions #**   This is the number of partitions. All the columns in a table have the same number of partitions.

- **Columns #**   This is the number of columns.

- **Encoding**   This describes the encoding of the columns selected, which could be HASH or VALUE. If you apply this measure to a group of columns with different encoding types, it displays Many.

You can group measures using a variety of attributes, which are already used in the PivotTables included in the VertiPaq Analyze workbook. The most important attributes are included in the Columns and Columns Segments tables. The following Columns attributes are available:

- **Tables-Columns**   This is a hierarchy with two levels, Table and Column, corresponding to the table and column names in the tabular model.

- **COLUMN_ENCODING**   This corresponds to the encoding type of a column, which can be HASH or VALUE, and can be used as a filter. This differs from the Encoding measure, which displays the encoding of the selected columns.

- **Data Type**   This corresponds to the data type of a column. The values available in VertiPaq are:

  - **DBTYPE_CY**   This corresponds to the Currency type in DAX, which is a fixed decimal number with four decimal digits of fixed precision, internally stored as an integer.

  - **DBTYPE_DATE**   This corresponds to the Date data type in DAX, which is internally stored as a floating point.

  - **DBTYPE_I4**   This does not have a corresponding data type in DAX. It is a 32-bit integer that is used for internal structures only. (You might find an internal column called *RowNumber* for each table here, but in certain models, these columns are stored as DBTYPE_I8.)

- **DBTYPE_I8**   This corresponds to the Whole Number data type in DAX, which is internally stored as a 64-bit integer.

- **DBTYPE_R8**   This corresponds to the Decimal Number data type in DAX, which is internally stored as a 64-bit floating point.

- **DBTYPE_WSTR**   This corresponds to the Text data type in DAX, which is internally stored as a Unicode string (16 bits per character). A string column is always hash-encoded in VertiPaq.

The following attributes are available in Columns Segments, which are useful to analyze the compression applied to columns of a tabular model:

- **BITS_COUNT**   This is the number of bits used to store the data ID in a column's segment. For value encoding, this is related to the range of values in the column for the segment. For hash encoding, the index pointing to the dictionary position corresponds to a value internally stored as value encoding. Thus, a segment can have fewer bits if the values referenced in the dictionary have been created in a contiguous area. Parallel processing of multiple partitions can affect this order, so in very large tables (billions of rows), you might want to prepopulate the dictionary of columns used to partition the table (usually date-related columns).

- **BOOKMARK_BITS_COUNT**   This is an estimate of the number of RLE bits in the segment.

- **COMPRESSION_TYPE**   This is always NOSPLIT for regular columns and C123 for internal columns (row number). It is reserved for internal use by VertiPaq.

- **PARTITION_NAME**   This is the name of the partition, as defined in the tabular model.

- **SEGMENT_NUMBER**   This is an integer number identifying the segment in the table.

- **TABLE_PARTITION_NUMBER**   This is an integer number identifying the partition in the table. This number is generated by SSAS.

- **VERTIPAQ_STATE**   This is the state of the VertiPaq compression for a segment. It can be set to the following states:

  - **COMPLETED**   This states that the VertiPaq compression completed successfully.

  - **TIMEBOXED**   This states that the VertiPaq compression was timeboxed. If you find many columns with this state in the data model, you might consider reprocessing the table with an increased value for the ProcessingTimeboxSecPerMRow setting in the SSAS properties. This will provide more time to complete the compression process and produce a better compression.

  - **SKIPPED**   This states that the column was not used by the VertiPaq clustering algorithm, which determines the degree of compression for each column. This always happens for internal columns, such as RowNumber, and could also happen for other columns, such as a high-cardinality column that contains a floating-point number. A column with hash encoding can have a SKIPPED state.

Memory usage in VertiPaq

All the database columns are stored in memory, making this the most relevant factor of memory consumption. In addition, VertiPaq needs other memory during a table refresh (we call this the *processing phase*) and when querying the tables.

Data memory usage

A common question when designing a database-based solution is how to forecast the database size, from which you derive disk and memory sizing. Knowing the database size is important when assessing the amount of memory required to run Analysis Services, which uses VertiPaq to store the database in memory. However, with this engine, answering this question is not easy.

Estimating database size is a relatively easy exercise for a relational database in SQL Server. This is because almost all the data is usually stored in a small number of tables. You can estimate the size of each table by calculating the product of the number of rows multiplied by the size of each row. The number of rows is usually estimated (for example, the number of customers, the number of transactions in five years, and so on), whereas the size of the row depends on the number of columns and their types. Having a sample set of data is often sufficient to make a good estimation of the average row size (you might have variable-length columns), including indexes. Detailed techniques for making such estimations are well known and documented. A good starting point is *http://msdn.microsoft.com/en-us/library/ms187445.aspx*.

With VertiPaq, estimating database size is a much more difficult exercise because it is very difficult to know in advance what the most important drivers are that will affect the database size. In fact, the number of rows is no longer the most important factor for determining the size of a table! The table size in VertiPaq is determined by a combination of the following factors:

- The number of columns
- The cardinality of each column
- The data type of each column (for strings, the average size is relevant)
- The number of rows

Not only do you have many variables to consider, but there is also no linear formula that produces an estimate, when starting from these values. If you are only interested in the size of the bigger tables within a database, you can get a rough estimate by using the following formula:

$$RowCount * \left(RowIterationCost + \sum_{c=0}^{columns} AverageDictionaryCost(c)\right)$$

This formula is not easy to apply. The average column cost can be quite different among columns, and it largely depends on the size of the dictionary, which is based on the number of distinct values in the column. You can see that adding rows to a table does not necessarily mean that you have a linear growth of the table size. In fact, if you add rows that use existing values in column dictionaries, you use only the first part of the multiplication (RowCount). If you add values that also increase the dictionary size, the AverageDictionaryCost for affected columns will increase, which results in a product that grows faster. Finally, the effect of adding a column depends on the size of the dictionary, so adding a column with low cardinality costs less than adding a column with high cardinality.

This is a general principle that helps you to estimate. However, it is much harder to translate these general concepts into concrete numbers because the dictionary cost depends on many factors, such as different data types, dictionary strategies, string length, and so on. VertiPaq automatically uses different types of dictionaries, depending on the type and data distribution of each column.

For these reasons, we suggest basing any estimation on a heuristic approach. Use a significant amount of real data and measure the size of a processed table. Then double the number of rows and measure the increment in size. Double it again, and then measure again. You will obtain a more accurate estimate in this way than by using a theoretical approach that is difficult to apply if you do not know data distribution. VertiPaq Analyzer helps you get these metrics after each test.

Processing memory usage

During processing, every table is read from the data source and loaded in memory to create the dictionary of unique values and the related index for each column. If you already have the table in memory and you do not clear the table from the VertiPaq database before proceeding, you will have two copies of the table until the process transaction commits. If you enable memory paging in Analysis Services and have enough virtual memory available, the process might succeed even if you do not have enough memory to store two copies of tables that are part of the processing batch. But if Analysis Services starts paging, query and processing performance might suffer. You should measure memory consumption during processing to avoid paging, if possible.

> **Note** VertiPaq is designed and optimized to have the whole database loaded into memory. To store more data and improve performance, data is also kept compressed while in memory, and dynamically uncompressed during each query. This is why fast CPUs with high memory bandwidth are required. Analysis Services can handle the paging of data to disk, but this should be limited to scenarios in which the paging activity is temporary. You can disable paging by setting the Memory\VertiPaqPagingPolicy advanced property to 0. (The default is 1, which enables this behavior.) For a more detailed discussion of VertiPaq memory settings, see *http://www.sqlbi.com/articles/memory-settings-in-tabular-instances-of-analysis-services*.

If multiple tables or partitions are processed in the same processing batch, they are processed in parallel by default in SSAS 2016. Previous versions of SSAS Tabular processed partitions of a table serially, allowing only multiple tables to be processed in parallel.

Every partition that is processed is divided into segments, each with 8,000,000 rows. After a segment is read, each column is processed and compressed. This part of the processing can scale on multiple cores and requires more memory, depending on the number of distinct values that are present in the segment. For this reason, as you saw in Chapter 3, "Loading data inside Tabular," sorting a table might reduce the memory pressure during processing and queries, requiring less memory to store data. Reading a smaller number of distinct values per segment improves the compression rates and memory used. Ideally, you would obtain the best results by first sorting the table using the column with the smaller number of distinct values and then including other columns until you arrive at the column with the maximum granularity. However, this sorting might be too expensive for the data source. You should find the right tradeoff for tables that require more segments to be processed. This consideration is less important for partitions smaller than 8,000,000 rows because they will always process a single segment and will not have the issue of distributing values across different segments for the same partition.

Important　You can optimize compression for tables with more than 8,000,000 rows by providing sorted data to Analysis Services. In Tabular, you can specify for each partition a SQL statement that contains an ORDER BY condition. Optimizing such a query in the relational database is not discussed here, but it is something to consider to keep the processing time at a reasonable level.

Querying memory usage

Every query performs one or more scans of the columns involved in the query. Some query constructs create memory pressure because they must store both temporary and intermediate results. When running very complex queries on large tables, you might observe very high memory pressure caused by the internal materialization of data when expressions cannot be managed by keeping the data in a compressed form. This could be critical if you do not have enough memory available. You should monitor memory pressure during queries to correctly size the memory available to Analysis Services. Concurrent users can increase the memory pressure if complex queries run simultaneously.

Note　High memory pressure is caused by particularly complex DAX queries. Many queries do not require much memory even when they operate on very large tables. This warning is applicable to potentially critical conditions that might be raised by a single query that exhausts server resources. A complete description of DAX queries that can increase materialization, and how to control this effect, is included in *The Definitive Guide to DAX*, published by Microsoft Press. In general, materialization is an issue related to specific DAX queries, not just to the tabular model.

Understanding processing options

You have learned how the VertiPaq engine uses memory. In this section, you will see the actions performed during table processing, what resources are required during this operation, and the differences between the processing options.

Every table in a tabular model is copied to an internal structure for the VertiPaq engine unless DirectQuery is being used. This operation is called *data processing*, and it can occur at different levels of granularity: database, table, and partition. There are no constraints on the process order, and you can process lookup tables after related tables. The storage is by column, and every column has its own data. The real dependencies are calculated columns, which must be refreshed after processing any table that is directly or indirectly referenced by the DAX expression that defines the calculated column.

> **Note** In a multidimensional model, you must process the dimensions before the measure groups, and you might have to process a measure group after you process a dimension, depending on the type of processing. In a tabular model, this is not required, and processing a table does not affect other processed tables. It is your responsibility to invalidate a table containing data that is no longer valid. Integrity issues are the responsibility of the source system, and these errors will not be picked up by processing a tabular model as they would be in a multidimensional model.

In this chapter, the processing options are discussed at a functional level. You can perform many (but not all) of these operations through the SQL Server Management Studio (SSMS) user interface. In Chapter 11, "Processing and partitioning tabular models," you learned how to use these features correctly, depending on the requirements of specific tabular models. In Chapter 13, "Interfacing with Tabular," you will learn how to control process operations in a programmatic way by accessing all the available features.

What happens during processing

When you execute a full process on a tabular database, every partition of every table is processed, and all the calculated columns are refreshed. However, you might want to control this operation to optimize the processing time and memory required, especially for larger models. For example, you can process only those tables that have been updated on the data source, and by using partitioning, you can limit the table-refresh operation to only the part of the table that contains changed data. Because each table is processed independently of other tables, you can examine the process operation at a table level. The same operation is repeated for every table involved in a process batch.

A table or partition process operation is divided into the following two steps:

1. **Process data**   The rows are sequentially read from the source table. If the process is on a table, a single dictionary is created for each column, and data files are created for each partition and column. If the process is on a partition, and a dictionary already exists, new values are added to the dictionary. In addition, existing values are kept in the dictionary even if they no longer exist in any source-table rows. This update of the dictionary can cause fragmentation, which you can eliminate with a specific operation that you will learn about in the next section. The data files of the processed partition are always rebuilt.

2. **Process other structures**   Many objects can be created or refreshed only after data processing has completed. Some of these structures can belong to tables other than those that have been processed. These structures are as follows:

   - **Calculated columns and tables**   All the calculated columns that have been processed must be refreshed. Moreover, any calculated column or calculated table that contains an expression with a direct or indirect dependency on a processed table must also be refreshed. The calculated columns must be calculated for all the partitions of a table, regardless of the partitions that have been processed. Calculated columns are split into the same number of segments of the table they belong to. However, calculated tables are split into segments according to the setting of the DefaultSegmentRowCount VertiPaq property.

   - **Relationships**   If the table contains references to other lookup tables, the internal structures must be rebuilt, and either that table or the lookup table must be processed. However, the cost of rebuilding relationship structures depends on the size of the dictionary of the involved column—not on the table size or the number of partitions.

   - **Hierarchies**   Attribute and user hierarchies in a table have structures that must be rebuilt after the data has been processed.

There are specific instructions to control these two steps of a process operation. In fact, the processing of other structures is usually done after all the data processing has been completed. Processing operations are memory-intensive and processor-intensive. During data processing, partitions are loaded serially, but other parts of the processing can use additional cores if available. Moreover, different tables can be processed in parallel, which might increase the memory requirements. You can control the process operation to avoid a high peak level of memory usage.

Because of this condition, Analysis Services might use paging during processing to access the physical memory available to complete the operation. However, if Analysis Services receives a query on the existing tabular model that has been paged during a process operation, you might observe a severe degradation in query performance that also affects processing time. You must measure the peak level of memory usage and the paging activity during the processing operation. If the processing operation exhausts server memory resources, you must adopt countermeasures.

Available processing options

Several processing options can be applied granularly to one or more objects. A more detailed operational guide is available in Chapter 11, and further details can be found in the blog post at *https://blogs. msdn.microsoft.com/cathyk/2011/09/26/processing-tabular-models-101/*.

In general terms, for each table, you can perform one of the following operations:

- **Process Data**   This operation reads from the data source and then populates a partition or a table. After that, the related structures of the table involved (even if you have loaded only a single partition) are no longer valid and require a Process Recalc operation.

- **Process Recalc**   This refreshes all the table-related structures (calculated columns, calculated tables, indexes, relationships, and hierarchies) when the underlying data in the partition or tables is changed. This operation can be directly executed only at the database level, affecting all the structures of all the tables that require refreshing. If you want to limit the process to only the affected objects after a single table has been changed (without refreshing the structures that have been invalidated and that need updating later), you must use the Process Full or Process Default processing options. These internally perform a recalculation of only those objects that have been invalidated by other operations.

- **Process Full**   This performs both a Process Data and a Process Recalc of the related structures. When it is requested at a database level, it rebuilds all the tables. When it is executed on a table or partition, it performs a Process Data operation on the requested object. It is followed by a Process Recalc operation that is limited to the structures that are related to the table involved in the first operation. Process Add is a special case of Process Full, because it runs in an incremental process that adds rows to an existing partition. If you are executing Process Full or Process Add operations on two or more tables in separate transactions, these operations might generate several Process Recalc steps of the same structures in other tables. An example is when you have a calculated column in another table that depends on the data from the table that is being processed by one of these commands.

- **Process Defrag**   This optimizes the table dictionary and rebuilds table data for all the partitions. If you process data at a partition level, you might end up with a fragmented dictionary that contains entries that are no longer used in the table. For example, suppose you remove a partition from a table. All the values that were used only in that partition will still be part of the dictionaries of hash-encoded columns even though they are no longer referenced by the column's data structures. This does not affect the correctness of the query result, but it does consume more memory and might indirectly affect performance. Process Defrag might be an expensive operation for a large table. This operation can be executed at the table or database level. (The latter is not exposed in the SSMS user interface.)

As a rule, to minimize processing time when you do not have to fully process the whole database, you should use Process Data for tables or partitions that must be refreshed. After all the data has been loaded, you can perform a single Process Recalc at the database level, processing the affected structures only once. In this way, if a calculated column depends on two or more modified tables, it will also be refreshed just once. However, some structures (indexes and calculated columns of processed and related tables) will not be available from the first Process Data operation until the Process Default completes at the database level unless they are executed in a single transaction. This requires more memory because two copies of data will be stored in memory during processing. Choosing other strategies, such as performing Process Full on single partitions or tables in separate batches, might require a longer time because the related structures will be processed more than once. However, it will reduce or eliminate the period of time during which the tabular model is unavailable.

> **Note** Compared to a multidimensional model, the processing options in tabular models are simpler and easier to manage. You do not have the strong dependencies between dimensions and measure groups. The dependencies affect the structures that require refreshing, even if the relationships between the tables and the formulas in calculated columns define the dependencies between those tables. However, because these operations have a column granularity, the actual cost is limited to the parts of the table that require refreshing. Moreover, the unavailability of data in a tabular model can be limited to calculated columns that require refreshing rather than affecting the whole table, as you might expect if you come from a multidimensional background.

Summary

In this chapter, you saw that VertiPaq is an in-memory, column-oriented database, and you learned the internal structures used to store data. Because the VertiPaq engine stores data in memory, it is critical to understand how data is compressed and which columns cause additional memory pressure (usually because of their data-dictionary size). Finally, you learned how VertiPaq processes data and how to control the process phases to minimize the latency and optimize the data structures.

Interfacing with Tabular

You can create an Analysis Services solution by using existing development and client tools, such as SQL Server Data Tools (SSDT), Power BI, or Excel. Using the libraries supported in script and programming languages, you can customize these solutions. In this chapter, you will learn about these libraries for defining models and performing administrative tasks. To better understand this chapter, you will need a basic knowledge of PowerShell and/or managed languages, such as C#.

The goal of this chapter is to introduce all the libraries available to programmatically access tabular models in Analysis Services so you will be able to evaluate the correct approach based on the requirements. You will find several links to documentation and examples throughout the chapter to help you understand all the details and possible parameters of available functions.

This chapter does not cover implementing query support from client code (which is possible using the ADOMD.NET managed library) or the native Analysis Services OLE DB Provider (also known as MOLAP provider). Documentation for these topics can be found at *https://msdn.microsoft.com/en-US/library/bb500153.aspx*.

> **What's new in SSAS 2016**   SSAS 2016 introduces a new library, called Tabular Object Model (TOM). This chapter, which is brand new, covers the architecture of this library, including several examples on using it with C# and PowerShell.

Introducing the AMO and TOM libraries

Analysis Services has a generic API called Analysis Management Objects (AMO) to administer both tabular and multidimensional deployments. Certain classes are shared between the two modes, whereas others are specific to each model type. The specific API for tabular models is included in an extension of AMO called Tabular Object Model (TOM). It is correct to reference both APIs as AMO, even if TOM is used only to create and manage Tabular metadata objects. To make a distinction between APIs for multidimensional and tabular models, however, it is common to use AMO for Multidimensional, and TOM for Tabular. Nevertheless, TOM still uses the AMO libraries that are shared between the two modes.

Starting with Analysis Services 2016, the original AMO library was divided into the following different assemblies:

- **Core (Microsoft.AnalysisServices.Core.dll)**   This contains classes common to both Tabular and Multidimensional.

- **TOM (Microsoft.AnalysisServices.Tabular.dll)**   This includes classes to create and manage a tabular model.

- **AMO (Microsoft.AnalysisServices.dll)**   This includes classes to create and manage a multidimensional model.

- **Json (Microsoft.AnalysisServices.Tabular.Json.dll)**   This is an assembly used internally by TOM that controls the serialization of metadata objects.

The TOM library can only manage tabular models with a compatibility level of 1200 or higher. If you want to manage models with the compatibility levels of 1050 through 1103, you need the AMO library. You can find more details on assembly dependencies and deployments at *https://msdn.microsoft.com/en-us/library/mt707783.aspx*.

As you will see later, there are classes with the same names defined in different namespaces to avoid name conflict between AMO and TOM libraries. Depending on the compatibility level you want to support in your code, you must create a class instance from either the `Microsoft.AnalysisServices` namespace (AMO, for compatibility levels 1050 through 1103) or the `Microsoft.AnalysisServices.Tabular` namespace (TOM, for compatibility levels 1200 or higher).

Introducing AMOs

This section identifies the specific set of classes and assemblies that are shared between multidimensional and tabular models. Analysis Services Management Objects (AMOs) include classes defined in two assemblies: AMO (Microsoft.AnalysisServices.dll) and Core (Microsoft.AnalysisServices.Core.dll). This division is required for compatibility with existing code that is designed for former versions of AMO. It supports access to SSAS databases with the compatibility levels of 1050 through 1103. Legacy code directly references only the AMO assembly and the `Microsoft.AnalysisServices` namespace.

For example, the AMO assembly code in Listing 13-1 connects to the Tabular instance of Analysis Services on the local machine, iterates the databases, and displays the list of dimensions for each one. Such code works for both Tabular and Multidimensional instances of Analysis Services. For a Tabular instance, each table corresponds to a dimension in the metadata that is provided to AMO.

LISTING 13-1 Script PowerShell\List Tabular Tables 1103.ps1

```
[System.Reflection.Assembly]::LoadWithPartialName("Microsoft.AnalysisServices")
$server = New-Object Microsoft.AnalysisServices.Server
$server.Connect("localhost\tabular")
foreach ( $db in $server.Databases ) {
    $db.Name
    foreach ( $table in $db.Dimensions ) {
        "-->" + $table.Name
    }
}
```

When connecting to a Tabular instance, the output includes the list of tables in databases with compatibility levels 1050 through 1103. There are no entries for databases with the compatibility level 1200 or higher. For example, in the following output there are three databases: AdventureWorks (with compatibility level 1103), Contoso, and Budget (both with compatibility level 1200). Only the AdventureWorks tables are included in the following output:

```
AdventureWorks
-->Currency
-->Customer
-->Date
-->Employee
-->Geography
-->Product
-->Product Category
-->Product Subcategory
-->Promotion
-->Reseller
-->Sales Territory
-->Internet Sales
-->Product Inventory
-->Reseller Sales
-->Sales Quota
Contoso
Budget
```

To access tables with compatibility level 1200 or higher, you must use the TOM assembly to get the Server and Database class instances from a different namespace. AMO exposes metadata for multidimensional models, because it was originally designed for that type of database. Previous versions of Analysis Services leveraged this existing infrastructure to expose database entities. When you access the compatibility levels 1050 through 1103, you must map tabular entities to the multidimensional concepts. For example, every table in a tabular model corresponds to a dimension in a multidimensional one. This book does not cover these legacy database models. For more information, you can reference the documentation at *https://msdn.microsoft.com/en-us/library/hh230795.aspx*.

> **Note** If you want to manage tabular models with compatibility levels 1050 through 1103, we suggest using the Tabular AMO 2012 library, which is available on CodePlex at *https://tabularamo2012.codeplex.com/*. This library is an AMO wrapper for multidimensional models, which exposes an object model close to the one provided by TOM.

Introducing the TOM

Tabular models with the compatibility level of 1200 or higher can be managed through the TOM library, which includes classes in three assemblies: Core, TOM, and Json. You only need to reference the AMO assembly if you want to access metadata from older compatibility levels, such as the Dimensions collection, which is shown in the previous example.

The TOM assembly defines all the classes in the `Microsoft.AnalysisServices.Tabular` namespace, whereas the Core assembly contains classes in the following two namespaces:

- **Microsoft.AnalysisServices.Core** This includes an abstract definition of the `Database`, `Role`, `Server`, and `Trace` classes. You do not need to reference such a namespace in your code. These classes are implemented in the `Microsoft.AnalysisServices` AMO assembly namespace and in the `Microsoft.AnalysisServices.Tabular` TOM assembly.

- **Microsoft.AnalysisServices** This includes objects for managing traces, security, XMLA commands, connections, impersonation, and more. These entities are shared between AMO and TOM libraries.

If your solution only references the TOM and Core assemblies, you can import both namespaces, but only a compatibility level of 1200 and higher will be supported. You might reference both AMO and Core assemblies, but in this case, you must consider possible ambiguity in class references. For example, suppose you create a script or tool that supports both the 1103 and 1200 compatibility levels. If so, you must be careful in choosing the namespace from which you reference the `Database`, `Role`, `Server`, and `Trace` classes.

The code in Listing 13-2 references only the TOM assembly. It connects to the Tabular instance of Analysis Services on the local machine, iterates all the databases, and for each one, displays the list of tables included in the model.

LISTING 13-2   Script PowerShell\List Tabular Tables 1200.ps1

```
[System.Reflection.Assembly]::LoadWithPartialName("Microsoft.AnalysisServices.
Tabular")
$server = New-Object Microsoft.AnalysisServices.Tabular.Server
$server.Connect("localhost\tabular")
foreach ( $db in $server.Databases ) {
    $db.Name
    foreach ( $table in $db.Model.Tables ) {
        "-->" + $table.Name
    }
}
```

This code only works for Tabular instances of Analysis Services, and its output only includes the list of tables of a model in compatibility levels 1200 or higher. Such a list is empty for databases in compatibility levels 1050 through 1103. For example, the following output shows three databases: AdventureWorks (with a compatibility level of 1103), Contoso, and Budget (both with a compatibility level of 1200). Only the tables from Contoso and Budget are included in the output.

```
AdventureWorks
Contoso
-->Date
-->Sales
-->Currency
-->Product
-->Promotion
-->Store
Budget
-->Product
-->Date
-->Sales
-->Territory
-->Budget
```

As you see, supporting both compatibility models requires additional coding and the management of different implementations of the same abstract classes. For the remainder of the chapter, we will consider how to interface with compatibility level 1200 or higher. In this scenario, you reference only the Core and TOM libraries, creating instances of Server, Database, Role, and Trace classes from the Microsoft.AnalysisServices.Tabular namespace.

The object hierarchy of the classes available in the TOM library is shown in Figure 13-1. The Server class is the root of the hierarchy. It has a Databases property with a list of Database instances. The Database class has a Model property, which contains an instance of the Model class. This is the entry point for the metadata information that is specific to a tabular model with a compatibility level of 1200 or higher. Most of the other properties of the Server and Database classes are common to other tabular and multidimensional models.

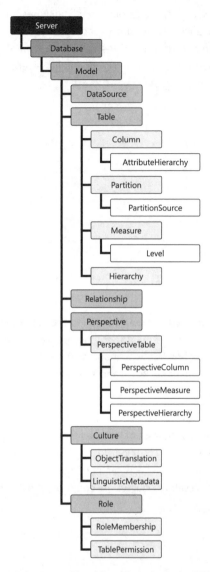

FIGURE 13-1   The object hierarchy in the TOM library.

If you want to look for valid tabular databases in an SSAS instance, you should first check the Server-Mode property of the Server class. If it is Tabular, then you should analyze the StorageEngineUsed property of the Database class. For a tabular model, its value can be InMemory for compatibility levels 1050 through 1103, or it can be TabularMetadata for compatibility levels 1200 or higher. However, if you connect to an SSAS instance in Tabular mode, you can simply check whether the Model property is null before accessing it. While PowerShell automatically applies these checks, you need to be more explicit when writing similar code in C#. Listing 13-3 shows how you might check that the Model property is not null rather than evaluating the StorageEngineUsed property.

LISTING 13-3   Models\Chapter 13\List Tabular Tables 1200\List Tabular Tables 1200.cs

```csharp
using System;
using Microsoft.AnalysisServices;
using Microsoft.AnalysisServices.Tabular;

namespace ListTables {
    class Program {
        static void Main(string[] args) {
            Server server = new Server();
            server.Connect(@"localhost\tabular");
            if (server.ServerMode == ServerMode.Tabular) {
                foreach (Database db in server.Databases) {
                    Console.WriteLine("{0}:{1}", db.ToString(), db.StorageEngineUsed);
                    if (db.StorageEngineUsed == StorageEngineUsed.TabularMetadata) {
                        foreach (Table d in db.Model.Tables) {
                            Console.WriteLine("--> {0}", d.Name);
                        }
                    }
                }
            }
            server.Disconnect();
        }
    }
}
```

Assembly references and namespace ambiguity

The C# code in Listing 13-3 compiles correctly if you reference the Core (Microsoft.AnalysisServices.Core.dll) and TOM (Microsoft.AnalysisServices.Tabular.dll) assemblies in your project. If you want to support compatibility level 1200 and higher, as well as compatibility levels 1050 through 1103, then you must also reference the AMO assembly (Microsoft.AnalysisServices.dll). This raises a problem, however, when you have the following two using statements in your code:

```csharp
using Microsoft.AnalysisServices;
using Microsoft.AnalysisServices.Tabular;
```

In this situation, the Server, Database, and Trace classes are defined in both namespaces, through different assemblies. You must disambiguate their instance by using the explicit class name (such as Microsoft.AnalysisServices.Server or Microsoft.AnalysisServices.Tabular.Server) or by creating an alias. For example, the previous code sample might have the following using statements from the TOM assembly to disambiguate Server and Database classes:

```csharp
using Microsoft.AnalysisServices;
using Microsoft.AnalysisServices.Tabular;
using Server = Microsoft.AnalysisServices.Tabular.Server;
using Database = Microsoft.AnalysisServices.Tabular.Database;
```

However, the easiest way to avoid ambiguity is to reference Core and TOM assemblies in your project only, without referencing the AMO one. This is the best practice when you only need to support compatibility levels 1200 and higher.

The Model class contains the same entities that are described in Chapter 7, "Tabular Model Scripting Language (TMSL)." In fact, TMSL is just the materialization of the object graph that is included in the Model class. In the section "Automating project deployment" later in this chapter, you will find functions to both read a model.bim file in memory by populating a Model class instance and create a model.bim file by just persisting the state of a Model instance. In fact, you can create and manipulate a tabular model without actually connecting to an SSAS instance. When you read the database metadata from a server, you have an object graph describing the database model. Any changes applied to this object graph are local to your code until you apply the changes to the server by invoking the SaveChanges method of the Model instance. For example, the script in Listing 13-4 adds a Margin measure to the Sales table in the Contoso database.

LISTING 13-4 Script PowerShell\Add Margin Measure.ps1

```
[System.Reflection.Assembly]::LoadWithPartialName("Microsoft.AnalysisServices.Tabular")
$server = New-Object Microsoft.AnalysisServices.Tabular.Server
$server.Connect("localhost\tab16")
$db = $server.Databases["Contoso"]
$model = $db.Model
$tableSales = $model.Tables["Sales"]
$measureMargin = New-Object Microsoft.AnalysisServices.Tabular.Measure
$measureMargin.Name = "Margin"
$measureMargin.Expression = "[Sales Amount] - [Cost]"
$tableSales.Measures.Add( $measureMargin )
$model.SaveChanges()
```

When you invoke SaveChanges, the TOM library manages the communication to the SSAS instance by using XMLA and JSON protocols. The following sections provide a short description of these protocols to help you better understand the content of certain trace events if you use the SQL Server Profiler (as explained in Chapter 14, "Monitoring and tuning a Tabular service"), but you can safely ignore this underlying communication by using TOM.

TOM and XMLA

The TOM library uses the industry-standard XML for Analysis (XMLA) protocol to communicate with an SSAS instance, as described here: *https://msdn.microsoft.com/en-us/library/ms977626.aspx*. To manage tabular objects, Microsoft extended the XMLA protocol to add the SQL Server Analysis Services Tabular protocol (MS-SSAS-T) for use with compatibility levels 1200 and higher. For more information, see *https://msdn.microsoft.com/library/mt719260.aspx*.

TOM and JSON

The metadata of tabular models is structured as JSON documents, which can be transferred using a JSON syntax that adds command and object model definitions. This syntax is described in Chapter 7.

When you use the TOM library, the communication with SSAS uses the MS-SSAS-T protocol over the wire, not TMSL. Nevertheless, both TOM and TMSL share the same object structure (tables, columns, partitions, and so on) and the same operations (create, delete, and refresh). When you use TMSL, you send commands in JSON format over the wire to the SSAS server. If you use the Profiler to analyze the SSAS instance events, you will see different content in the resulting capture than when you execute the same logical operations by using the TOM library and TMSL scripts.

Should you use TOM or TMSL to interface with a Tabular instance? The answer depends on your requirements. A TMSL script can be easily executed through SQL Server Management Studio (SSMS) or a SQL Server Agent job. You can also execute a TMSL script in PowerShell by using the `Invoke-ASCmd` cmdlet or the `Execute` method of the `Microsoft.AnalysisServices.Tabular.Server` class in the TOM library. However, TMSL defines operations only at the database, table, partition, or role level. When you need to operate at a finer grain, you should consider using TOM. For example, if you want to add, change, or delete a single measure or column in a table, you can easily apply the individual changes by using TOM, whereas you must include the entire table definition when using TMSL.

Finally, it is important to note that you can generate a TMSL script by using the TOM library. For example, you can create a model dynamically by using the TOM classes. Then you can generate a TMSL script to create, delete, or alter a tabular object by using one of the methods included in the `JsonScripter` class. This class is described at *https://msdn.microsoft.com/en-us/library/microsoft. analysisservices.tabular.jsonscripter.aspx.*

Introducing the TMSL commands

A TMSL command is a JSON document that describes the request of an operation to an SSAS Tabular instance. You can use TMSL to alter objects in a database, refresh data, manage databases, or execute multiple operations to control the parallelism of the execution. For example, the TMSL command in Listing 13-5 requires a full process of the Contoso database.

LISTING 13-5 Script TMSL\Process Contoso Database.xmla

```
{
  "refresh": {
    "type": "full",
    "objects": [
      {
        "database": "Contoso",
      }
    ]
  }
}
```

As you can see, a TMSL command does not contain references to a specific server, and is executed by the SSAS instance receiving it. You can find a description of the available commands in Chapter 7 in the section "TMSL commands."

You can create a TMSL script by using the TOM library and the JsonScripter class without connecting to a server. To do so, you must include the minimal definition of object entities in a Model object that is within a Database instance. For example, the C# code in Listing 13-6 generates a TMSL command to refresh two tables (Sales and Customer) in the Contoso database.

LISTING 13-6   Models\Chapter 13\Generate TMSL Refresh\Generate TMSL Refresh.cs

```
using System;
using Microsoft.AnalysisServices.Tabular;

namespace Generate_TMSL_Refresh {
    class Program {
        static void Main(string[] args) {
            Database dbContoso = new Database("Contoso");
            dbContoso.Model = new Model();
            Table tableSales = new Table { Name = "Sales" };
            Table tableCustomer = new Table { Name = "Customer" };
            dbContoso.Model.Tables.Add(tableSales);
            dbContoso.Model.Tables.Add(tableCustomer);
            string tmsl = JsonScripter.ScriptRefresh(
                new Table[] { tableSales, tableCustomer },
                RefreshType.Full);
            Console.WriteLine( tmsl );
        }
    }
}
```

The tmsl string is assigned to the TMSL script, as follows:

```
{
  "refresh": {
    "type": "full",
    "objects": [
      {
        "database": "Contoso",
        "table": "Sales"
      },
      {
        "database": "Contoso",
        "table": "Customer"
      }
    ]
  }
}
```

The previous example illustrates that you do not need a connection to SSAS to generate a TMSL script. However, you can obtain the same result by connecting to an existing database using TOM, and then using the model entities that are populated when you connect to the database. If you are already using TOM, you can apply changes and send commands by using the native TOM functions, which is more efficient and provides more control. You should generate TMSL when you do not have direct access to the SSAS instance to execute the command (for example, scheduling the execution by using a SQL Server Agent job).

Creating a database programmatically

Using TOM, you can create a complete database programmatically. You only need to reference the Core and TOM assemblies. Then you can apply the using Microsoft.AnalysisServices.Tabular directive in your source code so that only the classes for tabular models will be used. In the following example, you will create a database with just two tables from Contoso (Sales and Customer), with a relationship between the two tables and a measure to compute Sales Amount.

You can use the default values of a new instance of the Model class, but you must define at least one data source to retrieve data for your tables. Once completed, add an instance of the Database class to a Server object that is connected to an SSAS Tabular instance. The sample code in Listing 13-7 creates a connection to a ContosoDW database that is hosted on Microsoft SQL Server.

LISTING 13-7 Models\Chapter 13\Create Tabular Database\Create Tabular Database.cs

```
// Create the model and data source
Model smallModel = new Model();
smallModel.DataSources.Add(
    new ProviderDataSource() {
        Name = "ContosoDW",
        ConnectionString = @"Provider=SQLNCLI11;Data Source=localhost;" +
            @"Initial Catalog=ContosoDW;Integrated Security=SSPI;" +
            @"Persist Security Info=false",
        ImpersonationMode = ImpersonationMode.ImpersonateServiceAccount
    });
```

While Model should include a list of tables, it is useful to create the table columns first, storing their references to specific variables. This makes it easier to reference the same columns in tables and relationships. (See Listing 13-8.)

LISTING 13-8 Models\Chapter 13\Create Tabular Database\Create Tabular Database.cs

```
// Create columns for all the tables
Column customerKey = new DataColumn {
    Name = "CustomerKey", SourceColumn = "CustomerKey", DataType = DataType.Int64 };
Column customerName = new DataColumn {
    Name = "Name", SourceColumn = "Name", DataType = DataType.String };
Column salesCustomerKey = new DataColumn {
    Name = "CustomerKey", SourceColumn = "CustomerKey", DataType = DataType.Int64 };
Column salesDate = new DataColumn {
    Name = "Order Date", SourceColumn = "Order Date", DataType = DataType.DateTime };
Column salesQuantity = new DataColumn {
    Name = "Quantity", SourceColumn = "Quantity", DataType = DataType.Int64 };
Column salesUnitPrice = new DataColumn {
    Name = "Unit Price", SourceColumn = "Unit Price", DataType = DataType.Decimal };
```

Even though it is not necessary, you can create tables separately to make it easy to reference them. Every table must have a name, one (or more) columns, and at least one partition. In Listing 13-9, the partitions for both the Customer and Sales tables use the ContosoDW data source previously created in the Model object.

LISTING 13-9 Models\Chapter 13\Create Tabular Database\Create Tabular Database.cs

```
// Create tables
Table tableCustomer = new Table {
    Name = "Customer",
    Columns = { customerKey, customerName },
    Partitions = {
        new Partition {
            Name = "Customer",
            Source = new QueryPartitionSource() {
                DataSource = smallModel.DataSources["ContosoDW"],
                Query = @"SELECT [CustomerKey], [Name] FROM [Analytics].[Customer]"
            }
        }
    }
};
Table tableSales = new Table {
    Name = "Sales",
    Columns = { salesDate, salesCustomerKey, salesQuantity, salesUnitPrice },
    Measures = {
        new Measure {
            Name = "Sales Amount",
            Expression = "SUMX ( Sales, Sales[Quantity] * Sales[Unit Price] )",
            FormatString = "#,0.00"
        }
    },
    Partitions = {
        new Partition {
            Name = "Sales",
```

```
                    Source = new QueryPartitionSource() {
                        DataSource = smallModel.DataSources["ContosoDW"],
                        Query = @"SELECT TOP (1000) [CustomerKey], [Order Date], "
                                + @"[Quantity], [Unit Price] FROM [Analytics].[Sales]"
                    }
                }
            }
        };
```

You can add the Customer and Sales tables and their relationship to the model using the code in Listing 13-10. Note that you only need the two columns to create the relationship because the underlying tables are inferred from the columns.

LISTING 13-10 Models\Chapter 13\Create Tabular Database\Create Tabular Database.cs

```
// Add tables and relationships to the data model
smallModel.Tables.Add(tableCustomer);
smallModel.Tables.Add(tableSales);
smallModel.Relationships.Add(
    new SingleColumnRelationship {
        FromColumn = salesCustomerKey,
        FromCardinality = RelationshipEndCardinality.Many,
        ToColumn = customerKey,
        ToCardinality = RelationshipEndCardinality.One
    });
```

Finally, as shown in Listing 13-11, you create the Database object and assign it to the Model property (the object populated with tables and relationships).

LISTING 13-11 Models\Chapter 13\Create Tabular Database\Create Tabular Database.cs

```
// Create database
Database smallContoso = new Database("Contoso Small");
smallContoso.Model = smallModel;
```

The call to the Update method shown in Listing 13-12 is required to transfer the changes to the SSAS instance. If you do not call the method, the changes will remain local to the TOM library.

LISTING 13-12 Models\Chapter 13\Create Tabular Database\Create Tabular Database.cs

```
// Remove and create a new database using TOM
// Connect to an existing server
Server server = new Server();
server.Connect(@"localhost\tab16");
```

```
// Add the new databases to the database collection
server.Databases.Add(smallContoso);

// Update the complete database metadata
smallContoso.Update(
    Microsoft.AnalysisServices.UpdateOptions.ExpandFull,
    Microsoft.AnalysisServices.UpdateMode.CreateOrReplace);
```

You can also refresh the database by using the RequestRefresh and SaveChanges methods from the Model object. The SaveChanges operation shown in Listing 13-13 starts on the server that was invoked, whereas RequestRefresh prepares the request on the TOM library only.

LISTING 13-13   Models\Chapter 13\Create Tabular Database\Create Tabular Database.cs

```
// Refresh the data in a new database
smallContoso.Model.RequestRefresh(RefreshType.Full);
smallContoso.Model.SaveChanges();
```

As an alternative to the Update operation, you can generate the TMSL script by using the code sample shown in Listing 13-14.

LISTING 13-14   Models\Chapter 13\Create Tabular Database\Create Tabular Database.cs

```
// Generate and display the TMSL script
// Note: We do not execute this TMSL. We use the TOM API instead, which
//        internally communicates by using a different protocol
string tmsl = JsonScripter.ScriptCreateOrReplace(smallContoso);
Console.WriteLine(tmsl);
```

This option does not require a connection when you use the Server class. It can be executed or scheduled by using one of the techniques described in Chapter 7 in the section "TMSL commands."

The tabular model created in this example is very simple, and it uses the minimal set of object properties. Depending on your requirements, your code will populate a larger number of properties for each entity.

Automating data refresh and partitioning

Data refresh and partition management are two operations that are typically automated by using one or more different tools. For a tabular model, the most common techniques are TMSL scripts and TOM libraries, called by PowerShell or managed languages such as C#. A complete list of tools and techniques is described in Chapter 11, "Processing and partitioning tabular models," in the "Processing automation" section. Chapter 11 also includes a "Sample processing scripts" section, which includes TMSL and PowerShell examples to process databases, tables, and partitions.

When automating partition management, you must use TOM through a PowerShell script or a C# program. In the section "Sample processing scripts" in Chapter 11, you will find a complete PowerShell script to maintain a fixed number of monthly partitions in a table by removing older partitions and creating new ones automatically, based on the execution date. If you want a more complex and configurable general-purpose tool to manage partitions, consider the AsPartitionProcessing tool, available as an open source project from the Analysis Service development team at *https://github.com/Microsoft/Analysis-Services/tree/master/AsPartitionProcessing*. Its associated whitepaper, "Automated Partition Management for Analysis Services Tabular Models," includes more details and best practices about partition management.

Analyzing metadata

You can iterate databases and entities in each model's database to extract certain information about the tabular model, such as tables, measures, calculated columns, and partitions. You can use this information to customize the user interface of a reporting tool or to automate the manipulation of existing tabular models (as described in the next section). For example, the code sample in Listing 13-15 displays the list of databases on a particular SSAS instance.

LISTING 13-15   Models\Chapter 13\Display Tabular Metadata\Display Tabular Metadata.cs

```
using System;
using Microsoft.AnalysisServices.Tabular;

namespace Display_Tabular_Metadata {
    class Program {
        static void Main(string[] args) {
            Server server = new Server();
            server.Connect(@"localhost\tabular");

            ListDatabases(server);
        }
        private static void ListDatabases(Server server) {
            // List the databases on a server
            Console.WriteLine("Database (compatibility) - last process");
            foreach (Database db in server.Databases) {
                Console.WriteLine(
                    "{0} ({1}) - Process:{2}",
                    db.Name, db.CompatibilityLevel, db.LastProcessed.ToString());
            }
            Console.WriteLine();
        }
    }
}
```

The following output shows the compatibility level and the last-processed date and time for each database on the server. (Your output will reflect the databases on your server.)

```
Database (compatibility) - last process
Contoso VertiPaq (1200) - Process:10/16/2016 7:24:05 PM
Contoso DirectQuery (1200) - Process:12/6/2016 3:48:38 PM
Contoso (1200) - Process:12/26/2016 10:02:58 AM
Partitions (1200) - Process:12/10/2016 4:38:41 PM
Contoso Small (1200) - Process:12/27/2016 1:19:57 PM
```

By navigating the Model object properties, you can retrieve tables, columns, relationships, and so on. The code sample in Listing 13-16 displays the DAX formulas used in the measures and calculated columns of the tables in the tabular model.

LISTING 13-16   Models\Chapter 13\Display Tabular Metadata\Display Tabular Metadata.cs

```csharp
using System;
using Microsoft.AnalysisServices.Tabular;

namespace Display_Tabular_Metadata {
    class Program {
        static void Main(string[] args) {
            Server server = new Server();
            server.Connect(@"localhost\tabular");

            foreach (Database db1 in server.Databases) {
                if (db1.CompatibilityLevel >= 1200) {
                    ListMeasures(db1);
                    ListCalculatedColumns(db1);
                }
            }
        }
        private static void ListCalculatedColumns(Database db) {
            Console.WriteLine(
                "List of calculated columns in database {0} of server {1}",
                db.Name, db.Server.Name);
            foreach (Table t in db.Model.Tables) {
                foreach (Column c in t.Columns) {
                    CalculatedColumn cc = c as CalculatedColumn;
                    if (cc != null) {
                        Console.WriteLine(
                            "'{0}'[{1}] = {2} {3}",
                            t.Name, cc.Name, cc.Expression,
                            cc.IsHidden ? "[Hidden]" : "");
                    }
                }
            }
            Console.WriteLine();
        }
        private static void ListMeasures(Database db) {
            Console.WriteLine(
```

```
            "List of measures in database {0} of server {1}",
            db.Name, db.Server.Name);
        foreach (Table t in db.Model.Tables) {
            foreach (Measure m in t.Measures) {
                Console.WriteLine(
                    "'{0}'[{1}] = {2} {3}",
                    t.Name, m.Name, m.Expression,
                    m.IsHidden ? "[Hidden]" : "");
            }
        }
        Console.WriteLine();
    }
  }
}
```

The following output for this code sample shows the isolated rows that are related to the Contoso DirectQuery model:

```
List of measures in database Contoso DirectQuery of server DEVELOPMENT\TABULAR
'Sales'[Sales Amount] = SUM ( Sales[Line Amount] )
'Sales'[Cost] = SUM ( Sales[Line Cost] )
'Sales'[Margin] = SUM ( Sales[Line Margin] )
'Sales'[Sales Amount Original] = SUMX (
        Sales,
        Sales[Net Price] * Sales[Quantity]
    )
'Sales'[Cost Original] = SUMX ( Sales, Sales[Unit Cost] * Sales[Quantity] )
'Sales'[Margin Original] = [Sales Amount] - [Cost]
'Sales'[Calc Amount] =  SUM ( Sales[Calc Line Amount] )

List of calculated columns in database Contoso DirectQuery of server DEVELOPMENT\TABULAR
'Sales'[Calc Line Amount] =  Sales[Net Price] * Sales[Quantity]
```

After you retrieve the Model object from a Database, it is relatively easy to navigate the collections of the TOM classes, retrieving all the details about the entities you want to analyze.

Manipulating a data model

Using TOM, you can apply changes to an existing data model. For example, you might want to dynamically change measures and columns without having to redeploy the entire data model. However, it is important to remember that the user needs administrative rights in the tabular database to be able to alter its data model.

For example, the C# code sample in Listing 13-17 adds a measure to a model running on Analysis Services. (You can find similar examples in PowerShell at *https://www.sqlbi.com/articles/adding-a-measure-to-a-tabular-model/.*)

LISTING 13-17   Models\Chapter 13\Add Measure\Add Measure.cs

```csharp
using System;
using Microsoft.AnalysisServices.Tabular;

namespace AddMeasure {
    class Program {
        static void Main(string[] args) {
            string serverName = @"localhost\tabular";
            string databaseName = "Contoso";
            string tableName = "Sales";
            string measureName = "Total Sales";
            string measureExpression =
                "SUMX ( Sales, Sales[Quantity] * Sales[Net Price] )";

            string serverConnectionString =
                string.Format("Provider=MSOLAP;Data Source={0}", serverName);

            Server server = new Server();
            server.Connect(serverConnectionString);

            Database db = server.Databases[databaseName];
            Model model = db.Model;
            Table table = model.Tables[tableName];
            Console.WriteLine("Adding measure");
            table.Measures.Add(
                new Measure { Name = measureName, Expression = measureExpression }
            );
            model.SaveChanges();
        }
    }
}
```

Similarly, you can add a calculated column to a table. In this case, it is necessary to calculate the calculated column first to make it available for query. By invoking the RequestRefresh method before SaveChanges, you ensure that the two operations are executed within the same transaction. The C# code in Listing 13-18 adds a Rating column to the Product table.

LISTING 13-18   Models\Chapter 13\Add Calculated Column\Add Calculated Column.cs

```csharp
using System;
using Microsoft.AnalysisServices.Tabular;

namespace AddCalculatedColumn {
    class Program {
        static void Main(string[] args) {
            string serverName = @"localhost\tabular";
            string databaseName = "Contoso";
            string tableName = "Product";
```

```
                string columnName = "Rating";
                string measureExpression =
                    "VAR CustomerRevenues = CALCULATE ( [Sales Amount] )"
                  + "RETURN SWITCH ( TRUE(),"
                  + "            CustomerRevenues >= 10000, \"A\","
                  + "            CustomerRevenues >= 1000, \"B\","
                  + "            \"C\""
                  + "        )";

                Server server = new Server();
                server.Connect(serverName);
                Database db = server.Databases[databaseName];
                Table productTable = db.Model.Tables[tableName];

                Console.WriteLine("Creating rating column");
                productTable.Columns.Add(
                    new CalculatedColumn {
                        Name = columnName,
                        Expression = measureExpression
                    }
                );

                // Include an automatic refresh of the table
                productTable.RequestRefresh(RefreshType.Calculate);
                db.Model.SaveChanges();
            }
        }
    }
```

Note If you want to apply the changes to the SSAS instance in separate transactions, you need to call the SaveChanges method each time you want to commit to the database.

Automating project deployment

In this section, you will see how to use the TOM library to copy a database between different servers and deploy a model.bim file to the desired server and database name. These examples will show the flexibility and control of the TOM library compared to the TMSL script and deployment wizard covered in Chapter 11.

Copying the same database on different servers

The script in Listing 13-19 copies the definition of the Contoso database from Server1 to Server2, in the corresponding SSAS Tabular instances. This technique copies only the metadata, and requires a full refresh of the destination database to make the data available for query.

LISTING 13-19 Script PowerShell\Copy Database.ps1

```
[System.Reflection.Assembly]::LoadWithPartialName("Microsoft.AnalysisServices.
Tabular")
$sourceServer = New-Object Microsoft.AnalysisServices.Tabular.Server
$destServer = New-Object Microsoft.AnalysisServices.Tabular.Server
$sourceServer.Connect("SERVER1\tabular")
$destServer.Connect("SERVER2\tabular")
$sourceDb = $sourceServer.Databases["Contoso"]
$destDb = $sourceDb.Clone()
$destServer.Databases.Add( $destDb )
$destDb.Update( "ExpandFull" )
```

If you want to copy the database on the same server, you need to change its name and ID. Usually, both properties have the same value. However, changing just the Name property is not enough because the ID property is not renamed automatically. Thus, if you want to rename a database before copying it, you must assign both the Name and ID properties before the Databases.Add method, as shown in the following code:

```
$destDb.Name = "Contoso2"
$destDb.ID = "Contoso2"
```

Deploying a model.bim file by choosing a database and server name

In Chapter 11, you learned how to automate deployment to a production server using standard tools. By using TOM, you have an additional tool to automate the deployment. Using the JsonSerializer class, you can load the model.bim file into a Database object and then deploy it using the same methods as copying a database between two servers. As you can see from the C# code sample in Listing 13-20, loading the database into memory from a model.bim file requires two lines of code and that you save the Database object to the model.bim file.

LISTING 13-20 Models\Chapter 13\Deploy BIM File\Deploy BIM File.cs

```
        static Database ReadDatabaseFromBimFile(string path) {
            string modelBim = File.ReadAllText(path);
            Database database = JsonSerializer.DeserializeDatabase(modelBim);
            return database;
        }

        static void WriteDatabaseToBimFile(Database database, string path) {
            string modelBim = JsonSerializer.SerializeDatabase(database);
            File.WriteAllText(path, modelBim);
        }
```

Using this technique, you can read a database from a model.bim file and deploy it to a specific server. You can also change the database name by overriding the ID and Name database properties, as shown in the C# example in Listing 13-21.

LISTING 13-21 Models\Chapter 13\Deploy BIM File\Deploy BIM File.cs

```
using System;
using System.IO;
using Microsoft.AnalysisServices.Tabular;

namespace DeployBimFile {
    class Program {
        static void Main(string[] args) {
            string serverName = @"localhost\tabular";
            string databaseName = "Contoso from BIM file";
            string bimFilename = @"c:\temp\model.bim";

            Console.WriteLine("Reading {0} file", bimFilename);
            Database database = ReadDatabaseFromBimFile(bimFilename);

            Console.WriteLine(
                "Renaming database from {0} to {1}", database.Name, databaseName);
            database.Name = databaseName;
            database.ID = databaseName;

            Console.WriteLine("Connecting to {0}", serverName);
            Server server = new Server();
            server.Connect(serverName);

            Console.WriteLine("Deploying database {0}", database.Name);
            server.Databases.Add(database);
            database.Update(Microsoft.AnalysisServices.UpdateOptions.ExpandFull);
        }
        // Insert ReadDatabaseFromBimFile and WriteDatabaseToBimFile definitions here
    }
}
```

You can use the same methods in the PowerShell script shown in Listing 13-22.

LISTING 13-22 Script PowerShell\Deploy BIM to Database.ps1

```
[System.Reflection.Assembly]::LoadWithPartialName("Microsoft.AnalysisServices.
Tabular")
$serverName = "localhost\tabular"
$dbName = "Contoso from BIM file"
$bimFilename = "c:\temp\model.bim"

$modelBim = [IO.File]::ReadAllText($bimFilename)
$db = Microsoft.AnalysisServices.Tabular.JsonSerializer]::DeserializeDatabase($modelBim)
```

```
$db.ID = $dbName
$db.Name = $dbName

$server = New-Object Microsoft.AnalysisServices.Tabular.Server
$server.Connect($serverName)

$server.Databases.Add( $db )
$db.Update( "ExpandFull" )
```

After you load the model.bim file into memory by using the DeserializeDatabase method, you have access to the Model object and can alter any property, such as data source connections, security roles, partitions, or any other entity in the model.

Summary

This chapter discussed using the AMO and TOM libraries to administer and manipulate a tabular model and the differences in the libraries required to manage different tabular compatibility models. The TOM library provides you full control over the deployment and customization of a tabular model, which you can also manipulate offline by using the Model object. Using the examples shown in this chapter, you should be able to customize an existing tabular model or create a new model from scratch.

CHAPTER 14

Monitoring and tuning a Tabular service

Now that you have seen how to build a complete tabular solution, this chapter provides information on how to monitor its behavior and guarantee that your solution is running at its best. In Chapter 12, "Inside VertiPaq," you saw how the tabular engine uses memory to process and query databases. This chapter shows you how to monitor the resources used by the system. It also shows you how to change some of the parameters to optimize SQL Server Analysis Services (SSAS) and memory use.

What's new in SSAS 2016 There are no important differences with previous versions of Analysis Services for monitoring and tuning an instance in Tabular mode. However, this chapter has been updated to include references to extended events and related tools.

Finding the Analysis Services process

Analysis Services is a process running as a service under the Microsoft Windows operating system (OS). It starts as soon as the OS starts and normally waits to receive commands, answer queries, process databases, and perform its work. The process's name is MSMDSRV.EXE (Microsoft Multidimensional Server), and you can verify its existence by opening Windows Task Manager's Services tab, as shown in Figure 14-1.

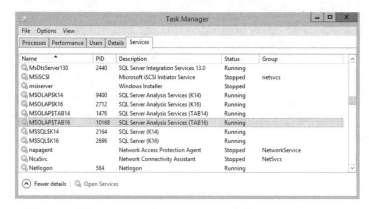

FIGURE 14-1 Windows Task Manager showing, among other services, SSAS Tabular.

You can see in Figure 14-1 that there are several instances of SSAS: two running Tabular (TAB14 and TAB16) and two running Multidimensional (K14 and K16). If you want to see the process that is running Tabular, right-click **MSOLAP$TAB16** (or MSOLAP$TABULAR; the name after the dollar sign is the name of the Tabular instance you installed) and choose **Go to Details**. Task Manager opens the Details tab, highlighting msmdsrv.exe, the Tabular instance of MSMDSRV, as shown in Figure 14-2. (Note that if the process is impersonating a different user, you must run Task Manager as the administrator to see the user name.)

Note The name of an Analysis Services instance is chosen during the installation operation. In this book, we use the Tabular and Multidimensional instance names to identify the corresponding roles of the different SSAS instances. However, you can choose different instance names during the installation.

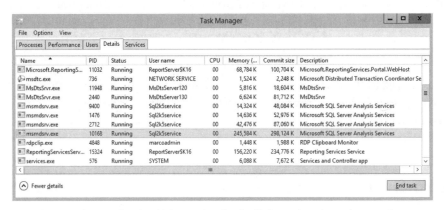

FIGURE 14-2   The Details tab, which contains detailed information about the msmdsrv.exe process.

SSAS, like any other Windows process, consumes resources by asking for them from the Windows OS. It is important to monitor whether it has enough resources to run optimally to ensure that the system is always responsive. The easiest tool for monitoring Tabular is Task Manager. It already provides much of the information about memory and CPU use and is available to any user on any Windows installation, without requiring special knowledge or administrative rights. Nevertheless, to fine-tune a solution, you will need more advanced tools and a deeper knowledge of the SSAS internals.

Warning   When you use Task Manager to monitor SSAS, the server should not be running other time-consuming processes. Otherwise, your observations will be contaminated by the other tasks that are consuming the server resources.

Because it is an in-memory columnar database, SSAS Tabular is easy to monitor because it primarily uses two kinds of resources: memory and CPU. The disk use of SSAS Tabular is not very important to monitor because disk activity only happens during processing. So, the activity is when the database is written to disk and when the database is being loaded, as soon as the first user accesses the database after the service starts. Both activities are sequential reads and writes, which are very fast operations on normal disk systems. Random I/O might occur during the processing, but only if there is not enough memory to complete the operation and if some data must be paged on disk.

Resources consumed by Analysis Services

Analysis Services consumes resources provided by the Windows OS. The first level of monitoring is looking at the behavior of SSAS Tabular as you would with any other process running on the server. Every process consumes CPU, memory, and I/O bandwidth. SSAS Tabular is particular because it is hungry for CPU processing and memory, but it does not demand much I/O bandwidth throughout.

CPU

Analysis Services consumes CPU processing during two operations: processing and querying. Not all the operations performed by SSAS Tabular can scale over multiple cores. The process of a single partition reads data sequentially, but the compression of the columns in each segment can be parallelized.

The process of a single partition reads data sequentially, but the compression of the columns in each segment can be parallelized. Usually the process of a single partition creates spikes in CPU use at the end of each segment (by default it is 8,000,000 rows). If you process multiple partitions in parallel (from the same tables or from different tables), then the CPU consumption can increase. In general, you should not increase the parallelism if, during a process operation, you already saturate the CPU available. However, you should consider increasing the parallelism if your system has a low use of CPU during the entire process operation.

During querying, SSAS consumes CPU to scan compressed data in the memory and to perform the calculations that are requested by a query. Every query has a part of the execution that can scale up on multiple cores (the storage engine, which uses internal calls to VertiPaq), and another part that is sequential (the formula engine, which manages uncompressed data that is returned by VertiPaq or by external SQL queries in DirectQuery mode). Queries that have a bottleneck in the formula engine will use no more than the equivalent of one core. As shown in Figure 14-3, on an eight-core server, you will see a constant consumption of one-eighth of our available CPU, which is 12 to 13 percent. (You might see a higher percentage because of the time spent by other processes.)

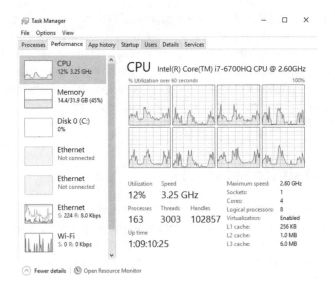

FIGURE 14-3 The Performance tab in Task Manager, which contains detailed information about the CPU.

In such cases, you must optimize the DAX expression so that the execution requires less resources than the formula engine. In general, SSAS can consume a lot of CPU resources during processing and, depending on the conditions, while running the queries. You need to bear this in mind when specifying servers for SSAS to run on or deciding if SSAS should be installed on the same server as other CPU-intensive applications.

Memory

Analysis Services uses memory for a lot of different purposes—even if for a tabular model, most of the memory is probably used to store the columnar database that is managed by VertiPaq. It is not the goal of this book to explain all the details of Analysis Services' memory settings or how to tune them. For most scenarios, the default settings are good enough. However, it is important to understand what happens when SSAS requests the memory from the OS because that memory is not always physical RAM. This could have important consequences like increased paging of memory to disk.

Analysis Services, like any other process in Windows, requires memory from the OS, which in turn provides blocks of virtual memory. Each process has a separate address space, called a *virtual address space*. Each allocation made by a Windows process inside the virtual address space gets a part of the OS virtual memory, which might correspond to either the physical RAM or the disk paging file. It is up to the OS to determine whether a page of memory (which corresponds to 4 KB) is in physical RAM or is moved to the paging disk file. This concept is very important, especially when you have several other services running on the same server, like Reporting Services, Integration Services, and the relational engine of SQL Server itself.

Note The memory allocated by SSAS might be paged to disk due to other process activities, and this is partially controlled by some memory settings. An explanation of these settings is available in the section "Understanding memory configuration" later in this chapter, and in the MSDN Library at *https://msdn.microsoft.com/en-us/library/ms174514.aspx*.

To understand how much virtual and physical memory a process is using, it is important to know how to read the numbers provided by Task Manager. The total amount of virtual memory requested by a process is displayed in a Commit Size column. The total amount of physical RAM consumed exclusively by a process is displayed in a Memory (Private Working Set) column.

The virtual memory manager in Windows is a complex system that aims to optimize the use of physical memory by sharing the data between processes whenever possible. In general, however, it isolates each virtual address space from all the others in a secure manner. Therefore, it could be difficult to interpret the counters we just mentioned. It could also be useful to recap how virtual memory allocation works in Windows, focusing mainly on memory that is allocated privately by a process, such as SSAS allocating RAM for VertiPaq and other internal structures.

When a process allocates private memory, as SSAS does when it requires space for its data, it is requested from virtual memory. When that memory is written, the OS ensures that the page is in physical RAM. When there is not enough RAM to hold all the virtual memory pages that are used to run the processes, the OS moves older pages from RAM to disk. These pages will be recalled from disk as soon as a process needs to read or write data there. This activity is called *memory paging*, and you want it to happen as little as possible. One way to stop it from happening is to remove the paging file from the OS. You do this by using the no-paging file setting, but we do not recommend using this option on a server running SQL Server or Analysis Services. Another option is to use VertiPaqPagingPolicy in mode 0, as explained later in this chapter.

Thus, you have a paging file and you need to optimize its use. Ideally SSAS should not use it at all. If SSAS were the only process running on the system, it would be sufficient to set its memory limits to a value that does not exceed the amount of physical RAM on the system. In fact, the default settings of SSAS are below this limit, but they do not consider that other memory-hungry processes may run concurrently on the same machine. For example, it is quite common to have both SQL Server and Analysis Services running on the same machine. Think about what would happen when you processed a cube, which of course would mean that SSAS would need to query the fact table in SQL Server: Both services require memory, and paging to disk could be unavoidable. There is a difference between SQL Server and Analysis Services in terms of memory management. SQL Server can adapt the amount of virtual memory it requests from the OS to the amount of physical RAM available to it. SSAS is not as sophisticated as SQL Server and does not dynamically reduce or increase the size of its requests for memory to the OS based on current available physical memory.

The memory requested by a process is always requested as virtual memory. In situations where the virtual memory allocated by SSAS is much larger than the available physical RAM, some SSAS data will be paged to disk. If you use VertiPaqPagingPolicy in mode 1, this could happen during processing or for queries that are creating materialization that is too large, even if an out-of-memory error is more likely in the latter case. You should avoid these situations by configuring Analysis Services' memory settings (which we discuss in the "Understanding memory configuration" section later in this chapter) so that they limit the amount of memory that can be allocated by it. However, when no other processes are asking for memory, you might find that limiting Analysis Services' memory use prevents it from using extra memory when it needs it—even when that memory is not used by anything else. We will explore the available memory options for Analysis Services and see how to monitor its memory use in the "Understanding memory configuration" and "Using memory-related performance counters" sections later in this chapter, respectively.

I/O operations

Analysis Services generates I/O operations in two ways:

- **Directly** A direct I/O request from SSAS is made when it needs to read data from or write data to disk and when it sends query results back to the client. This involves an inter-process communication (typically made through the network's I/O operations).

- **Indirectly** The indirect I/O requests generated by SSAS come from paging-disk operations. It is very important to be aware that this can happen. You cannot see these operations using the performance counters you might typically monitor for SSAS. Paging operations are not visible to the SSAS process and can be seen only by using the appropriate OS performance counters, like **Memory: Pages/Sec**.

In its regular condition, SSAS performs direct I/O requests only when it reads the database at services startup or during a restore or when it writes data during processing and the backup operation. The only other relevant I/O activities performed by SSAS should be indirect and caused by paging.

Another I/O operation generated by Analysis Services is the transfer of query results to the client. Usually this is not a slow operation, but if a query returns a very large number of rows, the query response time might be affected by the time needed to transfer the result from the server to the client. Take a look at the network traffic to understand if this is a possible issue.

 Note In general, it is not very important to monitor I/O operations that are performed by an SSAS Tabular service.

Understanding memory configuration

Because memory is so important to Tabular, being able to monitor how much memory is used and learning how to configure memory use is a very important topic. In this section, you learn about the main tools available to configure and monitor memory that is used by a Tabular instance.

First, it is important to understand that SSAS uses memory during the two following phases:

- **Processing**   During processing, SSAS needs memory to load data and create dictionaries and related data structures before it flushes them to disk. In addition, if the database being processed already contains some data, it must hold the previous version of the database until the transaction commits and the new database is ready to query. Refer to Chapter 12 for more information about the internal structure and processing.

- **Querying**   During a query, SSAS sometimes needs memory to hold temporary data structures that are needed to resolve the query. Depending on the database size and query shape, these data structures might be very big. Sometimes they are much bigger than the database itself. Later in this chapter, in the "Using memory-related performance counters" section, you will see an example of a complex query that uses a lot of RAM.

Memory settings in Tabular are configured in the msmdsrv.ini file, which contains the whole SSAS configuration. You can edit the file manually to change the memory settings, but the easiest way to read or modify the content of the configuration is to right-click the server in the Object Explorer pane of SQL Server Management Studio (SSMS) and choose **Properties**. The Analysis Services Properties dialog box opens (see Figure 14-4). From there, you can make most of the SSAS configurations.

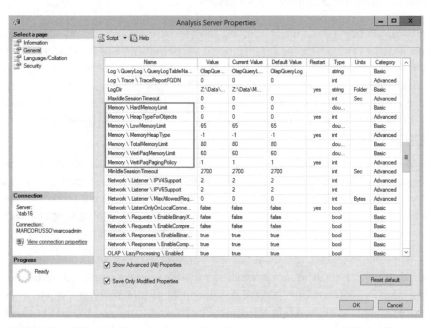

FIGURE 14-4   The Analysis Server Properties dialog box, which contains all the configurations of SSAS.

In the highlighted box, you see the following memory settings for SSAS. (Note that to display all these settings, you must select the Show Advanced (All) Properties check box.)

- **HeapTypeForObjects**   Choose the heap system to allocate objects of a fixed size, such as instances of classes in C++ (which is the language used by Microsoft to write Analysis Services). The possible values are as follows:

  - **0**   Use the Windows Low-Fragmentation Heap (LFH), which is the default in SSAS Tabular 2016.

  - **1**   Use the custom heap implementation of Analysis Services.

- **MemoryHeapType**   Choose the heap system to allocate objects of a dynamic size, such as strings, vectors, bytes, and so on. The possible values are as follows:

  - **–1**   This choice is made automatically by SSAS Tabular (the default in SSAS Tabular 2016).

  - **1**   Use the custom heap implementation of Analysis Services.

  - **2**   Use the Windows LFH.

  - **5**   This is a hybrid allocator (new in SSAS Tabular 2016).

- **VertiPaqPagingPolicy**   This is the first setting you need to learn. It can have a value of 0 or 1. We refer to its value as mode 0 or mode 1. In mode 0, all the VertiPaq data is locked into memory, whereas in mode 1, the data is not locked. This allows the VertiPaq in-memory engine to page data on disk if the system is running out of memory. More specifically, in mode 1, only hash dictionaries are locked. Data pages can be flushed to disk. This enables VertiPaq to use more memory than is available. Keep in mind that if paging occurs, performances will suffer a severe degradation. The default value is mode 1.

- **VertiPaqMemoryLimit**   If you choose mode 0, VertiPaqMemoryLimit defines the total amount of memory VertiPaq can lock in the working set (the total that can be used for in-memory databases). Remember that the Analysis Services service might use more memory for other reasons. In mode 1, it defines a limit for the physical memory that is used by VertiPaq, which allows paging for the remaining memory (virtual committed memory) above this limit.

  The VertiPaqPagingPolicy setting provides a way to prevent VertiPaq data from interacting badly with the memory-cleaning subsystem. In mode 1, it causes the cleaner subsystem to ignore the memory allocated for VertiPaq data beyond VertiPaqMemoryLimit when calculating the price of memory. In this mode, the server's total memory use can exceed the physical memory. It is constrained primarily by the total virtual memory, and it pages data out to the system page file.

  If you want to reduce the memory for an instance of Analysis Services, it makes sense to set VertiPaqMemoryLimit to a number that is lower than LowMemoryLimit (see the upcoming bullet).

- **HardMemoryLimit**   This is the maximum memory that SSAS can allocate. If SSAS exceeds the hard memory limit, the system aggressively kills the active sessions to reduce memory use. Sessions killed for this reason receive an error that explains the cancellation due to memory pressure. With VertiPaqPagingPolicy in mode 0, it is also the limit for the maximum working set of the process. If HardMemoryLimit is set to 0, it will use a default value midway between the high memory limit and the total physical memory (or the total virtual address space, if you are on a 32-bit machine on which the physical memory exceeds the virtual memory).

- **LowMemoryLimit**   This is the point at which the system starts to clear caches out of memory. As memory use increases above the low memory limit, SSAS becomes more aggressive about evicting the cached data until it hits the high/total memory limit. At this point, it evicts everything that is not pinned.

- **TotalMemoryLimit**   If memory use exceeds the total memory limit, the memory manager evicts all the cached data that is not currently in use. TotalMemoryLimit must always be less than HardMemoryLimit.

The HeapTypeForObjects and MemoryHeapType settings are important for memory-management performance and stability. The new defaults in SSAS Tabular 2016 are usually the best choice for most of the server, whereas upgrades from previous versions might keep settings that could create memory fragmentation after extensive use. More details on these problems are available at *https://www.sqlbi. com/articles/heap-memory-settings-for-analysis-services-tabular-2012-2014/*.

> **Important**   If you upgraded previous versions of Analysis Services to SSAS Tabular 2016, you should change the MemoryHeapType setting to the new default value of –1. The previous default value of 2 creates memory fragmentation that slows down the process and query performance. If you experienced an improved performance after a service restart in previous versions of Analysis Services, you were likely affected by this problem. If you do not modify the MemoryHeapType setting, you might experience the same performance degradation in SSAS Tabular 2016.

How aggressively SSAS clears caches depends on how much memory is currently being allocated. No cleaning happens below the LowMemoryLimit value, and the level of aggression increases as soon as the memory use approaches the TotalMemoryLimit value. Above the TotalMemoryLimit value, SSAS is committed to clearing memory, even if the panic mode only starts after the HardMemoryLimit value.

All the limit values are expressed as numbers. If their value is less than 100, it is interpreted as a percentage of the total server memory. (On 32-bit systems, the maximum available memory can be up to 2 GB, regardless of the memory installed on the system.) If it has a value greater than 100, it is interpreted as the number of bytes to allocate.

Important The value of these parameters, if greater than 100, is in bytes. If you use 8,192, you are not allocating 8 GB. You are allocating 8 KB, which is not so useful. If you provide the wrong values, SSAS will not raise a warning. Instead, it will try to work with the memory you made available to it.

When SSAS is working, it requests memory from the OS to perform its tasks. It continues to use memory until it reaches the TotalMemoryLimit value. Nevertheless, as soon as the LowMemoryLimit value has been reached, SSAS starts to reduce memory use by freeing memory that is not strictly necessary. The process of reducing memory (which means cache eviction) is more aggressive as the system moves toward the TotalMemoryLimit value. If SSAS overcomes the TotalMemoryLimit value, it becomes very aggressive. When it reaches the HardMemoryLimit value, it starts to drop connections to force memory to be freed.

Because cache-eviction decisions and hard-limit enforcement are normally done based on the process's total memory use, it has been necessary to change that calculation when allowing databases to exceed physical memory in Tabular. (Remember that previous versions of Analysis Services supported only multidimensional models.) Therefore, when VertiPaqPagingPolicy is in mode 1, which indicates that memory can grow beyond the total physical memory, the system tracks the total memory used by VertiPaq as a separate quantity. (This is reported in the MemoryVertiPaq* counters that you can analyze in Performance Monitor.) If the total memory used by VertiPaq exceeds the VertiPaqMemoryLimit value, the memory used by VertiPaq in excess of the limit will be ignored for the purpose of determining what to evict.

The following example demonstrates these concepts. Suppose VertiPaqMemoryLimit is set to 100 GB, LowMemoryLimit is 110 GB, and TotalMemoryLimit is 120 GB. Now assume that VertiPaq data structures are using 210 GB of memory and the process's total memory use is 215 GB. This number is well above the TotalMemoryLimit value (and probably above the HardMemoryLimit value), so ignoring VertiPaqMemoryLimit, the cleaning would be very aggressive and would kill sessions. However, when PagingPolicy is set to 1, the memory used by VertiPaq in excess of the limit is ignored for the purpose of computing memory pressure. This means that the number that is used is computed according to the following formula:

```
+ <Total Memory>           + 215GB
- <Total VertiPaq Memory>  - 210GB
+ <VertiPaqMemoryLimit>    + 100GB = 105GB
```

Because this value (105 GB) is below the LowMemoryLimit value (110 GB), the cache is not cleaned at all.

Note As you have probably noticed, this chapter covers how the SSAS engine behaves with memory and how to configure it. This chapter does not cover how to reduce memory use by using a correct database design. If you need some hints on this, see Chapter 15, "Optimizing tabular models."

Using memory-related performance counters

Now that you have learned how memory parameters can be set, you will learn how to monitor them by using performance counters. To obtain a very useful graphical representation of the memory use in SSAS, you can use Performance Monitor. Performance Monitor is a Windows utility that can show you many counters that programs make available to monitor their behavior. SSAS offers many interesting and useful counters.

If you open Performance Monitor, you must add the SSAS memory-related counters to the graph. If the instance is called Tabular, as in our example, you can find the counters under the MSOLAP$TAB16:Memory tree of the counter hierarchy. (If your instance is the default, the name will be MSAS11:Memory.) As shown in Figure 14-5, you see the Add Counters dialog box with the desired counters already selected.

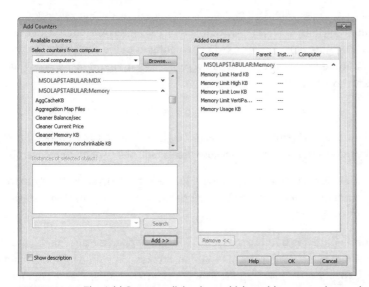

FIGURE 14-5 The Add Counters dialog box, which enables you to choose the counters to add to the graph.

Because the values are in kilobytes, you must adjust the counter scale to make it fit into the chart and to ensure that all the counters use the same scaling. For these counters, a scale of 0.00001 is a good choice. The chart, immediately after a service restart, is shown in Figure 14-6.

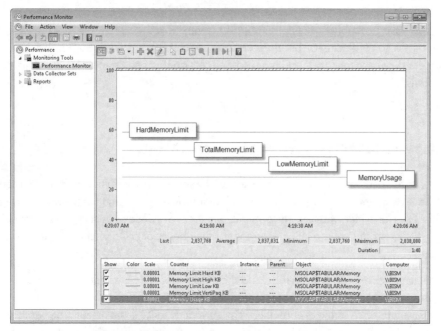

FIGURE 14-6 The counters on the chart, which clearly show the boundaries of memory use.

The chart was drawn using a computer with 8 GB of RAM. We changed the default values for the parameters by setting HardMemoryLimit to 70, TotalMemoryLimit to 55, and LowMemoryLimit to 45. When values are smaller than 100, these numbers are used as percentages of the available memory (8 GB). The server has been configured in mode 0, so no paging will happen. Figure 14-7 shows what happens if you execute a query requiring a lot of memory.

The query failed to execute. The following analysis is of the five points highlighted in the chart:

1. **The query starts**   Then, the LowMemoryLimit value having been reached, the cleaner starts to clean some memory by using a graceful tactic (because there is still plenty of memory available).

2. **The TotalMemoryLimit value has been surpassed**   The cleaner works aggressively to free memory because it is using too much memory. Cache is being cleared, and the query starts to suffer in performance.

3. **The HardMemoryLimit value has been surpassed**   This can happen because of the speed at which the memory is requested during query execution. It takes some time for the cleaner to start. Nevertheless, now the cleaner is very aggressive. In fact, after point 3, a large amount of memory is cleared.

4. **Even if the cleaner has tried its best to reduce the memory use, the query is still asking for memory**   The connection is closed. There is no way to give it the memory it needs because it is over the HardMemoryLimit.

5. **The connection has been closed**   All the memory requested by the query is cleared, and SSAS can work normally.

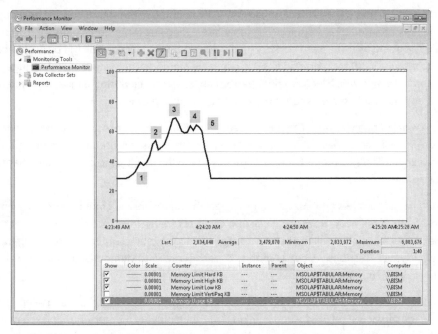

FIGURE 14-7 An analysis that highlights some important steps during a complex query execution.

Now, check the same query, on the same server, running in mode 1. In this mode, SSAS can page out memory to use more memory than the physical RAM available. The first part of the chart is shown in Figure 14-8.

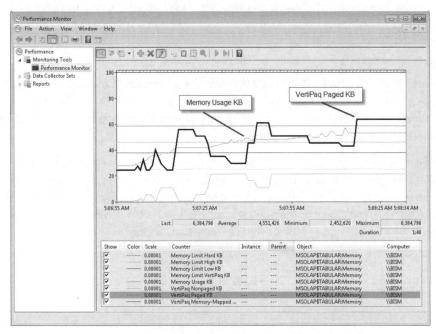

FIGURE 14-8 Mode 1 is selected, with VertiPaq paging out data to free memory.

In the chart, the highlighted line is the VertiPaq Paged KB counter, which shows how many kilobytes of pageable memory are used by the engine. The other interesting line is Memory Usage KB. You can see that SSAS is not going over the HardMemoryLimit value, so the connection will not be dropped. Nevertheless, to avoid using RAM, VertiPaq is using pageable memory. The system is paging huge amounts of memory to disk, which leads to poor performance. Moreover, during paging, the system is nonresponsive, and the whole server is suffering from performance problems.

This example is deliberately flawed. The query needed 15 GB of RAM for execution, and trying to make it work on an 8-GB server was not a very good idea. Nevertheless, it is useful to understand the difference between mode 0 and mode 1 and to learn how to use the counters to check what is happening to the server under the covers.

Using mode 1 has advantages and disadvantages. It lets the server answer complex queries even when it is running out of memory. However, it can also cause severe performance problems—not only for the complex query, but also for all the users who are running the much lighter queries. Using mode 0, the server is always very responsive, but as soon as it reaches the HardMemoryLimit value, it will close connections due to memory pressure.

Correctly setting the mode in a production server is a very complex task that requires a deep understanding of how the server will be used. Keep in mind that Tabular is very memory-hungry. You need to carefully check the memory use of your queries before correctly sizing the memory for the production server.

Memory-usage complexity

You might wonder how complex this query was and how important testing your queries correctly before going into production is. The query we used to produce these charts is as follows:

```
EVALUATE
ROW ( "Distinct", COUNTROWS ( SUMMARIZE ( Numbers, Numbers[Num1], Numbers[Num2] ) ) )
```

This query runs on a database with 100,000,000 rows and a distribution of Num1 and Num2. This guarantees that the result is exactly 100,000,000 (there are a 100,000,000 combinations of Num1 and Num2), which causes the server to run out of memory. The database size is 191 MB, but the engine needs 15 GB to complete the query.

The reason the server runs out of memory is that the engine has to materialize (spool) the complete dataset to perform the computation. Under normal circumstances, the materialization leads to much smaller datasets. It is very unlikely that you want to compute a distinct count of a 100,000,000-row table, knowing that the result is exactly 100,000,000. Keep in mind that, in rare circumstances, spooling temporary tables might consume quite a bit of memory.

Using dynamic management views

SSAS makes available a set of dynamic management views (DMVs), which are useful for gathering precise information about the status of a database or an instance of SSAS. The information provided by DMVs is reset at service startup, so it can show very interesting statistics about the use of SSAS since its last restart.

There are many DMVs, and you can find a detailed description of each one at *https://msdn.micro-soft.com/en-us/library/ms126221.aspx*. A selection of the most interesting DMVs is shown later in this section. If you want to list all available DMVs, you can execute the following query from inside an MDX query panel in SSMS:

```
SELECT * FROM $SYSTEM.DISCOVER_SCHEMA_ROWSETS
```

A simpler way to see the list of the available DMVs is to switch to the DMV pane in DAX Studio. As shown in Figure 14-9, the DMV pane contains the same names returned by the DMV above. You can double-click one of these names to get the corresponding statement to query the DMV ready to be executed.

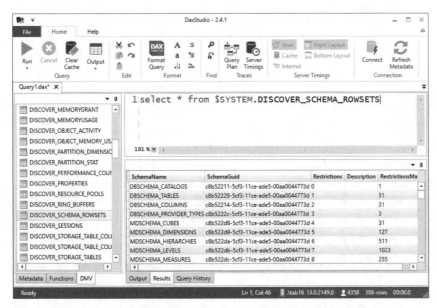

FIGURE 14-9 The DMV pane in DAX Studio, which shows all the available DMVs.

Although we will not provide a complete description of all the available DMVs, we will briefly discuss some of the queries to give you a better idea of the kind of information you can obtain by using DMVs.

As a first example, the following query retrieves the activity executed on different objects in the database since the service startup. It is useful to see the objects in your instance on which the engine has spent more time:

```
SELECT TOP 10
    OBJECT_ID,
    OBJECT_CPU_TIME_MS
FROM $system.DISCOVER_OBJECT_ACTIVITY
ORDER BY
    OBJECT_CPU_TIME_MS DESC
```

The result is the set of the 10 objects on which the SSAS instance has spent the most time (expressed in CPU milliseconds).

> **Note** You cannot use the full SQL syntax when querying the DMV. You have only a subset of SQL available, and features such as JOIN, LIKE, and GROUP BY are not available. DMVs are not intended to be used in complex queries. If you need complex processing, you should issue simple queries and then process the results further.

All the DMVs return many columns, most of which are useful for Multidimensional. (There are several columns that show numbers related to I/O, which, in Tabular, are of no use.) This is a clear indication of the big difference between Tabular and Multidimensional. In Tabular, because all the data should be in memory, there should be no I/O at all, and the system maintenance and optimization are greatly reduced. All you need to do is optimize the DAX queries and make sure that enough memory is available in the system.

Because memory is so important to Tabular, a very useful function of DMVs is gathering memory occupation by object. The DMV that returns this information is DISCOVER_OBJECT_MEMORY_USAGE. In the information you get with this DMV, there are both SHRINKABLE and NONSHRINKABLE memory usages. In the following query, there is an ORDER BY on the NONSHRINKABLE memory size. Note that in Multidimensional, the SHRINKABLE column is always empty; you must use the NONSHRINKABLE column to get meaningful values. For example, you might run the following query:

```
SELECT * FROM $system.DISCOVER_OBJECT_MEMORY_USAGE ORDER BY OBJECT_MEMORY_NONSHRINKABLE DESC
```

As a result, you will receive the list of all the objects currently loaded, along with the amount of memory they are using, as shown in Figure 14-10.

A big difference between using this view and the other views used by VertiPaq Analyzer is that you have a single complete view of the memory used by the service, regardless of the single database. You can analyze this view by using a Power Pivot for Excel data model called BISM Server Memory Report, created by Kasper De Jonge and available at *http://www.powerpivotblog.nl/what-is-using-all-that-memory-on-my-analysis-server-instance/*. The technique of extracting data from DMVs used in this workbook was the inspiration behind the creation of VertiPaq Analyzer, which seeks to provide a more detailed analysis of a single database.

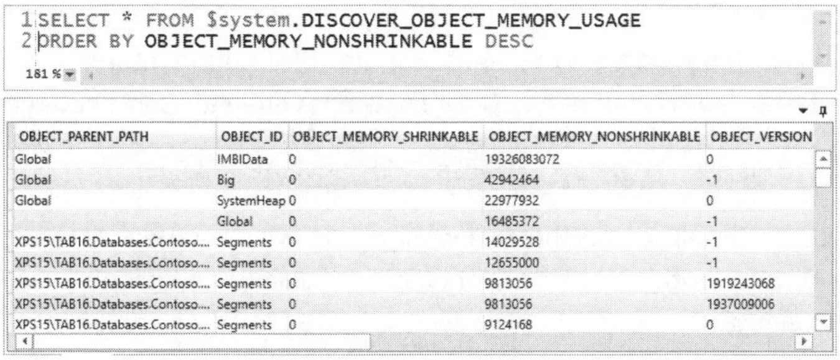

FIGURE 14-10 The DMV pane in DAX Studio, which shows all the available DMVs.

Interesting DMVs to monitor a Tabular service

The most interesting DMVs you can use to monitor the state of an instance of Analysis Services Tabular that runs on a server are a subset of those with the DISCOVER prefix. In the following list, you will find a selection of these DMVs. The list does not include other DMVs with the same prefix that are useful to analyze the size of objects in the databases (which is already covered by VertiPaq Analyzer) and to get other metadata from the system (a list of keywords, profiler events, and others).

You should use the following DMVs for troubleshooting:

- **DISCOVER_CONNECTIONS** This lists the connections that are currently opened on the server. You can see the name of the user connected, the timestamp of the last command sent, and other counters. This could be useful to make sure there are no clients connected before restarting the service.

- **DISCOVER_COMMANDS** This shows the last command sent for each connection. It could be a command currently executing or the last command executed if the connection is idle.

- **DISCOVER_DB_CONNECTIONS** This provides resource use and activity information about the currently opened connections from SSAS Tabular to an external database. (Usually, during a database process operation, SSAS retrieves data from the other databases.)

- **DISCOVER_LOCKS** This returns information about current locks on the server. There are different types of locks in SSAS Tabular, but like SSAS Multidimensional, these locks manage the conflict between process operations and queries. If a long process operation blocks many of the queries, or a long-running query is blocking a process, you use this DMV to identify the operations responsible for the lock.

- **DISCOVER_MEMORY_USAGE** This provides the memory-usage statistics for the objects allocated by Analysis Services.

- **DISCOVER_OBJECT_MEMORY_USAGE** This returns information about memory that is allocated for specific objects.

- **DISCOVER_SESSIONS**   This provides resource use and activity information about the currently opened sessions on the server. It provides more details than the information returned by DISCOVER_CONNECTIONS because SSAS might have more sessions within the same connection.

- **DISCOVER_TRANSACTIONS**   This lists the pending transactions on SSAS Tabular.

An open source tool, SSAS Activity Monitor, uses these views and helps you to monitor the current activity on Analysis Services. It works for both Multidimensional and Tabular instances, and is available at *https://www.sqlbi.com/tools/ssas-activity-monitor/*.

Automating monitoring info and logs acquisition

The tools we have seen so far are useful to monitor what is happening and what will happen on Analysis Services Tabular. However, a common requirement is trying to understand what happened in the past, whether it was two minutes ago, two days ago, or two weeks ago. If you did not collect the data, you will have very little information to analyze. For this reason, it is better to acquire the logs that will help you in future investigations.

Performance counters

The performance counters that are available from the OS are visible in Performance Counter, which is a snap-in for Microsoft Management Console (MMC). In reality, these performance counters are available through a set of APIs, and there are third-party tools that can access them, too. However, in this book, we use Performance Monitor to show them. The concepts related to each counter described are valid, regardless of the tool used to display them.

> **Note**   There are differences in the Performance Monitor user interface, depending on which version of Windows you have, but they are not significant for the purposes of this chapter.

Performance Monitor can display performance-counter data captured in real-time. It can also be used to display a trace session of the performance-counter data that is recorded by using the Data Collector Sets feature. This trace data is very useful for monitoring a production server to detect bottlenecks and to measure the average workload. We suggest reading the documentation at *https://technet.microsoft.com/en-us/library/cc749337.aspx* to understand how to make good use of Data Collector Sets.

It is a good idea to keep a data collector active on a server that is running SSAS Tabular, as shown in Figure 14-11. You should include the Memory and Processor counters from the OS (selecting those we mentioned in this chapter), certain Process counters (at least those related to memory and CPU), and specific counters from Analysis Services instances that you want to monitor (they have the prefix MSO-LAP$ followed by the name of the instance). In the latter group of counters, the more interesting for

SSAS Tabular are Connection, Locks, Memory, Processing, and Storage Engine Query. Because all these counters produce a certain amount of data, you should consider the sample interval for a production server in minutes (because it will be always running). The same sample should be seconds when you need to analyze a specific problem in detail (for example, a database process operation), which enables and disables the Data Collector for the minimum amount of time necessary.

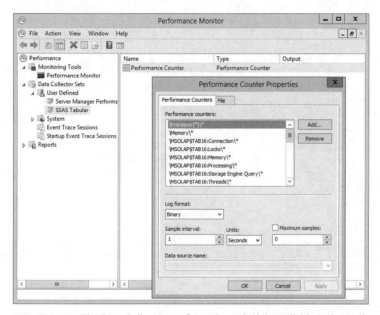

FIGURE 14-11 The Data Collector configuration, which is available in the Performance Monitor snap-in.

SQL Server Profiler

Microsoft SQL Server Profiler is a tool for capturing database engine trace information, but it is still supported for Analysis Services workloads. (See more info at *https://msdn.microsoft.com/en-us/library/ms181091.aspx*.) It is a good idea to create one or more templates for SSAS Tabular including only the events you are interested in for query and process analysis. For example, Figure 14-12 shows a simple set of events to monitor for capturing long-running queries and information about process operations.

> **Note** Certain feature sets of SQL Server Profiler, including Database Engine Trace Capture, Trace Replay, and the associated namespace, will be deprecated in the version after SQL Server 2016. However, SQL Server Profiler for the Analysis Services workloads is *not* being deprecated, and it will continue to be supported.

The events chosen in a profiling session are, in fact, classes of events. For each class, there are many actual events that can be generated. These events are shown in the EventSubClass column in SQL Server Profiler, which is shown in Figure 14-13.

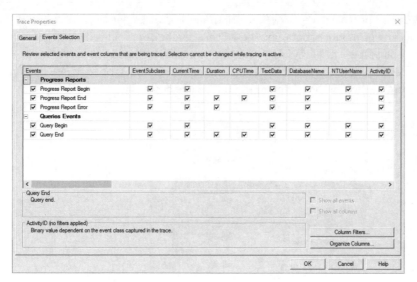

FIGURE 14-12 The events selected in SQL Server Profiler for monitoring queries and processing.

EventClass	EventSubclass	Current Time	TextData
Progress Report End	44 - Compress Segment	2016-07-28 12:09:14.000	Finished compressing segment 0 of column 'StoreKey' for the...
Progress Report End	44 - Compress Segment	2016-07-28 12:09:14.000	Finished compressing segment 0 of column 'Unit Cost' for th...
Progress Report End	44 - Compress Segment	2016-07-28 12:09:14.000	Finished compressing segment 0 of column 'Net Price' for th...
Progress Report End	44 - Compress Segment	2016-07-28 12:09:14.000	Finished compressing segment 0 of column 'DueDateKey' for t...
Progress Report End	44 - Compress Segment	2016-07-28 12:09:14.000	Finished compressing segment 0 of column 'PromotionKey' for...
Progress Report End	43 - Analyze\Encode Data	2016-07-28 12:09:14.000	Finished Analyzing\Encoding segment 0 for the 'Sales' table...
Progress Report End	1 - Process	2016-07-28 12:09:14.000	Finished processing the 'Sales' partition of the 'Sales' ta...
Progress Report End	59 - Tabular object processing	2016-07-28 12:09:14.000	Finished processing partition 'Sales' of table 'Sales'.
Progress Report End	17 - ReadData	2016-07-28 12:09:16.000	Finished reading data for the 'Sales' table 'Sales 2' parti...
Progress Report Begin	43 - Analyze\Encode Data	2016-07-28 12:09:16.000	Analyzing\Encoding segment 0 for the 'Sales' table 'Sales 2...
Progress Report Begin	53 - VertiPaq	2016-07-28 12:09:16.000	Compression started for the segment 0 of the 'Sales' table...
Progress Report End	53 - VertiPaq	2016-07-28 12:09:16.000	Compression for the segment '0' of the 'Sales' table 'Sales...
Progress Report Begin	44 - Compress Segment	2016-07-28 12:09:16.000	Compressing segment 0 of column 'CurrencyKey' for the 'Sale...
Progress Report Begin	44 - Compress Segment	2016-07-28 12:09:16.000	Compressing segment 0 of column 'ProductKey' for the 'Sales...
Progress Report Begin	44 - Compress Segment	2016-07-28 12:09:16.000	Compressing segment 0 of column 'StoreKey' for the 'Sales' ...
Progress Report Begin	44 - Compress Segment	2016-07-28 12:09:16.000	Compressing segment 0 of column 'RowNumber-2662979B-1795-4F...
Progress Report Begin	44 - Compress Segment	2016-07-28 12:09:16.000	Compressing segment 0 of column 'CustomerKey' for the 'Sale...

Compression for the segment '0' of the 'Sales' table 'Sales 2' partition completed in '2635' steps with '745' clusters computed in total. Execution hasn't b...

FIGURE 14-13 There are different event subclasses for each event class.

Looking at these events in SQL Server Profiler is not particularly easy. Saving the trace data to a SQL Server table is a good idea because it enables you to query and report on it much more easily. To save a captured trace session, open the **File** menu, choose **Save As**, and select **Trace Table**. You could also choose to save a trace session in advance by selecting the **Save to Table** option in the Trace Properties dialog box that is shown when you define a new trace session.

The trace events that you might be interested in are listed below. Event classes and subclasses are identified by an integer value when saved in the SQL Server log tables. These definitions are available in the following DMVs in Analysis Services: DISCOVER_TRACE_EVENT_CATEGORIES and DISCOVER_TRACE_COLUMNS.

The events that are relevant for processing operations are as follows (the corresponding integer value appears in parentheses):

- **Command Begin (15) and Command End (16)** These contain only one interesting subclass event, as follows:

  - **Batch (12)** This contains the XMLA command sent to Analysis Services to process one or more objects.

- **Progress Report Begin (5) and Progress Report End (6)** These contain several subclass events that apply mainly to processing operations for a tabular model. Following are the subclass events that are relevant to processing:

  - **Process (1) and Tabular Object Processing (59)** These notify the process of single objects (database, table, partition, and segment). One process can invoke other process operations. For example, processing a table will execute the process of every partition of the table. Tabular Object Processing is new to SSAS Tabular 2016 for model compatibility 1200.

  - **ExecuteSQL (25)** This contains the syntax sent to the data source to query data (which is actually a SQL syntax for a relational database).

  - **ReadData (17)** This shows in the IntegerData column the milliseconds required to read the data from the data source. Usually this event has the longest duration, even if the CPU consumption is a fraction. This is because SSAS Tabular is waiting for data from the data source most of the time.

  - **Analyze\Encode Data (43)** This reports the activity of compression for a segment, which includes VertiPaq and Compress Segment events.

  - **VertiPaq (53)** This reports the activity of the compression made by VertiPaq.

  - **Compress Segment (44)** This notifies the compression of each single column in each segment.

  - **Hierarchy Processing (54), Relationship Build Prepare (46), and Build Relationship Segment (47)** These are events related to the calculation of hierarchies and relationships in the data model.

  - **Tabular Transaction Commit (57)** This indicates the final commit operation, which could be long when there are long-running queries that must complete before the process commit takes place.

The events that are relevant for analyzing the query workload are as follows:

- **Query Begin (9) and Query End (10)** These usually include only one subclass event, which corresponds to the type of the query received: MDXQuery (0) or DAXQuery (3). The Query End event contains the total duration of the query. It could be the only event you want to collect in long-running logs so you can identify the slow-running queries and users affected. The other events are interesting for analyzing single queries in more detail.

- **DAX Query Plan (112)** This contains two subclasses that are raised for every query. Be careful about intercepting this event; the query plan is represented with a text string that can be extremely long, and its construction can slow down the activity on a server. Activating this event in a profiling session can slow down all the queries sent by any user to that server. Activate it only if necessary and for a limited time on a production server. The subclasses are as follows:

  - **DAX VertiPaq Logical Plan (1)** This contains the logical query plan for the MDX or DAX query to Tabular.

  - **DAX VertiPaq Physical Plan (2)** This contains the physical query plan for the MDX or DAX query to Tabular.

- **VertiPaq SE Query Begin (16) and VertiPaq SE Query End (16)** These contain the following two interesting subclass events:

  - **VertiPaq Scan (0)** This contains an xmSQL query, which is sent by the formula engine to the VertiPaq storage engine.

  - **Internal VertiPaq Scan (10)** This contains an xmSQL query, which is generated to solve part or all of the VertiPaq Scan request made by the formula engine. Every VertiPaq Scan event generates one or more Internal VertiPaq Scan events.

- **VertiPaq SE Query Cache Match (16) and VertiPaq SE Query Cache Miss (16)** These have no related subclass events and notify cache match and miss conditions.

- **Serialize Results Begin (75) and Serialize Results End (77)** These have no related subclass events. They mark the start and end of the query results that are being sent back to the client. A large result from a query could take a long time to be serialized and sent to the client.

A sort of nesting of events can be seen in the trace data. For example, the Process event for a database initiates several other Process events for related objects such as the tables, partitions, and segments in that database. The outermost events have an execution time (the Duration column, in milliseconds) that includes the time taken for all the operations executed within those events. Therefore, the values in the Duration and CPU columns for different events cannot easily be summed because you must be careful not to sum events that might include each other.

ASTrace

Using SQL Server Profiler to capture trace data is a good option if you want to create a trace manually, but it is not the best way to automate the trace-data capture on a production server. A useful tool is ASTrace, which is part of the Microsoft SQL Server Community Samples for Analysis Services, available from *http://sqlsrvanalysissrvcs.codeplex.com*. ASTrace captures an Analysis Services trace and logs it into a SQL Server table.

This utility runs as a Windows service that connects to Analysis Services. It creates a trace and logs trace events into a SQL Server table by using the SQL Server Profiler format. To customize the trace (for example, to filter on certain events), you can use a standard trace template authored with SQL Server Profiler. Running as a service, this tool does not require a logged-in user, unlike SQL Server Profiler.

Flight Recorder

Flight Recorder is a feature of Analysis Services that maintains a log of all events that have occurred in the recent past. This might be useful when investigating crashes or performance problems. It works by running a trace. By default, it does not capture all the events and keeps data for only a limited time so as not to fill the disk with the trace data. However, you can customize it by changing both the length of time it keeps the data and the events it records. You must remember, though, that Flight Recorder can affect performance. The more events it records, the more I/O operations are required to update the trace files it generates. Moreover, certain events could slow down all the queries sent by the users. For example, the DAX Query Plan really slows down queries with a complex query plan.

You can open Flight Recorder trace files with SQL Server Profiler. They are stored in the OLAP\Log folder (usually found at C:\Program Files\Microsoft SQL Server\MSAS13.*TABULAR*\OLAP\Log, where *TABULAR* is the name of the instance of SSAS Tabular). You can customize the trace definition used by Flight Recorder by defining a SQL Profiler template in the same way you can for ASTrace.

Extended Events

Analysis Services, like SQL Server, has an alternative API to capture trace events other than the SQL Server Profiler: Extended Events. This includes all the events provided by the profiler. It also includes a set of additional events that are useful for debugging for programmers who write the internal code of Analysis Services, but are not so useful for BI developers.

If Extended Events traces the same events that are of interest to us as SQL Server Profiler, why should you should consider changing? The reason is that the standard trace events (managed by SQL Server Profiler) are more expensive to manage. They create an additional overhead on the server. In contrast, events in Extended Events are lighter and have fewer side effects with respect to server performance. Moreover, capturing these events does not require an additional process of listening to Analysis Services as it does for standard trace events. (You saw earlier that ASTrace is an additional service.) However, Extended Events is not commonly used in Analysis Services because it lacks a quick and intuitive user interface to start interactive sessions and to analyze the data collected in recorded sessions. SQL Server 2016 added some features in SSMS to manage Extended Events through a graphical user interface, but they are still not mature enough to replace SQL Server Profiler completely.

The lack of a good user interface does not greatly affect the requirements for collecting the events of a production server. In this case, a low impact in performance is as important as the availability of tools that automate the monitor and export the raw data to an analytical platform. Because Extended Events is more of an API than user interface, this is probably the best choice for implementing an infrastructure that will constantly monitor a production server.

SSAS Events Analyzer is an open source set of batches and analytical tools that collect and analyze Extended Events for Analysis Services. It is available at *http://www.sqlbi.com/tools/ssas-events-analyzer/*. If you need a step-by-step tutorial for Extended Events for Analysis Services 2016, read the article at *https://blogs.msdn.microsoft.com/analysisservices/2015/09/22/using-extended-events-with-sql-server-analysis-services-2016-ctp-2-3/* and the MSDN documentation at *https://msdn.microsoft.com/en-us/library/gg492139.aspx*.

Using Extended Events, you will collect and manage the same events described in the SQL Profiler section, but using a collection technology that is more efficient and has a lower overhead on the server.

Other commercial tools

Few vendors provide commercial tools for monitoring Analysis Services Tabular. As of this writing (March 2017), only two tools provide these services: SQL BI Manager from Idera (*https://www.idera.com/productssolutions/sqlserver/sql-server-business-intelligence/*) and SQL Sentry Performance Advisor (*http://www.sqlsentry.com/products/performanceadvisor/ssas*). We do not have specific experience in these tools, and this list might not be complete by the time you read this book. We have listed these resources in case you want to consider a commercial product to manage monitoring operations for Analysis Services.

Monitoring data refresh (process)

When you deploy a tabular model by using the default in-memory storage (VertiPaq), you have a copy of the data that has to be refreshed periodically using a process operation. In Chapter 11, "Processing and partitioning tabular models," you saw the different processing strategies and operations you can use. After you deploy a model and execute a process operation, you might want to monitor it to optimize the process performance or use it for troubleshooting.

Processing data in a tabular model is a stressful operation for the server. CPU and memory are used intensively. In addition, to accelerate the completion time, you also must make sure the throughput of data transfer between data sources and the Tabular instance is optimal because this is often the bottleneck of the process.

You can use different tools to collect the information you need to control the behavior of SSAS Tabular while processing the data. In general, you should increase the CPU consumption to parallelize the process. That way you can control it so the memory required by SSAS Tabular does not exceed the physical RAM available.

Performance counters for monitoring a data refresh

You can use Task Manager for a first look at the performance of a server. You can easily see in the Performance tab whether you are saturating the cores available (the CPU use). You can identify the msmdsrv.exe process by looking at the memory that is required for the OS (Commit Size). Analyzing paging with Task Manager might not be simple. You have more counters in Performance Monitor, which we introduced in the previous section of this chapter.

You must monitor the use of memory and CPU, and the throughput transfer speed between the data sources and SSAS Tabular. You saw a few memory counters in the Performance Monitor in the section "Using memory-related performance counters" earlier in this chapter. This section focuses on the counters that are relevant for a process operation, without further examples of user interface.

The first element to control is the memory. You should avoid memory paging (which occurs when there is not enough physical memory to complete an operation). For this reason, you should monitor the following counters in the Memory category. These provide information about the overall consumption of memory, regardless of the consumer (a process, a driver, or the OS itself):

- **Pages/Sec**   This is the number of pages read from and written to disk, to resolve hard page faults. Access to a page of virtual memory that has been paged to disk generates this type of event. The cause is insufficient physical RAM to satisfy all the memory requests. If this happens, you should apply a technique that will lower the memory pressure, which is described in Chapter 15, "Optimizing tabular models."

- **Committed Bytes**   This is the amount of virtual memory requested by all the running processes. If this value is higher than the amount of available physical RAM, then data has been paged to disk. However, if the Pages/Sec rate is low or null, the data paged to disk is not used often. As long as that data does not need to be accessed, this situation will not result in performance problems. If the data paged is from databases that are not queried during a nightly batch, nobody will recognize the issue. However, the first user who queries the database will hit a very slow response time because data must be restored in physical RAM from the paging file to execute a query.

The Process category contains other counters related to memory. These include memory counters and others that are useful for analyzing the state of an Analysis Services instance:

- **Virtual Bytes**   This is generally not so useful because it represents the amount of virtual memory used for both private allocations and file mapping (including the executable files).

- **Page File Bytes and Private Bytes**   These are usually very similar for Analysis Services. They correspond to the Commit Size counter you have seen in Task Manager.

- **Page File Bytes Peak**   This is very important because it reports the maximum value reached by Page File Bytes from the start of the process execution, regardless of when you started monitoring. If Page File Bytes Peak is higher than Page File Bytes, then there has been a reduction in the amount of memory requested by Analysis Services. But, because this peak has been reached before, this usually implies that it can be reached again in the future.

- **Working Set**   This corresponds to the Working Set (Memory) value in Task Manager.

- **Working Set–Private**   This corresponds to the Memory (Private Working Set) value in Task Manager.

- **Working Set Peak**   This is the maximum value reached by Working Set since the start of process execution, regardless of when you started monitoring. This value can be higher than the actual Working Set counter because, even if a process has not released memory that was previously allocated, part of that memory may have been paged due to memory activity by other processes. If this happens with Analysis Services, you could investigate what other processes are requesting memory that is concurrently on the same server.

Profiler events for monitoring a data refresh

You can capture trace profiler events from Analysis Services with several tools: SQL Profiler, ASTrace, Flight Recorder, and Extended Events. Regardless of how you collect this data, to monitor a process operation, you must focus on a certain subclass of events. You cannot sum the duration and CPU time between different subclasses because certain subclasses include others. Unfortunately, this hierarchical nature of the events is not represented in the data model of the profiler events you receive.

When you process an object in SSAS Tabular, the following events are raised (the corresponding integer value appears in parentheses):

- **Command End (16)/Batch (12)**   This is the high-level batch that starts a process operation. The duration reported is the amount of time spent completing the process, whereas the CPU time is not a valid indication. This event includes the time of all the other Progress Report End events executed internally.

- **Progress Report End (6)/Process (1)**   This reflects *most* of the time required for the process, minus the time to save the file and to wait for the lock to switch the processed objects so that they become available for querying. This event includes both the duration and CPU time of the other events in the Progress Report End class and different subclasses (ReadData, Analyze\ Encode Data, Commit, and Tabular Object Processing).

- **Progress Report End (6)/ReadData (17)**   This is the time spent reading data from the data source.

- **Progress Report End (6)/Analyze\Encode Data (43)**   This is the time spent finding the best encoding and compression for the data.

- **Progress Report End (6)/VertiPaq (17)**   This is the time spent compressing data in VertiPaq for each object. This time is included in the Analyze\Encode Data subclass event.

- **Progress Report End (6)/Compress Segment (17)**   This is the time spent compressing each segment by VertiPaq. This time is included in the VertiPaq subclass event.

- **Progress Report End (6)/Tabular Object Processing (59)**   This is the time spent computing hierarchies and relationships.

- **Progress Report End (6)/Commit (6)** This is the time spent compressing each segment in VertiPaq. This time is included in the VertiPaq subclass event.

- **Progress Report End (6)/Tabular transaction commit (57)** This is part of the time spent committing the transaction. It is already computed in the Commit subclass event.

- **Progress Report End (6)/Sequence point (58)** This is an event related to the completion of a sequence of internal events.

Usually the main parts of a process operation are the ReadData and the Analyze\Encode Data subclass events. Drilling down in the single events of each subclass, you can identify the objects (tables or partitions) that get most of the time of a process operation.

If the bottleneck is the ReadData operation, you must improve the speed of the data source. However, if the CPU time of ReadData is very close to the duration, then the bottleneck is the connection and/or the driver on the client side (Analysis Services). You can improve the speed by increasing the parallelism of the process (by processing more partitions in parallel) or by increasing the clock speed of the Analysis Services server.

When Analyze\Encode Data is the bottleneck and your process runs using all the cores available (you observe a 100 percent CPU time during the process for Analysis Services), then you can try to increase the number of CPUs available to Analysis Services or increase the clock speed. When this is not possible, you can improve the speed by lowering the number of columns imported. (This reduces the memory pressor and the work required to compress each segment.)

In an ideal condition, the commit time is close to zero seconds, but in the case of long-running queries in execution, the process operation might have to wait before completing the commit phase. If you notice a large amount of time spent during commit, you might consider moving the process operation to a different time slot to avoid conflicts with other queries that are running on the same data model.

These are just basic suggestions for starting the optimization of the process operation. By investigating specific bottlenecks, you might find other techniques to apply to specific data models. For example, you might consider changing the segment size or the parallelism of the process to better balance the memory and the CPU available on a server. The goal of this chapter is to provide you with the tools to understand what is going on and to locate the bottlenecks, which are the longer and harder activities, especially when you need to optimize a process operation.

Segment size and partitioning strategy

You have seen that increasing the segment size could increase the compression, which reduces the memory footprint of a database. However, a larger segment size requires more memory to read uncompressed data for the segments that are processed on a server. This increment must be combined with the parallelism of the operations you run. For example, if you have a single table made by 100 segments, or you have several large tables in your database, a single process operation will parallelize all the partitions included in the process. If you do not have enough memory to keep the uncompressed data of all the segments processed in parallel, you might experience slower processing time because of the paging, or you might receive an out-of-memory error that will stop the process.

When you want to improve the performance of a process operation for a large database, you should consider all the implications of a change in parallelism and/or segment size. You should also measure the effects of the different settings so you can document the reasons you make a certain optimization choice. In this way, a future change in hardware might revise the assumptions used to perform the optimization, which would cause you to evaluate whether a new optimization might be productive (before actually repeating the collection of performance counters and trace events).

Monitoring queries

When users query a tabular model, you might want to analyze the overall level of use by answering the following questions (and others):

- How many users access the service?

- Who are the users running the slowest queries?

- At which time does the server have the peak workload?

You saw earlier in this chapter that SSAS Activity Monitor can help you analyze existing connections to an SSAS instance. This section is focused on the analysis of the data collected on a server, analyzing the past workload and identifying possible bottlenecks in queries, before the users of the system call support because of bad performance.

The most important information to collect is probably a trace of the queries sent by the users to the server. However, a minimal set of performance counters could be helpful in identifying critical conditions that are caused by a high number of concurrent queries or by particularly expensive queries that require temporary memory because of large materialization.

Performance counters for monitoring queries

You can use the same counters described in the "Monitoring data refresh (process)" section to monitor the resources of the OS that are consumed at query time.

In ideal conditions, you should not see a particular increase in memory consumption when the user queries a data model. However, the following two main effects could decrease perceived performance:

- A DAX expression that creates a large materialization will use a large amount of memory for the duration of the query execution. Different parts of the DAX engine (the formula engine and the storage engine) communicate by exchanging uncompressed data in memory. In particular, the storage engine materializes uncompressed data for the formula engine, which executes the final part of the expression evaluation. In certain conditions (such as complex queries or badly written DAX code), this materialization could require too much memory, generating a slower response time, or, in the worst case, an out-of-memory error. In this case, you should modify the DAX code for measures and queries to minimize the required materialization.

- Other services running on the same server might consume physical RAM, paging part of the data that is managed by Analysis Services. When paging occurs, subsequent queries on the same data will be much slower. The VertiPaq engine is optimized for the data stored in physical memory, but if paging happens, the algorithm used by the DAX engine might have a severe decrease in performance.

In both cases, you will have high pressure in memory and possibly paging activities, which are easy to detect by collecting performance counters from the OS. Thus, you can use the same Data Collector Sets configuration that you defined to monitor a data refresh. You can also use them to monitor the behavior of the server under a query workload that is generated by the users.

Profiler events for monitoring queries

You always use the same tools to capture trace profiler events from Analysis Services: SQL Profiler, ASTrace, Flight Recorder, and Extended Events. However, you need to be very careful to keep these recording systems active on a production server because they might affect the performance perceived by the users. The number of events generated by a process operation is smaller and usually does not have a big impact on the overall duration of monitored operations. This is because a single-process operation usually requires minutes, if not hours. A single query is possibly a quick operation, hopefully running in less than 2 seconds. You will find most of the queries running in only a few milliseconds. Adding an overhead to these operations could be very dangerous for the performance. For these reasons, we suggest gathering the minimum number of events, such as one event per query, to retrieve the user, time, duration, CPU, and text of the query.

In practice, you should capture only the following trace profiler event during queries:

- **Query End (10)**   The only subclasses you should consider are MDXQuery (0) and DAXQuery (3). You might observe a SQLQuery (2) subclass event; it shows DMV queries that are usually not useful for monitoring the server's activity.

By collecting these events, you can analyze how many queries have been generated by which users and accurately identify slow-running queries. Having the DAX or MDX statement available in the log enables you to replicate the query behavior in an environment where you can use more diagnostics, and you can then optimize the query. For example, DAX Studio provides an environment that automatically collects detailed trace profiler events that are helpful in the optimization process. It would be too expensive to collect these events on a production server for every single query. You might see a trace volume increase of two orders of magnitude doing that. For this reason, intercepting only Query End is a suggested practice if you want to monitor queries running on an SSAS Tabular server.

Performance analysis and optimization of individual queries

After you identify a query that is too expensive, the next step is to optimize it. Analysis Services Tabular does not have specific techniques for optimizing query performance apart from changing the DAX expression of measures that are involved in the query itself. You cannot create indexes or aggregations as you might want to do in relational databases and multidimensional models, respectively.

Optimizing DAX requires a deeper knowledge of the language and the data model. Often, you must rewrite some of the DAX expressions to obtain the same result and to generate a different (and more efficient) query plan. This is usually very hard without being able to make some assumptions about the data model (and the data it contains), which usually requires the competency of one of the developers of the data model. In other words, query performance optimization for a tabular model is a difficult operation for a DBA to execute without knowing the details of the underlying data model.

For these reasons, to optimize individual queries for a tabular model, we suggest our book *The Definitive Guide to DAX* (Microsoft Press). The book contains several chapters dedicated to the performance optimization of DAX expressions. It describes tools, techniques, and the best practices for getting the most out of the DAX language.

Summary

In this chapter, you learned how to monitor an instance of SSAS Tabular by collecting the performance counter and trace profiler events to locate bottlenecks in queries and processing operations. You saw how to use tools such as Performance Monitor, Data Collector Sets, SQL Profiler, and Extended Events. Now you know which counters, events, and DMVs you should consider, depending on the analysis you must perform. For a production server, you should consider a continuous data-collection strategy to find bottlenecks in data-refresh tasks and to locate slow-running queries in the user's workload.

Optimizing tabular models

A tabular data model can be optimized in different ways, depending on its characteristics and its main goal. In this chapter, you will see a checklist and numerous good practices that are common to any data model. It is important that you understand the concepts explained in Chapter 12, "Inside VertiPaq," before reading this chapter. After that, there are sections specific to Analysis Services, related to large databases and near–real-time solutions. You will find numerous considerations and suggestions for those particular scenarios. The goal of this chapter is to provide specific information for optimizing data models for Analysis Services. We will consider scenarios that are unlikely to happen by using Power BI and Power Pivot for Excel. (Additional information about the generic optimization of tabular models is also available in the book *The Definitive Guide to DAX* in Chapter 14, "Optimizing data models.")

> **What's new in SSAS 2016**   This is a new chapter for this second edition of the book. Most of the content would be valid also for previous versions of Analysis Services, but the previous edition did not include a specific chapter about the optimization of data models. A limited number of hints were included in a more generic chapter about optimization and monitoring.

Optimizing data memory usage

As you saw in Chapter 12, the memory used to store a table depends primarily on the dictionary cost of each column, and the memory size is directly related to the performance in VertiPaq. Now you can learn how to choose the data type and the content to be stored in a column to reduce the memory footprint and improve the performance in VertiPaq.

The cardinality of a column directly affects its size in VertiPaq. Its actual cost also depends on the data type of the column. The combination of these two factors (cardinality and data type) determines the actual memory cost, and you should control both to achieve optimization.

Removing unused columns

To optimize a tabular model, VertiPaq Analyzer (*http://www.sqlbi.com/tools/vertipaq-analyzer/*) provides you with a variety of useful information. You should start looking for the most expensive columns in the entire database, removing those that are not necessary for the analysis. For example, you will discover that a timestamp or primary key in a fact table consists of columns with a high cardinality, which are very expensive. So, removing them from the data model will not limit the data analyst, but it will free a lot of memory.

The next step in the optimization is locating the columns with a higher cardinality, making sure they are really required. This is particularly important for the columns used in the relationships between tables. For a relationship, a cardinality greater than 1,000,000 could affect the performance of all the queries involved in such a relationship, even in an indirect way.

Reducing dictionary size

You can reduce the dictionary cost by reducing its size. This can be achieved mainly by reducing the cardinality of a column.

The first suggestion is to remove the columns that contain data that is not relevant for analysis. This is something you probably already do when you design a relational data warehouse or data mart. However, the goal in a relational database is to minimize the size of each column without worrying too much about its cardinality, provided the chosen data size can represent the value. In contrast, with VertiPaq, the cardinality of a column is much more important than its data type.

For example, adding an INT column in SQL Server might seem better than adding eight columns of the type TINYINT. You should save half the space. This is the reason for creating junk dimensions in a star schema. (You can read more at *http://en.wikipedia.org/wiki/Dimension_(data_warehouse)*.) In VertiPaq, the cardinality of a column is more important than the data type for its storage cost. Therefore, you might find that you do not save space by using the junk-dimension approach. This is not a general rule, and you should test it on a case-by-case basis. The point is that when using VertiPaq, you should not make the same assumptions that you make when you are working with a relational database.

A column with a unique value for every row is most likely the most expensive column in your table. You cannot remove keys from tables that are used as lookup tables, such as the dimension tables of a star schema. However, if you have a star schema and an identity column on the fact table (usually used as a primary key), you can save a lot of space by removing the identity column from the fact table imported in VertiPaq. More importantly, you can reduce the percentage of increase when adding more rows to the table.

From a performance point of view, a calculated column might be expensive when it creates a large dictionary. This might be unnecessary if you have a simple expression involving only columns from the same table in which the calculated column is defined. For example, consider the following calculated column:

```
Table[C] = Table[A] * Table[B]
```

The number of distinct values for the C column is a number between 1 and the value of MaxDistinctC, which is calculated as follows:

```
MaxDistinctC := DISTINCTCOUNT ( Table[A] ) * DISTINCTCOUNT ( Table[B] )
```

Thus, in the worst-case scenario, you have a dictionary with a size that is orders of magnitude larger than the dictionaries of the separate columns. In fact, one of the possible optimizations is removing such a column and splitting the content into separate columns with a smaller number of distinct values.

The next step in this optimization is reducing the number of values of a column without reducing its informative content. For example, if you have a DATETIME column that contains a timestamp of an event (for example, both date and time), it is more efficient to split the single DATETIME column into two columns—one for the date and one for the time. You might use the DATE and TIME data types in SQL Server, but in VertiPaq, you always use the same date data type. The date column always has the same time, and the time column always has the same date. In this way, you have a maximum number of rows for date, which is 365 multiplied by the number of years stored, and a maximum number of rows for time, which depends on the time granularity (for example, you have 86,400 seconds per day). This approach makes it easier to group data by date and time even if it becomes harder to calculate the difference in hours/minutes/seconds between the two dates. However, you probably want to store the difference between two DATETIME columns in a new VertiPaq column when you read from your data source instead of having to perform this calculation at query time.

> **Note** You must transform a DATETIME column into separate columns—one for date and one for time—using a transformation on the data source, like a SQL query. This is another reason you should use views as a decoupling layer, putting these transformations there. If you obtain them by using a calculated column in Tabular, you still store the DATETIME column in VertiPaq, losing the memory optimization you are looking for.

A similar approach might be possible when you have a column that identifies a transaction or document and has a very high cardinality, such as an Order ID or Transaction ID. In a large fact table, such a column might be a value with millions, if not billions, of distinct values, and its cost is typically the highest of the table. A good practice would be to remove this column from the tabular model. However, if you need it to identify each single transaction, you might try to lower its memory cost by optimizing the model schema. Because the cost is largely due to the column dictionary, you can split the column value into two or more columns with a smaller number of distinct values, which can be combined to get the original one. For example, if you have an ID column with numbers ranging from 1 to 100,000,000, you would pay a cost of nearly 3 GB just to store it on a disk. By splitting the value into two numbers ranging from 1 to 10,000, you would drop the cost below 200 MB, saving more than 90 percent of the memory. This requires the execution of a simple arithmetical operation to split the value by writing data to the table and to compose the original value by reading data from the table, as shown in the following formulas:

$$LowID = ID - 10,000 \left\lfloor \frac{ID}{10,000} \right\rfloor$$

$$HighID = \frac{ID}{10,000}$$

$$ID = HighID * 10,000 + LowID$$

These formulas can be translated into the following DAX expressions:

```
HighID = INT ( [ID] / 10000 )

LowID = MOD ( [ID], 10000 )
```

Note   You can find a further discussion of this optimization technique at
http://www.sqlbi.com/articles/optimizing-high-cardinality-columns-in-vertipaq.

Important   Splitting a column into multiple columns to lower its cardinality is an optimization that you should consider only for measures or attributes that are not related to other
tables. This is because relationships can be defined by using a single column and implicitly
defining a unique constraint for that column in the lookup table.

A similar optimization is possible when you have other values in a fact table that represent measures
of a fact. For example, you might be accustomed to storing the sales amount for each row or order. In
Figure 15-1, a typical Sales table is shown.

Quantity	Unit Price	Line Amount
1	100	100
2	100	200
1	60	60
3	60	180
2	60	120

FIGURE 15-1   A typical Sales table with redundant information.

The Line Amount column is obtained by multiplying Quantity by Unit Price. However, if you have 100
possible values in the Quantity column and 100 possible values in Unit Price, you would have up to 10,000
unique values in the Line Amount column. You can optimize the memory footprint by storing only Quantity and Unit Price in VertiPaq. You obtain the total Sales Amount by using the following measure:

```
Sales[Sales Amount] :=
SUMX ( Sales, Sales[Quantity] * Sales[Unit Price] )
```

You will not have any performance penalty at query time by using this approach because the
multiplication is a simple arithmetical operation that is pushed down to the VertiPaq storage engine,
and it is not in charge of the formula engine. The benefit of this approach is that you pay the cost of
two columns of 100 values each, instead of the cost of a single column with a cost that is two orders of
magnitude larger (10,000 instead of 200).

Important In a multidimensional model, you must use a different approach, storing only the measures that can be aggregated. Thus, in Multidimensional, you must choose Quantity and Line Amount to get better performance. If you are accustomed to building cubes by using Analysis Services, you should be careful when using the different design pattern that you have in Tabular.

A further optimization is reducing the precision of a number. This is not related to the data type but to the actual values stored in a column. For example, a Date column in VertiPaq uses a floating point as internal storage, in which the decimal part represents the fraction of a day. In this way, it is possible to also represent milliseconds. If you are importing a DATETIME column from SQL Server that includes milliseconds, you have many rows displaying the same hour/minute/second value (which is the common display format) because they are different values internally. Thus, you can round the number to the nearest second to obtain a maximum of 86,400 distinct values (seconds per day). By rounding the number to the nearest minute, you would obtain a maximum of 1,440 distinct values (minutes per day). Thus, reducing the precision of a column in terms of the actual value (without changing the data type) can save a lot of memory.

You might use a similar approach for the other numeric values, although it might be difficult to use for numbers that are related to financial transactions. You do not want to lose any decimals of a measure that represent the value of an order. However, you might accept losing some precision in a number that, by its nature, can have an approximation or an error in the measure, or a precision that is not relevant to you. For example, you might save the temperature of the day for every sale transaction of an ice cream shop. You know there should be a correlation between temperature and sales, and the actual data might represent that in detail, helping you plan ice-cream production based on the weather forecast. You could achieve this by connecting a good digital thermometer to your cash system that stores the temperature with two decimals for every transaction. However, this approach would result in a very high number of values, whereas you might consider the integer part (or just one decimal) to be enough. Rounding a number helps you save a lot of space in a column, especially for a decimal number that is stored as a floating point in your data source.

Choosing a data type

In a relational database, such as SQL Server, every data type might have a different size because of the range of values it can represent, not because of the actual data stored. In VertiPaq, the differences in size are less relevant, and the choice of a data type must be based only on the range of values that the column has to represent.

From the point of view of the internal storage, there are two categories of data types. The first category includes all the following numeric data types:

- **Whole Number** This stores 64-bit integer values.

- **Decimal Number** This stores 64-bit real numbers, which are limited to 17 decimal digits.

- **Currency** This stores numbers with four-decimal digits of fixed precision by using an underlying 64-bit integer value.

- **Date** This stores dates and times by using an underlying real number.

- **Binary** This stores images or similar large chunks of binary data—also called *binary large objects*, or *BLOBs*.

All the numeric data types have an overall dictionary-related storage cost in the range of 20 to 30 bytes, which includes the value and indexes cost. Thus, the memory required to store a dictionary with 1,000,000 numbers is approximately 20 to 30 MB. The actual value might vary because different dictionary storage types can be used for numeric data types, depending on the data distribution.

The second category of data types includes strings. Every string is compressed in data, and the memory required for the dictionary-related storage can be estimated by considering a typical overhead cost of 16 bytes per string. The cost must be summed to the size of the string value (which is stored as Unicode in the dictionary with a minimal compression, consuming up to 16 bits for each character). The final dictionary cost for string columns depends on the length of the strings. You can safely assume that it is unlikely a string will have a dictionary-related cost lower than 20 bytes, whereas its actual cost depends on the average string length. As a rule, you can estimate the cost of a string to be 16 bytes plus the string length. Thus, if you have 1,000,000 strings with an average length of 50 characters, you might expect an average dictionary cost of 66 bytes per string, which results in a 60–70 MB dictionary.

> **Important** The memory cost of a column is calculated by the dictionary and values index. The latter depends on the number of rows and values in the dictionary and data distribution. It is much harder to estimate the size of the values index of a column in VertiPaq.

Even if a numeric column sometimes has a larger dictionary-related storage size than a corresponding string column (you can always convert a number to a string), from a performance point of view, the numeric column is faster. The reason for a larger memory footprint is related to attribute hierarchies that are not always included in the table-scan operations that VertiPaq makes. Thus, you should always favor a numeric data type if the semantic of the value is numeric because using strings would produce a performance penalty.

> **Tip** You can use a string data type instead of a numeric one if the semantic of the column does not include an arithmetical operation. For example, the order number might be expressed as a string even if it is always an integer. This is because you will never sum two order numbers. However, if you do not really need the order number in your tabular model, the best optimization is to remove the column.

There is no reason to choose between numeric data types based on their memory footprint. The choice must be made by considering only the range of values that the numeric column represents (including significant digits, decimal digits, and precision). To represent a null value, VertiPaq uses the boundary values of the range that can be expressed by a numeric type. Importing these values might raise a Value Not Supported error, as described at *http://msdn.microsoft.com/en-us/library/gg492146.aspx*.

Reducing a database size by choosing the sort order

As mentioned in Chapter 12, the run-length encoding (RLE) algorithm's efficiency strongly depends on the table's sort order. Obviously, all the columns in the same table are sorted in the same way because, at some point during the querying, VertiPaq might have to match different columns for the same row. So, in large tables, it could be important to determine the best way to sort your data to improve RLE efficiency and to reduce the memory footprint of your model.

When SSAS reads your table, it tries different sort orders to improve compression. In a table with many columns, this is a very expensive operation. SSAS then sets an upper limit to the time it can spend finding the best sort order. By default, the decision of this timeout to Analysis Services and the effective value can change with different versions of the engine. Currently, it is 10 seconds per every 1,000,000 rows. You can modify its value in the ProcessingTimeboxSecPerMRow entry in the advanced properties of the SSAS service, as shown in Figure 15-2. (The value –1 corresponds to the default value, which assigns the decision to Analysis Services.)

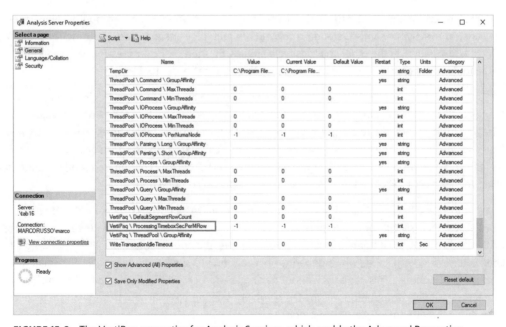

FIGURE 15-2 The VertiPaq properties for Analysis Services, which enable the Advanced Properties.

> **Note** SSAS searches for the best sort order in data, using a heuristic algorithm that also considers the physical order of the rows it receives. For this reason, even if you cannot force the sort order used by VertiPaq for RLE, you can provide it to the engine data sorted in an arbitrary way. The VertiPaq engine will include a sort order in the options to consider.

To obtain maximum compression, you can set the value to 0, which means SSAS stops searching only when it finds the best compression factor. The benefit in terms of space usage and query speed can be relevant, but at the same time, the processing will take much longer.

Generally, you should try to put the least-changing columns first in the sort order because they are likely to generate many repeating values. Moreover, a sort order for the table or for a single partition will certainly affect the distribution of data across the segments. (You learned about segments in Chapter 12.) Keep in mind that finding the best sort order is a very complex task, and it makes sense to spend time on it only when your data model is really large (in the order of a few billion rows). Otherwise, the benefit you get from these extreme optimizations is limited.

After all the columns are compressed, SSAS completes the processing by building calculated columns, calculated tables, hierarchies, and relationships. Hierarchies and relationships are additional data structures that VertiPaq needs to execute queries, whereas calculated columns and calculated tables are added to the model by using DAX expressions.

Calculated columns, like all other columns, are compressed after they are computed. Nevertheless, they are not exactly the same as standard columns. In fact, they are compressed during the final stage of processing, when all the other columns have already finished their compression. Consequently, VertiPaq does not consider them when choosing the best sort order for the table.

Suppose you created a calculated column that resulted in a Boolean value. Having only two values, the calculated column could be compressed very well (1 bit is enough to store a Boolean value). Also, it is a very good candidate to be first in the sort order list, so that the table shows all the FALSE values first, and later it only shows the TRUE values. But being a calculated column, the sort order is already defined and it might be the case that, with the defined sort order, the column frequently changes its value. In that case, the column results in a less-than-optimal compression.

Whenever you have the chance to compute a column in DAX or SQL, keep in mind that computing it in SQL results in slightly better compression. However, many other factors may drive you to choose DAX instead of SQL to calculate the column. For example, the engine automatically computes a calculated column in a large table, which depends on a column in a small table, whenever the small table has a partial or full refresh. This happens without having to reprocess the entire large table, which would be necessary if the computation was in SQL. If you are seeking optimal compression and/or processing time, this is something you should consider.

Understanding why sorting data is important

The memory required for each column in VertiPaq depends on the number of distinct values of that column. If a column has only three values, it can be compressed to a few bits. If, however, the column has many values (as it happens, for example, for identity values), then the space used will be much higher. Because this evaluation happens at the segment level, the number of distinct values should not be counted for the whole table, but for each segment. Each segment is processed and compressed individually. By default, tables up to 16,000,000 rows will always fit a single segment (tables made by two segments of 8,000,000 rows are merged into a single table), whereas bigger tables can span several segments.

Before processing a segment, VertiPaq uses a highly-sophisticated algorithm to find the best way to sort the rows so that similar rows appear near each other in the sequence. Improving homogeneity reduces the distribution of distinct values. It also greatly improves the compression of the segment, resulting in less memory usage and better performance during queries. Thus, sorting a segment is not very useful because VertiPaq reverts sorting due to its internal consideration.

Nevertheless, sorting the whole table, when it is bigger than a single segment, can reduce the number of distinct values for some columns inside a segment. (If, for example, you have a mean of 4,000,000 rows for each date, sorting by date reduces the number of distinct dates to two for each segment.) A sorted table creates homogeneous segments that VertiPaq can better compress. Both the size of the database and the query speed of the tabular model benefit from this.

Because all these considerations apply to big tables, we recommend a careful study of the best clustered index to use for the table. Issuing an ORDER BY over a table by using keys that do not match the clustered index might slow the processing because SQL Server will use the temporary structures to materialize sorted results. Finally, remember that a partition is a boundary for a segment. So, if you have multiple partitions, you control the sort order at the partition level, but the partition itself keeps a separation between the segments.

Improving encoding and bit sizing

With the information available in VertiPaq Analyzer, you might consider certain advanced optimization techniques. For example, the use of hash encoding for a high-cardinality column might be unnecessary. You might save the space for the dictionary by enforcing the value encoding. This usually results in a larger data size, but removes the requirement of a lookup in the dictionary during the scan (to retrieve the actual value). So, you should measure the two conditions to evaluate whether it is a real performance improvement. Because you cannot enforce the encoding in a tabular model (maybe a future release of SSAS Tabular will introduce a setting to control that), you must suggest to the engine which choice you prefer. The encoding is chosen by reading the first rows of the first partition, so you might create a dummy partition that contains rows that drive the choice toward value encoding by using values included in a small range (making the dictionary unnecessary). However, you should consider that encoded values can have only a 32-bit storage, so any column requiring more than 32 bits to express the actual values must use hash-encoding.

In large tables, with more than 200–300,000,000 rows, further optimization is possible when trying to reduce the number of bits used in each segment. For example, if you partition by month, every segment should have only a limited number of values—assuming you read each partition using an ORDER BY statement in SQL, which guarantees reading data in a certain sort order. If the partitions are processed one at a time, the dictionary of a hash-encoded date column will be created incrementally, using the days of each new month. However, if you process several partitions in parallel, then the dictionary could add new dates without any order, resulting in ranges of internal IDs for each segment that are larger than required. A possible workaround could be prepopulating the dictionary, creating a temporary partition that sequentially loads all the dates that will be loaded in the following process operations. However, these optimizations are really necessary only for very large tables. You should measure the possible advantages before implementing techniques that increase the complexity of the process operation.

Optimizing large dimensions

Even in small and medium data models, the presence of a single large dimension can affect performance in a negative way. For example, consider a Products table with attributes such as Category, Subcategory, Model, and Color. This model works well whenever the cardinality of the relationship is not too large. By large, we mean more than 1,000,000 unique values in the entity key. However, when you have more than 100,000 unique values, you already enter a warning area in terms of performance.

To understand why the cardinality of a relationship is important for performance, you must know what happens when you apply a filter on a column. Consider the schema shown in Figure 15-3, where you have the Sales table with relationships to the Product, Customer, and Date tables. When you query the data model by filtering customers by gender, the engine transfers the filter from Customer to Sales by specifying the list of customer keys that belong to each gender type included in the query. If you have 10,000 customers, any list generated by a filter cannot be larger than this number. However, if you have 6,000,000 customers, a filter by a single gender type might generate a list of unique keys, resulting in around 3,000,000 unique values. Having numerous keys in a relationship always has an impact on performance, even if in absolute terms. The impact also depends on the version of the engine and on the hardware (CPU clock, cache size, or RAM speed) you are using.

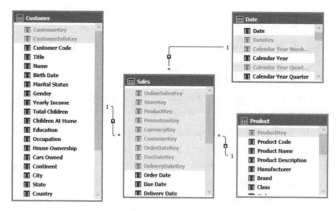

FIGURE 15-3   The Sales table, which has relationships with the Product, Customer, and Date tables.

What can you do to optimize the data model when a relationship involves millions of unique values? After you measure performance degradation that is not compatible with your requirements, you can consider some form of denormalization that reduces the cardinality of the relationship or removes the need of any relationship at all (in certain queries). In the previous example, you might consider denormalizing the Gender column in the Sales table if it is the only case where you need to optimize performance.

If you have more columns to optimize, you might consider creating another table comprised of the Customer table columns that users query often and have a low cardinality. For instance, you can create a table with Gender, Occupation, and Education columns. If the cardinality of these columns is 3, 6, and 6, respectively, a table with all the possible combinations will have 108 rows (3 x 6 x 6). A query on any of these columns will be much faster because the filter applied to Sales will have a very short list of values. In terms of usability, the user will see two groups of attributes for the same entity, corresponding to the two tables: Customer and Customer Info. This is not an ideal situation. For this reason, you should consider this optimization only when strictly necessary. It is important that both tables have a direct relationship with the Sales table, as shown in Figure 15-4.

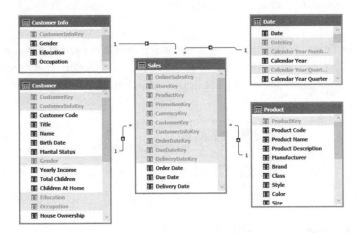

FIGURE 15-4 The Customer and Customer Info tables, which have a relationship with Sales.

You should evaluate the CustomerInfoKey column that is added to the Sales table before you import data in the large Sales table so that it is a native column. However, you might obtain it in a calculated column by using the following DAX expression, even if it would be expensive for every refresh operation:

```
Sales[CustomerInfoKey] =
LOOKUPVALUE (
    'Customer Info'[CustomerInfoKey],
    'Customer Info'[Gender], RELATED ( Customer[Gender] ),
    'Customer Info'[Occupation], RELATED ( Customer[Occupation] ),
    'Customer Info'[Education], RELATED ( Customer[Education] )
)
```

Note The examples in the companion content for this chapter create the Customer Info view and the relationships with CustomerInfoKey by using SQL queries that would not be efficient in a real large data model. You should consider a more efficient implementation of ETL in a real-world data model to avoid a bottleneck process while loading data from the fact table.

On the topic of user experience, you should hide the columns denormalized in the Customer Info table from the Customer table itself. Showing the same attributes (Gender, Occupation, and Education) in two tables would generate confusion. However, if you hide these attributes from the client in the Customer table, you cannot show in a query (and especially in a PivotTable) the list of customers with a certain occupation. If you do not want to lose this possibility, you must complicate the model with one inactive relationship, and then activate it in when you need to. That would show all the attributes in the Customer table and hide the Customer Info table from the client tools. This approach becomes completely transparent to users, who will continue to see all the customer's attributes in a single table (Customer).

Figure 15-5 shows that the Customer Info table has an active relationship with the Sales table and an inactive relationship with the Customer table. This latter relationship has a bidirectional filter propagation. The Gender, Education, and Occupation columns are visible in the Customer table, and the Customer Info table is hidden.

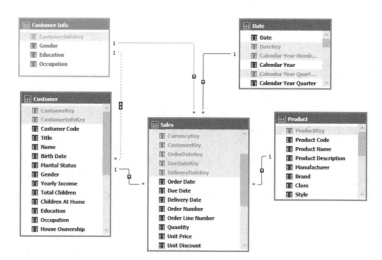

FIGURE 15-5 An inactive relationship that connects the Customer and Customer Info tables.

You can enable the relationship between Customer Info and Customer in case a filter is active on Gender, Education, or Occupation, and there are no filters active on other columns of the Customer table. Unfortunately, the DAX code that is required will explicitly test all the visible columns of the Customer table, as you see in the following definition of the measures required to calculate Sales Amount:

```
Sales[IsCustomerInfoFiltered] :=
ISFILTERED ( Customer[Gender] )
    || ISFILTERED ( Customer[Education] )
    || ISFILTERED ( Customer[Occupation] )

Sales[IsCustomerFiltered] :=
ISFILTERED ( Customer[Address Line 1] )
      || ISFILTERED ( Customer[Address Line 2] )
      || ISFILTERED ( Customer[Birth Date] )
      || ISFILTERED ( Customer[Cars Owned] )
      || ISFILTERED ( Customer[Children At Home] )
      || ISFILTERED ( Customer[City] )
      || ISFILTERED ( Customer[Company Name] )
      || ISFILTERED ( Customer[Continent] )
      || ISFILTERED ( Customer[Country] )
      || ISFILTERED ( Customer[Customer Code] )
      || ISFILTERED ( Customer[Customer Type] )
      || ISFILTERED ( Customer[Date First Purchase] )
      || ISFILTERED ( Customer[House Ownership] )
      || ISFILTERED ( Customer[Marital Status] )
      || ISFILTERED ( Customer[Name] )
      || ISFILTERED ( Customer[Phone] )
      || ISFILTERED ( Customer[State] )
      || ISFILTERED ( Customer[Title] )
      || ISFILTERED ( Customer[Total Children] )
      || ISFILTERED ( Customer[Yearly Income] )

Sales[Sales Amount Raw] :=
SUMX (
    Sales,
    Sales[Net Price] * Sales[Quantity]
)

Sales[Sales Amount] :=
IF (
    AND ( [IsCustomerInfoFiltered], NOT [IsCustomerFiltered] ),
    CALCULATE (
        [Sales Amount Raw],
        USERELATIONSHIP ( Customer[CustomerInfoKey], 'Customer Info'[CustomerInfoKey] ),
        CROSSFILTER ( Sales[CustomerKey], Customer[CustomerKey], NONE )
    ),
    [Sales Amount Raw]
)
```

If you have a filter applied to the Customer table that only affects the columns that are also in the Customer Info table, then you execute a CALCULATE function. The CALCULATE function activates the relationship between Customer and Customer Info, which disables the relationship between Sales and Customer. In this way, Customer Info receives the correspondent filter applied to the Customer table and automatically propagates such a filter to the Sales table. Using a relationship based on Sales[CustomerKeyInfo] is less expensive than the one used by Customer (which is based on Sales[CustomerKey]).

If a filter is active on one or more columns that are unique to the Customer table, then the engine must process a list of CustomerKey values in any case. So, the filter applied by Customer Info would be redundant and would not improve the performance. Unfortunately, to apply this optimization, you must apply this DAX pattern to all the measures that might involve customer attributes.

Designing tabular models for large databases

In the previous section of this chapter, you learned the fundamentals for optimizing memory usage in a tabular model. In general, reducing the memory footprint of a data model has the side effect of improving query performance. However, certain assumptions are true for small and medium databases, but they could be false for large databases. In this context, a large database contains at least one table with 1,000,000,000 rows or more. We consider tables with 100-200,000,000 rows as medium sized. If you do not have large tables, the optimizations described in this section could be counter-productive.

Optimizing compression by splitting columns

You have seen that splitting a numeric column into two columns can reduce the dictionary size. For example, consider a table containing billions of rows, each with a transaction amount expressed in a currency value, with two decimal points. Suppose you have 6,000,000,000 rows in a Sales table, whereas the Amount column contains 700,000 unique values with a range between 0.01 and 99,999,999.99, as shown in the following recap:

Column	Unique Values	Minimum Value	Maximum Value
Amount	700,000	0.01	99,999,999.99

Your original measure is a simple DAX expression, such as the following:

```
Sales[Total Amount] :=
SUM ( Sales[Amount] )
```

Even if you do not have the quantity and price, you might consider storing the decimal part in another column so that by summing both you will obtain the original value. In other words, you will have two columns with a distribution that is similar to the one described in the following table, where the number of unique values in AmountHi depends on the distribution of the data. However, it is likely to be between one and two orders of magnitude lower than the following original column:

Column	Unique values	Minimum value	Maximum value
AmountHi	10,000	0	99,999,999
AmountLo	100	0.00	0.99

You can expose the same results by using the following measure:

```
Sales[Total Amount] :=
SUM ( Sales[AmountHi] ) + SUM ( Sales[AmountLo] )
```

This approach is likely to save memory, especially if the original column was using dictionary encoding instead of value encoding. But does this correspond to a performance improvement at query time? The answer is that it depends. You should measure the performances of the two approaches with your real data to get a good answer. However, in general, we might say that for a small to medium data model, the difference would be minimal. If the absolute execution time is below 100 milliseconds, then probably any difference would not be appreciated by end users. Thus, for a small model, this optimization could be effective, but only if it saves memory.

In a large data model, you should consider that the engine is required to scan two columns instead of one. If you have eight cores available and your table has 30,000,000 rows, scanning two columns at the same time requires scanning four segments for two columns, using all the cores. If you scan a single column, you do not use half the cores available, but the execution time should be small enough that nobody cares. But if you have 6,000,000,000 rows, then you have more than 700 segments to read for each column. In this case, you would not have any spare CPU capacity to use, and the additional column is likely to slow down the calculation instead of improving it (regardless of the fact that the overall memory footprint was lower, and assuming you reduced the memory footprint, which is not guaranteed).

To give you some numbers, we have seen cases where it was possible to save several gigabytes of RAM by splitting the column similar to the Sales table described before, but this produced an increase of 15–20 percent of query time. Also, the memory saved really depends on other columns of the table, so it is hard to provide a guideline that is valid for any data model. If you have a large data model, we suggest you do your own benchmark before considering optimizations based on column splitting.

Optimizing the process time of large tables

A large table with billions of rows requires time and the processing of server resources. This is true for any table, but a large table might require additional considerations related to the memory available.

Reducing the number of columns

Every column in the table requires memory to read the uncompressed original value from the data source. The more the columns, the larger the memory buffer required to store all the rows of a segment in memory. Reducing the columns will reduce the memory pressure, the complexity of the compression algorithm, and the overall process time. It is easy to underestimate this requirement. A table reading 100 columns from SQL Server can easily require 1 KB of RAM to read one row, so the buffer to read a segment from such a table requires 8–9 GB of RAM.

Reducing calculated columns

Calculated columns are evaluated for the entire table, regardless of the partitions processed. For example, if you process a monthly partition of a 6,000,000,000 row table that contains data for 5 years, you probably have an average of 100,000,000 rows per partition. Thus, even if you process only 100,000,000 rows, each calculated table computes the DAX expression for 6,000,000,000 rows every time. Moreover, if you have more than one calculated column in the same table, each calculated column is processed in a sequential way, one after the other.

You do not take advantage of the multiple cores available when you compute multiple calculated columns for a single table. A good practice is to avoid creating calculated columns in a fact table.

Adapting parallelism to available RAM

In Analysis Services 2016, you can process multiple partitions of the same table in parallel. This was not possible in previous versions of Analysis Services. By default, processing a table that has multiple partitions invokes the process of multiple partitions in parallel. Consider that every partition processed in parallel requires its own buffer to read uncompressed data from the data source. Increasing the parallelism of the process operation for a single table requires a larger amount of physical memory available. You should consider this and evaluate whether to limit the parallelism of the process operation to avoid memory paging conditions (lower performance) and out-of-memory errors.

Aggregating fact tables at different granularities

Even if VertiPaq guarantees excellent performance in storing all the data in RAM in a compressed way, there are volumes of data that are too big to guarantee a good interactive experience for the user browsing data. If you assume that a good user experience requires every query to run in less than 2 seconds, you might assume that the storage engine cost of a query should be within the range of hundreds of milliseconds. You should measure the performance of your data model on your server to establish the storage engine cost for scanning an entire table. To give you an idea of the numbers, we included the following table of a typical range of scan time for a column, depending on the number of rows in the table:

Size (Rows)	Storage Engine Scan Time (ms)
10,000,000	0–20
100,000,000	10–200
1,000,000,000	100–2,000
10,000,000,000	1,000–20,000
100,000,000,000	10,000–200,000

As you can see, when you have more than 1,000,000,000 rows, you enter a warning zone. And when a table has more than 10,000,000,000 rows, you have little hope of providing a good interactive user experience. Even if the performance might be satisfactory for certain queries, if you want to guarantee that the user can drill down in a PivotTable without having to wait several seconds for every click, you should consider an optimization technique that would be absolutely counter-productive to smaller data models. For example, consider the star schema shown in Figure 15-6. You see only Sales, Product, and Date in the diagram, but you might have other dimensions as well.

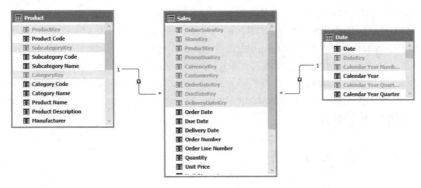

FIGURE 15-6 A simple star schema for a large fact table.

If the Sales table has 10,000,000,000 rows, any navigation across the Product dimension could take several seconds. For example, the PivotTable shown in Figure 15-7 would require a complete evaluation of the Sales table to provide a small number of rows. If such a navigation (by category and subcategory) is frequent, and other Product attributes are explored only after a selection of a certain subcategory (such as product name, color, size, and so on), then you might wonder how to optimize such a frequent query pattern.

Row Labels	Sales Amount
⊞ Audio	$384,518.16
⊞ Cameras and camcorders	$7,192,581.95
⊞ Cell phones	$1,604,610.26
⊞ Computers	$6,741,548.73
⊞ Games and Toys	$360,652.81
⊟ Home Appliances	$9,600,457.04
⊞ Air Conditioners	$712,451.93
⊞ Coffee Machines	$974,725.18
⊞ Fans	$133,137.15
⊞ Lamps	$1,112,452.14
⊞ Microwaves	$763,859.16
⊞ Refrigerators	$1,864,739.74
⊞ Washers & Dryers	$3,045,477.38
⊞ Water Heaters	$993,614.37
⊞ Music, Movies and Audio Books	$314,206.74
⊞ TV and Video	$4,392,768.29
Grand Total	$30,591,343.98

FIGURE 15-7 A PivotTable that browses data by category and subcategory.

One possible optimization is to reduce the number of rows in the Sales table, modifying its granularity. For example, if 90 percent of the queries require only the category and subcategory of products (without analyzing other product attributes), then you might create a Sales table that aggregates data by subcategory. You would use the table whenever the query does not require additional details. To be effective, the ratio between the products and subcategories should be at least one or two orders of magnitude. A simple relationship of 100 products per subcategory is not enough. You also need existing transactions for most of the product references. Otherwise, the aggregation at the fact-table level would not be effective. If this assumption is possible, then you can apply a variation of the technique you saw previously to optimize large dimensions.

Figure 15-8 shows a Product Subcategory table that contains only the Subcategory and Category attributes from the Product table. These attributes are still visible through the Product table, so the implementation of this optimization is transparent to end users. The Product Subcategory table has a relationship with the SalesBySubcategory table, which contains the same data as Sales aggregated by Product Subcategory. If our assumption is correct, such a table will have around 100,000,000 rows instead of the 10,000,000,000 rows of Sales. Both the Product Subcategory and SalesBySubcategory tables are hidden from client tools.

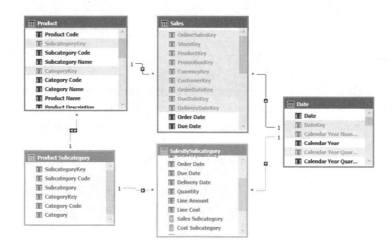

FIGURE 15-8   A bidirectional filter that connects Product to Product Subcategory.

In the example in the companion content, the Product Subcategory table is generated by a view in the SQL Server database, whereas the SalesBySubcategory table is obtained by using a calculated table that is defined by the following DAX expression:

```
SalesBySubcategory =
SUMMARIZECOLUMNS (
    Sales[StoreKey],
    Product[SubcategoryKey],
    Sales[PromotionKey],
    Sales[CurrencyKey],
    Sales[CustomerKey],
    Sales[OrderDateKey],
    Sales[DueDateKey],
    Sales[DeliveryDateKey],
    Sales[Order Date],
    Sales[Due Date],
    Sales[Delivery Date],
    "Quantity", SUM ( Sales[Quantity] ),
    "Line Amount", [Sales Amount Product],
    "Line Cost", [Cost Product]
)
```

> **Note** The aggregation obtained in the example (included in the companion content) does not reduce the rows with a ratio of 1:100 because the source table is smaller than what is required for the initial assumption. Nevertheless, the example shows a technique that should be used with very large tables, which would not be practical to provide as complete examples in this book.

Using a calculated table to evaluate the aggregated table could be slow and expensive, so you should consider whether to use a similar approach or a preparation of the aggregated data on a SQL Server table. A calculated table cannot be partitioned, so an external computation is necessary whenever you need to partition the table with an aggregation.

At this point, you can create internal measures that aggregate columns on both the SalesBySubcategory and Sales tables, exposing only a final Sales Amount measure to the user. Sales Amount chooses the measures based on SalesBySubcategory whenever possible, relying on the original calculation from the Sales table when product details other than category and subcategory are required. The following expressions define these measures:

```
SalesBySubcategory[Sales Subcategory] :=
SUM ( SalesBySubcategory[Line Amount] )

Sales[Sales Amount Product] :=
SUMX ( Sales, Sales[Net Price] * Sales[Quantity] )

Sales[IsProductFiltered] :=
ISFILTERED ( 'Product'[Available Date] )
    || ISFILTERED ( 'Product'[Brand] )
    || ISFILTERED ( 'Product'[Class] )
    || ISFILTERED ( 'Product'[Color] )
    || ISFILTERED ( 'Product'[Manufacturer] )
    || ISFILTERED ( 'Product'[Product Code] )
    || ISFILTERED ( 'Product'[Product Description] )
    || ISFILTERED ( 'Product'[Product Name] )
    || ISFILTERED ( 'Product'[Size] )
    || ISFILTERED ( 'Product'[Status] )
    || ISFILTERED ( 'Product'[Stock Type] )
    || ISFILTERED ( 'Product'[Stock Type Code] )
    || ISFILTERED ( 'Product'[Style] )
    || ISFILTERED ( 'Product'[Unit Cost] )
    || ISFILTERED ( 'Product'[Unit Price] )
    || ISFILTERED ( 'Product'[Weight] )
    || ISFILTERED ( 'Product'[Weight Unit Measure] )
)

Sales[Sales Amount] :=
IF (
    NOT ( [IsProductFiltered] ),
    [Sales Subcategory],
    [Sales Amount Product]
)
```

The IsProductFiltered measure returns TRUE whenever the current filter requires the details of Product and returns FALSE if the query only requires data that is aggregated by subcategory. Thus, the Sales Amount measure returns the value computed by the Sales Subcategory measure when IsProductFiltered is FALSE. Otherwise, it returns the value provided by the Sales Amount Product measure. Figure 15-9 shows the values computed by all these measures that are navigated by Category, Subcategory, and Product Name. Only the Sales Amount measure should be visible to users.

	Row Labels	Sales Amount	Sales Amount Product	Sales Subcategory	IsProductFiltered
2					
3	⊟Audio	$384,518.16	$384,518.16	$384,518.16	FALSE
4	⊞Bluetooth Headphones	$124,450.79	$124,450.79	$124,450.79	FALSE
5	⊞MP4&MP3	$170,194.00	$170,194.00	$170,194.00	FALSE
6	⊟Recording Pen	$89,873.37	$89,873.37	$89,873.37	FALSE
7	WWI 1GB Digital Voice Recorder Pen E100 Black	$2,634.84	$2,634.84	$89,873.37	TRUE
8	WWI 1GB Digital Voice Recorder Pen E100 Pink	$2,995.20	$2,995.20	$89,873.37	TRUE
9	WWI 1GB Digital Voice Recorder Pen E100 Red			$89,873.37	TRUE
25	WWI 4GB Video Recording Pen X200 Red			$89,873.37	TRUE
26	WWI 4GB Video Recording Pen X200 Yellow	$6,541.60	$6,541.60	$89,873.37	TRUE
27	⊞Cameras and camcorders	$7,192,581.95	$7,192,581.95	$7,192,581.95	FALSE
28	⊞Cell phones	$1,604,610.26	$1,604,610.26	$1,604,610.26	FALSE
29	⊞Computers	$6,741,548.73	$6,741,548.73	$6,741,548.73	FALSE
30	⊞Games and Toys	$360,652.81	$360,652.81	$360,652.81	FALSE
31	⊞Home Appliances	$9,600,457.04	$9,600,457.04	$9,600,457.04	FALSE
32	⊞Music, Movies and Audio Books	$314,206.74	$314,206.74	$314,206.74	FALSE
33	⊞TV and Video	$4,392,768.29	$4,392,768.29	$4,392,768.29	FALSE
34	Grand Total	$30,591,343.98	$30,591,343.98	$30,591,343.98	FALSE

FIGURE 15-9   A PivotTable that browses data by category and subcategory.

Optimizing performance of a large fact table by creating aggregations at different granularities is an expensive operation, which requires certain assumptions about data distribution and frequent query patterns performed by users. This technique has been successfully applied in production databases with tens of billions of records. However, you should consider it as a last resort. The preferred method is to try to reduce the granularity read from the data source.

Designing tabular models for near–real-time solutions

Analysis Services Tabular provides a semantic model that enables an end user to navigate into data. It uses clients such as Excel PivotTables and Power BI, without knowing the query language required by the original data source. However, the data sources used in a tabular model could change over time, and Tabular might not have the latest data available. In this section, we consider the options available to reduce the delay between data changes made on the data source and the availability of the correspondent data in the tabular model.

Note   The definition of *near–real-time* corresponds to delays that are measured in seconds to minutes, whereas a *real-time* system usually corresponds to delays measured in milliseconds or less. For this reason, in this section we discuss near–real-time.

Choosing between DirectQuery and VertiPaq

The first option for implementing a near–real-time system would certainly be to implement the tabular model using DirectQuery. This removes the delay required to process the data on SSAS Tabular. Every query sent to Analysis Services is transformed into one or more SQL queries that are sent to the data source, so you can keep the delay at a minimum. If the performances provided by your relational data source are good enough for your requirements, then DirectQuery moves the challenge to keep the data up to date on the relational-database side. Often, however, the relational database used as a data source for the tabular model is a data mart produced as a result of an ETL process, which means that data does not change continuously on the data source.

If you have a set of tables (in a relational data source) that change continuously, and you implement a DirectQuery model on top of it, you have the minimum possible delay between the data updates and the availability of data in the tabular model. If you otherwise have discrete updates, even at a relatively high frequency (such as every 5 minutes), then you should consider both VertiPaq and DirectQuery as possible alternatives.

If you use DirectQuery, and Tabular receives a request during a data update, you might have more than one SQL query sent to the relational database for the same DAX/MDX processed by SSAS. You should consider whether this could produce some inconsistency in the result. Usually, this is not a problem for a simple sum of a column in a table. But, if you are relating different tables and you have different measures working at different granularities, you might combine data read at different stages of the data update that is executed on the relational database.

If you process data by using VertiPaq, you create a snapshot of the data at a certain point in time (the process event), and you can guarantee that you have a consistent view by using snapshots or transaction isolation levels. However, even if you do not use any of these tools, the process operation performed by VertiPaq reads every table only once during a process operation. This reduces the risk of inconsistencies, which are generated by multiple reads of the same table in different moments. The risk exists in DirectQuery because a single DAX/MDX query might generate more than one SQL query. Moreover, the result of a SQL query could be temporarily cached by Analysis Services when you use DirectQuery, so you should figure out whether this could affect the correctness of your results.

> **More information** More details about the behavior of DirectQuery are available in the whitepaper "DirectQuery in Analysis Services 2016" at *http://www.sqlbi.com/articles/directquery-in-analysis-services-2016/*.

If you choose DirectQuery, the consistency and latency of the data will depend mainly on the implementation of the relational database. If you choose VertiPaq, then you must make sure that the time required to process the data is less than the interval of maximum delay that your users are expecting as a near–real-time requirement. For example, if you want to provide data newer than 15 minutes, then the time required to process data must be lower than 15 minutes. You must optimize the process operation to guarantee this level of service.

In the remaining part of this chapter, you will learn how to manage a near–real-time solution by using VertiPaq.

Using partitions

In Chapter 11, "Processing and partitioning tabular models," you learned how to define a partitioning strategy and to automate the related process operations. This section assumes you are already well-versed on the topic of partitions, focusing only on the specific processing requirements of near–real-time solutions.

To reduce processing time, the first goal is to reduce the number of objects to process. For example, consider a classical star schema made by the Sales, Product, Customer, Store, and Date tables. The near–real-time requirement is having the data updated in the tabular model within 15 minutes. During the day, you might have new products and new customers, but processing the Sales, Product, and Customer tables in a continuous way could be challenging. For example, how do you identify a new customer or a new product? The cost for detecting whether these conditions exist could be expensive. Also, there is a risk of creating inconsistent data if you have a bug in the update logic.

Usually, it makes sense to reduce the area subject to updates. You might insert new transactions in the Sales table without creating new products and new customers every 15 minutes. You could keep this activity in the nightly process, which also rebuilds all the transactions of the day, applying all the data quality controls that would not be possible with frequent updates. All transactions related to new products or new customers would be included in the grand total, but it would not be possible to identify a new customer or a new product until the day after. Most of the time, this is an acceptable tradeoff.

To lower the process time, you do not process the entire Sales table every 15 minutes. Instead, you process only a subset. This is done by either reprocessing a partition or by adding new rows to the partition that contain the most recent data.

In any case, it is a good idea to have a starting point, in the morning, with the result of a nightly process operation that updates all the tables in the tabular model. From this starting point, every 15 minutes, the Sales table must be updated with the most recent transactions. You can achieve this by using the following two possible approaches:

- **ProcessData for daily partition**   With this approach, you create an empty partition in the Sales table that includes only the transactions of the day during the nightly process. You process the entire partition every 15 minutes. The processing time might increase over the course of the day because you reprocess all the rows of the day at every update. This approach should be considered when the time required to process all the transactions in one day is considerably smaller than the update interval. For example, to reach our goal of 15 minutes, we should have a partition process time of no more than 3–4 minutes at the end of the day. If you can process 10,000 rows per second on your server, you can manage up to 2,000,000 rows per day. An advantage of this approach is that any update to the transactions made within the day is automatically reported in the next data refresh.

- **ProcessAdd for new transactions** You can use the ProcessAdd command to add rows to an existing partition. For example, you might add rows to the partition of the current month, or to the single partition of the entire Sales table, if you did not use partitions. Every ProcessAdd operation clones the existing partition and then appends data to that clone (after decompressing the last segment of data). However, multiple merges of partitions produce a suboptimal storage, so you must make sure that the nightly batch will rebuild the partition, which restores it to an optimal state. You should consider the ProcessAdd approach whenever the ProcessData of a daily partition is too slow for your requirements. You also should consider that updates made to the transactions already processed will not be reported in the model until the day after unless you implement the generation of compensating transactions. We suggest that you consider the ProcessData of a daily partition whenever possible. This is because the ProcessAdd approach is more error-prone, even if it can provide a lower latency with large amounts of data to process.

Figure 15-10 shows a possible partitioning schema for the Sales table.

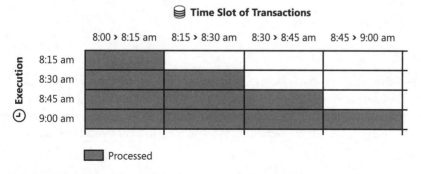

FIGURE 15-10 The definition of multiple partitions for the Sales table, and a single partition for other tables.

By using ProcessData, you schedule the same event multiple times over a day. The result is that the partition you process continues to grow over the day, requiring more time for every ProcessData, as shown in Figure 15-11.

ProcessData
Sales Table

| TODAY PARTITION |

Time Slot of Transactions

	8:00 › 8:15 am	8:15 › 8:30 am	8:30 › 8:45 am	8:45 › 9:00 am
8:15 am	Processed			
8:30 am	Processed	Processed		
8:45 am	Processed	Processed	Processed	
9:00 am	Processed	Processed	Processed	Processed

Execution

☐ Processed

FIGURE 15-11 The sequence of events using ProcessData for daily partition.

By using the ProcessAdd approach, you have a faster operation to execute every 15 minutes because every row is processed only once, as shown in Figure 15-12. However, every ProcessAdd creates a new partition that is merged with the previous ones, and you do not automatically fix transactions that have been modified after the first process. Every ProcessAdd should include a predicate that correctly filters the rows to process. If the predicate reads the data that you have already processed in previous ProcessAdd operations, this would result in duplicated transactions stored in the Sales table.

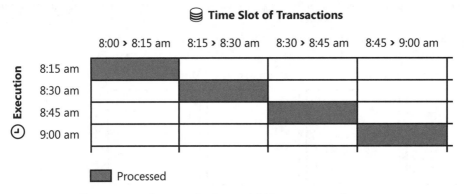

FIGURE 15-12 The sequence of events using ProcessAdd for new transactions.

Reducing recalculation time

First you process the data using the ProcessData or ProcessAdd operation, as described in the previous section. Then you need to update additional data structures to make the data available to the user. The structures requiring an update are as follows:

- Calculated columns
- Calculated tables
- Relationships
- Hierarchies

All these entities are processed at the table level, and they are not just for the partition you updated. By using the ProcessDefault command at the database level, only the entities that have been affected by a process operation will be updated. To reduce the time required by this update, you must minimize the side effects of the frequent process operations that you perform in a near–real-time solution.

Calculated columns and calculated tables

Calculated columns are evaluated at the table level. It is a good practice not to include calculated columns in a table where you have partitions that you refresh often. In the previous example, you should not have a calculated column in the Sales table.

You should also avoid references to the Sales table that are also made in calculated columns included in other tables. For example, the following DAX expression in a calculated column of the Customers table should be recalculated every time there is an update in the Sales table:

```
Customer[Total Sales] =
SUMX (
    RELATED ( Sales ),
    Sales[Quantity] * Sales[Unit Price]
)
```

In a similar way, any reference made to the Sales table in a DAX expression for a calculated table would compute the calculated table again, at every update of the Sales table.

You should consider moving these calculations to the SQL query so they are no longer automatically updated at every refresh during the day. Transforming a calculated column in a native column has the side benefit of better compression, but you lose the automatic update and consistency that is guaranteed by a calculated column. However, this is a feature that might have an impact on the process time. You must carefully measure the time required (you can analyze this using Profiler events) to make sure this will not exceed the time available in the process window.

Relationships

Every relationship in the data model corresponds to a small structure that maps the IDs of the two columns involved in the relationship. When you update a partition using either the ProcessData or ProcessAdd operation, all the relationships involved with the target table must also be updated. Because the cost of updating a relationship depends on the number of unique values in the underlying columns, updating a fact table often has a higher cost for refreshing relationships when there are large dimensions involved in the data model.

If the cost of updating relationships affects the process time in a negative way, you might remove relationships with the largest dimensions by replacing them with a slower filter implemented in DAX. The side effects are the highest maintenance required for writing DAX queries and a negative impact in query performance. This choice should be considered only in extreme cases. You might need to create a separate table instead of a separate partition for the daily data if you are affected by this problem. In this way, you can keep the existing relationships in the original fact table, and then remove the relationships only from the table that contains daily data. This approach still requires more DAX code (summing the results from the original fact table and from the new daily table), but it limits the performance impact on the smaller daily fact table.

Hierarchies

VertiPaq creates additional structures for the attribute hierarchies, user hierarchies, and columns decorated with the Sort By Column property. All these structures related to a table must be rebuilt when one or more partitions of the table are updated. The cost of updating these structures mainly depends on the number of unique values included in the columns involved. So, you should avoid having these structures active on the high-cardinality columns of the tables that you update often.

You can choose not to create user hierarchies and not to assign the Sort By Column property to the columns of the fact table, but you still have the attribute hierarchy for every column of a table, even if you do not need it. For this reason, you should try to avoid high-cardinality columns in the tables that must be updated often to reduce the time required to build attribute hierarchies.

> **Important** As explained in Chapter 12, a future release of Analysis Services might introduce a setting to disable the creation of attribute hierarchies. If this setting becomes available, it will be important to use it in tables that are updated often in a near–real-time solution.

Managing lock during process

During a process operation, the current version of the tables in the database are available for queries. The process creates a new copy of the partitions that are involved in the process and a copy of all the additional structures that must be updated as a side effect. It is a good idea to include the ProcessData or ProcessAdd request in the same transaction of a subsequent ProcessDefault at the database level. In this way, the database is always available, and it presents a consistent situation.

As soon as the process completes and the new data is ready, the commit operation requires a pending commit lock on the database, which will generate an exclusive write lock over the database. All the queries have a shared lock. So, to commit the process, all the running queries must be completed first, and the new queries need to wait until the commit completes. The running queries must be completed within a certain amount of time, as defined by the ForceCommitTimeout setting, which has a default of 30 seconds. If this timeout expires, running queries are cancelled and the commit takes place.

You also have a setting that cancels the process operation if the pending commit lock is still active after a certain timeout. This setting is named CommitTimeout and its default is 0, which means there is no timeout to complete the process operation.

In a near–real-time solution, you should ensure that ForceCommitTimeout has a value that is compatible with the refresh cycle. For example, you should not set ForceCommitTimeout to 600 (corresponding to 10 minutes) when your refresh cycle is 5 minutes. It is a good idea to avoid long-running queries in a database that is updated often in a near–real-time solution. Setting ForceCommitTimeout to 30 or to a lower value will give the proper precedence to the scheduled process operations.

Summary

In this chapter, you learned how to optimize a generic tabular model, starting with concepts that are common to other products that use the VertiPaq engine, such as Power BI and Power Pivot. You learned how to implement large dimensions (with millions of rows) in an effective way, and you applied and extended this technique to optimize very large databases by managing fact tables with more than 10,000,000,000 rows. Finally, you were guided in the design of tabular models, which are optimized for near–real-time solutions, evaluating the choices available between DirectQuery and VertiPaq, and then implementing the optimizations required in an effective VertiPaq implementation.

Choosing hardware and virtualization

To obtain the best performance from a tabular model, you must make the proper choices in terms of hardware and, if used, virtualization. These concepts were introduced in Chapter 1, "Introducing the tabular model," but they are important enough to deserve a separate discussion.

In this chapter, you will learn the trade-offs to consider when using a virtualization environment and why controlling certain hardware characteristics, such as the CPU clock, memory speed, and NUMA architecture, can make the difference between a successful Tabular solution and a poorly implemented one.

> **What's new in SSAS 2016**   This is a new chapter for this second edition of the book. Most of the content (besides the NUMA section) would also be valid for previous versions of Analysis Services, but the previous edition did not include a specific chapter about hardware and virtualization, which is an important topic for Analysis Services running in Tabular mode.

Hardware sizing

When you plan a tabular model deployment, you often need to provide the necessary hardware for the server. A tabular model server can have very different requirements from a relational database server. There are also significant differences between servers that are optimized for tabular and multidimensional models. In this section, you will see techniques for correctly sizing a server for a Tabular instance of Analysis Services that manages a database deployed in-memory by using VertiPaq. DirectQuery databases also have different needs and minimal resource requirements for Analysis Services, as you will learn in the "Hardware requirements for DirectQuery" section later in this chapter.

The first question is whether you are using existing equipment or selecting new hardware. The problem with using a virtual machine for a Tabular solution is that, often, the hardware has already been installed, and you can influence only the number of cores and the amount of RAM assigned to your server. Unfortunately, these parameters are not particularly relevant for performance. In this situation, you should collect information about your host server's CPU model and clock speed before deployment.

If you do not have access to this information, you can find the CPU model and the clock speed under the Performance tab in Task Manager on any virtual machine running on the same host server. With this information, you can predict the performance and compare this to the performance on an average modern laptop. Unfortunately, this comparison may show that performance will be worse on the virtual machine. If so, you may need to sharpen your political skills and convince the right people that running Tabular on that virtual server is a bad idea. If you find the performance acceptable, you will only need to avoid the pitfalls of running a virtual machine on different NUMA nodes. This will be discussed further in the "Virtualization" section later in this chapter.

Assuming you can influence the hardware selection, you must set priorities in this order:

1. CPU clock and model

2. Memory speed

3. Number of cores

4. Memory size

Notice that disk I/O performance does not appear in this list. Although there is a condition (paging) in which disk I/O affects performance, the concern is minimal when selecting hardware. Ideally, you should size the RAM so that paging is no longer an issue. This will be covered in greater detail in the "Memory speed and size" section later in this chapter. Allocate your budget on CPU speed, memory speed, and memory size, and do not be concerned with disk I/O bandwidth unless you want to reduce the time required to load a database in memory when the service restarts.

You might wonder why memory size is the fourth priority in hardware selection and not the first one. The reason is that having more RAM does not improve the speed of a tabular model. You certainly need enough RAM to load the database in memory. In many scenarios, the RAM can be expanded later. A bad choice of CPU and memory speed, however, is often irreversible. Modifying this requires the replacement of the entire server. Moreover, you can optimize the RAM consumed by carefully choosing the columns to import and improving the compression rate. Having an adequate amount of available memory is critical, but a server with more RAM can be a slower server for Tabular because of the particular architecture (NUMA) required for managing large amounts of RAM, as you will see in the following sections.

CPU clock and model

Analysis Services Tabular runs DAX and MDX queries, using an architecture with two main modules: the *formula engine* and *storage engine*. These modules have different roles, and a basic understanding of their behavior is important to grasp the performance impact of certain hardware choices. The size of the tabular model and the complexity of the DAX expressions might increase the priority of certain characteristics over others in your CPU selection.

Single-thread versus multi-thread operations

Every query starts its execution in the formula engine, which runs operations in a sequential way by using a single thread. The formula engine requests data from the storage engine, which is different between in-memory and DirectQuery models. A database running in-memory uses VertiPaq as a storage engine, which can execute operations in parallel on multiple threads, but it must return data to the formula engine as a single dataset. With DirectQuery, the storage engine requests are made to an external database in the form of SQL queries, and they do not use Tabular service resources other than the RAM that is required to store the SQL query results.

All the remaining operations that are executed by the formula engine run in a single thread. Because the formula engine cannot use the cache to store DAX query results, the CPU clock speed becomes critical. The VertiPaq cache stores only the results from storage engine requests, running the formula engine code in every DAX query execution. A separate formula engine cache exists for MDX queries.

At query time, the only advantage to having multiple cores is to parallelize the storage engine part of a single query. The storage engine does not split the execution into multiple threads unless there are two or more segments in a table. For these reasons, scalability over multiple cores is effective only for very large tables. Raising the number of cores will improve performance for a single query, but only when it hits a large table. In theory, this includes more than 16,000,000 rows, but in practice you should see visible differences when you have more than 100–200,000,000 rows.

Multiple concurrent queries can be executed in parallel, and each one uses its own instance of the formula engine. Thus, the single-thread formula engine bottleneck applies only to a single query, but the presence of multiple cores can improve the ability to serve multiple concurrent queries. However, in terms of scalability, a higher number of cores might not improve performance if users access the same tables simultaneously and contend for access to shared RAM at the storage-engine level. A better way to increase the number of concurrent users is to use more servers in a load-balancing configuration.

Tabular model users have very demanding performance requirements, expecting any query to run in less than 2 seconds to achieve a positive interactive user experience. For this reason, a query's single-thread operation could easily become the bottleneck of a slow-running query. After you optimize the DAX expression, the only way to improve the performance of these queries is to use a faster CPU with a higher clock rate and a better architecture. A higher number of cores for a single socket does not help to improve these queries.

The database process operation has very different characteristics from queries. During a process, a single-thread operation reads rows from the data source, but at the end of each segment, most of the subsequent operations, such as compression, take advantage of multiple cores. Because you can process multiple tables and/or partitions in parallel, it is much easier to take advantage of multiple cores during a process than during a query.

Clock speed, cache size, and the number of cores

The most important factors that affect the speed of code running in the formula engine are the CPU clock and model. Different CPU models might have varying performance at the same clock rate, so considering the clock alone is not enough. The best practice is to run your own benchmarks by measuring performance in queries that stress the formula engine. You can find an example of a DAX query that stresses the formula engine at *https://www.sqlbi.com/articles/choose-the-right-hardware-for-analysis-services-tabular/.* We suggest you create your own benchmarks to validate the hardware you want to use for your tabular model.

In general, CPUs have a classification between families. For example, Intel has i3, i5, and i7 families for desktop; m3, m5, and m7 for mobile; and E3, E5, and E7 for servers. (You can find them described at *http://ark.intel.com/.*) AMD has its own families, described at *http://www.amd.com/en-us/products/processors.* Usually, a higher family number corresponds to better performance and a higher cost, but this is not necessarily true for Tabular. The notion of performance for a CPU is usually measured by the number of instructions that can be executed in a unit of time, using *all* the available cores. For a single query in Tabular, you will often use only one of the available cores. As such, when we compare CPUs of the same family, we give a higher priority to the CPU clock speed than to the number of cores.

An important difference between CPU families is the cache size. Although memory speed is important, even the fastest available RAM is slower than the CPU clock. To prevent the CPU from continuously waiting for data from RAM, modern CPUs have several cache levels, named L1, L2, and L3. L1 and L2 are typically private to each core, while L3 is shared across cores of a single socket. In more recent CPUs, Intel has implemented a feature called *SmartCache*, which dynamically assigns cache to each core depending on the requests. This is a good feature for a tabular model because a single-thread operation can benefit from a large cache at the CPU level.

In general, Intel Xeon E5 and E7 series processors are used on servers, and it is very common to find clock speeds around 2 GHz, even with a very high number of cores available. You should look for a clock speed of 3 GHz or more whenever possible. Another important requirement is a larger cache size at the CPU level. This is especially important for large tables and relationships between tables that are based on columns that have more than 1,000,000 unique values. Usually, desktop processors have much smaller cache sizes, even if the clock speed is higher than server CPUs.

We have observed that modern Intel i7 series CPUs, running on 3 GHz or more, provide very good performance. These CPUs are optimized for desktop workload, and you rarely find them on a server. The best performance/cost ratio on Intel's server families is on E5, where you can find clock rates of 3 GHz or more, with up to 12 cores in the same socket. The E3 family is inexpensive, but the cache size is limited, so it should be considered only for small and simple tabular databases. The E7 is very expensive. It usually provides a large cache and numerous cores, but it has a relatively low clock speed.

As mentioned, the number of cores is not the first priority. However, when you choose a CPU, you also select the number of cores available in one socket. A higher number of cores usually corresponds to a lower clock speed, and the trade-off is convenient only for storage-engine operations on large tables (more than 100–200,000,000 rows). If your databases do not have large tables, you should give a higher priority to the clock speed. If your queries are primarily in the storage engine, then sacrificing clock speed to increase the number of cores might be worth the effort.

Finally, remember that the concept of "modern" is relative. Look for the CPU model release date, and consider anything that has been released in the last 18–24 months to be modern. For older models, verify whether there is a new generation and compare CPU benchmarks (single-thread operations) to other CPUs. (If you make in-house tests with benchmarks, using your own data, then that will be more relevant than published benchmarks.)

Memory speed and size

Memory is the most critical resource in a Tabular instance. Data is stored in physical memory, and SQL Server Analysis Services (SSAS) also uses RAM to create temporary structures to handle complex queries. In Chapter 12, "Inside VertiPaq", you learned how to measure the storage size required for a tabular model stored in memory by using VertiPaq Analyzer.

To process the model and avoid paging operations, you need at least two or three times the space required to store a compressed database in memory, particularly if you run ProcessFull operations on the whole database and keep previous versions available for querying during process operations. For large databases, alternative options are available that lower the memory required to keep the database available for querying during process operations. These include clearing the database from memory before the process and using a separate process server that is synchronized with the query server when the processed data is ready.

Any query can require a temporary peak of memory usage to store the partial results that are required to solve the complete query. Simple queries require minimal memory, but more complex queries might be expensive from this point of view. This cost is difficult to estimate because it depends on the number of concurrent queries that Analysis Services receives. It is also difficult to provide a guideline for sizing memory depending on concurrent users. It is better to follow a heuristic approach, measuring memory consumption in the expected workload, as discussed in Chapter 14, "Monitoring and tuning a Tabular service."

> ## More RAM does not improve speed
>
> Having enough memory will guarantee that your queries will come to an end, but increasing the available RAM does not produce any performance improvement. The cache used by Tabular does not increase when more RAM is available. However, low available memory might affect query performance in a negative way if the server starts paging data. You should ensure there is enough memory to store all the data within your database to avoid materialization during query execution.

Memory size is an important requirement, but not all memory is the same. In Tabular mode, memory speed is more important than in other types of servers. Memory bandwidth is a key factor for Tabular performance, and it can cause a severe bottleneck when querying a large database. Every operation made by the storage engine accesses memory at a very high speed. When RAM bandwidth is a bottleneck, you will see CPU usage instead of I/O waits. Unfortunately, we do not have performance counters monitoring the time spent waiting for RAM access. In Tabular, this time can be relevant and difficult to measure.

Slow RAM speed primarily affects the storage-engine operations, but it also affects formula-engine operations when it works on a large materialization that is obtained by a storage-engine request.

> **Note** Memory bandwidth is the rate at which data is transferred between the RAM and CPU. It is expressed in bytes/second, even if the common naming convention (such as DDR, DDR2, DDR3, DDR4, and so on) provides a nominal MHz rating (that is, DDR3-1600) that corresponds to the number of transfers per second. The higher this number, the higher the memory bandwidth is. You can find more information at *http://en.wikipedia.org/wiki/DDR_SDRAM*.

You can observe performance differences with greater memory bandwidth that are more significant than those obtained by using a faster CPU clock. Thus, you should carefully consider the memory bandwidth of your system, which depends on RAM characteristics, CPU, chipset, and configuration. This could be as important, if not more so, than the CPU clock. A fast CPU clock rate becomes useless if the RAM speed is insufficient.

In general, you should get RAM that has at least 1,600 MHz. If the hardware platform permits, though, you should select faster RAM (1,833, 2,133, or 2,400 MHz). At the time of this writing, there are servers with a maximum speed of 2,400 MHz.

NUMA architecture

Non-uniform memory access (NUMA) is an architecture in which a single server has two or more CPU sockets, each with a local amount of RAM that is also accessible from other sockets through a slower communication process. In other words, the memory access time depends on the memory location, relative to the processor. For example, Figure 16-1 shows a server with four CPU sockets and 1 TB of RAM with a NUMA architecture.

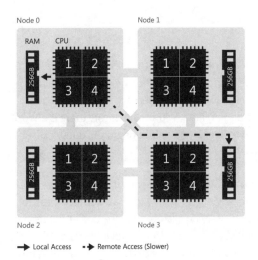

FIGURE 16-1 A server with 1 TB of RAM in a NUMA architecture with four sockets.

If every CPU socket has eight cores, then you have a server with a total of 32 cores. The RAM is split across the sockets, and each one has 256 GB of local memory. Under NUMA, a processor can access its own local memory faster than the memory local to another processor. For example, a thread running in node 0 core can access a structure allocated in node 3 RAM, but its access time will be slower than accessing data allocated in the RAM that is tied to node 0 itself. A NUMA-aware application controls memory allocation and code execution, so code using a certain structure in memory will be executed on the same socket (CPU node) that accesses data locally, without paying the traversal cost of the longer path to reach data.

Analysis Services 2016 in Tabular mode is a NUMA-aware application if you applied the Service Pack 1 or you have a later build or version. Previous versions of Analysis Services Tabular were not NUMA aware, even if NUMA is supported by Windows at the operating-system level. However, even though new versions of Analysis Services are NUMA-aware, you still should carefully evaluate whether to use multiple NUMA nodes for Tabular.

Without NUMA support, you might have threads in the storage engine running on a node other than the one with local access to the data to scan. NUMA support improves the chances that the storage engine will consume data from the node closest to the RAM storing the data. However, even with NUMA support available in SSAS 2016 SP1, the data cache could be materialized by the storage engine in an area of memory separate from the node where the thread with the formula engine will consume it.

When data is read or written by a node that is not the local one, the result is a slower execution time that, in the worst conditions, could double compared to one obtained in ideal conditions (the code and data running on the same NUMA node). Thus, we suggest choosing a non-NUMA server for Analysis Services–dedicated machines. If this is not possible, and multiple services run on the same server, then it might be better to run an Analysis Services Tabular instance on processors belonging to the same NUMA node. You can control this by using the settings described in the "NUMA settings" section later in this chapter. Because these settings are global for the SSAS instance, you should consider using a NUMA configuration with multiple nodes only for large databases.

You can find more details about NUMA architecture in the "Hardware Sizing a Tabular Solution (SQL Server Analysis Services)" whitepaper, available at *http://msdn.microsoft.com/en-us/library/jj874401.aspx*. If you use more than one node for Analysis Services, you should measure whether the benefits of using more NUMA nodes are worth the additional cost of accessing remote nodes, which could still happen for the data materialized for the formula engine.

The benefits of the improvements for NUMA architecture introduced by Service Pack 1 could be visible only for large database on four or more NUMA nodes, but it is also possible that two NUMA nodes could provide some benefits, depending on your workload. For this reason, we suggest you benchmark the results of different configurations, comparing the use of SSAS Tabular on a single node with the use of the same instance on multiple nodes with the same hardware.

Disk and I/O

If the server has only a Tabular Analysis Services instance, but the data sources for your tabular models (such as Microsoft SQL Server) are on other servers, disk access will be limited to service startup, first database access, and database process tasks.

When you start the Analysis Services service, only the metadata from attached databases is read from disk. At the first access of any object, the entire database is loaded into physical memory with read-only storage access. In this scenario, elapsed time depends on the sequential I/O performance and data-transfer rates. For very large databases (several gigabytes of size with a slow disk subsystem), the time required could range between a few seconds to a few minutes. After the database has been loaded, it remains in memory until it is detached. Connecting SQL Server Management Studio (SSMS) to a Tabular Analysis Services instance and browsing the list of databases is sufficient to load all the databases into memory.

To process a database, write operations to storage are required. Multiple tables can be processed with concurrent write operations over multiple files. Thus, you have read and write operations over I/O. Each file is read or written from beginning to end. While both read and write operations are handled sequentially for each file, these operations are never handled concurrently over the same file. As such, disk performance is not a very important factor for a Tabular instance of Analysis Services, even if concurrent write operations occur when processing multiple tables. It may be better to allocate more of your hardware budget to higher-end processors and RAM than to expensive storage area networks (SANs).

I/O operations in a Tabular instance

Random I/O is not used in Tabular. A good sequential I/O throughput can improve startup time, but there are no effects on query time if you do not consider the first access to a database. During a process operation, all write operations will be sequential if you have enough RAM. If you do not have enough available physical memory to store both the processed and replaced data, random I/O paging operations can occur. The only reason for random access is the presence of many small files, as the access order could be different from the physical storage order. With enough RAM available, however, files will always be accessed sequentially.

Hardware requirements for DirectQuery

Tabular databases running in DirectQuery mode have much lower memory requirements than those running in memory using VertiPaq. However, because DirectQuery mainly replaces the VertiPaq storage engine, many operations are still executed in the formula engine. For this reason, if you can run Tabular with a smaller amount of memory for DirectQuery, having a fast CPU clock speed is important to prevent the formula engine from becoming the bottleneck for complex queries.

You should also consider the connection between the Analysis Services and the relational data source as the critical point of a DirectQuery-based solution. The I/O between the two processes should run with a low latency and a high bandwidth. Hosting the relational database on the same physical machine running SSAS Tabular could be the ideal solution. If this is not possible, consider a dedicated connection or a solution that does not use a physical connection that could be saturated by other concurrent activities.

It is beyond the scope of this book to discuss the hardware requirements of relational database servers used for DirectQuery. Your requirements will depend on the workload and on the server product used. It is worth mentioning that to obtain the corresponding features using an in-memory tabular database, you generally need more expensive hardware for a relational database than for an SSAS Tabular database. DirectQuery is not generally an option to save money unless it is reusing existing hardware.

Optimizing hardware configuration

After you have selected the hardware, you need to ensure it is properly configured. There are three configurations to check on a server running Tabular: power settings, hyper-threading, and NUMA settings.

Power settings

The most important configuration to check on a server running SSAS Tabular is power settings. You must ensure that any power-saving or low-power modes are disabled. Checking the operating system (OS) settings might not be enough, however, especially if you run SSAS Tabular on a virtual machine. You will also need to check the power-management options in the server BIOS settings.

The impact of these settings is huge, with poor performance observed in an incredibly high number of instances on SSAS Tabular servers. The VertiPaq engine uses the available CPU for a short period, and the latency that increases the CPU speed is too large for the timings involved for its operations.

Underestimating the impact of power settings can lead to problems. One common mistake is assuming the power settings were correctly configured during installation. Often, the reality is that the new server's default setting is a power-saving mode that is never modified after the initial setup. For some servers, you need to modify the BIOS settings and restart the server to configure the power settings, but for hardware that enables remote management, you can change the settings online. On an HP Blade server, for example, you might have a remote management interface that is similar to the one shown in Figure 16-2.

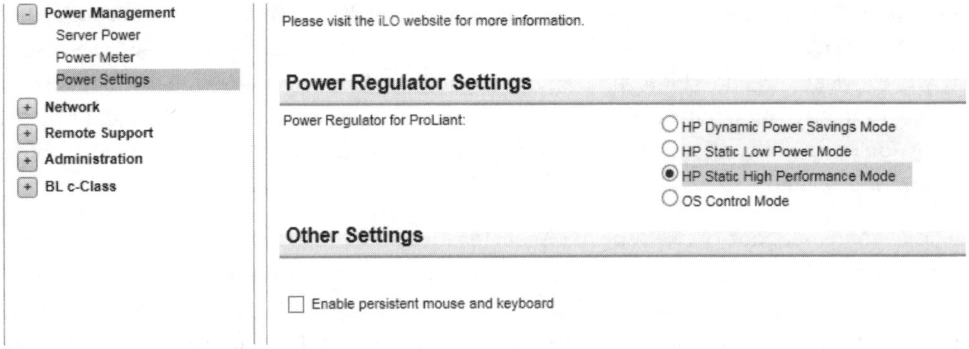

FIGURE 16-2 The power settings in the BIOS of an HP Blade server.

The correct setting is HP Static High Performance Mode. The two settings above it should be avoided for Analysis Services Tabular. You will need to check for similar settings in your hardware. If you do not have physical access to the hardware, you should run a performance assessment. Look at the server configuration and then validate the CPU benchmark against the technical specs. You can use the information available at *https://www.cpubenchmark.net/* as a reference, running the same CPU tests on your hardware. Remember that the tests related to single-thread execution are the most important. If the numbers do not match, then check the power-settings configuration.

The cost of power-saving mode on a server

We examined several real-world scenarios where we found issues with the power settings for SSAS Tabular. In one of them, a server had the Dynamic Power Savings Mode option enabled and cut several DAX query execution times between 13 and 50 percent. It is hard to predict which query type benefits more because there are heavy queries running on the formula engine for several seconds that saved between 14 and 49 percent of execution time. In any case, the negative impact of a power-saving setting can double the wait time of a query, especially for small databases. We all want to lower energy consumption, but certain power settings do not fit well with the typical workload of SSAS Tabular. It is possible that new servers and technologies will be unaffected by this problem, but current anecdotal experiences suggest that it is wise to check this issue carefully.

Hyper-threading

Despite the many articles that suggest disabling hyper-threading for maximum performance, the reality is that many benchmark runs have shown better performance with hyper-threading enabled, whereas other benchmarks have shown a penalty between 1 and 8 percent. With no clear results, we usually keep hyper-threading enabled. You should perform specific benchmark runs on your databases and hardware and consider disabling hyper-threading if the performance advantage exceeds 10 percent in your scenarios.

NUMA settings

You can control the nodes used by Analysis Services on a NUMA server by using the GroupAffinity setting in the advanced properties. In particular, for a Tabular instance, you can set the affinity mask for the following properties:

- **ThreadPool\Query\GroupAffinity**   This setting controls the threads dispatching the workload of the formula engine.

- **VertiPaq\ThreadPool\GroupAffinity**   This is the thread pool executing the scans performed by the storage engine.

It is suggested that you use the same affinity mask for both settings, using cores of the same node. More details about these settings are available at *https://msdn.microsoft.com/library/ms175657.aspx*.

Virtualization

Running Analysis Services Tabular on a virtualized server is not an issue in itself. The performance penalty for running on a virtual machine is between 1 and 3 percent under ideal conditions. The real issue is that, often, you have access to a virtual machine without any information or control over the hardware that is used for the host virtualization environment. In these cases, poor performance could result from the same hardware issues described previously: slow clock speed, slow memory, NUMA architecture, or wrong BIOS power settings.

To optimize performance from a virtualized environment, you must make sure that:

- You do not overcommit memory on the host server.

- You commit the memory to the virtual machine so it is never paged.

- You do not allocate more cores on a virtual server than those available in a single socket.

- You only allocate cores from a single NUMA node (single socket).

- You set an affinity mask for the cores running on the same NUMA node (single socket).

- You set memory affinity for the NUMA node.

If you are unsure about any of the above points, you should ask your virtual environment administrator for assistance. Different virtualization products (such as VMware and Hyper-V) have different configurations, and it is outside the scope of this book to provide more details about these settings. However, it is important to clarify at least two of these concepts so you might recognize the symptoms in case these settings have not been properly configured on your server.

Splitting NUMA nodes on different VMs

Previously in this chapter, you learned how a NUMA architecture might negatively affect SSAS Tabular performance. If you have a server with two or more sockets with NUMA architecture, the easiest way to avoid performance degradation is to create one virtual machine for every socket and assign to it only the cores and memory of a single NUMA node. In this way, each virtual machine will have processors and memory from a single NUMA node, which removes the risk of potentially executing code in a node that is not local to the data.

You can also choose to assign a smaller number of cores to a single virtual machine than those available on a single socket. In any case, if a VM will run an SSAS Tabular instance, all its cores should be assigned to the same NUMA node. In our experience, it is very common to find virtual machines with cores running on different NUMA nodes, even if a single node can support running all the cores of the VM. Do not assume that, by default, your virtualization host will allocate all the cores to the same NUMA node. This happens only when you explicitly define a constraint to obtain such a behavior.

If you want to assign more than one NUMA node to a virtual machine, then make sure this hardware is visible to the virtual machine and follow all the suggestions for a NUMA architecture described in previous sections of this chapter.

Committing memory to VMs

One goal of a virtualization environment is to optimize the use of available resources: CPU, memory, and I/O. For this reason, it is relatively common to overcommit the memory on the host server. This means the sum of the memory allocated to all the virtual machines is higher than the available physical memory on the host server. When this happens, the OS running on the virtual machine manages the physical memory, whereas instead, the memory could have been paged to disk while not in use.

Usually, this approach can slow down virtual machines that are not often used, providing more CPU time and memory to those virtual machines that run with a more continuous workload. Unfortunately, an SSAS Tabular instance uses memory in a unique manner, potentially scanning a huge amount of memory over a small amount of time, and then staying idle until the next query is received. Because all the algorithms in SSAS Tabular assume that the compressed data is available in physical memory, at worst, you might observe that a relatively fast query requires more time to be completed. For this reason, you should make sure the memory allocated to virtual machines running SSAS Tabular instances cannot be paged out. Usually, this is not the default, so you will need to explicitly request this behavior from your system administrator.

Scalability of an SSAS Tabular solution

When you need to scale a solution, you generally have two choices:

- **Scale-up** This involves adding more RAM and CPUs to create a more powerful server.
- **Scale-out** This involves adding more servers with less RAM and CPUs.

For SSAS Tabular, there are constraints to consider that might favor one direction over another.

You can easily duplicate a single database on other servers using the backup/restore or database-synchronization features available in Analysis Services. You can duplicate the same database across multiple servers (scale-out) to increase the number of concurrent users and the availability of the service. Alternatively, you can increase the resources for a single server (scale-up) to support a larger database or add smaller databases. However, because available RAM is one of SSAS Tabular's more critical resources, it is usually easier to add more servers for many SSAS Tabular databases than to try to load and process all the tabular databases onto a single server.

In the following sections, you will learn the suggested best practices for two common cases of SSAS Tabular solution scalability.

Scalability for a single database (large size)

If you have a large tabular database with tables containing billions of rows, you can only try to scale-up your solution with a bigger server. Usually, the driving factor in buying a new server is memory require-ment. When looking for a server with 1 TB of RAM or more, you will likely get a NUMA architecture with two, four, or more sockets. As you have seen in this chapter, this is not always a good idea for a tabular model. A better option is to obtain a single socket server with enough RAM to load the entire database into memory. If this is not possible, before considering a NUMA architecture, try to determine whether you can optimize the required memory by removing unused rows or optimize existing columns in the data model.

If you have a large database, you will probably need a large number of cores. In this case, a NUMA architecture could provide better query performance. However, you should measure whether there is a real benefit, comparing configurations using one or more NUMA nodes. You should also consider im-plementing optimizations for large databases as described in Chapter 15, "Optimizing tabular models."

If you have multiple databases, you should consider splitting them into separate instances of SSAS Tabular, running on separate NUMA nodes.

Scalability for large user workload

An easier scenario to manage is one with many concurrent users. It is frequently better to opt for a scale-out solution, getting more servers running the same tabular database, with a load balancer that distributes the workload across multiple nodes. In this scenario, you might have a large server dedicated to processing databases, while the queries are redirected to smaller servers that receive a synchronized copy of the data from the process server at scheduled intervals.

You can find more details about this approach in the article "High availability and Scalability in Analysis Services," at *https://msdn.microsoft.com/en-us/library/mt668924.aspx.*

Summary

In this chapter, you learned how to select the hardware for a Tabular server. Choosing the right CPU model and faster RAM is important. Although, this may be an inexpensive option, it could differ from company provisioning. You also learned the pros and cons of a virtualized environment for Tabular and how to correctly configure a server to avoid common pitfalls with default configurations. Finally, you saw a few scale-up and scale-out scenarios using SSAS Tabular.

Index